YALE HISTORICAL PUBLICATIONS
MISCELLANY, 134

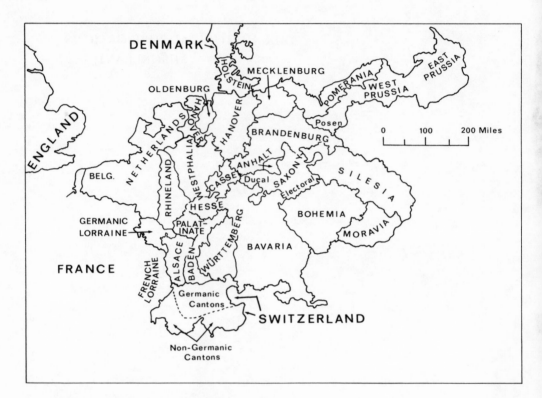

Principal Pre-Eighteenth-Century Germanic States

Caspar Schwenckfeld
Reluctant Radical

HIS LIFE TO 1540

R. EMMET McLAUGHLIN

YALE UNIVERSITY PRESS
NEW HAVEN AND LONDON

Designed by Sally Harris
and set in Electra type by
Graphic Composition, Inc., Athens, Georgia
Printed in the United States of America by
Vail-Ballou Press, Binghamton, N.Y.

Library of Congress Cataloging-in-Publication Data

McLaughlin, R. Emmet, 1950–
    Caspar Schwenckfeld, reluctant radical.

    Bibliography: p.
    Includes index.
    1. Schwenckfeld, Caspar, 1489–1561. 2. Reformation
—Biography. I. Title.
BX9749.S36M35 1986   284   85-20330
ISBN 0–300–03367–2 (alk. paper)

The paper in this book meets the guidelines for
permanence and durability of the Committee on
Production Guidelines for Book Longevity
of the Council on Library Resources.

10 9 8 7 6 5 4 3 2 1

Contents

Maps

Preface

Biography is a hazardous business, especially when the subject lived before the modern age. Many historians doubt its usefulness; it is elitist and antidemocratic, and it misses the large-scale, long-term movements that are the stuff of real history. Others, while accepting the value of the genre, may have unrealistic expectations. Sixteenth-century figures did not divulge their innermost fears and aspirations with great regularity. Even Luther, who was more outspoken than most, is hard to capture in the flesh. Caspar Schwenckfeld was no easier, and in many ways more difficult. The facade that he presented to the world rarely allowed a glimpse of irrational dreams, fears, and desires—what we moderns tend to consider the inner man. Given these limitations, speculation can easily outstrip evidence and produce pure fantasy. And while a certain interest might be satisfied by peeping into Schwenckfeld's psyche in this way, I am not sure that it would serve any historical purpose.

My goals instead were these: I wanted to reconstruct the stages of Schwenckfeld's development from a landed noble and courtier of Germany's eastern periphery to a notorious religious radical in Germany's southern heartland. I also wanted to understand how larger social, political, and religious forces molded the man. Finally, I wanted to establish the details of his reform activity. I felt that the accomplishment of these goals would make a contribution to our understanding of the German Reformation.

Since his own time Schwenckfeld has been the subject of comment, abuse, and praise.[1] Works of scholarly merit have examined aspects of his theology. But the only full biography of the man, Selina Gerhard Schultz's *Caspar Schwenckfeld von Ossig (1489–1561), Spiritual Interpreter of Christianity, Apostle of the Middle Way, Pioneer of Modern Religious Thought*, though still a valuable reference tool, is too much the product of pious admiration and lacks critical and analytic rigor. Despite the detailed scholarship on him, therefore, Schwenckfeld remains an elusive figure. Known to all scholars of the Reformation at

---

1. For a review of the literature, see Maron 1961a, 10–32.

least by name, Schwenckfeld has always been difficult to classify. Historians have not integrated him effectively into the larger religious and
historical context; he has been one of those pieces left over after the
puzzle is complete.

Some word should be said about the chronological limits of this
study, which ends in 1540 although Schwenckfeld did not die until
1561. Schwenckfeld lived seventy-two years and for forty of them he
was active in the Reform. His collected works fill nineteen huge volumes in the *Corpus Schwenckfeldianorum*. To have covered his entire
life with the care and detail useful to scholars was simply not feasible.
1540 was chosen as the break-off point because by that year all of the
major elements in Schwenckfeld's theology had received their first full
formulation. Furthermore, the events surrounding the christological
debates of 1538–39 led Schwenckfeld to reevaluate his own vocation.
From that period we can date the beginning of Schwenckfeld's self-
conscious public ministry. But stopping at 1540 has a great disadvantage which may not be obvious. I am reminded of the Chinese curse
"May you live in interesting times." The first half of Schwenckfeld's
career, though undoubtedly the most important for an understanding
of his growth as a reformer, lacks the excitement and daring of his life
after the Schmalkaldic War. These later years are filled with code
names, narrow escapes, and secret journeys. In the period covered by
this study Schwenckfeld's life, if not placid, was certainly orderly, and
well within the pale of respectability. The contrast between his inner
spiritual development and his outward manner does provide some en-
ergy for the narrative, but hardly enough to compare with the adven-
tures of a Müntzer or a Hoffmann or a John of Leyden. Schwenckfeld's
experiences were closer to those of more staid and established reformers like Butzer, Brenz, and Bugenhagen.

With regard to the perennial problem of orthography: Personal
names are in the German or Latin forms that occur most often in primary and secondary sources. Place names are given in German unless
English equivalents exist. Citations in the original languages are limited to the footnotes and retain the spelling and punctuation of the
originals. All translations in the text are mine unless otherwise noted.

I owe a debt of gratitude to many individuals and institutions. I have
profited greatly from the advice of Professors Steven Ozment and
Heiko A. Oberman. Peter C. Erb and the Schwenkfelder Library,

Pennsburg, Pennsylvania, have provided invaluable assistance. The generosity of the government of the Federal Republic of Germany made possible a year in Germany. My thanks also go to the libraries and staff of Yale University Library; Harvard University Library; Princeton Theological Library; the University of Chicago Library; Universitätsbibliothek Tübingen; Universitätsbibliothek Freiburg im Breisgau; Staatsbibliothek Preussischer Kulturbesitz, Berlin; Bayerische Staatsbibliothek, Munich; Herzog-August-Bibliothek, Wolfenbüttel; and Staatsarchiv, Weimar. A special word of appreciation is owed to Professor Lee Hopple of Bloomsbury State University, Bloomsbury, Pennsylvania, for permission to use the maps which he prepared for the Schwenckfeld Commemorative Colloquium in September 1984.

Abbreviations

In citations of multivolume works, the first number given indicates the volume, and the numbers following refer to pages. Line numbers, when supplied, follow a colon. Volumes from the *Corpus Schwenckfeldianorum* are indicated by Roman numerals. Thus TA 7, 237:24–26 refers to volume 7 of *Quellen zur Geschichte der Täufer*, page 237, lines 24–26. CS I, 12, 38 refers to volume 1 of *Corpus Schwenckfeldianorum*, pages 12 and 38.

AMKG	*Archiv für mittelrheinische Kirchengeschichte.* Speyer, 1949–.
ARG	*Archiv für Reformationsgeschichte.* Gütersloh, 1903–.
ASKG	*Archiv für schlesische Kirchengeschichte.* Hildesheim, 1949–.
BWKG	*Blätter für württembergische Kirchengeschichte.* Stuttgart, 1886–90, n.s. 1897–.
CR	*Corpus Reformatorum.* 101 vols. Zurich and Berlin, 1834–1982.
CS	*Corpus Schwenckfeldianorum.* 19 vols. Leipzig, 1907–61.
CVGEKS	*Correspondenzblatt des Vereins für Geschichte der Evangelischen Kirche Schlesiens.* Breslau and Liegnitz, 1882–1911.
JSKG	*Jahrbuch für schlesische Kirchengeschichte.* Düsseldorf, 1882–.
Lenz	Max Lenz, ed. *Briefwechsel Landgraf Philipps des Grossmüthigen von Hessen mit Bucer,* Part 1. Leipzig, 1880.
ME	*Mennonite Encyclopedia.* 4 vols. Scottsdale, Ariz., 1955–59.
MQR	*Mennonite Quarterly Review.* Goshen, Indiana. 1927–.

PL	*Patrologiae cursus completus, series Latina,* ed. Jacques Paul Migne. 221 vols. Paris, 1844–1903.
Schiess	Traugott Schiess, ed. *Briefwechsel der Brüder Ambrosius und Thomas Blaurer 1509–1548.* 2 vols. Freiburg im Breisgau, 1908, 1910.
Schuler and Schulthess	Melchior Schuler and Johannes Schulthess, eds. *Huldrici Zuingli Opera.* 8 vols. Zurich, 1828–42.
TA 1	Quellen zur Geschichte der Wiedertäufer. Vol. 1, *Herzogtum Württemberg,* ed. Gustav Bossert. Leipzig, 1930.
TA 2	Quellen zur Geschichte der Wiedertäufer. Vol. 2, *Markgraftum Brandenburg (Bayern I. Abteilung),* ed. Karl Schornbaum. Leipzig, 1934.
TA 4	Quellen zur Geschichte der Täufer. Vol. 4, *Baden und Pfalz,* ed. Manfred Krebs. Gütersloh, 1951.
TA 7	Quellen zur Geschichte der Täufer. Vol. 7, *Elsass, I. Teil, Stadt Strassburg, 1522–1532,* ed. Manfred Krebs and Hans Georg Rott. Gütersloh, 1959.
TA 8	Quellen zur Geschichte der Täufer. Vol. 8, *Elsass, II. Teil, Stadt Strassburg, 1533–1535,* ed. Manfred Krebs and Hans Georg Rott. Gütersloh, 1960.
Th. B.	Thesaurus Baumianus, 26 vols., MS Strassburg BNU.
Vad. Br.	*Vadianische Briefsammlung,* ed. Emil Arbenz and Hermann Wartmann, 7 vols. St. Gall, 1890–1913.
WA	*Luthers Werke. Kritische Ausgabe.* 60 vols. to date. Weimar, 1883–.
WA Br	*Luthers Werke. Kritische Ausgabe. Briefe.* 17 vols. Weimar, 1883–.
WA Deutsche Bibel	*Luthers Werke. Kritische Ausgabe. Deutsche Bibel.* 12 vols. Weimar, 1883–.

WA Tischreden	*Luthers Werke. Kritische Ausgabe. Tischreden.* 6 vols. to date. Weimar, 1883–.
ZBKG	*Zeitschrift für bayerischen Kirchengeschichte.* Nürnberg, 1926–.
ZGO	*Zeitschrift für die Geschichte des Oberrheins.* Karlsruhe and Heidelberg, 1850–.
ZVGS	*Zeitschrift des Vereins für Geschichte Schlesiens.* Breslau, 1855–1943.
ZWLG	*Zeitschrift für württembergische Landesgeschichte.* Stuttgart, 1937–.

PART I

SILESIA

(1489–1529)

1 Courtier
(1489–1521)

Schwenckfeld was for many years a courtier in the courts of princes and had not concerned himself much with Holy Scripture.—Schwenckfeld to Nicholaus Rhediger, November 1556

On May 18, 1529, Wolfgang Capito wrote to Ulrich Zwingli to announce the arrival of yet another religious refugee in Strassburg. Capito described the visitor as "a truly noble man. He is completely filled with the spirit of Christ. . . . Certainly he is a distinguished witness for Christ."[1] Glowing praise notwithstanding, in journeying to Strassburg Caspar Schwenckfeld von Ossig,[2] at age thirty-nine, a Silesian noble, courtier, and counselor to princes, had begun a lifelong exile from his native land. Hunted by Catholics, Lutherans, and Reformed, in conflict with the Anabaptists, at odds even with his fellow spiritualist Sebastian Franck, Schwenckfeld trod an increasingly lonely path throughout southern Germany until his death in Ulm in 1561. It was probably in that city, far from Silesia, that he was laid to rest in an unmarked grave.

Capito's first comment on his new guest and future antagonist provides an important key to Schwenckfeld's career and personal fate. Was it possible in Reformation Germany to be all three: "truly noble," "filled with the spirit," and a "distinguished witness for Christ"? The attempt brought Schwenckfeld much inner turmoil, while making his position in both church and secular society increasingly untenable.

He was born in late November or early December 1489 on the ancestral estate of Ossig, a village located half a mile from Lüben, Lower Silesia.[3] The Schwenckfelds had long been established in Schweidnitz, Upper Silesia, at least since the thirteenth century. Caspar

---

1. TA 7, 237:24–26.

2. Although the name Schwenckfeld is spelled in a variety of ways, sometimes within a single document (CS I, 117–18), the spelling most widely accepted is the one used here. The monuments of the family in Silesia as well as two autograph letters of Schwenckfeld attest to this spelling (CS I, 12, 38). Cf. Hampe 1882, 6; Schneider 1862, 2–3, 27 n. 10.

3. For Schwenckfeld's date of birth, see S. Schultz 1946, 1; Hampe 1882, 6; Hoffmann 1897, 6.

Schwenckfeld sprang from a cadet branch of the family that had taken possession of Ossig early in the fifteenth century.[4] He was the oldest of at least three children, with a brother Hans and a sister Anna.[5]

Schwenckfeld probably received his earliest education in Lüben and the city school of Liegnitz at SS. Peter-Paul. The teaching method and curriculum were fairly typical of late medieval schools, humanist pedagogy not yet having made its influence felt.[6] In 1505, at the age of fifteen, Schwenckfeld began his university studies at Cologne.[7] We have no information about his program of studies. But since his name was not on any of the matriculas, it is probable that he, like many another young nobleman, merely engaged a tutor to guide him through the arts course. In 1507 Schwenckfeld's name appeared in the rolls of the University of Frankfurt an der Oder. Again, there was no record of what he studied. The three years or so between his stay in Frankfurt and the beginning of his career at court remain unaccounted for. However, since Schwenckfeld later claimed to have attended other unspecified universities, it is probable that he spent the time making the educational grand tour of Germany. Overall there was nothing unusual in Schwenckfeld's wanderings.[8] To attend a number of universities over a period of five or six years without acquiring an academic degree was not unusual for a man of his class and ambitions.

If Schwenckfeld was a fairly typical student from a noble family, what did he study? We can assume he followed the basic arts program required of all at the university, but beyond that we are left with conjecture. It is most unlikely, as some scholars have speculated, that Schwenckfeld studied theology.[9] None of his later writings betray an acquaintance with scholastic method or theological content, and he himself liked to claim an inability to understand "schul Theologia."[10]

4. S. Schultz 1946, 4; Hampe 1882, 3–6; Konrad 1917, 2; Sinapius 1720, 861. The fourteenth-century inquisitor Johann Schwenckfeld does not seem to have been a member of the family. Schneider 1862, 18 n. 1.
5. S. Schultz 1946, 2; Hampe 1882, 6.
6. S. Schultz 1946, 3–4; Hoffmann 1897, 6; Hampe 1882, 7. Though he may have studied for a time with Dr. Bartholomaeus Ruersdorf, provost of the Liegnitz chapter, there is no evidence that Ruersdorf was humanistically inclined (F. Bahlow 1918, 24–25; Kluge 1917, 221–22).
7. For Schwenckfeld's university education, see S. Schultz 1946, 4. Suggestions that Schwenckfeld studied at Leipzig and Erfurt (Hampe 1882, 7; Anders 1867, 7; Otte 1936, 5) are mere conjecture.
8. For a profile of the student body at Frankfurt an der Oder, see Kliesch 1961. According to Kliesch (p. 66) only 20 percent of the students at Frankfurt received degrees. See p. 34 on the number of universities attended by students.
9. Otte 1936, 3–5; Kadelbach 1860, 1; Kluge 1917, 221–22.
10. CS VII, 585.

The study of canon law, on the other hand, would have made more sense for a nobleman planning to serve in the court of a Silesian prince. The relations between church and state were particularly strained in that region on the eve of the Reformation, and a knowledge of church law might have proved useful.[11] Furthermore, a young noble making his way in the world would always have to reckon with the possibility of high ecclesiastical preferment,[12] and in the early sixteenth century canonists were considered more suitable episcopal timber than were theologians.[13] Unfortunately, Schwenckfeld's writings betray no expert knowledge of canon law. When he used the *Decretum* it was as a handy compilation of patristic citations.[14] If Schwenckfeld did hear an occasional law lecture it would probably have been during his year at Frankfurt, since that university had one of the finest schools of canon law north of the Alps.[15]

Frankfurt was also an early center of humanism.[16] Schwenckfeld, however, showed no signs of a serious involvement in the scholarly side of humanism. He learned no Greek until study of the Bible required it. He studied Hebrew even later than he did Greek. His early letters to a bona fide humanist, Johannes Hess, are examples of typical late medieval Latin.[17] Schwenckfeld was much taken by the writings of Ulrich Hutten, but it is clear that he was impressed more by Hutten the zealot than by Hutten the literary stylist.[18] But although Schwenckfeld could never be termed a humanist himself, some of his closest friends and colleagues were. Humanism was therefore one

11. After a period of open warfare between the secular princes and the church during which the nobles and rulers of Silesia denied the church any protection, in effect outlawing it, an agreement was reached in 1504. The Kolowrat Treaty remained a bone of contention until the Reformation rendered it superfluous.

12. Jakob Salza, bishop of Breslau during the early years of the Reformation, was of the same class as Schwenckfeld and attained his episcopal rank through years of loyal secular service. Erhardt von Queiss, bishop of Pomersania and chancellor to one of Schwenckfeld's patrons, Friedrich of Liegnitz, pursued much the same course.

13. For the situation in England see Dickens 1974, chap. 3. In like manner the Breslau cathedral chapter had not a single theologian (Engelbert 1960, 147).

14. See, for example, his *Eyn kurtzer Auszug auss dem Bäbstlichen Rechten der Decret und Decretalen*, ca. June 1530 (CS III, 753–811). This work was merely a reworking of a collection by Lazarus Spengler. Schwenckfeld's later correspondence (1538) with a lawyer at the imperial court in Speyer, though dealing with issues of marriage law, is noteworthy solely for its nonlegal tone (Nicolaus Maior to Schwenckfeld, Cod. Aug. 37.27.2, 555–56; Schwenckfeld to Maior, CS VI, 176–92).

15. Kliesch 1961, 17.

16. Kliesch 1961, 61.

17. CS I, 16.

18. CS I, 11:15, 17. Did Schwenckfeld know Hutten personally? It is possible because both men studied at Cologne in 1505. Hutten also spent the winter of 1506–07 at Frankfurt an der Oder. (S. Schultz 1946, 4; Holborn 1937, 29).

among many influences to which Schwenckfeld was exposed as a literate, well-traveled noble of early sixteenth-century Germany.

Schwenckfeld was an educated man, but no scholar. He was also not a follower of any school or movement. Unlike the scholastically trained Luther, for instance, he was not caught up in the school traditions, the controversies of the *Viae*, or the ongoing discussion of seemingly transcendent or transhistorical issues in theology or philosophy. Lacking this anchor in the intellectual tradition, Schwenckfeld was more easily moved by the rush of events. This did not make him inconsistent or inconstant. But it did encourage him to weigh "eternal" ideas or doctrines by the standard of the temporal, the concrete, the contemporary. Luther's gospel message would be so weighed and eventually found wanting.

The young man of twenty-one who returned to Silesia in 1510–11 was in no sense atypical. Born of an old, established family, trained in the customary fashion, and ready to embark on the expected career at court, Caspar Schwenckfeld von Ossig gave no sign that his life would differ significantly from the lives of his by now long-forgotten peers.

Late medieval Silesia was the stage upon which Schwenckfeld played out the first ten years of his reforming career. Its fragmented political structure, its depressed economic conditions, and its fierce anticlericalism guided Schwenckfeld's choices, determined the scope of his activities, and left a deposit of experience, perceptions, and preconceptions which marked him for the rest of his life. The land was, in many ways, father to the man.

Silesia is a land gathered around the river Oder and its tributaries. Stretching from the mountains of Bohemia to the Mark of Brandenburg, in the sixteenth century Silesia was a German salient jutting into Slavic Europe. Poland lay to the east, Hungary and Moravia to the south, Bohemia to the southwest. The bridge to Germany was formed by Saxony on Silesia's northwestern border and Brandenburg due north. Initially settled by German colonists in the thirteenth century, Silesia was predominantly German in population and, at least for the upper classes, wholly German in culture by the sixteenth century. But it remained a border region nonetheless, and this one fact determined its fate throughout the late Middle Ages.

The Hussite wars of the early fifteenth century had left large areas of Silesia devastated and depopulated. A renewed struggle with Georg

Podiebrad, the heretic-king of Bohemia, in the third quarter of the century incurred new damage, while preventing any recovery from earlier losses. Indeed, throughout the later Middle Ages, Silesia had been the coveted prize of all its neighbors. At times controlled by Poland, Bohemia, and Hungary, at times autonomous, Silesia became the cause and the battlefield for wars among those powers. Only in 1527, when Ferdinand the Habsburg became overlord by virtue of his title as King of Bohemia, was some stability provided.

Though primarily an agricultural region, Silesia had one other important economic resource—trade. The chief city of the region, Breslau, with some thirty thousand inhabitants, rivaled the great imperial cities in wealth, prestige, and autonomy.[19] Since Silesia had little manufacture of its own, Breslau and the other cities depended on their geographical position as points of transit from east to west and from south to north. The transshipping of Hungarian copper was particularly vital. An attempt by Bishop Turzo of Breslau in 1514 to redirect that trade around the lands of Friedrich II of Liegnitz plunged those two magnates into war.[20] This reliance on its neighbors had been a heavy burden for Silesia and left it vulnerable to outside pressure. Schwenckfeld's fate in Silesia was determined by that vulnerability; in turn, he would conclude that the Reformation movement could not rest on political power. The Hussite wars had broken commercial ties with Bohemia, never to be fully reestablished. An incipient nationalism in Poland also led to clashes over trade. Later, an embargo by Catholic Poland was always a viable threat against the Protestant burghers of Breslau. It was therefore advantageous for all concerned that from 1474 until 1527 Silesia, though nominally a Bohemian possession, was in fact ruled by Hungary, its chief source of trade. Although this connection also provided Silesia with its first effective ruler in over a century in the person of Matthias Corvinus, after that sovereign's death in 1490 a succession of incapable or underaged rulers, whose limited abilities and energies were concentrated on stemming the Turkish advance, left Silesia to its own devices.

War, devastation, political uncertainty, and the lack of any effective central power produced chaos. The unsettled conditions made it dif-

19. Knörrlich 1957, 18–19. Knörrlich estimates the total population of Silesia at one million in the early sixteenth century.
20. Meyer 1903, 119–20. Bishop Turzo was a member of the Hungarian Turzo family, partners with the Fuggers in exploiting the copper mines of Hungary.

ficult to maintain a peasant work force and impossible to attract new settlers. The decline in revenues hit lay and clerical sectors alike.[21] Much of the bitterness of the clashes between secular and spiritual powers in the pre-Reformation period can be traced to competition for the drastically reduced wealth to be got from the land. But perhaps the group that was most affected, and whose reaction was most destructive to the welfare of the Silesian community as a whole, was the nobility. It was from this class that Schwenckfeld came, and he always felt he belonged to it.[22]

In search of new sources of revenue, some knights declared war on their neighbors, the cities, while others simply resorted to highway robbery.[23] No knights-errant, they were noted for their cruelty and their delight in killing or mutilating their victims. But brigandage was not the only career possible for a young noble. Others sought to serve in the courts of the territorial princes of the region. No less violent and greedy than the nobility, these princes did eventually impose a measure of security upon the land.[24] Much as the territorial princes of the empire became the foci of power, so too, but on a smaller scale, did the various hereditary princes of Silesia. Among other things, they would determine the course of Silesia's Reformation. It was in service to such princes that Schwenckfeld sought to advance his career.

By March 10, 1511, he was serving at the court of Karl von Münsterberg-Oels (1476–1536).[25] Having recently united these two principalities and rented their gold mines to the Fuggers, he set out to make himself noticed in Silesia.[26] He was ambitious, extravagant, and a lover of courtly splendor. (By his death he had managed to construct the most extensive and the most costly palace in Silesia, and he left his

21. Meyer 1903, 35–36.
22. CS XIV, 47:28–32.
23. There is the case of Adam Schwob, who was at war with Liegnitz and Breslau for many years in the latter part of the fifteenth century, and whose activities occasioned much correspondence between the king of Bohemia, the duke of Saxony, and the rulers of Brandenburg and Anhalt (Meyer 1903, 14–18; see also Knörrlich 1957, 13). On the unenviable life of a landed noble, see Ulrich von Hutten's letter to Willibald Pirckheimer, October 1518, in von Hutten 1859, 195–217. Though Hutten undoubtedly exaggerates the inconveniences and dangers, he does much to dispel any romantic notions.
24. In many cases the princes were the worst offenders against the peace. The league of Silesian cities formed in 1509 to suppress highway robbers felt constrained in 1512 to choose Friedrich of Liegnitz as its head. In so doing they ended the war that Friedrich had been waging with Breslau, the most important of the league's members (Knörrlich 1957, 13).
25. S. Schultz 1946, 5; Otte 1936, 5–6; Hoffmann 1897, 6–7.
26. Knörrlich 1957, 30 n. 9; Aubin 1938, 382–83.

heirs so saddled with debts that they were forced to pawn Münster-berg.)[27]

Shortly after Schwenckfeld's arrival at the court of Oels, Karl and his cousins, the brothers Georg of Brieg and Friedrich of Liegnitz, became embroiled with the bishop and chapter of Breslau.[28] King Wladislaw of Bohemia and Hungary, at that time overlord of Silesia, had granted the church immunity from all local taxes on March 27, 1511. The three cousins had ignored the royal grant and demanded payment. When the church refused, Georg of Brieg took up arms and waged open war on the church. He declared the subjects of the cathedral chapter his enemies, seized their cattle, and threatened the church's peasants with expulsion. Georg was finally paid off in 1514.

The princes' readiness to use force against the church testifies to the weakness of the central power as well as to their lack of regard for the church. Although economic factors account for most of the tension between secular and spiritual authorities, another factor fueled the conflict. Karl of Münsterberg-Oels, Georg of Brieg, and Friedrich of Liegnitz were all grandchildren of Georg Podiebrad, the Bohemian king whose posterity had been banned "in perpetuum" from all public office by papal decree in 1496.[29] Although the ban had finally been lifted in 1507,[30] the memory still rankled.

The incident in 1511 was not an isolated one. Georg and his brother Friedrich had already threatened the church's peasants with war in 1499–1500 over their failure to pay ducal taxes.[31] Georg's relations with the church deteriorated so far that the Breslau cathedral chapter would have refused him Christian burial in 1521 had his brother Friedrich not been the most powerful ruler in Silesia.[32] Schwenckfeld therefore grew to political manhood in an atmosphere marked by a

27. Knörrlich 1957, 31; Schimmelpfennig 1884, 147–48, 161.
28. Meyer 1903, 141–42.
29. Rosenberg 1767, 4. The text of the condemnation states: "exuitur regia potestate, omnibus Iuribus privatur, ipsi filii, et tota regia posteritas in perpetuum inhabiles ad omni dignitates, honores et officio pronunciatur."
30. The ban may have been lifted as a result of Friedrich's pilgrimage to the Holy Land. Karl of Münsterberg-Oels was informed of the papal absolution on "Donnerstag nach Kreuzerhohung" 1507 by his brother Albrecht (Schimmelpfennig 1884, 127). Friedrich's pilgrimage began in Silesia in March 1507. He had returned to Venice in November 1507. Since the return trip to Silesia would last about a month, there would have been little time to procure the absolution and still get word to Silesia before the end of the year. Perhaps the pilgrimage was a thanks offering and not a requirement for absolution (Meisner and Röhricht 1878, 101–31).
31. Meyer 1903, 112–13.
32. Konrad 1917, 6.

bitter—and active—anticlericalism. It was as much a part of his identity as his noble escutcheon.

In 1515 Schwenckfeld left Oels to join the court at Brieg.[33] Georg's court was noted for its gaiety and license in a time when the corruption of court life was proverbial.[34] Much addicted to the splendor and magnificence of the knightly ideal brought into vogue by Emperor Maximilian, he spent vast sums on horses, armor, and feasting.[35] Georg died in 1521, still a relatively young man, "destroyed by drinking and pleasures" (corruptus crapula et voluptatibus).[36] Free now to seek a new lord, Schwenckfeld, nearly thirty-two, joined the entourage of Friedrich of Liegnitz, Georg's brother and heir. The exact date is unknown, but by October 1521 he was an established member of the court.[37]

Schwenckfeld's ten-year apprenticeship had made of him a polished and assured courtier. This calling—much discussed, much praised, and much condemned in the sixteenth century[38]—required, like the professions of medicine and law, a remolding of character on the part of its practitioners in addition to the discrete skills demanded. One did not just practice law, medicine, or the arts of courtly behavior. One became a lawyer, a doctor, or a courtier. This was especially true for courtiers because in a real sense personality was their most important commodity. Forerunners of Castiglione's cortegiano can be traced as

33. S. Schultz 1946, 5; Hampe 1882, 8.
34. Hoffmann 1897, 7; Knörrlich 1957, 31.
35. Schönwälder 1855, 321.
36. Georg died May 20, 1521. Hoffmann 1897, 7.
37. Various dates for Schwenckfeld's move to Liegnitz have been suggested. Hampe (1882, 8) puts forward 1516. Hoffmann (1897, 8) and S. Schultz (1946, 5) believe 1518 to be more probable. F. Bahlow (1918, 26) feels that Schwenckfeld transferred to Liegnitz as a result of his religious awakening, an event which Bahlow correctly dates to 1519. But since Schwenckfeld himself gives no information on the subject, only a terminus ante quo is certain. This is provided by his first letter to Johannes Hess of October 1521 (CS I, 10–12). The death of Georg of Brieg seems a more likely cause for shifting to the court of Georg's heir than would Schwenckfeld's religious conversion. After all, Georg was indifferent to the Lutheran movement (Schönwälder 1855, 315), while Friedrich at first was actively opposed to it (S. Schultz 1946, 10). Furthermore, Brieg was an early Lutheran center. Georg's wife, Anna, joined in early support of the Wittenberg movement. Her brother was rector at Wittenberg in 1519 and accompanied Luther to the Leipzig Debate (Hartmann 1928, 12). In any event, to use Schwenckfeld's religious experience as a means of dating his shift to Liegnitz, and then to take that shift as revealing Schwenckfeld's character is to argue in a circular fashion, as does, e.g., F. Bahlow 1918, 26.
38. On Castiglione's Cortegiano and its influence, see Loos 1955; Mazzeo 1965, 131–60; Barker 1948, 124–58. On the origins of the German medieval courtier ideal, see Jaeger 1977 and Jaeger 1983. The courtier mode was also the subject of criticism (Uhlig 1973). For the best analysis of court life and courtier mentality, see Elias 1969. For the imperial court in this period, see Müller 1982, esp. pp. 22–79.

far back as the tenth-century German imperial court. And though modified under the impact of late medieval chivalry and Renaissance humanism, the figure of the model courtier remained surprisingly constant until the end of the ancien régime.

Function determined character. Above all, the courtier was to be a boon companion and intimate counselor to the ruler. In most cases this required that the courtier be of the nobility himself. Although low-born favorites and servitors abounded in the Middle Ages, they almost invariably occasioned disparaging comment. Noble descent lent a self-assurance that was lacking in the arriviste. Capito was to complain that Schwenckfeld, because he was noble, simply expected to be taken seriously.[39] High birth did not suffice, of course; in Capito's words, "vir *vere* nobilis." It was a matter of both show and substance, but could best be described as "style." Natural good looks were to be complemented by tastefully expensive clothing and ornament. The ability to dance well, to sing or play a suitable instrument, was valuable. Skill at the chase or in jousting was in demand at some courts. More important was elegance of manner and manners joined to conversational skill and wit. In the hothouse atmosphere of the court, language was the successful courtier's most important tool. Flattering the ladies, entertaining the prince, arguing policy, defending against the inevitable backbiting—all required volubility, precision, and eloquence. As Bugenhagen would learn to his dismay, Schwenckfeld possessed a finely honed skill in argument and conversation. Zwingli left his one meeting with Schwenckfeld feeling that he had barely escaped the lion's jaws.[40] Poor Martin Frecht was repeatedly embarrassed before the Ulm city council. Martin Butzer saw friends and followers weakened or turned away. Other theologians simply fled.

As far as education was concerned, the courtier was to be the gifted amateur, a well-rounded, well-read man who was informed, but no pedant. Wearing one's learning lightly became an art form to which Castiglione gave a name, *sprezzatura*. The courtier's words were enhanced by what one can only call a "presence." There was a certain gravity, not dour or grim, but a quiet seriousness which lent weight to

39. TA 1, 992, Capito to Johann Jakob Truchsess von Rheinfelden, May 21, 1534.
40. "Satis notus est mihi Schwenckfeldius, quem ex uno colloquio, quod mihi cum illo fuit, velut ex ungue leonem emensus sum. . . . Fidit ille non veritate, sed elegantiae, cum civilium morum, tum sermonis germanici, qua eloqui venuste potest quicquid cogitaverit" (TA 7, 282, 10–18).

his views and wishes. In Schwenckfeld's case this gravity assumed ever more somber hues as cares and years began to burden him.

Schwenckfeld's persona as a courtier was a mixed blessing for the man himself and for any who sought to understand him. His charm and native dignity attracted many followers and impressed even his enemies. But it was based on a deeply rooted, perhaps on occasion unconscious, drive to please, to establish ties of friendship or agreement, to "become all things to all men" (1 Cor. 9:22). Coupled with a horror of open or bitter disagreement, another product of his court days, he tended to accentuate the common ground which he shared with his opponents.[41] Even when it became clear that the differences which separated were greater than at first he supposed, he refused to indulge in the vicious polemic characteristic of the age. His restraint only served further to confuse and infuriate his enemies. And it tends to bestow an air of unreality about the man and his writings, something like watching a violent television scene with the sound turned off. This bell-jar effect is heightened by the internal silence, the rarity of personal commentary in his letters. He does speak of his hopes and fears, but his grief is a composed grief, his joy a decorous joy. As with other public figures of the early modern period, Schwenckfeld can be understood as a carefully groomed and crafted public personage who remained a public person even in some of his most private moments.

The harmony that Schwenckfeld wished upon the world around him was a reflection of the inner harmony that defined the style of the courtier.[42] Each of the many elements of that ideal was subordinated to a larger, more pleasing whole. The Aristotelian mean was the measure of virtue, and too great a knowledge or too limited a skill would disturb the carefully maintained symmetry and balance. But Schwenckfeld's conversion experience, his subsequent absorption in theology, and his increasingly pronounced piety conspired to disturb that balance, creating an internal psychological flywheel which propelled Schwenckfeld forward by fits and starts.

This internalized social pressure—the competing demands to be a polished courtier and a good Christian—was reinforced by a more

41. "The nature of court life itself favored the stifling of conflict, not the open airing of it" (Jaeger 1983, 310). Schwenckfeld's irenicism was not a family trait. His younger brother, Hans, a somewhat more typical Junker, once tried to run down the local Lutheran pastor with his horse (Fleischer 1975, 258).

42. See Mazzeo 1965, 146–47.

fundamental condition which may have been innate, or may have been the product of his personal trials. Capito, a learned and observant man with whom Schwenckfeld lived for two years, has provided a capsule analysis, written in 1534 in an effort to warn a correspondent against Schwenckfeld:

He is a melancholic. For this reason he is stubborn in his opinions, and is fearful [*forchtsam*] and suspicious for no good reason [*da nichts zu besorgen*]. It is characteristic of *serodiscentia*, that is, of those who come to learning late, that such people believe that what they have just learned no one knows. And they proclaim it so pompously [*brachtlich*].[43]

Despite its bias Capito's assessment is illuminating; many of Schwenckfeld's actions fit this description, and some of his own remarks lend support. *Melancholia* was a technical term describing both a physiological state and a psychological condition.[44] Beginning with ancient Greek writers and continuing through medieval and Renaissance medical traditions, certain widely accepted characteristics had been ascribed to melancholia. The preponderance of black bile (*melaina kole*) produced a personality bearing some similarity to that of a manic-depressive, though by no means as violent in its alterations. Periods of lassitude and depression were followed by bursts of activity and inspiration. The condition was often associated with intellectual or creative preeminence. Students and scholars were thought subject to it by reason of overlong and overstrenuous study. Aristotle claimed that all extraordinary men in philosophy, politics, poetry, and art had been melancholics.[45] Goethe's Faust is the best literary portrayal of one. Whatever modern psychology would make of its causes, *melancholia* described a cluster of personal characteristics which premodern men recognized in some of their contemporaries.

Schwenckfeld's religious experience in Silesia was marked by periods of quiescence, almost retirement, punctuated by episodes of revelation and bursts of activity. His behavior during the 1530s, after his exile, cannot be fully explained. A quiet period from 1529 through

43. TA 1, 992.

44. Capito himself was described as melancholic (Friedman 1983, 35). For a short history of the concept *melancholia*, see Heger 1967, 23–37. For the best overall treatment of melancholy in the period, see Klibansky et al. 1964.

45. Actually this statement was found in the pseudo-Aristotelian *Problemata physica*, bk. 30, chap. 1 (Heger 1967, 25).

1532 was followed by Schwenckfeld's dramatic involvement in the Strassburg synod and his trip to Augsburg in 1533. Another four years of relative peace was ended by his departure from Ulm in 1539. What provoked Schwenckfeld, who had maintained a good relationship with the Ulm city council, to place that body in an untenable position and force them to ask him to leave the city, is not entirely explicable.

Capito's comment on Schwenckfeld's educational shortcomings was not repeated by others of the period and is exactly what one would expect from a humanist. Although Schwenckfeld did eventually learn Greek and Hebrew, his strength lay always in the vernacular.[46] Nonetheless, this was no impediment. It was perhaps rather an advantage since it enabled him to reach a broader audience than could the latinate humanist theologians who opposed him in the South. He was also a more skilled and imaginative theologian than any of those opponents, with the possible exception of Butzer. Recognizing this, they avoided attacking him by name in print until 1540. His ability served only to exacerbate the fear and jealousy that motivated many of his clerical opponents. Schwenckfeld's troubles were as much the product of personality clashes as theological differences.

The strain of a long "identity crisis," the surges of his melancholic disposition, and the challenges of the evolving reform movement conspired to evoke at least three experiences (in 1519, 1525, and 1527) which he termed divine visitations, *Heimsuchungen*. Beginning with his conversion, each represented a new stage in his religious commitment, and each marked his decision to proceed in the face of his own uncertainty and to overcome his own reluctance to commit himself more fully.[47]

46. He was already using his Greek before leaving Silesia (CS III, 479:39–480:1). One of the reasons Schwenckfeld went to Augsburg in 1533 was to continue his study of Hebrew with Bonifacius Wolfhart (CS V, 106:14–24).

47. A later work (1529?), "Of the stages of rebirth and of God's work with the poor sinner whom he has accepted into grace for Christ's sake" (CS III, 571–75), certainly incorporated Schwenckfeld's own religious odyssey. The dating is admittedly speculation on the part of the editors, but it clearly seems to be from the post-Silesian era. According to that description Schwenckfeld's first *Heimsuchung* was indeed a visitation. Drawn by the Father, Schwenckfeld suddenly realized his own sinfulness, was overcome with repentance, and yearned for reconciliation with God and a new Christian life. Given the extravagance of Karl of Münsterberg-Oels and the ill repute of Georg of Brieg, such a reaction seems quite appropriate. Remorse was followed by rebirth in the consolation of the gospel. A new Christian life was made possible by the increasing knowledge which the divine light and the word of God imparted. Growing wisdom, faith, and knowledge, the contemplation of the sweetness of the law and of Christ was followed by the cross and persecution. Confirmed in faith, the Christian confessed publicly. Revelations, new understanding, were the Christian's lot. Finally there came a "sealing of faith," an absolute certitude of salvation and a wish to shed this body of death and return home

What marked the courtier Schwenckfeld most was his ambition. Schwenckfeld was the elder son, yet it was he who went to university and then entered court service, while his younger brother Hans was left behind to tend the family properties.[48] In choosing the court of Karl of Münsterberg-Oels Schwenckfeld was associating himself with a rising star in the Silesian firmament. In 1515 Karl was made first counselor to King Wladislaw, in effect prime minister.[49] Ferdinand of Austria later appointed Karl provincial governor (*Oberlandeshauptmann*), his highest representative in Lower Silesia.[50] If, as most scholars have assumed, Schwenckfeld left Karl's service in 1515, Karl's appointment to the royal court may have been the reason. By becoming a royal counselor and by residing at the royal court, Karl effectively removed himself from the Silesian political scene. In Silesia the king had at his disposal relatively little patronage and even less land with which to reward his servants. Karl himself received only a salary for his services. And since his salary was often in arrears, and his duties more expensive than remunerative, he died leaving many debts. His heirs had to pawn half their inheritance to Friedrich of Liegnitz, who had wisely stayed at home tending his own garden.[51] Schwenckfeld chose to imitate Friedrich, not Karl.[52]

Schwenckfeld's next master, Georg of Brieg, was a natural choice. Schwenckfeld's property at Ossig lay in Georg's domain. Service to this prince would at the very least strengthen Schwenckfeld's influence in his own home region. But it was Schwenckfeld's transfer to the court of Friedrich II of Liegnitz that was his greatest coup.

Friedrich II (1480–1547) was the older brother of Georg of Brieg, and the grandson, through his mother, of King Georg Podiebrad of Bohemia.[53] Because of his lineage and his close ties to the royal courts of eastern Europe (he had lived at the court of King Wladislaw until his father's death required him to return to Liegnitz), Friedrich was a

---

to heaven with Christ. As something of an anticlimax, the reborn Christian must await God's call, continually fighting the old flesh.

48. Knörrlich 1957, 30.

49. Schimmelpfennig 1884, 138.

50. Schimmelpfennig 1884, 145–46.

51. Schimmelpfennig 1884, 145–46.

52. Aside from the salary, gifts, and food allowance which Schwenckfeld received as a member of court, he may also have been granted lands by Friedrich. S. Schultz (1946, 3) believes that Schwenckfeld owned lands in Wohlau. At least it is certain that he spent some time there. Wohlau was purchased by Friedrich II in 1523, and the first Schwenckfeld letter from Wohlau is dated March 20, 1527 (CS II, 608:8). For the structure, staff, and salaries of the Liegnitz court in 1564, see Scriptores 1856, 214–19.

53. On Friedrich see F. Bahlow 1918, 24–25; Engelbert 1963, 163.

power to be reckoned with in Silesia. Friedrich's ambition and his importance in Silesia was reflected in the marriages he contracted. In 1515 he married Elisabeth, the sister of King Wladislaw and daughter of King Kasimir IV of Poland, but unfortunately she died two years later. Friedrich's second marriage was of more lasting significance. On November 14, 1518, he wed Sophie, the daughter of Markgraf Friedrich V of Brandenburg and sister of Markgraf Georg of Brandenburg. This was the beginning of a connection with the Hohenzollern family which would determine many of Friedrich's political and religious policies.

By 1521 Friedrich was also *Oberlandeshauptmann* for Lower Silesia,[54] an office created by Matthias Corvinus in 1474 in an attempt to exert royal influence and impose order. Silesia suffered from a checkered constitutional past. Originally a part of the Greater Polish Kingdom of the Piast dynasty in the tenth and eleventh centuries, in the twelfth century it became one of the almost independent Polish duchies produced by the Piast practice of dividing lands equally among all male heirs.[55] Within Silesia itself the fragmentation continued, producing at first two and then increasing numbers of independent duchies. Each duke was completely sovereign within his own domain, possessing full regalian rights of coinage, mining rights, and powers of high and low justice.[56] Internecine warfare was endemic. The power vacuum attracted outside interference, resulting in a loose vassalage to the Hohenstaufen German emperors in the late twelfth and thirteenth centuries. The fourteenth century witnessed Silesia's incorporation into the Bohemian crown lands by the Luxemburgers King John and Emperor Charles IV. These strong kings actually ruled in Silesia, providing the first centralized administration. But in the years between the death of Charles IV in 1378 and the accession of Matthias Corvinus in 1469—nearly a century—the land lacked a strong, universally recognized overlord. Eventually, in response to Hussite threats and the growing chaos in the countryside, the dukes gathered at meetings called *Fürstentage*, where provisional and usually short-lived alliances

54. Various dates are proposed for Friedrich's term of office. Engelbert (1963, 165) asserts that Friedrich received the post in 1516. Knörrlich (1957, 11) believes 1518 is more accurate. 1519 has also been suggested (Aubin 1938, 239). It is certain that Friedrich held the office in 1519 since Albrecht von Brandenburg-Ansbach addressed a letter in that year to him using the title (Krämer 1977, 9). On the nature of the office, see Knörrlich 1957, 10.

55. On Silesia's inner development, see Rachfahl 1894. On its relationship to the German state, Poland, Bohemia, and Hungary, see Kutscha 1924.

56. See Menzel 1964.

were formed. To head the military forces and to preside over legal pro-
cesses a *Hauptmann* was chosen. When the Hungarian king Matthias
Corvinus sought to gain real administrative control of Silesia he
adapted this structure, making the *Oberlandeshauptmann* a royal ap-
pointee.

In the early years of the sixteenth century there were actually two
such positions, one each for Upper and Lower Silesia. These officials
were to enforce the king's peace in the lands under their jurisdiction.
In addition, and indeed far more important, the provincial governor
called the *Fürstentag* at the king's behest, arranged its agenda, and cast
the deciding ballot.[57] These gatherings pledged taxes, offered allegiance to newly enthroned overlords, and sought to bring a measure of
unity and peace to the land. The *Fürstentag* was the only effective
organ of government above the level of the local prince. The provincial governor thus occupied a mediating position, representing the
king's interests to the estates and the estates' interests to the king. Because royal power was never really effectively exercised in Silesia, the
provincial governor had to rely on his own resources for executing
whatever duties were assigned to him. In effect, this meant that the
most powerful secular ruler in the region was chosen for the position.
When the existence of Protestant principalities had become a reality,
the Habsburg penchant for combining religious and political aims led
to a policy, after 1536, of appointing the bishop of Breslau to the
post.[58] Ferdinand of Austria had learned by experience how important
the office could be. Until he was replaced in 1527, Schwenckfeld's
patron Friedrich used his post to block Catholic efforts to suppress the
young Lutheran movement.[59] It was also under his leadership that the
Grottkau *Fürstentag* of 1524 in effect gave legislative sanction to Protestant activities.

In 1521 when we find him in Liegnitz, Schwenckfeld's ambition

57. The bishop of Breslau usually presided. There were three *curia*, each having one vote.
The first *curia* comprised the princes, including all the dukes, the city of Breslau as "prince" of
the Breslau principality, the bishop of Breslau as prince of Neisse-Ottmachau-Grottkau, and
the four nonducal lordships of Wartenbeg, Pless, Thachtenberg, and Militsch. The second
curia was composed of representatives of the lords, prelates, and knights of the directly held
royal principalities of Schweidnitz-Jauer, Glogau, and Troppau, as well as of the Breslau principality. In the third *curia* were representatives of the cities in the royal principalities.

58. Knörrlich 1957, 22.

59. Knörrlich (1957, 11) believes that Friedrich held office only until 1524, but there is
evidence that Friedrich was *Oberlandeshauptmann* until August 1526 (Engelbert 1963, 142).
Since Ferdinand of Austria did not appoint Karl of Münsterberg-Oels to the post until March
1527 (Schimmelpfennig 1884, 145–46), Friedrich would have remained *Oberlandeshauptmann* de facto if not de jure until that time.

and talents had become harnessed to the furtherance of the gospel and the kingdom of his new prince, Christ.[60] Schwenckfeld's decision to join Friedrich's court, and his efforts to win Friedrich for the evangelical cause, would in large measure determine the success of the Reformation in Silesia. As Wolfgang Knörrlich has pointed out, Schwenckfeld could have picked no better place from which to help the Lutheran party.[61]

Schwenckfeld's religious conversion, or *Heimsuchung*, in 1519 was sudden and, unlike Luther's, preceded by no prolonged personal crisis.[62] Although he was occasionally hesitant, he experienced no recurring attacks of doubt (*Anfechtungen*) concerning his salvation as did the Saxon reformer. Before 1519 he was a typical courtier, not much concerned with religion but caught up instead in the round of courtly life.[63] Despite later rhetorical self-accusation, however, it is unlikely that Schwenckfeld was a depraved "courtesan."[64] Even his new religious intensity didn't move him to leave court service immediately. The shift to Liegnitz was not an attempt to find a more Christian setting in which to live and work. Despite the tendency of later historians to portray Friedrich of Liegnitz as a particularly pious prince, the evidence suggests that this could only be in comparison to his profligate brother.[65] It was, in fact, while at Friedrich's court that Schwenckfeld

60. For one instance among many of Schwenckfeld's view of Christ as his prince, see CS XVI, document 1045. On the dating of Schwenckfeld's move to Liegnitz, see note 37, above.

61. Knörrlich 1957, 16.

62. F. Bahlow (1918, 25–26) is undoubtedly correct in placing Schwenckfeld's conversion in 1519. Cf. Ecke 1911, 48–49; Furcha 1970, 13; Hampe 1882, 8; Hirsch 1922, 153; Hoffmann 1897, 10; Lashlee 1969, 34; Otte 1936, 7; Pietz 1959, 9; Weigelt 1973, 4. See also CS I, 248:17–20; CS XIV, 795:18–24. All of Schwenckfeld's comments on the experience refer to its suddenness; cf. CS VI, 490:9–19; CS IV, 775:21–31; CS V, 535:13–16; CS IX, 60:36–61:3.

63. Schwenckfeld admitted he had little interest in the Bible during his years at court (CS XIV, 876:29–31). He also admitted having spent his youth *uppigklich* (CS IV, 781:15–17).

64. Schwenckfeld on his sinful youth: CS VI, 609:13–17; CS IX, 421:10–16; CS XI, 583:14–16; CS XII, 133:22–25. These passages have the ring of self-deprecation and evangelical humility. He also claimed, however, that he had lived blamelessly (*gegen jederman unverweiss-lich zuehalten*). CS VI, 489:20–24. This may mean that he simply maintained good friendly relations with all he met, while not claiming to have led a morally spotless life. Since this passage formed part of an apology to the duke of Württemberg, Schwenckfeld's peaceful demeanor rather than his abstemiousness may have been the more important issue.

65. Johannes Hess, during a colloquy with Bohemian Brethren in 1540, recounted how Friedrich of Liegnitz had at one time planned to institute a strict church discipline in his lands, assuming, however, that he as prince would himself be exempt. Hess had replied, "Dass, Euer Gnaden, durchlauchtiger Fürst, Ihr selbst Euch zuerst dem Urteil unterwerfen und aus der Kirche ausgeschieden werden muesset, wegen dieser und jener Dinge, welche ich ihm aufzaehlte" (Rezek 1884, 292). Since Friedrich had already accepted the Augsburg Confession the previous year (F. Bahlow 1918, 133), the "Dinge" which Hess mentioned would probably

made his most critical remarks about court life. But whatever the pit-falls that court life presented, the court remained the focus of Schwenckfeld's activity in Silesia, even after he had retired to his own estate.[66]

While Schwenckfeld was being reborn through penitence and faith, the whole of Silesia was shaken by events in Wittenberg and elsewhere in the empire. Shortly after publication, the Ninety-five Theses appeared in Breslau and the rest of Silesia.[67] Nonetheless, there was no immediate recognition that Luther posed a threat to the church in Silesia. The cathedral chapter may well have been initially favorable to him; the bishop, Johann Turzo, was indifferent.[68]

The Lutherans' first foothold in Silesia was in the villages and country seats of the Junkers, often Hussite. Lutheran preachers began to appear there in 1518.[69] Throughout the Reformation era the landed nobility provided protection and support for dissident, and often radical, groups on their country estates, beyond the reach of urban magistrates and princely bureaucrats. One might almost term it a Junker Reformation which stood alongside the more significant urban and princely ones. Schwenckfeld and his followers were to profit handsomely from the wayward independence of landed nobles in both Silesia and southern Germany.

The Protestant movement in Silesia gathered steam in 1519. Adam Dyon opened a publishing house in Breslau in that year and began printing Luther's works, along with those of Eck, Karlstadt, and Mosellanus.[70] Silesians began to flock to the University of Wittenberg,

---

have been related to Christian living and not doctrine. Schwenckfeld, when relating his life's history, includes his years at Friedrich's court as ones spent frivolously (CS IV, 781:15–17). Finally, while still associated with the Liegnitz court Schwenckfeld bemoaned his fate to Hess and looked forward to release from his captivity at court (CS I, 37:9–12). For a standard view of "Friedrich the Pious," see S. Schultz 1946, 9.

66. In this Schwenckfeld was very much like Ulrich von Hutten, who despite his distaste for court life, and his expressed preference for the quiet leisure of contemplation, nonetheless recognized the importance of the court in practical political matters. Cf. Holborn 1937, 89–100.

67. Hartmann 1928, 10.

68. On the early attitude of the cathedral chapter, see Meyer 1903, 164. On Johann Turzo's inactivity, see Hoffmann 1897, 14–15.

69. On the priority of rural preaching, see Knörrlich 1957, 36. The first Protestant preaching took place in 1518 at the castle of Freiherr Georg von Zedlitz at Neukirche in Jauer (Weigelt 1973, 25). On the early stages of Protestant preaching, see Aubin 1938, 239; Hoffmann 1897, 9–10; Schneider 1862, 3.

70. Later Dyon was joined by K. Lyblich, who printed works by Haetzer, Zwingli,

including the Protestant leaders Schleupner and Moibanus of Breslau, and the future Catholic bishop of Breslau Balthasar von Promnitz, all of whom matriculated in 1519. Valentin Trotzendorf, later famous as the head of the Goldberg school and a determined Lutheran opponent of Schwenckfeld, also went off to study at Wittenberg.[71]

At the court in Brieg, which had direct ties with the university (the brother of the reigning princess was rector in 1519 and accompanied Luther to Leipzig), Caspar Schwenckfeld, then thirty, was immediately caught up in the excitement.[72] Responding with enthusiasm to Luther's challenge, he feverishly read the Bible; at the pace of four chapters a day he was able to complete the whole of Scripture in one year.[73] He also formed a small Bible study group composed of three pastors with whom he could discuss his insights.[74] The establishment of such groups, later including more and more laity and assuming wider social and religious functions, became the pattern of Schwenckfeld's pastoral activity. For a man whose theology, and especially whose ecclesiology, has been branded as individualist, Schwenckfeld was rarely an isolated figure, even if his contact with others could at times be maintained only by a voluminous correspondence.

After the first flush of success, the Lutheran movement in Silesia ran into opposition. In 1520, even before the papal ban against Luther was published, the Breslau chapter began to move against the new sect, and the bishop successfully pressured Breslau into banning the publication of Protestant materials by Adam Dyon.[75] The minutes of the Breslau chapter meetings reveal the revival of Hussite activity in the area, activity which must have caused grave concern for all the rulers, secular or spiritual, in Silesia, since Silesia had borne the brunt of Hussite depredations in the preceding century.[76] With the fear of popular unrest and social upheaval widespread, the efforts to control

---

Schwenckfeld, and Crautwald. In 1520 the bishop pressured the city into prohibiting this printing, but they resumed in 1521. See Volz 1967; F. Bahlow 1918, 20; Erdmann 1887, 2.

71. Schneider 1862, 3.

72. See note 37, above.

73. CS XVI, 795:18–24. Schwenckfeld later advised a slower, more careful reading.

74. The three were Arnold of Ossig, Ambrosius Creusing, and Egetius of Wohlau. Konrad 1917, 79.

75. Already on May 11, 1520, the chapter had received permission from Bishop Turzo to proceed against Luther's writings and followers (Konrad 1917, 16). The papal bull *Exsurge Domine* was only published at Rome on June 15, 1520; it didn't reach Luther until October 10, 1520; and excommunication was pronounced on January 3, 1521. On the publishing ban, see Volz 1967, 105–08.

76. F. Bahlow 1918, 22–23.

the new movement met no resistance. And no secular ruler had as yet espoused openly the Lutheran cause. Fortunately for the Protestants, however, on August 2, 1520, Bishop Johann Turzo died, and Jakob Salza, his successor, was not duly consecrated until September 1, 1521.[77] This paralyzed the church's efforts in much the same way as did the vacancy in the empire after the death of Emperor Maximilian. In the intervening year the Lutheran message quietly spread throughout the region.[78]

77. See Otto 1872. Although the Chapter had elected Salza, a Silesian, to the episcopal throne, the election was at first voided by the papacy at the insistence of the powerful house of Brandenburg, which wanted the post for one of its members. Eventually the city of Breslau, with the financial help of the Fuggers, got Salza confirmed.

78. Among others Valentin Crautwald, Schwenckfeld's future collaborator, was converted to Luther's cause in 1520 (Weigelt 1973, 7–11). Johannes Hess, the Reformer of Breslau, was also corresponding with Wittenberg, especially Melanchthon, during this period (Kretschmar 1960, 36).

2 Reformer
(1521–1524)

I am carrying out our intention to put together a few points on the matter of the reform of the Christian estate, to be laid before the Christian nobility of the German nation, in the hope that God may help his Church through the laity, since the clergy, to whom this more properly belongs, have grown quite indifferent.—Martin Luther, To the Christian Nobility of the German Nation, *1520*

Had Luther . . . settled back comfortably in some safe place, we laymen would not have so great a share in the evangelical teaching today. How I wish that we had its fruit in life and morals.—Schwenckfeld to Johannes Hess, June 1522

Silesian Reformation

Had things eventually gone differently for Caspar Schwenckfeld, in his old age he might have looked back upon the early 1520s as the years in which he was happiest and most fulfilled. He was still young and at the height of his powers, he had a cause, and he had vast new realms in which to exercise his abilities and his ambitions. Though thrilled and propelled by Luther's writings (especially *On the Freedom of a Christian* and *To the Christian Nobility of the German Nation*), he had not yet begun to ponder and weigh them. Practical reform, action not contemplation, was what was needed. Though there were no detailed maps on which to plot that reform, the way seemed obvious and there was always the Wittenberg compass, Luther. It was an adventure which fascinated a whole generation of young Germans, Schwenckfeld among them.

Schwenckfeld was the model of a religiously active layman. Few other nonclerics can have worked as hard, in so many ways, and with such success as he did. He used his position at court to further the political aims of the reformers, and as lord of the village he reformed Ossig by fiat. He also began his long career as goad and critic to the clergy, while at the same time competing with them as lay preacher. There was little time for reflection. In addition to the inner strain under which he increasingly struggled, his relationship with the Protestant ministry was also bound to suffer, for whatever their praise of an active Protestant laity, there were limits beyond which activity became presumption.

Fresh from his rapt reading of Scripture and Luther, Schwenckfeld launched himself on a series of missionizing campaigns. Mixing instruction, preaching, admonition, and consolation, he brought the reformers' message to the Silesian countryside. As elsewhere in Germany there was a severe shortage of capable reforming clergy, especially outside the cities. Although it is clear that Schwenckfeld addressed entire communities,[1] the focus of his efforts was upon the local lords and rural pastors. These formed a network of support for the early Lutherans and the later Schwenckfelders.

The Catholic hierarchy, which had combatted lay preaching for centuries, naturally complained of Schwenckfeld's behavior. On the other hand, Wittenberg, at least initially, gave him its blessing.[2] The latter was important, because preaching formed the core of Schwenckfeld's very Lutheran conception of the goal of the reform. It was to free "the pure word of God and the gospel of Christ without any human addition," so that it might be preached to the betterment and salvation of all.[3] He shared with Luther an optimistic trust in the power of the preached word. Schwenckfeld, in his devotion to the gospel, in his confidence in the success of its dissemination, and in his expectations of its beneficent effects, was one of Luther's most faithful and successful followers in Silesia.

On his own estates at Ossig he was able to go a bit further. Exercising his *jus patronatus* over the parish church and his nearly total authority

1. While scholars agree that in this early period Schwenckfeld was active as a lay preacher, neither the dates nor the locations of such preaching have been determined. Knörrlich (1957, 35) limits Schwenckfeld's activity to a brief period in 1523 in Liegnitz alone. The date is surely wrong, as a letter to Hess testifies (CS I, 12:18–20). Weigelt (1973, 19–20) is closer to the truth in dating Schwenckfeld's preaching to his printed *Address to the Sisters of the Convent at Naumburg am Queiss*, 1523 (CS I, 117–24). There are also reports that Schwenckfeld preached in Lüben, a half-mile from Ossig, helping the aged pastor there (Klose 1963, 190; Hoffmann 1897, 13). It is also likely that he preached at the court of Anna of Lüben, the widow of Georg Brieg, and a faithful follower of Schwenckfeld until her death. Though not limited to the upper classes, Schwenckfeld's audiences did include princes, bishops, and lords. He claimed to have preached to large public gatherings until forced by royal pressure to stop (CS XIV, 290:20–33).

2. Schwenckfeld hinted at the bishop's disapproval in a letter to Hess (CS I, 37:1–6). In Bishop Salza's 1524 response to the demand for the free preaching of the gospel, the prelate remarked that he had never opposed it, but was opposed to letting anyone preach who felt like it (F. Bahlow 1918, 41). King Ferdinand in his mandate of 1528 would once again emphasize the illegality of unauthorized preaching (Rosenberg 1767, 425). For Bugenhagen's comments during Schwenckfeld's visit to Wittenberg in 1525, see CS II, 262: 10–11. In 1544 Schwenckfeld claimed that Luther had once expressed his approval in a letter which is no longer extant (CS IX, 82:1–4).

3. CS I, 244:4–8. In 1523–24, Breslau also replied to charges of innovation with the claim that they merely wanted the free preaching of the gospel according to Scripture, and not any man's doctrine (Kretschmar 1960, 101–02). The Grottkau *Fürstentag* of January 1524 phrased its demands in much the same manner (F. Bahlow 1918, 36–38).

over the subject peasantry, he appointed one of his Bible-study companions as pastor and began to dismantle some of the more marginal
Catholic *"ceremoniales."*[4] The latter move was especially daring for the
early 1520s, and Schwenckfeld was even chided by some Protestant
clergy.[5] He was imitated by none.

In fact, the Lutheran sympathizers among Silesia's clergy seemed to
Schwenckfeld an especially timid lot. For a long time, Johannes Hess,
the eventual reformer of Breslau, absolutely refused to leave the relative safety of the court of Oels, where he served as tutor to Prince Karl's
son Joachim, to take up the admittedly exposed position as head of the
church in Silesia's largest and most important city.[6] Schwenckfeld's letters to him in 1521–22 are a blend of flattery, prophetic exhortation,
and a waspish, impatient sort of wit.[7] They are very effective, and the
fact that Hess responded only with embarrassed ill humor, while
choosing to remain safely at Oels, is a measure of his perhaps well-
grounded fears. In any event, Schwenckfeld would expend much effort during his career trying to persuade Protestant ministers to have
the courage of their convictions and not let what he considered a spe-
cious common sense overwhelm their desire for thoroughgoing reform.

But in 1521–22 Hess had good reason to fear for his own safety and
for the future of the reform as a whole. Luther himself was missing,
"kidnapped" by his friends after the Diet of Worms and held safe but
incommunicado for half a year. In Luther's absence the political ad-
venturism of Ulrich von Hutten and Franz von Sickingen and the religious radicalism of the Wittenberg movement had threatened to lead
the reform into dangerous and unwise paths. Expelled from Witten-

---

4. CS I, 11:20–21. Anders (1867, 620) gives 1523 as the year that Ossig was made Protestant, but he cites no evidence. Knörrlich (1957, 35) distinguishes between the minor changes
instituted in 1521 and the Protestantization of Ossig in 1523. But I think it more accurate to
say that Schwenckfeld introduced Protestant doctrine and practice, so far as that doctrine and
practice had already developed. Subsequent changes in Ossig reflected evolution within the
Protestant movement, not a separate stage of Protestantization.

5. See CS I, 11:20–21, for Hess's reaction.

6. For Hess's biography see Köstlin 1864–65, 97–137, 181–265. Johannes Hess had been
an important member of the humanist circle which Bishop Turzo of Breslau had gathered about
him. He had studied at Leipzig (1506–10) and Wittenberg (1510–11) before becoming secretary
to Turzo in 1513. In 1514 he was named tutor to Joachim, accompanying the young prince in
his round of universities before settling at Oels in 1518. On a prolonged journey in 1519 he
visited Bologna, where he received a doctorate in theology. On the return trip Hess stopped at
Wittenberg, this time meeting Luther and forming a fast and enduring friendship with the
young Melanchthon. In Oels again, Hess was ordained by his patron Turzo.

7. See his letters of October 14, 1521, and June 13, 1522 (CS I, 10–13, 35–38).

berg at Luther's return, the too fervent strain of reform began making its appearance elsewhere, including Breslau, where its virulence in 1522 was a matter of increasing concern to Wittenberg.[8]

The Catholic opposition was also making progress. Luther had been excommunicated by Rome in January 1521 and had been placed under the imperial ban three months later. Following the empire's lead, King Louis of Hungary, at that time overlord of Silesia, issued a harsh mandate against Luther, his writings, and his followers. The contested episcopal election in Breslau finally ended with the consecration of Jakob Salza in September 1521. One of the firstfruits of the Catholic revival was the bishop's order in 1522 to arrest Ambrosius Creusing, another member of Schwenckfeld's Bible study group, for preaching Lutheran heresy in Wohlau.[9]

Schwenckfeld was keenly aware that the reform movement in Silesia sorely needed protection and the leadership of a commanding clerical figure who would establish pastoral and theological order. He tried to lure Hess to Liegnitz and dangled before him the prospect of a "fat bishopric" (*pingui episcopatu*).[10] But Hess, a colorless and unimaginative journeyman reformer, refused to have greatness thrust upon him, even after he became the leading Lutheran minister in Breslau. Schwenckfeld himself never seems to have entertained seriously the idea of being ordained. Although the threat of episcopal and papal discipline to which ordination would have exposed him may have played a role in this decision, Schwenckfeld's own self-confidence and satisfaction with his lay role shines through all he wrote.[11] He simply had no inclination or desire for clerical status.

He was also much more valuable where he was—at the side of the prince, manipulating events behind the scenes. There were four prominent secular powers in Silesia: Karl of Münsterberg-Oels, the

8. Melanchthon to Hess, March 25, 1522 (CR I, 566–67) and December 4, 1522 (CR I, 584).

9. Schwenckfeld refers to it in CS I, 37:2–3.

10. CS I, 37:24–28.

11. See his explanation in CS I, 36:1–3. The earlier literature on Schwenckfeld had assumed that Schwenckfeld was a canon at Liegnitz (Hampe 1882, 10; Kadelbach 1860, 1; Kluge 1917, 222–23; Sinapius 1720, 863; Wachler 1833, 210). The earliest mention that I have found is in Sinapius, but since Christoph Schultz (1942, 32) also offers the information, it may well be derived from an earlier Schwenckfelder tradition. Though it is always possible that Schwenckfeld held minor orders, I agree with Hoffmann 1897, 6, and F. Bahlow 1918, 26, on the basis of the above cited passage, that Schwenckfeld was neither a canon nor a cleric in higher orders.

city of Breslau, Friedrich of Liegnitz, and the bishop of Breslau. Schwenckfeld's energies were directed toward aligning this constellation of political authority in support of religious reform. The successes and failures of the Reformation in Silesia were, therefore, personal events for him.

In many ways the political landscape determined the form that the Reformation took in Silesia, as elsewhere. City, court, and countryside had their own patterns. Schwenckfeld would always be at home in the latter two, but his affinity for the city was minimal. Breslau developed its own autonomous reform, beyond the influence, and one suspects, the grasp, of the junker courtier Schwenckfeld. By its very nature Breslau was alien and vaguely hostile, and it provided Schwenckfeld a foretaste of his experience in southern Germany.

Both Schwenckfeld and Wittenberg applied pressure on Hess to win to the cause Karl of Münsterberg-Oels, the first of the four powers, but without great success.[12] Karl, whose religious proclivities ran along moderate Hussite lines, was intrigued by the reformers' advocacy of communion with bread and wine for the laity, the central demand of the Hussite Utraquists. He maintained a benevolent neutrality toward the reformers until 1525, but thereafter religious and political developments transformed him into a leading, if not particularly effective, defender of the Catholic order.

Breslau proved more fruitful ground. From early on, Luther's writings had been known in the city. Many of Breslau's leaders—members of the city council, clerics, humanists, and lawyers—had been sympathetic. Itinerant preachers, many of them Franciscans, laid the foundation for popular support. Nonetheless, it was an old problem that brought matters to a head and made Breslau one of the strongholds of reform in Silesia.

For years, Breslau, Liegnitz, and the episcopal seat of Neisse had been troubled by the constant bickering of the two wings of the Franciscan order, the Conventuals (Reformed) and the Bernhardines (Observant).[13] This posed a constant threat to the peace, while the burden of supporting two competing convents also began to prove too much for the host cities. In 1516 Breslau, the bishop, and Friedrich of Liegnitz had got permission to forcibly unite the two under the stricter

12. CS I, 11:19–20; WA Br 2, 482.
13. For history of the dispute, see Scholz 1874.

Observant rule. For some reason the papal order was never executed. The Breslau city council took the matter up again in 1522, but this time the plan was to consolidate the two warring factions under the rule of the Conventual friars. The reason for the change was not hard to find. The Conventual friars were members of the Saxon province, and, as the Breslau town fathers readily admitted, had been openly preaching the Protestant gospel for some time.[14] In fact, the first truly public Protestant sermon in Breslau was delivered by the representative sent from the Saxon province to oversee the transfer of the Bernhardines.[15] The latter would have nothing to do with their heretical brethren and promptly left the city, on June 21, 1522.[16] As a result of their representations to King Louis and the support of the Breslau cathedral chapter, the Hungarian monarch immediately ordered Friedrich of Liegnitz and Kasimir of Teschen, provincial governors of Lower and Upper Silesia, to marshal forces for a march on the city. Georg of Brandenburg-Ansbach, the King's guardian and a Lutheran, averted disaster for the city, but Breslau had to pay for its temerity with the pledge in March 1523 of one thousand horses for the Turkish war.[17]

But having taken that first decisive public step, the Breslau city council could not draw back. Encouraged by the council's action, religious passions threatened to get out of hand within the city, and a radicalism dangerous to both religious and social order manifested itself. And though the city had bought its peace over the affair of the Bernhardines, the Catholic forces were alerted to the Lutheran tendencies in the city's policy. At the insistence of the Breslau cathedral chapter, on April 7, 1523, King Louis of Hungary reissued his 1521 mandate against the Lutherans. King Sigismund of Poland was also induced to write the city council later that year.[18] Friedrich of Liegnitz, himself under pressure, issued pointed warnings to Breslau to put its house in order.[19] This the city proceeded to do.

14. Scholz 1874, 373.
15. Konrad 1917, 24–26.
16. Meyer (1903, 26–29) maintains that the manifest immorality of the monks caused their expulsion. Since the Bernhardines were admittedly the more rigorous of the two parties this hardly seems likely. The monks were probably expelled both for political reasons (Engelbert 1960, 153–58) and as a result of Catholic-Protestant tensions (F. Bahlow 1918, 50–51).
17. Engelbert 1960, 159–60.
18. F. Bahlow 1918, 35–36; Engelbert 1963, 168–69; Hoffmann 1897, 22.
19. F. Bahlow 1918, 34–35; Engelbert 1963, 168; Knörrlich 1957, 53.

On May 6, Hess was offered the pastorate of Mary-Magdalen.[20] Once again he refused to be drawn out, citing the very radicalism which the city council hoped to temper through Hess's presence. Hess's reluctance may also have stemmed from the fact that the city council's offer was illegal. The cathedral chapter, not the city, held the rights of patronage and appointment to Mary-Magdalen. Eventually Bishop Salza, himself disregarding the illegality of the appointment, joined the chorus urging Hess. Hess took up his post in the fall of 1523. Earlier that year (June 12) the city council had also forcibly consolidated all charities into one common chest.[21] Breslau was clearly establishing itself as an avowedly Protestant city in the Lutheran mold.

The events in Breslau conform closely to the pattern of the "Urban Reformation." In Liegnitz, on the other hand, reform was at the behest of the prince. The focal point of Protestant activity, and Schwenckfeld's, was Friedrich's palace, which appropriately enough was located just outside the city's walls. Friedrich's mandates were separately issued and applied in Liegnitz, Wohlau, and Brieg, the three main cities in his duchy. The Reformation in Liegnitz (which was the name of both the city and the larger ducal state) was therefore a territorial and not a purely urban event. Princely power imposed reform on not-unwilling cities and countryside alike. Both the centrality of the court and the importance of the countryside brought Schwenckfeld's strengths into play.

Within a year of his arrival at Liegnitz Schwenckfeld had overcome Friedrich's initial aversion to the reform movement and served as "mid-wife" to the prince's own conversion.[22] Friedrich soon showed himself a committed, if prudent, patron of the reform in Liegnitz. In June 1522 he appointed Fabian Eckel to the Marienkirche, the post which Hess had refused, making Eckel the first Protestant preacher in Liegnitz.[23] The reissue of the royal mandate against the Lutherans in

20. On this whole episode see Kretschmar 1960, 67–73. Cf. WA Br 3, 143, and CR I, 624–43.

21. Kretschmar 1960, 74–77.

22. CS I, 36:1–13. The earlier literature agreed in placing Friedrich's conversion in 1521: F. Bahlow 1918, 27; Hoffmann 1897, 12; Otte 1936, 14. But Knörrlich (1957, 48) is surely correct in admitting that no more precise dating than 1521–22 can be put forth. Friedrich may have been Lutheran as early as Pentecost 1522 (June 8) when Fabian Eckel gave the first Protestant sermon from the chancel of a Liegnitz church (F. Bahlow 1918, 34).

23. For Friedrich's role in appointing Eckel along with other Protestant pastors like Rosenhayn, see Knörrlich 1957, 49. Already in 1522 Eckel also had an assistant direct from Wittenberg (F. Bahlow 1918, 34, 50).

April 1523 gave him pause, but after consulting his allies and in-laws, the Hohenzollerns of Brandenburg,[24] and observing the failure of enforcement by the royal administration, Friedrich rapidly picked up the pace. He appointed two Wittenberg graduates, Trotzendorf and Helmrichten, to the staff of the Goldberg school. In December, Johann Sigismund Werner, a fiery Lutheran, was called from Goldberg to become court preacher. Also in December, Valentin Crautwald, trilingual humanist and a Lutheran, was made a canon at Liegnitz and immediately began to lecture on Paul.[25] Friedrich went still further, requiring that all clerics procure ducal licenses to collect their rents, debts, and income.[26] He also usurped the patronage of churches on the lands of the various military orders and began to replace incumbents with Protestants.[27]

By the end of 1523, then, Breslau and Liegnitz were firmly attached to the reform movement, while Karl of Münsterberg-Oels remained uncommitted though favorably disposed. There remained only one figure of importance who stood outside the movement. This was the bishop of Breslau, whose dual role as territorial prince and head of the Silesian church made him either a most attractive candidate for conversion or a most formidable opponent. The new year saw efforts both to woo and to coerce the bishop, with Schwenckfeld playing a key role.

In 1524 Schwenckfeld published his first two major tractates. They were destined to become landmarks in the Silesian Reformation and personal milestones in Schwenckfeld's own development. The six months which separated them (January 1–June 11) saw the triumph of the Protestant party in Silesia. The first of these tractates was an open letter to the bishop of Breslau and in it Schwenckfeld pleaded the Protestant case, urging Bishop Jakob Salza to join the movement. The second, *The Admonition concerning Abuse*, was addressed to Friedrich of Liegnitz and the Protestant clergy, and in it Schwenckfeld began his criticism of the now triumphant reform party. In both, Schwenckfeld argued as a good Lutheran seeking the middle way between a hypocritical Catholic moralism and an equally hypocritical Protestant lax-

24. Duke Georg of Brandenburg-Ansbach, a prominent Silesian landholder, and his brother Wilhelm, canon at Mainz and Cologne. Both Schneider (1862, 6–7) and Kluge (1917, 278) see this meeting as decisive for Friedrich's more forward policy toward the reform. But he did not make any new moves until the end of the year.
25. Rosenberg 1767, 40; F. Bahlow 1918, 45–47.
26. Engelbert 1963, 168–69.
27. Von Velsen 1931, 6.

ity.[28] Both his concrete proposals for reform and his theological positions were molded by the desire to avoid the Scylla of the Catholic
tyranny of conscience through works righteousness, and the Charybdis
of a *sola fide* antinomianism. At the same time, in the practical political realm he hoped to steer a narrow course which would allow the
free preaching of the gospel, the reform of ecclesiastical institutions
and ceremonies, and the reformation of life and morals, without disturbing the precarious social and political balance and causing unrest
and revolution (*aufruhr*). These concerns mark him as a fairly typical
reformer of the early 1520s.

Schwenckfeld's New Year's Day Letter was a major political event.[29]
It announced, in effect, that the *Fürstentag* appointed for January 17,
1524, was to be a showdown between the reformers and their secular
allies on the one hand, and the church and Catholic party on the
other. The two signatories were Schwenckfeld and his neighbor Hans
Magnus Axleben of Langenwald. Hans, like Schwenckfeld, was of the
landed nobility and also had very close ties to the court of Liegnitz.[30]
There would have been no mistaking that they spoke for Liegnitz and
wide sections of the nobility. They obviously hoped to detach Bishop
Salza from the papal party, to seize the "high ground," and through
him to gain control of the church in Silesia.[31] They reminded him
that the papacy had opposed his election to the episcopacy, and that
only the support of his friends in Silesia had helped him overcome that
obstacle.[32] They preyed upon any latent anticlericalism that the recently ordained Salza might still possess, and tried to play the bishop
off against his own clergy, primarily the cathedral chapter.[33] Appealing
to progressive ideals which they imputed to him, and to his sense of
duty as bishop, they urged him to break with Rome and embark immediately upon an independent course of reform.[34] Should he do so,
they assured him, he would have the support of the secular estates in

28. CS I, 62:15–17.
29. CS I, 242–83.
30. CS I, 359–60; Hoffmann 1897, 20. Hans Magnus von Axleben accompanied Friedrich
on his 1507 pilgrimage to the Holy Land, while Hans's father, Christopher Magnus von Axleben, *Landeshauptmann* of Liegnitz, remained behind as regent.
31. CS I, 242:25–26, 244:4–8, 246:26–34, 248:26–31, 280:18–20.
32. CS I, 276:30–278:8, 282:5–7.
33. CS I, 246:5–12, 248:11–15.
34. On Salza's episcopal duty, see CS I, 280:7–17; cf. F. Bahlow 1918, 38–40. On immediate episcopal reform: CS II, 96:3–14. Erhardt von Queiss, the bishop of Pomersania since
1523, was a close friend and sometime court colleague. Schwenckfeld may have had him in
mind as an example (Knörrlich 1957, 66–67).

Silesia.[35] Implied was a threat by those same estates if he should resist. Salza's reply was noncommittal.[36] At the *Fürstentag* the bishop and cathedral chapter requested time to consider both the secular estates' demands and Friedrich's efforts to supervise clerical incomes.[37] A new *Fürstentag* was appointed for April 11.

During the interim more pressure was brought to bear on the already beleaguered Catholic party. In January Breslau began to seize church property, a turn of events that disturbed even the Protestant Hess.[38] On Easter Sunday, March 27, incendiary Lutheran sermons were preached by monks in Breslau.[39] Even more unsettling were that day's events in Liegnitz, where the Eucharist was given in both kinds to the laity.[40] Bishop Salza was particularly concerned with the situation and on April 2 sent a forceful letter to the newly elected Pope Clement VIII describing the dangerous state of affairs in his diocese.[41] The Breslau chapter noted on April 4 that there were disturbances in the streets and attacks on clergy. Despite this, on the same day both bishop and chapter decided that the demands of the secular estates must be refused.[42]

On the first day of the *Fürstentag* the bishop announced the decision, and on the day following, the assembled princes and nobles adopted a resolution, based on that of the Nürnberg *Reichstag* of the previous year, allowing the free preaching of the pure word of God. The Breslau chapter immediately began transferring the cathedral jewels and other valuables to Neisse for safekeeping.[43]

The Breslau city council submitted its own list of demands to the

35. CS I, 280:23–25.
36. CS II, 94:17–31.
37. F. Bahlow 1918, 40, 89.
38. Luther wrote to Hess on January 27, and on March 12, 1524, presumably in reply to the latter's complaints concerning the Breslau city council's depredations. Luther gave cold comfort (WA Br 3, 240, 253).
39. Engelbert 1961, 171.
40. See F. Bahlow 1918, 70–71; Hampe 1882, 10; Hoffmann 1897, 25; Otte 1936, 24–25; Schneider 1862, 4–5; Weigelt 1973, 20–21.
41. Salza had some ideas for remedying the situation. He suggested the calling of a council, the remedying of gravamina, the enlistment of men like Erasmus to lead a reform, and limitations on the mendicants. Though Salza probably knew of the content of Hess's *Axiomata* (Luther surely did by March 21, 1524, WA Br 3, 253) no mention is made of doctrine (Engelbert 1961, 165–70). It is interesting that when Ferdinand of Austria first became involved with Silesia he acted as if the Reformation there was merely a continuation of the severe lay-cleric struggles of the pre-Reformation era (Rosenberg 1767, 408).
42. Engelbert 1961, 171.
43. On the bishop's response, see F. Bahlow 1918, 40–41. For the *Fürstentag* decree see CS II, 90:17–92:8. On the transfer of the church treasures, see Engelbert 1961, 171.

bishop on April 15. Had they been granted, the council would in effect have gained control of the church within Breslau's walls.[44] The bishop's reply, if there was one, is lost. The council decided to proceed anyway and staged a disputation between Hess and an assortment of Catholic nonentities (April 20–23).[45] More like Luther's defense at Leipzig than Zwingli's exposition in Zurich, the Breslau Disputation was a scholarly debate held in Latin. The topics dealt with praxis.[46] What Hess's arguments did was justify the council's program. They systematically undercut the authority, function, and hieratic character of the priesthood. Breslau thus presents a classic example of an urban Reformation. The final step came in September when the council ordered all preachers to follow Hess in all points of doctrine.[47]

The refusal of the bishop to join the reform, or at the very least to take cognizance of the laity's complaints, also forced Friedrich to tighten his grip on the church in Liegnitz and reform it himself. He first united the two Franciscan houses under the rule of the Lutheran Conventuals and then expelled the unruly Bernhardines in June 1524. Their crime was their successful preaching against the Protestants.[48] It was increasingly clear to Friedrich that a laissez-faire attitude left the reformers hopelessly weak in the face of the still-powerful Catholic party. Schwenckfeld's second tractate, *Admonition concerning Abuse of Certain Important Articles of the Gospel*, must be understood against this background.[49]

44. Kretschmar 1960, 101–02. The city council demanded that (1) the free preaching of the word and true gospel be allowed, (2) the tithe and grain taxes be lowered, (3) the city council be given the right to appoint and replace both the pastors and schoolteachers, (4) all money for masses be applied to the pastor's salaries, (5) canons be allowed to serve as pastors in churches outside the city, but that they not be paid as if present in Breslau, (6) feast days be removed or limited in order to prevent the taking of people from their work, (7) the cathedral chapter's tavern be closed, (8) the head of the hospital of Saint Matthew render accounts to the council, and (9) ecclesiastical punishments cease in secular matters. The result was the economic dependence of the church upon the secular authorities.

45. On the Breslau Disputation see Engelbert 1961, 174–201; Konrad 1917, 50–56; Kretschmar 1960, 110–16.

46. Strangely, the doctrine of justification by faith alone was never expressly mentioned. Engelbert (1963, 176) points out that *sola fide* is implicit in much of what Hess says. This is especially evident in the article on the Eucharist (Konrad 1917, 52).

47. Konrad 1917, 59.

48. On the fate of the Bernhardines in Liegnitz, see F. Bahlow 1918, 51–52; Hoffmann 1897, 26; and Scholz 1874, 377–78. On the causes for the expulsion see CS II, 92:20–94:10. The decision to drive the monks out may not have been wise. Breslau's decision to do so a year earlier had loosed those staunch Catholics upon the rest of Silesia. In fact, it was a Breslau refugee, Friar Antonius, who was at the center of the Liegnitz troubles (Scholz 1874, 377–78).

49. CS II, 26–105.

In form a letter to Friedrich, it was in reality both an apology and a plan of action for the Liegnitz Reformation. Schwenckfeld described the abuses, complained of the failure of the Catholic clergy to remedy them, prescribed particular reforms, argued that it was Friedrich's duty to introduce them, and touted the personal qualities which made Friedrich especially suited for the task. Intriguingly, Schwenckfeld also went into some detail about the failings of the new reformed clergy, hence the title of the piece. This has led some scholars to conclude that Schwenckfeld was already moving beyond his early Lutheran position toward a more radical one. I will discuss this issue in more detail below, but it suffices to say here that the guiding purpose of the entire work was the establishment of a fairly typical Lutheran *Landeskirche* (territorial church) in the form taken by that phenomenon in the early 1520s. Schwenckfeld's criticism of the new clergy served only to underscore the necessity for Friedrich's intervention.

Within two weeks of the appearance of the *Admonition* Friedrich issued a mandate permitting open Protestant preaching in his lands.[50] Shortly thereafter the last Catholic pastor in Liegnitz left in protest. Friedrich replaced him with a Protestant.[51] In September Friedrich announced his refusal to aid the church in the collection of taxes, and he ignored the royal commands ordering him to render the church all necessary assistance.[52] Though at times more hesitant and circumspect in his actions than was the Breslau city council, Friedrich had also successfully taken control of the church within his domain.

Schwenckfeld's role in all of this is hard to define precisely, and the exact purpose and impact of the two treatises may still elude us. That the letter to Bishop Salza represented Friedrich's own position cannot be doubted. It was probably drafted at court, where Schwenckfeld on occasion seems to have served as secretary for religious correspondence.[53] It is true that he had retired from court life in 1522 or 1523 due to a progressive hearing loss, but this did not prevent him from

50. Knörrlich 1957, 81–82; cf. F. Bahlow 1918, 16. Engelbert (1963, 172–73) denies that such a mandate was ever issued. But Friedrich's remarks to Ferdinand in 1528 show that some such order was published (Rosenberg 1767, 429–31).

51. F. Bahlow 1918, 49. B. Ruersdorff resigned the pastorate of Peter-Paul-Kirche and was replaced by Wenzel Kuechler, a former Bernhardine monk converted by Hess at the Breslau Disputation.

52. Engelbert 1963, 173.

53. A letter from Friedrich to King Sigismund of Poland in November 1523 defending his religious policy bears startling resemblance in content and phrasing to both the Salza letter and the *Admonition* (Knörrlich 1957, 53).

extensive travels and repeated visits to Liegnitz. It may well be that he remained a counselor based at his own home. The *Admonition* may originally have been submitted to Friedrich as a memorandum, repeating Schwenckfeld's oral communication to the prince and based upon Schwenckfeld's personal observations on conditions in the countryside. Publication would have followed Friedrich's acceptance and paved the way for the June 24 mandate. Even without the evidence of the two treatises, however, one would have to assume that an advisor of Schwenckfeld's skill and ardor would exercise considerable influence on Friedrich's religious policies. Still, we must not credit Schwenckfeld with undue power or originality.[54] The Silesian reformations achieved many of the goals of pre-Reformation policy and did so in a way which was increasingly typical of Lutheran lands.

One aspect of that typicality was the increasing preponderance of the secular power. Schwenckfeld, who would later develop a surprisingly liberal conception of religious freedom, urged and participated in that tendency. To be sure he did have some misgivings even in the early years,[55] and his removal from Liegnitz tended to give him the outlook of one from the country, not the court. Nonetheless, he advised Friedrich to seize church property in order to rededicate it to its proper purposes. He insisted that it was Friedrich's duty to protect his subjects from Catholic error and provide them with the pure gospel. This involved, as Schwenckfeld explicitly admitted, the power to depose and appoint pastors.[56] At the same time, he denied the secular power any authority over people's souls and accorded congregations the right to choose their own pastors.[57] With an eye to the Catholic princes, he even argued that church reform proceed despite the opposition of constituted authority.[58] This inconsistency was widespread among the early reformers, Luther included.[59]

54. I see this tendency in some of the secondary literature, e.g., CS I, 216; Hoffmann 1897, 23, 28–29; Knörrlich 1957, 63; F. Bahlow 1918, 4, 401; Engelbert 1963, 174–75; Otte 1936, 22–23.

55. Schwenckfeld replied to charges that Friedrich had greedily confiscated church property with a half-hearted statement that he, Schwenckfeld, had no personal knowledge of any seizures. Immediately after, Schwenckfeld outlined the proper use of church goods. CS II, 34:22–23.

56. On the use of church property, see CS II, 34:22–33, 86:25–88:14. On the prince as provider of the gospel: CS II, 38:14–20. On the prince's duty to purge the unfit: CS II, 38:21–28.

57. CS I, 254:9–11, 16–19; CS II, 98:1–7.

58. CS II, 98:12–15.

59. On Luther's views, see Kühn 1923, 140–45, and Lecler 1955a, 57.

The entire problem centered on the phrase "the free preaching of the pure gospel of Christ according to Holy Scripture." Like Luther, Schwenckfeld believed Scripture to be sufficiently clear as to allow all reasonable people to grasp its message. There was only one gospel. The reformers did not preach Lutheran doctrine, but rather the truth of the gospel which Luther had confessed.[60] The secular authorities and the spiritual estate were required to ensure that the message of God and no other was preached, but they were not empowered to force belief in that message. Such unbelievers were not heretics but pagans, and therefore not subject to discipline for their beliefs, as long as no public disorder followed.[61] The Bernhardines had been driven from Liegnitz only when they disturbed the peace. But Catholics were not to be exiled if they practiced their religion quietly. Since the true gospel was so readily ascertainable, the secular authority could easily determine which ministers held false beliefs and could have them expelled. This would not conflict with each congregation's right to choose its own minister, because congregations too would judge on the same basis of pure doctrine. Schwenckfeld's Lutheran confidence in the clarity of the Scriptures expressed itself, therefore, in the practical realm of church order and discipline.

Schwenckfeld's reforming activity had three goals: that the consoling word of God be proclaimed to all; that there be correct worship of God; and that Christians lead a truly Christian life.[62] The principle determining both the necessity of particular reforms and the speed with which they were to be implemented was the priority of the inner over the outer, of the substance of faith over the external forms in which it was expressed.[63] Three factors—the welfare of the peasants, the ultimate goals of reform, and the precedence of inner spiritual change over outer formal change—shaped Schwenckfeld's reform program. "Rather we will not even spare our own goods, so far as our small means allow, in order that a Christian evangelical order according to God's Word, with neither uproar nor expulsion of priests, but rather with all patience and gentleness, be erected, at least in our villages."[64]

The rest of Schwenckfeld's practical reform program bears the im-

60. "Dz ich helffe die Lutheranischen sache (wie es etzliche nennen) wir heissens das Evangelion furdern" (CS II, 36:2–4). Cf. CS I, 254:25–256:2.
61. CS II, 98:12–15.
62. CS I, 254:25–256:2.
63. CS II, 86:8–41, 102:4–6.
64. CS I, 260:4–8.

print of his personal situation and experience. His focus was rural, and the object of his concern, quite paternalistic in its nature, was the subject peasantry who peopled the countryside.[65] He had no illusions about rural religious conditions, and the fact that he was lord of a village himself made him feel a particularly urgent responsibility to reform.

For Schwenckfeld, not surprisingly, the cause of the distressing decay of Christianity was an ill-educated duplicitous clergy who terrorized simple peasants with both superstition and Judaic legalities out of ignorance and greed.[66] To correct this Schwenckfeld offered two suggestions in his letter to the bishop of Breslau. First, lectureships should be provided so that both those seeking to become priests and those already ordained would receive instruction.[67] Schwenckfeld seems not to have had in mind a formal seminary structure, but a looser form of reading and exposition of the Bible. Johannes Hess had conducted such Bible sessions in Breslau in the summer of 1523. In Liegnitz, Valentin Crautwald began lecturing on Paul's epistles probably about the time Schwenckfeld was writing to the bishop.[68] The insistence upon education, formal or autodidactic, as the single most important tool for reform, was a hallmark of Schwenckfeld's thought during his Silesian years. Secondly, realizing that something must be done immediately to ameliorate the situation, he also suggested that unlearned priests be restricted to choir duty. The capable clergy were to be sent out into the countryside to become village pastors.[69]

Undoubtedly the minister's function as preacher was paramount. But because for Schwenckfeld Christian doctrine and Christian living were inextricably bound, the moral and religious example of the pastor was almost as important. It was a silent form of preaching. Even more crucial, the common parishioner would inevitably judge a minister's doctrine by his personal life.[70] Like the other reformers, Schwenckfeld

65. CS I, 250:3–6, 270:21–24, 272:33–274:7, 276:17–24; CS II, 38:14–20, passim.

66. On clerical oppression, see CS I, 276:17–24. On Catholics misusing or failing to use the Bible: CS I, 252:30–254:3, and CS II, 28:18–30:3. Bishop Salza seems to have been an exception (CS I, 246:13–16).

67. CS I, 272:30–32.

68. Luther, in a letter dated August 26, 1523, requested a copy of Hess's commentary on Solomon (WA Br. 3, 143). On Crautwald's lectures, see F. Bahlow 1918, 45–47; Eberlein 1903, 270.

69. CS I, 272:22–28.

70. On the importance of the minister's example, see CS II, 42:5–13. Justification and sanctification in Schwenckfeld's thought are discussed below. "Ich sage (bruder) man sicht gantz

supported clerical marriage as a remedy for the scandal of clerical con-
cubinage and as an answer to the question "How shall a poor village
pastor run his household without a wife?"[71] Schwenckfeld was obviously concerned with the very practical business of introducing the
Christian religion to the peasant countryside. The trying experience of
Andreas Karlstadt at Orlamuende and the continuing shortage of qualified ministers to serve the peasantry point out both the difficulty in
persuading clerics to settle in the villages and the real need for them to
do so.[72]

Concern for his "poor little folk" also prompted Schwenckfeld's demand for a vernacular liturgy. In his letter to the nuns at Naumburg
am Queiss in 1523 he called for prayers and psalms in the vernacular,
and in the *Admonition concerning Abuse* Schwenckfeld listed the use
of a German liturgy and of a German baptismal rite as matters of equal
importance with preaching the gospel, receiving both the bread and
wine in the Eucharist, and the right of priests to marry.[73]

The Eucharist was thus already an important issue. It is revealing,
however, that Schwenckfeld's concern centered not on the theological
significance of the Lord's Supper as such, but rather upon the financial
exactions which accompanied the Catholic doctrine of the Mass, as
well as other Catholic customs. To light votive candles, endow masses,
or make pilgrimages was easier than to lead a good Christian life, but
these practices impoverished the lower classes. Indulgences were just
another fraud, as was the system of "buying" the supposed good works
of the monks. These worthless practices were to be done away with,
and the Mass was to be said and the Eucharist administered only when
members of the congregation requested it and were present.[74]

genau auff wie denn der gemein man nicht so balde die lere mag fassen hott gross achtung auff
der lerer lebenn / und richt sich auch noch dem exempell etzlicher mossen" (CS II, 84:17–19).

71. CS I, 276:12–16.

72. On Karlstadt, see Sider 1974. For the religious condition of the peasantry later in the
century and even in the seventeenth century, see Strauss 1975 and Strauss 1978, 249–300. On
the difficulties of providing an effective body of ministers for the countryside, see Karant-Nunn
1978.

73. CS II, 98:28–100:3; cf. CS I, 276:25–27. Request for vernacular in the letter to the nuns:
CS I, 121:21–27. These reforms were so central that Schwenckfeld advised that the opposition
of secular power be ignored: CS I, 98:16–27. Luther had already published a German baptismal
service in 1523 (WA 12, 45).

74. On Catholic financial exploitation, see CS I, 260:11–14. Schwenckfeld also saw Friedrich's role as one of relieving the peasantry of unwarranted and useless religious exaction (CS
II, 38:14–20). On the impoverishment of the peasantry, see CS I, 250:21–34; on indulgences
and monastic good works: CS I, 274:7–11.

In Schwenckfeld's other reforms the Bible was usually the standard. For example, both clerical marriage and the distribution of the Eucharist in both kinds to the laity were supported by scriptural texts.[75] But his attacks on Catholic praxis were often based on empirical evidence. For example, although Schwenckfeld normally condemned the hasty and imprudent dismantling of the old church, he nevertheless urged the immediate removal of all religious images. It could be seen that the images pandered to a peasantry which was literally pagan.[76]

But to say that Scripture was to provide the measure of reform was not to furnish an unambiguous standard. While all the reformers agreed that those things which were commanded in Scripture must be done, and those things which were prohibited either avoided or discontinued, the status of the *adiaphora*, the indifferent things which were neither commanded nor forbidden, remained unclear. There was also the problem of timing, of the necessity of immediate reform as opposed to the desirability of tarrying for the weak. Luther showed his conservatism both in retaining many Catholic *adiaphora* and in avoiding hasty reform.[77]

Schwenckfeld's position was less clear. He did not deal at all with the question of things indifferent. Rather his attention was concentrated upon those clear cases of Catholic abuse which could be condemned on clear scriptural grounds.[78] Speed of reform was another matter, and here Schwenckfeld was a zealot. He had not tarried for the weak in reforming his own estates, and he had urged his bishop to follow his example.[79] One never knew when an individual, be it Schwenckfeld or the bishop, must face his maker in judgment for the souls entrusted to his care. Besides, delay served only to prolong darkness. Therefore, while Schwenckfeld did not call for the wholesale destruction of Catholic praxis and structure,[80] he did insist upon immediate reform of the most glaring abuses. On the other hand, he criticized those who needlessly destroyed everything. He objected not really to their haste, but to their motives and to their emphasis on outer

75. CS I, 274:31–276:4; CS I, 264:23–30.
76. Schwenckfeld's criticism of indiscriminate destruction is found in CS I, 272:31–276:4. Here Schwenckfeld agreed with Luther, who had said in the fourth Invocavit sermon that images must be removed if worshipped (WA 10, pt. 3, 30:17–31:3).
77. The best expression of Luther's position is found in his Invocavit sermons of 1522 (WA 10, III). Cf. Pelikan 1968, 92.
78. CS I, 264:23–30, 280:12–17; CS II, 86:8–21.
79. CS I, 280:12–17.
80. CS II, 102:4–6.

change at the expense of internal improvement. Given men of proper spirit, reform should proceed quickly. But, Schwenckfeld believed, any uproar that disturbed the social and political balance while claiming the gospel as warrant should be suppressed immediately by the secular power.[81]

Behind Schwenckfeld's insistence upon immediate reform was his personal knowledge of the situation in the countryside. Schwenckfeld did not fear scandalizing the peasantry by rash reforms. Rather the peasantry, as they then were, were a scandal to all Christians. More pagan than Christian, tyrannized and exploited by an ignorant and immoral clergy, the peasants were an indictment of both clerical and secular authorities, whose only escape from the punishment reserved for unfaithful shepherds was immediate reform.

Schwenckfeld's Lutheran Theology

A third goal of the Reformation, as Schwenckfeld saw it, was the reform of morals and the development of a truly Christian form of living. Schwenckfeld's concern with these and his hopes for improvement were shared by most of the early reformers.[82] But some have concluded that even in this early period Schwenckfeld was not truly a follower of Martin Luther because of the emphasis which he placed upon moral improvement, and the vigor with which he attacked those Lutheran preachers who, he felt, had perverted the doctrine of justification by faith alone into antinomianism.[83] Others, while not denying Schwenckfeld's reliance upon Luther's thought, argue that he misunderstood it and transformed it in ways which presage Schwenckfeld's later teachings.[84] A third group maintains, however, that Schwenck-

81. On the importance of internal versus external reform, see CS II, 86:8–21. On the urgency of reform despite opposition: CS II, 86:8–21, 98:16–22. On the suppression of uproar: CS II, 96:21–28.

82. See Strauss 1975 and Strauss 1978.

83. The clearest statement of this position is by Erb (1976, 225–26): "Thus, while Luther's works initiated a major change in Schwenckfeld's religious outlook . . . , Schwenckfeld himself cannot be described as a Lutheran. . . . His earliest works indicate that in him, Lutheranism was strongly redirected by a practical ethical humanism. . . . In his first major work, the "Ermanung des Missbrauchs" in 1524, he opposes Lutheranism directly on what are essentially ethical grounds, maintaining that Lutheran teaching on justification, the bondage of the will, the role of works, the law, and Christ's satisfaction result, although not so intended, in immoral libertarianism." Kluge (1917, 229) had said basically the same thing.

84. Maron (1961a, 157) argues that from the beginning Schwenckfeld reinterpreted Luther in a "vulgärmystischen" sense.

feld was still a faithful disciple of Luther in 1524.[85] A review of Schwenckfeld's early works proves this latter conclusion to be correct, though we must qualify such a position by stating that the Luther whom Schwenckfeld followed was the Luther of *Freedom of a Christian* (1520) and especially the *Commentary on the Seven Penitential Psalms* (1517).[86]

In the early years, of course, Schwenckfeld denied being a Lutheran, as did many others who feared to side openly with the excommunicate monk.[87] But this wasn't only dissembling. The whole point of the reform movement was that it wasn't just another new sect, but rather the authentic version of Christianity. To cite Luther in 1522, "I ask that men make no reference to my name, and call themselves not Lutherans, but Christians."[88] Only when Schwenckfeld later recognized Lutheranism as a sect could he admit that he had been in fact Lutheran.[89]

But it was as a still-faithful follower of Luther that Schwenckfeld published in 1524 his blistering attack on those who had debased the Lutheran message. He accused Protestant preachers of mishandling these five difficult points of doctrine: "That only faith justifies us; that we have no free will; that we cannot obey God's commandments; that our works are nothing; that Christ has paid our debt."[90] Since Schwenckfeld accepted these five points as true and beyond refutation, he did not try to prove them. Nor did he believe that these were sub-

85. Still the best treatment of Schwenckfeld's use of Luther is by Hirsch (1922, 145): "Bis in das Jahr 1525 hinein muss Schwenckfeld als Anhänger und schüler Luthers ohne eigentlich innere Selbständigkeit angesehen werden. Gewiss er nimmt Luthers Gedanken auf als ein Laie, d. h. mehr mit dem Gemüt und ohne Sinn fur scharfe Begriffsbestimmungen. Man täte ihm unrecht, wenn man sein Verhältniss zu Luthers Theologie zu bestimmen versuchte. Aber in Luthers Christentum steht er drin." Cf. Knörrlich 1957, 38, 40, 58, 76; Sippel 1911, 925; Ecke 1911, 58–69.

86. Schwenckfeld recommended Luther's *Commentary on the Seven Penitential Psalms* to all his friends (CS II, 82:12–20). Other sources were *To the Christian Nobility of the German Nation* (1520); *An Earnest Exhortation* (1522); *A Sermon on the Three Kinds of Good Life for the Instruction of Consciences* (1521); *The Invocavit Sermons* (1522); *Two Kinds of Righteousness* (1519); *The Magnificat* (1520–21); and *The Babylonian Captivity* (1520). For a fuller listing consult Hirsch 1922.

87. CS I, 254:25–256:2; CS II, 36:2–4. Cf. Friedrich's letter to King Sigismund of Poland, November 30, 1523: ". . . damit in meinen ambte nichts anders denn das heilege evangelium und lautere gottes wort, ohne Luthers und sonst menschlichen zusatz gepredigt wuerde" (CS XVIII, 3:16–28). It is generally assumed that Schwenckfeld had a hand in drafting this letter. See F. Bahlow 1918, 36–38; Kretschmar 1960, 101; Engelbert 1963, 169 n. 23.

88. WA 1, 685:4–6. Cf. Steck 1955, 63.

89. CS IV, 248:17–26, 677:1–6; XII, 971; XIII, 854:18–22; XIV, 802:17.

90. CS II, 42:20–44:2. Schwenckfeld drew points 2 and 4 from Luther (Hirsch 1922, 148–49).

jects best passed over in silence, as Erasmus suggested with regard to the issue of free will. Rather, he felt that it was absolutely necessary that they be preached.[91] His goal was to point out the difficulties which had to be faced in presenting these matters to "simple people," and to silence the unqualified before they led the people into a "fleshly freedom," or antinomianism.[92] He rightly feared the effect such preachers had upon the lives of their listeners, but he was even more concerned that their followers would fail to achieve a true, living, justifying faith.[93] The misunderstanding of the nature of true faith and its relation to good works jeopardized the entire gospel. Schwenckfeld was not just worried about immoral lives; he was anxious over lost souls.

Nonetheless, we must not ignore the extent of Schwenckfeld's dismay at the lack of visible improvement.[94] He was not alone, of course. Erasmus, Melanchthon, and even Luther complained bitterly about the state of the Protestant laity.[95] Still, though always expecting that visible improvement was just around the corner, Schwenckfeld came to terms with the problem by 1524. He cautioned that really very little time had passed to accomplish the great changes, that even Christ had been unable to change men's hearts in so short a time. Also, the apparent decline in public morality was deceptive. Hypocrites who had seemed pious under the Catholic regime had been stripped of their pretended sanctity by the gospel. In a sense the gospel made some men worse while making other men better.[96]

Despite Schwenckfeld's concern for the reform of morals, the primary goal of the preaching of the gospel remained for him, as for Luther, the consolation of consciences.[97] To Bishop Salza Schwenckfeld emphasized the differences separating the reformers from the Catholics on this point. The Catholics preach "themselves much more than Christ, and hell and purgatory much more in order to frighten the

91. CS II, 56:3–27.
92. CS II, 40:23–31; 52:24–27; 92:20–22. On the dangers of antinomianism, see CS II 62:3–12.
93. Schwenckfeld feared that these Protestants had a false, historical, Catholic type of faith (CS II, 46:14–19).
94. As early as 1522 he had expressed his disappointment to Johannes Hess (CS I, 36:19–21).
95. G. Eberlein 1900, 2, 4; Williams 1968, 5–8; Pelikan 1964, 92.
96. CS I, 270:15–31.
97. He expressed this concern to Hess (CS I, 35:5–6), to a despairing friend (CS I, 60:19–61:2), and to the nuns (CS I, 121:2–6). Sciegienny (1975, 32) is therefore wrong in denying that Schwenckfeld ever held *sola fide*, or that it is to be found in Schwenckfeld's letter to Bishop Salza.

common man, than heaven, and its promises, and God's goodness in order to console."[98] The Lutherans, on the other hand, want only "that his [Christ's] divine Word be preached in all the world as a consolation to all the grieved."[99]

Even in the *Admonition concerning Abuse*, which placed more weight upon the responsibilities of the Christian, Schwenckfeld rejoiced in the success with which the proponents of reform had released the "ensnared consciences" of the people.[100] Faith "brings the joy of the Spirit and peace of conscience" because the "faithful heart knows and feels the great inexpressible love and the gracious good will of the almighty God, his loving Father."[101] The joy, peace, and consolation of faith was caused by the sure knowledge that one was already saved, that one possessed heaven now, and not that one would be saved sometime in the future.[102] By contrast, under Catholic tutelage, no man could be certain whether or not God loved him, or as Luther would phrase it, whether he had a gracious God.[103] The focus of Schwenckfeld's thought was, therefore, justification by faith alone for the consolation of consciences.

That said, it must be admitted that in his major work, *Admonition concerning Abuse*, the emphasis was upon the nature of good works and their relationship to salvific faith. Because this tract was directed at the abuse of *sola fide* and associated doctrines, and because Schwenckfeld made no attempt to defend or define them, some have mistakenly seen it as an attack on Luther's core teachings. But what results from this admittedly practical, polemical work is a balanced consideration of works and faith which drew upon and compared favorably with Luther's *Freedom of a Christian* and *Commentary on the Seven Penitential Psalms*.

Law played the same role in Schwenckfeld's thought that it did in Luther's. Schwenckfeld's practical reform measures were designed to do away with the myriad laws with which the Catholic church ordered and, to Schwenckfeld's mind, oppressed Christian consciences.[104] Even when such Judaic human laws were removed, however, there

98. CS I, 254:28–29.
99. CS I, 254:28–29.
100. CS II, 36:7–16.
101. CS I, 50:4–8, 12.
102. CS I, 258:23–25.
103. CS II, 50:17–18.
104. CS I, 122:16–24, 256:14–18. On this distinction in Luther, see Pelikan 1968, 100.

remained the far more serious burden of divine law. For Schwenckfeld as for Luther, God's message to man was composed of law and gospel:[105] the law accused, condemned, and reduced the sinful man to despair; the gospel brought salvation, freedom from the law, and peace of mind. In the *Admonition* Schwenckfeld accused some Protestants whom he termed *Schwärmer* of confusing human and divine law, and of preaching the gospel to the exclusion of the law.[106] While the gospel freed all men from human ecclesiastical law and all believing Christians from the guilt of having disobeyed divine law, this did not mean that God's commandments, like church laws, were void. They were still binding, though no man had ever or would ever obey them perfectly.

Man cannot obey the law because in his fallen state he is by nature sinful: "But the will is a slave of our nature, and we are by nature sinners; thus our will is constrained to sin."[107] One could avoid visible external sins, like adultery and murder, but the inner sins of pride and self-love were ineradicable by man's own efforts.[108] The one law which man could never obey was the command "to love God with his whole heart, with all his might, with his whole soul" (Deut. 6:5).

Schwenckfeld's position on the role and nature of free will in man was drawn from Luther's *Commentary on the Seven Penitential Psalms*.[109] The free will which Adam possessed and then lost through the Fall was the indwelling of the Holy Spirit, not a human faculty at all. Faith was the return of that Spirit, and to the extent that the Holy Spirit reigned in the heart of the believer, free will was reinstated.[110] As Schwenckfeld emphasized again and again, all good works were done by God through man; man was a mere tool.[111] To the extent that man did good works God is active; to the extent that he sinned man himself was active.[112]

---

105. *CS* II, 68:28–31, 80:27–30, 80:36–82:2, 86:4–5.

106. *CS* I, 270:1–6; *CS* II, 82:7–11. For Schwenckfeld's use of the term *Schwärmer*, see *CS* II, 62:3–17.

107. *CS* II 58:17–19. Cf. *CS* I, 258:2–10.

108. *CS* I, 68:28–31, 256:37–258:10.

109. WA 1, 191:3–192:2.

110. *CS* I, 252:26–28; *CS* II, 60:1–4, 10–29.

111. *CS* I, 258:13–20; *CS* II, 70:33–72:4; 74:9–11; 76:9–12.

112. In passing, it is interesting to note that Schwenckfeld's earliest citation of Tauler is employed to assert that God must be the beginning, the middle, and the end of every good work. As yet Schwenckfeld had no "mystical" theology which would require Tauler's support. *CS* I, 252:26–28.

111111111111111111111111

Schwenckfeld's dependence on Luther appears even more strikingly in a statement which seems truly un-Lutheran. Describing the process by which a Christian grows in faith and good works, Schwenckfeld argued that "Adam must leave in order for Christ to enter."[113] This would seem to describe a process of *partim-partim* justification and/or sanctification. However, the sentence is almost an exact duplicate of Luther's phrasing in the *Commentary on the Seven Penitential Psalms*, "that Adam must leave and Christ enter, that Adam must disappear and Christ alone rule and exist."[114]

Two other passages which appeared in the *Admonition* and which would seem to run counter to Luther were in like manner drawn from the *Commentary on the Seven Penitential Psalms*. They both involve the life proper to a Christian possessed of a living faith.

> And therefore if we would participate in his [Christ's] satisfaction, we must love him and obey his Word. We must deny ourselves, bear our crosses and imitate [*noch folgen*] Christ. That is, we must be formed to the suffering of Christ, and bear all that the eternal God sends with patience and meekness. Indeed we must realize Christ's suffering in our own flesh. If any man would be resurrected into joy with Christ, he must first suffer unto death with him. If we would become like God [*gotformig*], we must first of all be like Christ [*Christformig*].[115]

Horst Weigelt has conjectured that Schwenckfeld's ideal of imitating Christ might have derived from late medieval mysticism, the *Devotio Moderna*, or scholasticism.[116] Although Weigelt may be correct about the ultimate provenance of the idea, its immediate source was Luther's *Commentary*. There Luther wrote of the *Christformig* man who suffered on both an inner and outer cross, so that the Old Adam would be crucified with Christ as a sacrifice.[117] In Schwenckfeld it takes this form:

> Whoever will follow the word in earnest must not avoid the cross, since the gospel is called by St. Paul a word of the cross (1 Cor.

---

113. CS I, 250:32–252:12.
114. WA 1, 186:25–29. Both Schwenckfeld and Luther qualified such statements by emphasizing that no man reaches perfection in this life and that a Christian's sins were still forgiven by the forensic imputation of Christ's merits. CS I, 258:13–20.
115. CS II, 80:17–26.
116. Weigelt 1973, 39.
117. WA 1, 194:37–39; 199:31–32; 216:28–32.

1:18). It brings the Old Adam an inner and outer cross, in order that he be completely destroyed by the power of the word, and that the spirit of Christ in true patience and resignation [*gelossenheit*] might be installed in man's heart.[118]

Schwenckfeld's use of *Gelossenheit* introduces another possible non-Lutheran conception,[119] but as used by Schwenckfeld[120] it is perfectly Lutheran—in the form which that theology took in the *Commentary*. For Schwenckfeld *Gelossenheit* meant a complete acceptance of God's will, a rejection of all external things and human efforts, including one's own, in the matter of salvation. Not a metaphysical doctrine as in the late medieval mystics, it described the subjective mental state of one whose faith and trust lay in God and not in man. Luther described the entire life of the Christian as a complete resignation in God's will, the acceptance of our worthlessness and the worthlessness of all external works, and a determination to offer ourselves to God, though of course never believing it to be a truly worthy sacrifice.[121]

For both Luther and Schwenckfeld, then, the faithful man, resigned to God's will, must of necessity produce good works.[122] Where these firstfruits of the Spirit were missing, both Luther and Schwenckfeld were agreed true faith was also lacking.[123] Schwenckfeld went even further and argued that the presence of good works could be a consolation to those doubtful of their own salvation, since God judged a man's faith by the fruit which it bore.[124] Such an approach to the relationship between faith and works in the salvific process did not really contravene the doctrine of justification by faith alone, since the works did not earn salvation but only attested to a faith which assured the sinner that Christ has saved him. Still, this emphasis on visible signs of faith and moral improvement did run counter to Luther's espoused

118. CS II, 30:3–8.
119. Weigelt (1973, 45) sees Schwenckfeld's use of *gelossenheit* as proof that Schwenckfeld used Tauler.
120. CS II, 30:3–8, 46:21–30, 60:10–29, 60:32–33, 68:12–14.
121. WA 1, 194:6–14; 210:10–13. Schwenckfeld does perhaps exceed Luther in the extent to which he believed man capable of casting aside self-love. *Gelossenheit* might include the *resignatio ad infernum* as its final stage (CS II, 68:12–14). It should be noted that Schwenckfeld limited himself to the feelings of the believer in this life. It is not clear whether he goes so far as to maintain that if the believer actually went to hell, he would still be oblivious to his fate.
122. CS I, 256:14–15; CS II, 74:13–15; *Two Kinds of Righteousness*, WA 2, 146:36–147:23; *Preface to the Epistle to the Romans*, WA Deutsche Bibel 7, 18:21–26.
123. CS I, 258:23–25; CS II, 48:18–27; 54:3–12; 76:14–17; WA 7, 59:26–33; 62:27–29; WA Deutsche Bibel 6, 10:3–5.
124. CS II, 76:14–35.

goal—the consolation of consciences oppressed by God's law and their own sinfulness.

The reason for this deviation lies in the purpose of the *Admonition concerning Abuse*. In his concern to avoid both Roman hypocrisy and Protestant antinomianism, and to follow Luther's "middle way" or "royal road,"[125] Schwenckfeld exceeded the limits of theological precision, much as Luther did in his polemical popular tracts. Works righteousness was opposed by an emphasis on faith, antinomianism by good works. Even so, Schwenckfeld was capable of a balanced treatment of the problem.

> Through this [faith] we become reborn and returned to that freedom which Adam had lost. This same spirit and righteousness we achieve only through a living faith in Christ. Where the spirit is, there also is freedom. We are driven by that same spirit, as St. Paul says, to do those good things freely and willingly which formerly were difficult or impossible for our nature. Through the same spirit we achieve an indifference [*gelossenheit*] toward all creatures, and indeed ourselves. We recognize the evilness of our nature, that all our being, and life, and even the best of our works are nothing but sin in God's eyes. Our will is then broken by that same spirit into the eternal unchanging will of God. And thus are we entirely renewed, so that no longer the Old Adam, but rather the spirit of Christ works and lives through us and in us. Now this faithful man says that he can do nothing good. Indeed, he does not do it, but rather the spirit of Christ does it through him. The faithful man, indeed, knows and recognizes through such works that he does possess true faith, even if at times he still falls into sin. As long as he rises up again (what he does not accomplish God will not reckon to him because of his faith) his fall will not damn him.[126]

On the key issues of Luther's own theology, Schwenckfeld was firmly rooted in the Lutheran tradition.

Two recent scholars, Gottfried Maron and Horst Weigelt, are of the opinion that already in Schwenckfeld's early reforming years three doc-

---

125. *CS* II, 62:15–17. Luther deals with the excesses of both Catholics and Protestants in *Freedom of a Christian*. He pointed to Paul's choice of a middle way (WA 7, 67:14–15; 70:3–29).

126. *CS* II, 60:10–29.

trines which were hallmarks of Schwenckfeld's later theology—insistence on the unmediated bond between God and the faithful man, a thoroughgoing dualism, and the denial of a salvific role for the Bible—were to be found in his writings.[127] It is tempting to read into Schwenckfeld's early statements his later positions. But, though there are formulations which could be understood in this manner, to do so would be to misunderstand the early Schwenckfeld.

Schwenckfeld does give occasion for such a misconstruction of his thought. He did distinguish between inner and outer sins,[128] a distinction drawn from Luther.[129] But that was merely to emphasize that one must eradicate not only externally visible sins but also the hidden sins of the soul before one could claim true holiness. Far more important was Schwenckfeld's repeated assertion that no external thing could confer salvation: "You should . . . not seek the salvation of your soul through external things, but through Christ, and with the Prophets raise your eyes and hearts to Him who lives in heaven."[130] This passage certainly reads like some of Schwenckfeld's later statements in which he denied that the Bible and the sacraments acted as means of grace. But in this period Luther's concerns were the measure of Schwenckfeld's. Schwenckfeld was merely worried by visible abuse:

A truly Christian life and existence does not stand in external appearance, hypocrisy, human laws, or trust in one's own efforts. As a result it is not bound to place, time, clothing, persons, foods, and the like. On the contrary it stands in the complete trust in God, through the knowledge of Jesus Christ, which now the Holy Spirit is beginning to bring forth in our hearts out [aus] of the hearing and diligent consideration of the word of God (Gal. 3:2).[131]

When Schwenckfeld spoke out against externals in religion, he was attacking the cultic, penitentiary, and monastic strictures of the Catholic church, and he echoed the criticism which Luther had directed at his too radical followers in Wittenberg: "Nay, my dear friends, the

127. Maron (1961a, 83, 98) finds Schwenckfeld espousing an unmediated relationship between God and the faithful as early as 1523. Weigelt (1973, 39–41) is more cautious, finding his evidence in 1524 and limiting himself to a "sehr wahrscheinlich."
128. CS I, 256:14–18.
129. WA 1, 188:24–26.
130. CS I, 62:12–33.
131. CS I, 118:7–25.

Kingdom of God consists not in outward things, which can be touched or perceived, but in faith."[132]

But the passage by Schwenckfeld brings a further problem concerning the role of the Bible and the preaching of the word. In his later writings Schwenckfeld would deny that either aided in the production of faith and, hence, justification.[133] He distinguished, on the one hand, the Bible and preaching of the gospel as the word of God, and on the other hand the indwelling glorified Jesus Christ, the consubstantial word of God. Only he who heard the inner word, Christ, and not the mere external word, was to be saved. Gottfried Maron finds this distinction between the external word and Christ the inner word in Schwenckfeld's thought already in 1524.[134] There would seem to be corroborative evidence in the passage cited above. For there Schwenckfeld employed a version of Galatians 3:2 that varied from Luther's. Luther's translation had said "preaching of the word." The version "hearing of the word" would later be used by Schwenckfeld to supplant the Lutheran emphasis on preaching with an emphasis on hearing, without recourse to human instruments, the inner word, Christ. These two points, the ambiguity of the phrase "word of God" and the early correction of a later disputed biblical text, would seem to mark Schwenckfeld as already straying from the Lutheran fold.

In fact they do not. Schwenckfeld used the Galatians passage without any comment on Luther's version. He was accustomed to using many different texts of the Scriptures, not merely Luther's. Schwenckfeld could have used or remembered another version without implying thereby a criticism of Luther or Luther's doctrines. It is well to remember that Luther's text was the aberrant one and not Schwenckfeld's. Furthermore, the assertion that Schwenckfeld already distinguished between substantial inner word and spoken or written outer word will not stand. Maron claimed that in his *Admonition concerning Abuse* Schwenckfeld had distinguished between "the word of God" and "Holy Scripture."[135] In actuality, twice in that work Schwenckfeld referred to the word of God and the holy gospel. In both contexts it is obvious that he meant by that something which could be studied and preached.[136]

---

132. WA 10, pt. 3, 43:5–6. Still stronger is Luther in *Freedom of a Christian* (WA 7, 51:35–52:4).

133. See McLaughlin 1979.

134. Maron 1961a, 175. Cf. CS II, 28, 38.

135. Maron 1961a, 175.

136. "Ja wolt got das unsere Bischoffe und seelsorger sich dermossen mit gottis worte und

The distinction is not between inner and outer words. The fact that he did not hasten to define his terms makes it likely that they were not of central importance. Perhaps he was merely differentiating between God's complete communication to man in the Bible and that part which concerned man's salvation in Christ. Or perhaps he was following Luther in distinguishing between the written form of God's word and the gospel as content.[137] In any event there is no sign of a dualism of inner word and outer word.

What does exist in Schwenckfeld's extant writings from this period is the insistence upon the necessity of "preaching and reading the pure gospel of Christ according to the Holy Scripture," or of preaching "the pure word of God and gospel of Christ without any human additions . . . because God's word is the only food of the soul through which it is nourished and receives eternal life, and upon which all Christian efforts shall be built as on an enduring rock."[138] There is an allusion here to John 6:28–35, a text which would be one of Schwenckfeld's favorites in the battle against the new idols—preaching and the Bible—but which is used to support the demand for both in this passage.

In a proper Lutheran manner Schwenckfeld also maintained the priority of Scripture over the church and the clarity of the self-interpreting Bible.[139] As a result Schwenckfeld was confronted with a problem that all the Reformers had to face. Despite the clarity of God's word, many supposed Christians refused to understand it, or what was worse, in their pride they rejected it. The devil also knew the Scriptures and used them for his own evil purposes. The dead letter of Scripture was in itself not sufficient.[140] At its heart, the problem was

dem heiligen Evangelio bekommerten" (CS II, 28:181–89). "Das Prediger und Pfarrer in gotis worte und dz heylige Evangelio zu predigen voreyniget wurden" (CS II, 38:21–25). Earlier in 1523 Schwenckfeld had described the prioress of Naumburg am Queiss as a "liebhaberinne des gottlichen wortes und Evangelii" in whose cloister "das Evangelium teglich gepredigt wird" (CS I, 119:13–21).

137. On Luther, see Pelikan 1968, 119; Pelikan 1964, 21. Cf. WA Deutsche Bibel 6, 6:22–8:2.

138. "Dz lauther Evangelio Christi noch ausslegung der heyligen Schrift . . . gepredigt und gelessen werden" (CS I, 246:21–25). ". . . das lauther gottis wort und Evangelion Christ ahn allen menschlichen zusatz zu predigen die weil denn gottis wort eine einige speiss der seelen ist / dormit sie sol ernert und ewig erhalten werden / dorauff auch aller Christen furnemen als auf einen bestendigen felssen erbawet sein soll" (CS I, 244:4–8). Cf. CS I, 252:30–32.

139. The church had not determined the canon of the Bible. Rather the canon and the church itself were established by Holy Scripture. CS I, 260:25–261:1, 262:32–264:7, 266:8–23.

140. CS II, 54:18–24. For the devil's misuse of God's word, see also CS II, 36:17–23.

caused by the Lutheran anthropology. How could fallen man, whose mind was clouded by sin and whose will was the devil's plaything, be expected to understand God's gracious word? And even more difficult, how could he accept the gospel even if he understood it? Not surprisingly, for Schwenckfeld, faith was the sole means of overcoming fallen man's handicaps. "Without faith, however, I can make use neither of God's grace, nor of baptism, indeed not even of God's word. I have no more than what I believe, be it God's grace or even justification itself. That is, unless he pours into our hearts (so that we may be certain) a living faith which alone justifies."[141] This is, of course, a circular argument: Faith is necessary to use God's word; one receives faith through God's word.

The solution to the problem lies in Schwenckfeld's identification of faith with possession of the spirit: "What is the spirit but faith in Christ."[142] In another passage he writes: "Beg God with all your heart for his Holy Spirit and a true living faith. . . . Through that spirit for the first time you will recognize your crimes and sinful life, and through the same spirit you will learn to seek forgiveness of sins from Christ alone."[143] Though Schwenckfeld would later separate spirit and Scripture, here he does not. Rather the spirit is viewed as working closely with God's word to produce a living faith. The spirit enables man to understand Scripture and to believe its message—*fides qua*. The Scriptures provide the objective content of faith—*fides quae*.

> It is not the fault of Scripture, therefore, that we do not understand, but rather our darkened hearts, which are burdened with self-love, covetousness, anger, impurity, and tyranny. Because of these the light can not enlighten. If we wish to see the light, we must first of all tear the veil from our eyes. . . . The spirit must do it . . . the flesh cannot. Thus will the Word of God alone be our judge.[144]

Schwenckfeld made no attempt to define in greater detail the exact relationship between word and spirit; much as in the Lutheran mold, the two are for him inextricably intertwined and symbiotic.[145]

141. CS II, 46:1–7.
142. CS I, 252:18–20.
143. CS II, 62:20–28.
144. CS I, 262:1–20.
145. See Pelikan 1968, 9; WA 6, 411:14–412:30, 573:3–4; WA 7, 58:19–21, 546:22–29. WA Deutsche Bibel 7, 6:14–23.

Both Schwenckfeld and Luther also emphasized the immediacy of the bond between the faithful Christian and God. This bond was the direct exercise of God's power through the Holy Spirit in the hearts of men, not some form of substantial union with the Godhead.[146] The spirit worked through man and in man, but did not become a part of man.

Given Schwenckfeld's mainstream Lutheran teachings on Scripture and the spirit, it is not surprising that his view of the church remained fairly conservative. In his letter to Bishop Salza in 1524, he wrote:

> We believe that in Scripture the Church is defined as a congregation or gathering of many or all hearts or souls who believe in Christ. Its head is Christ our Lord. . . . Such a Church is born only through God's word. And it is nourished and ruled by God's word. In short, they arrange everything according to the gospel, and all is judged according to the gospel. All men who have one baptism, one faith, and one spirit, wherever they live, in Rome or elsewhere, are all members of the same Church whose head is Christ. That is, the number of the predestined friends of God are the true Christian Church.[147]

Schwenckfeld actually gives two definitions here. The second, "the number of the predestined friends of God," should not be allowed to overshadow the first, "a congregation or gathering of many or all hearts or souls who believe in Christ." I do not agree with Gottfried Maron that in this passage we see already Schwenckfeld's tendency to concentrate "much more on an invisible ideal Church than on a real visible community of Christendom."[148] It is found in a work which is an exhortation to reform in general as well as a catalog of specific reforms for the very real, visible Silesian church. Nor had Schwenckfeld come to the point of demanding separation of the faithful from the impure, mass church. His choice of "*number* of the predestined friends of God" as a description of the Church Triumphant, is an antithetical construction to the separated *congregation* of the predestined, as Maron also

146. Schwenckfeld did not yet hold that a basically bipartite man (body and soul) became tripartite (body, soul, and spirit) with the reception of the spirit. I disagree with Weigelt (1973, 39–40), who finds this teaching already in 1524. The passage that best supports Weigelt's point of view can be found in CS II, 50:26–34. However, all Schwenckfeld did there was string together biblical texts (Rom 8:16, 1 Cor. 2:12, John 14:17, 1 Cor. 3:16). Cf. WA 1, 191:3–20.
147. CS I, 262:32–264:7
148. Maron 1961a, 117.

points out. Although Schwenckfeld agreed with Luther that real Christians were rare and known only to God, this did not lead him to repudiate the visible church as such.[149] A further sign of Schwenckfeld's belief in a visible church was his demand in 1524 for the institution of an evangelical ban,[150] something which made no sense if he repudiated a visible congregation.

His treatment of the Eucharist also reflects his adherence to a visible church. This sacrament was to become one of the chief points of difference between Schwenckfeld and Luther. And it was with the Eucharist that Schwenckfeld began his campaign against the visible, unspiritual elements in Christianity. But in the *Admonition concerning Abuse* he considered the necessity of establishing both forms—bread and wine—for the laity to be so great that he counseled proceeding even in the face of opposition by secular authorities.[151]

A. Kluge, with better right, argued that Schwenckfeld's views both on the vocation of ministers and on his own personal calling reveal the Silesian as early as 1522 "omitting all human mediation" and being "content with an inner calling through the spirit of God."[152] Kluge referred to Schwenckfeld's letter to Johannes Hess (June 13, 1522), in which Schwenckfeld urged Hess to come forward publicly and espouse the cause of reform. Schwenckfeld chided him for not believing that he, Hess, had received a special call. Did Hess expect a dove to descend from heaven? Didn't Hess know that all priests were ordained for the purpose of preaching? "You are called by God, I say, because you certainly have the word of God; and God wants his Church to be fed with this word."[153] Far from denying the validity of church orders, Schwenckfeld cited Hess's status as a priest, and later as a trained theologian, to argue that Hess should preach. This was not to say that all ordained priests have the word. It is the combination of human and divine callings that entitles a man to be a minister in God's Church; both God and the congregation must call an individual to his post.[154] There is nothing particularly radical in this. Luther had said as much already in 1522.[155] If anything, Schwenckfeld's remark about doves

149. For Schwenckfeld's view on the number of true Christians, see CS II, 88:21–25.
150. CS II, 90:17–92:8.
151. CS II, 90:17–92:8.
152. Kluge 1917, 226.
153. CS I, 35:8–18.
154. CS I, 254:9–11.
155. See Konrad 1917, 62.

from heaven tended to play down the importance of extra-eccle-
siastical callings.

But he does not rule them out. Schwenckfeld felt himself called. In
the letter to Hess Schwenckfeld explained that although he was not
prepared to enter orders himself, he could not remain silent. He must
seek the glory of the gospel as a layman. "In my opinion, those men
are called by the spirit of God who are urged by a secret impulse of the
spirit to utter his pure word."[156] A comparison of the Latin terms which
Schwenckfeld employed in this passage and the earlier one describing
Hess's calling is revealing. Hess is to teach (*docendi*), and Schwenckfeld to utter (*eloquantur*). Schwenckfeld claimed no right to the pulpit,
nor did he see himself as a priest capable of administering the sacraments or exercising pastoral care over a congregation. But as a Christian, it was his duty to proclaim the gospel and confess Christ openly:
"Although it is not sufficient for salvation, faith and divine truth must
be confessed orally and outwardly so that the office which we have
taken upon ourselves may be successful. Otherwise nothing will come
of it, and we will have to face a grievous reckoning."[157]

Here again Luther was Schwenckfeld's teacher. In *To the Christian
Nobility of the German Nation* Luther had insisted: "Therefore, it is
the duty of every christian to espouse the cause of the faith, to understand and defend it, and to denounce every error."[158] In the 1522 *Preface to the New Testament* Luther was to elaborate this theme and put
it in the context of the entire life of a Christian.

> If he has faith, the believer cannot be restrained. He betrays him-
> self. He breaks out. He confesses and teaches this Gospel to the
> people at the risk of life itself. His whole life and all his efforts are
> directed towards the benefit of his neighbor, and this is not just in
> order to help him to attain the same grace. But he employs his
> strength, uses his goods, and stakes his reputation, as he sees
> Christ did for him, and therefore follows His example.[159]

Or as Schwenckfeld would say:

> And so good works should come to pass in the simplicity of our
> hearts so that we praise God and do his will. And as Christ has

156. CS I, 36:1–13.
157. CS II, 94:22–25.
158. Luther 1970, 22. WA 6, 421:37–38.
159. Luther 1961, 18. WA Deutsche Bibel 6, 8:29–34.

served us with his body and life, so we should serve our neigh-bors.[160]

Through 1524 Caspar Schwenckfeld was still an apostle of Luther-anism in Silesia. He was an apostle and not a theologian. Even his most theological work of this period, *Admonition concerning Abuse*, limits itself to meeting certain practical problems which had arisen through what Schwenckfeld considered to be a misreading of Luther's message. But to say that Schwenckfeld was an apostle of Lutheranism or a follower of Luther is not to say that Schwenckfeld grasped Luther's theology in all its profundity and complexity. But then, none of Lu-ther's contemporaries could make that claim. And if the volume of scholarship on Luther being produced today is any indication, the claim still cannot be made.

The Luther that Schwenckfeld followed was the early Luther of the 1520 pamphlets and the *Commentary on the Seven Penitential Psalms*. The emphasis was on the free preaching of the word and the freedom of the Christian. Both were interpreted in practical ways and embodied in concrete reform proposals. The issue of Christian free-dom shows most clearly the way in which Schwenckfeld appropriated Luther's teachings. The Christian was free of all the petty, and not so petty, rules and expectations with which the medieval Catholic church had burdened him. As with other reformers of this early period—men like Zwingli and later Calvin—there was a drive toward simplicity in religion. And it was primarily those extraneous details, like pilgrim-ages, bells, candles, and churchings, that Schwenckfeld had in mind when he spoke of oppressed consciences. Only in the *Admonition con-cerning Abuse* did he begin to emphasize the oppressive aspect of God's law. Even there, he employed the law/gospel antithesis not so much to drive men to complete reliance on Christ, but rather to humble the newly freed Christian so that he might use his freedom wisely.

Schwenckfeld's personal experience differed from Luther's. The young noble had never been a monk's monk, and it is doubtful that he had exhausted the consolatory possibilities of late medieval Catholi-cism. His life at court would have confronted him with patent, visible sins. Turning away from that life and those sins, while difficult, was nonetheless marked by an obvious, perceptible improvement. After his conversion there were no *Anfechtungen*. There was no sense of a psy-chologically deeply rooted feeling of utter worthlessness such as Luther

160. CS II, 78:6–8.

experienced. Schwenckfeld never suffered from scrupulosity. On the other hand, he took the proffered consolation of Luther's message much more to heart than Luther himself had. As a result Schwenckfeld was completely convinced of his own salvation. Unlike Luther he did not have to struggle again and again to achieve that confidence. But having been assured of his own salvation through faith in Christ, having once and for all won that battle, there was nothing left to do but realize in his own life and in the life of the Silesian community the Christian ideal which God's grace had now made possible. Here again Schwenckfeld displayed a tendency that separated him from Luther. Schwenckfeld had great confidence in God's omnipotence. No matter how low man had fallen, God could and, in the case of true Christians, did restore him. After the truly incomprehensible miracle of justification by faith alone sanctification was something of an anticlimax, but it did happen. Perfection was of course not possible, but a visible piety and goodness certainly were.

Schwenckfeld's emphasis on the possibility and necessity of personal reform for the Christian New Man stemmed from his own religious *curriculum vitae*. Faith, a true living faith, was a deeply felt personal commitment to Christ and to the reform of his Church. This commitment entailed an earnestness which was reflected in the Christian's life. Schwenckfeld's own experience involved an increasing concentration on the more theological aspects of religion. His works after 1522 are more theological; his writings more deft and perceptive when dealing with theological issues. His retirement from court to his estates marked a turning point in this regard. At Ossig, away from the distractions of court, immersed in the Bible, isolated still further by his increasing deafness, Schwenckfeld became even more grave.[161] No longer did he write with the cocky sarcasm of his letters to Hess. Although the evidence is at best ambiguous he seems to have distinguished his 1519 conversion from a somewhat later reform in his way of life.[162]

He began to plumb the depths of teachings which, though fervently

---

161. See CS V, 30 n. He viewed his deafness as an act of God to wean him from the world.

162. In a confession submitted to Ulm on November 3, 1536, Schwenckfeld says, "Dann nachdem Ich das Evangelion Christi / auff seyner gnedigen haimsuchung one jedermans schaden oder nachthail angenommen / unnd demselbigen (one Roum zureden.) von funfftzehen Jaren her / vermittels der gnaden Gottes / gelebt . . ." (CS v, 535:13–16). The dating in some of Schwenckfeld's statements is only approximate. In other passages he places these events in 1523–24 (CS VI, 490:9–19; CS IX, 60:36–61:3). This would agree with the course of rebirth outlined by Schwenckfeld in 1529(?). Reform of life comes as late as step four (CS III, 572–73).

espoused, took time, experience, and meditation to grasp in all their profundity. The understanding that resulted penetrated Schwenckfeld's personality and began a process of increasing dissonance between deeply held religious convictions and ingrained social and ecclesiastical conventions. He remained a noble loyal to his class and its ideals and never for a moment considered casting off the courtier's persona and its privileges. But he was becoming increasingly drawn into theology and had always been more actively involved in the reform than was expected from one of his background. He was a reformer himself, and not merely a lay ally or auxiliary to other, clerical, reformers. As a result it was difficult, and it remains difficult, to bring his character into focus; it is too much the double exposure.

In the years through 1524, however, the contours of Schwenckfeld's personality and program still retained definition. He was the leading lay advocate of the Silesian Lutheran Reformation.

3 Bishop in Ossig
(1525–1526)

I was as good a Lutheran in that matter [the Eucharist] as one might wish. But because it pleased my God, because he looked upon me with the eyes of his mercy, suddenly he helped me—Schwenckfeld to Dr. Markus Zimmerman, June 1556

To our most beloved and pious brothers in Christ, Valentin Crautwald, bishop of the Church of Liegnitz, and Caspar Schwenckfeld, bishop in Ossig, and the other brethren throughout Silesia.—Zwingli, April 17, 1526

The years 1525–26 saw the greatest successes of the Silesian Reformation. But in the same years occurred the irreparable splintering of the reform movement, with Liegnitz assuming the lineaments of inchoate reformed Protestantism and Breslau becoming a bastion of Lutheranism.

The bishop of Breslau, cognizant of the weakness of the Catholic position in his diocese, sensibly withdrew into the safety of the principality Neisse-Ottmachau-Grottkau where he exercised secular rule in addition to his spiritual jurisdiction.[1] Jakob Salza was no "hot gospeler" of the Counter-Reformation, nor was he merely an ecclesiastical time-server. By birth a member of the landed nobility, by education a doctor of law, by long years' service an able administrator, the bishop of Breslau was quite incapable of putting up a doctrinal defense of Catholicism. He therefore sought to save what jurisdiction, property, and secular power still remained to the church in hopes of eventual reconciliation or, perhaps, reconquest. The other potential source of leadership for the embattled Catholics was the canons of the Breslau cathedral chapter. But they were separated from the bishop physically (he lived in Neisse, they in the espiscopal see Breslau) and alienated from him psychologically and politically by long, bitter pre-Reformation disputes. The bishop and the chapter never succeeded in forming an effective common front. The chapter itself was something of a prisoner in Protestant Breslau. In addition, neither bishop nor

1. For the state, organization, and reactions of the Silesian Catholic Church during the Reformation, see Sabisch 1975. For the initial years of the Reformation, see chap. 2 and 3, pp. 35–71.

chapter possessed the necessary bureaucratic mechanism for exercising control over the approximately eight hundred fifty parishes in the diocese. These were for the most part left to the various cities, princes, lords, and patrons. Although episcopal jurisdiction was not formally repudiated, the Catholic church in Silesia was reduced, in effect, to the status of one territorial church among many.

In Liegnitz Friedrich moved in 1525 to gain control of church finances, at first acting as arbitrator between the clergy and their debtors,[2] and then actually seizing and reassigning eccesiastical revenues.[3] In 1526 he ordered the confiscation of all church bells and the inventorying of chalices and other valuables, ostensibly to meet the Turkish threat after the disastrous defeat at Mohacs.[4] Friedrich also intervened in church praxis, regulating burial practices and granting Lutheran ministers dispensations from Catholic services.[5] And he began the process of purging Catholics and other dissidents from the clerical ranks.[6] Though Friedrich was careful to negotiate an agreement with Bishop Salza ratifying at least some of his actions,[7] the net result was the Protestantization of the church in his lands.

But the Protestant successes, in Silesia and in the empire, were already being undermined. The various social groups and religious parties that composed the reform movement began to go in separate ways, pursuing programs often mutually exclusive. The broken alliances which resulted produced clashes, in some cases cataclysmic, that determined the future course and complexion of the reform. Two of

2. Engelbert 1963, 174–75. The text of the agreement published in Brieg (May 23, 1525) and Liegnitz (June 19, 1525) can be found in F. Bahlow 1918, 155–56.

3. This was done by the mandate of September 15, 1525 (Engelbert 1963; Konrad 1917, 81). It was reissued for Brieg. Engelbert (1963, 176) sees this as a sign that Brieg was still largely Catholic and in need of special handling.

4. Engelbert 1963, 181. Although there was probably compelling reason for this (Breslau did the same thing), Friedrich's other seizures had made even his Protestant brother-in-law Georg of Brandenburg suspect his motives (Engelbert 1963, 181). The Reformation made Friedrich's fortune.

5. Engelbert 1963, 175–76; Konrad 1917, 81.

6. F. Bahlow (1918, 48–49) denies that force was used, but both the Breslau canons and even Friedrich himself give evidence to the contrary (Engelbert 1963, 176; CS III, 17:8–20). Otte (1936, 22–23) and Konrad (1917, 81) agree. Nonetheless, not all Catholic clergy were immediately expelled. The last Catholic canon of the Liegnitz chapter died in 1545 (F. Bahlow 1908, 145), and as late as 1529–30 two mass-priests were appointed to SS. Peter-Paul (F. Bahlow 1918, 6).

7. Salza had nothing to lose and much to gain. In return for granting the income of other clerics to Friedrich, he retained his own and also his nominal right of supervision (F. Bahlow 1918, 90–91). The cathedral canons never came to terms, but Friedrich unilaterally extended the agreement on debts to cover them as well (Engelbert 1963, 91).

those events, the Peasants' War and the eucharistic controversy, swept Schwenckfeld from his already shaky moorings and launched him in ever more radical directions.

Beginning in 1524 and lasting for two years, the Peasants' War threatened to destroy the very foundations of civil society in southern and central Germany, and the fears that it generated were keenly felt throughout the German-speaking lands and beyond. Combining some new religious demands with traditional economic and political grievances, the peasants vented their wrath at first on the church and the clergy, but soon extended their attacks to the nobility and other elements of the secular hierarchy.

Silesia escaped the cataclysm with only one minor, quickly suppressed uprising, in part because Breslau and Liegnitz had moved quickly to take control of the reform, thus damping the fires of unrest.[8] Friedrich of Liegnitz also took precautions, putting the entire principality on alert when the first reports were received. From this base he was able to assist his in-laws, the Brandenburg Hohenzollerns, by serving as a secure line of communication between that family's two branches in Prussia and Anhalt, both faced with serious peasant uprisings. The courier who raced between Liegnitz and Prussia, a member of the Prussian court, was a Schwenckfeld, probably Caspar's nephew.[9]

The Peasants' War posed a great challenge to the early Reformation and to those who supported it, because the rebels had claimed Scripture and Luther as judges of the justness of their cause. Luther, embarrassed and enraged at the presumption of the rebels and their misuse of Scripture, published *Against the Robbing and Murdering Hordes of Peasants* and called upon all good Christians to "smite, slay and stab [them], secretly and openly."[10] Luther's reaction, though repellent, was not totally ill-advised. The Peasants' War seemed to lend substance to Catholic criticism that the reform, if not seditious in itself, certainly provided occasion and encouragement to insurrection and social upheaval. This association threatened to undermine the widespread support that the reformers found among the upper classes, support which was essential to the success of the movement. It certainly contributed to the decision by Karl of Münsterberg-Oels to back

8. Schimmelpfennig 1884, 133.
9. Krämer 1977, 250–55, 257–260.
10. Sessions 1968, 38–39.

away from the reform.[11] Others, though remaining faithful to the cause, assumed a lower profile.[12] For those, like Schwenckfeld, who were personally caught up in the religious renewal, it was particularly pressing. After all, might not Scripture call for and the new religious situation actually entail a "new heaven and a new earth"?

Nothing Schwenckfeld wrote documents his inner turmoil; we have only the results. Schwenckfeld's reform program had never had any political components. Since Silesia was not part of the empire, the revival of that institution had played no part in his thinking, as it had in Hutten's.[13] Nor had he seen the reform as a way of bettering the lot of the lower nobility at the expense of either the church or the territorial princes, as had the supporters of the Knights' Rebellion. Schwenckfeld had abetted the princes and sought to win over the church. In this he was no different from the mass of the lower nobility.[14] What little social concern he demonstrated was for the peasantry, the "poor little people," whom the Catholic church had oppressed both religiously and financially. After 1525, however, the peasants *qua* peasants disappear altogether from his writings, with one exception. He once complained that they, along with the nobility, were taking advantage of the reform to play clerics off against one another in order to lower tithe assessments.[15] More normally he didn't even treat the rural lower classes as a socially or economically defined group. They became for him a religious category—Christians, yet abysmally ignorant and almost pagan.

This was typical of Schwenckfeld's wider vision of Christianity and the Reformation. Having decided to reaffirm his commitment to *religious* reform, he became curiously and willfully color-blind to its social consequences and corollaries. In his view, religion was concerned with the salvation of souls, not the reform of society; it dealt with the

11. Karl had personal acquaintance with the dangers of insurrection. He was the one who put down Silesia's only uprising, and his sister was driven from her home in Anhalt (Schimmelpfennig 1884, 133).

12. For example, Hartmuth von Kronberg, a noble propagandist for the Lutherans, suddenly stopped his literary production in the spring of 1525, though he remained a devoted Lutheran (Hitchcock 1958, 87).

13. Despite ephemeral ties in the twelfth and thirteenth centuries, Silesia never really belonged to the empire. Its sole point of contact was through the union with the Bohemian crown. To the extent that Bohemia was part of the empire, so too was Silesia. But imperial law and the decisions of the various *Reichstage* were not normative for Silesia. See Kutscha 1924.

14. On the reaction of the lower nobility to the Reformation, see Hitchcock 1958 and Press 1978.

15. CS III, 111:2–6.

morals of the individual, not the relations between the classes. For Schwenckfeld the separation of what Luther called the "Two Kingdoms" was complete, and he took as his own the medieval image of the Christian as a pilgrim who passed through this world, but was not really of this world.[16] Schwenckfeld did not reject the secular world; he ignored it. It rarely appeared in his writings.[17] His theology developed around an ever more thoroughgoing dualism which safely buffered the inner spiritual world of Christianity from intrusion by the external material world of everyday life. In turn, the world of power, politics, and privilege was freed from the demands of spiritual perfection. Schwenckfeld's social conservatism thus provided much of the impetus for his truly impressive religious radicalism. And because he became more deeply immersed in speculative theology as he withdrew from the world, to understand Schwenckfeld in these years it is necessary to study his theology.

Revelation and Breakthrough

Beginning in 1524–25 the reformers were forced to confront the fact that society as a whole was not becoming the Christian community which they all—somewhat inconsistently—had expected.[18] Luther began to see the need for secular intervention to harness the unregenerate herd, and Melanchthon, who may have suffered a severe personality crisis, was even more distressed.[19] Zwingli and the Anabaptists split over the pace of reform. The peasants rose, were defeated, and became disillusioned, while bitterness and apathy were becoming widespread. Neither Silesia nor Schwenckfeld escaped the general crisis.

> Not once, but often I was violently agitated and assaulted with something like pain because at that time still so few of those who heard the present preaching of the gospel showed any improvement. And if we should admit the truth (and I speak here of our

16. CS III, 460:10–17.

17. This may be the result of later editing, however. See Gottfried Seebass's paper in Erb 1985.

18. Luther's theology emphasized the sinful nature of fallen man even after his redemption through faith in Christ. Strauss 1978 makes much of the basic contradiction between Lutheran theology and a Lutheran pedagogical theory based on the malleability and educability of the young.

19. Strauss 1978, 6.

people), the longer it was preached, the worse they were, God help us. Therefore I suspected that there must be something lacking, whatever it could be, and that things were not as perfect as we allowed ourselves to think. And the Father of all mercy, who is present to all who in truth call to him with their whole heart, out of his fatherly goodness had directed that we should once again carefully consider the scriptures [to discover] whether there might be still some error remaining, and particularly in the article of the sacrament [the Eucharist]. Especially since we had been so far from the truth in the past, that it would be wise to suppose that we couldn't grasp all the truth so quickly. And if we err in this article, then we truly err grossly and sin, since we believe a creature to be the creator, and worship and reverence the work of our hands as if it were Jesus Christ, our God. Such a sin he could never forgive us in the future, because there is no error in our Christian faith to compare with it.[20]

The entire Protestant world had been caught up in the eucharistic controversy since autumn 1524, when Andreas Karlstadt had begun his spate of publications against the real presence. Luther replied in an open letter to the clergy of Strassburg and in the first installment of *Against the Heavenly Prophets*. Ulrich Zwingli joined the attack against the real presence in the *Commentarius de vera et falsa religione* (March 1525) and the *Subsidium sive coronis de eucharistia* (April 1525). By the summer of 1525 Protestants all over Germany were choosing sides.

In Silesia Karlstadt's and Zwingli's works were available and found a ready audience. Their supporters were numerous, and among them were many of Schwenckfeld's friends.[21] Schwenckfeld himself was well acquainted with their arguments, and although he did not agree with their own positive theology of the Eucharist, he did find their critique of the real presence persuasive and disturbing.[22] Finally, sometime

20. Schwenckfeld to Speratus October 1, 1526, CS II, 368:9–369:4.

21. WA Br 3, 315 (July 4, 1524), 418–19 (January 11, 1525), 433 (February 4, 1525), 527 (June 11, 1525), 555–56 (after August 15, 1525). Luther warned Johannes Hess about the new prophets on July 19, 1525 (Köhler 1924, 182). The opening salvo of the Lutheran counterattack came in the form of an open letter to Hess from Bugenhagen, *Contra novum errorem de sacramento . . .* , 1525. Ambrosius Creusing is suspected of being a follower of Karlstadt (Schneider 1862, 3–4). Bernhardinus Egetius was a Zwinglian (Crautwald to Egetius, December 10, 1525, CLM 718, 212v).

22. Schwenckfeld thought that Zwingli's teaching was basically that of the Bohemian Brethren (Schwenckfeld to Speratus, June 23, 1525, CS II, 122:11–125). Though Schwenckfeld did not mention Karlstadt here, he discussed him when he went to Wittenberg in December 1525

during the summer of 1525 it all became clear to him.[23]

> I was as good a Lutheran in that matter [the Eucharist] as one
> might wish. But because it pleased my God, because he looked
> upon me with the eyes of his mercy, suddenly he helped me. He
> cast the traitor Judas in my teeth, and made me consider what sort
> of companion he was, and how the devil after the meal had en-
> tered into him, John 13 [vs. 27], and whether such a person could
> also eat really and essentially the true body of Christ our Lord,
> King and Redeemer, and whether he could drink of his blood
> (which is a blood of the new eternal Testament), as the Lutherans
> even today believe. I went for a while, but not long, filled with
> such thoughts [Schwanger in meinem gemuet], until the spirit of
> the Lord came to my aid with his teaching in the sixth chapter of
> the Gospel of John [6:54] where he says: "whoever eats my flesh
> and drinks my blood, he shall have eternal life." Then I was
> helped by God's grace so that I was quite sure in my own heart
> that the traitor Judas (whom the Lord had already called a devil,
> John 6 [vs. 70], and in whom Satan had already begun the work
> of betrayal before the Last Supper) was by no means fed with the
> body and blood of Christ, because the body and blood of Christ
> are never without divine power, spirit and life, nor can they ever
> be, because the word was made flesh.[24]

Convinced that a physical real presence in the sacrament was impossible, he immediately wrote the twelve *Questiones*, or *Arguments
against Impanation*, which explained his discovery.[25] Schwenckfeld's
treatment of the Eucharist began with John 6:54–57.

> Unless you eat the flesh of the Son of Man and drink his blood,
> you will not have life in you. Whoever eats my flesh and drinks
> my blood has eternal life, and I shall raise him on the last day.

(CS II, 253:14–16; 281:6–282:2; cf. Schwenckfeld to Speratus, October 1, 1526, CS II, 369:5–
370:2). Schwenckfeld thought that Wittenberg had failed to meet Zwingli's objections (CS II,
122:11–125). Köhler 1924, 272, stretches the evidence too far when he labels Schwenckfeld a
Zwinglian "allem Anschein nach."

23. That is, between his two letters to Paul Speratus on June 23, and September 14, CS II,
113–25, 167–71.

24. Schwenckfeld to Dr. Markus Zimmerman, June 1556, in CS XIV, 802:17–34.
Schwenckfeld was probably drawn to the issue of Judas by his reading of Augustine's *Homilies
on the Gospel of John* (PL 35, 1611–12).

25. *Argumenta contra impanationem*, CS III, 498–507. For a detailed analysis of this document, see McLaughlin 1983, 98–102.

My body is truly a food and my blood is truly a drink. Whoever eats my flesh and drinks my blood remains in me and I in him.[26]

Schwenckfeld reasoned that if Christ's body and blood did convey salvation, then all who ate of it were in fact among the saved. Judas, the false apostle, had partaken of the bread and wine at the last supper, but the Bible states that it was the devil and not Christ who entered into him. Therefore, Christ's body and blood was not to be identified with the outward bread and wine of the sacrament. The unworthy, the unrepentant, and the unbelieving received the outer elements but not the inner flesh of Christ. The outer ceremony and the inner reception must be clearly and emphatically distinguished. According to Schwenckfeld it was the failure of the Lutheran preachers to make that distinction that led people astray. Many Lutherans were convinced that by participating in the Eucharist they were ipso facto saved. He argued that this outward, one might say *opus operatum*, formulation of Christianity was the principal cause of the Reformation's failure to reform individual Christians.

In summary, then, Schwenckfeld's arguments relied on John 6:54–57 as the proof text and maintained (1) the necessity of faith and the exclusion of the unworthy, (2) the radical distinction of inner and outer Eucharists, and (3) the centrality of Christ's flesh in the economy of salvation. Though directed against the Lutherans and Catholics, the twelve *Questiones* do not follow Karlstadt or Zwingli. Schwenckfeld did not rely on the argument that Christ's simultaneous presence both in heaven and on earth was a physical impossibility, since for Schwenckfeld Christ did indeed dwell both in heaven and in the heart of every believing Christian.[27] And his failure to cite Zwingli's favorite passage "But the flesh profits nothing" (John 6:63),[28] is even more easily explained; for Schwenckfeld the flesh, Christ's flesh, profited everything. It granted a new existence and eternal life. Schwenckfeld's interpretation of the relationship between faith and the sacrament was also different. While Karlstadt and Zwingli emphasized faith often to the exclusion of the reception of Christ's body and blood, for Schwenckfeld faith remained merely the instrument through which such a reception was effected. Faith was the means, not the end. The

26. Vulgate, my translation.
27. CS III, 503:10–26.
28. Maurer (1952, 19 n. 32) calls John 6:63 the center of the entire eucharistic controversy.

flesh and not the instrument was what truly mattered. The insistence upon a real, though spiritual, participation in Christ places Schwenckfeld in the late medieval Augustinian tradition along with Thomas a Kempis, Wessel Gansfort, Erasmus, the early Luther, and Johannes Oecolampadius.[29] It would eventually receive a new formulation with Calvin and the Reformed.[30] And it was this very conservative conception of the power of the flesh which, paradoxically, made it impossible for Schwenckfeld to accept the real presence.

Although the twelve *Questiones* went into some detail about the content of the Eucharist, they contained no attempt to deal with the disputed exegesis of Matt. 26:26, "Hoc est corpus meum." Schwenckfeld clearly felt that Luther, Zwingli, and Karlstadt had allowed themselves to become mired in the minutiae of logic-chopping philological scholarship. Breadth of vision was required in order to get to the heart of the matter. Once one had a true understanding of the sacrament based on all of self-interpreting Scripture, he argued, what need was there to worry about those few syllables?[31] And so he rejected Karlstadt's and Zwingli's tortured explanations, and of course Luther's and the Catholics',[32] while not bothering to provide his own.

For that he turned to a specialist, the trilingual humanist and lecturer of the Liegnitz chapter of the Holy Sepulcher Valentin Crautwald (1490–1545).[33] Crautwald became a key figure in the develop-

---

29. See McLaughlin 1983, 49. Zwingli differentiated his own position from one which claimed a spiritual eating of Christ's flesh (Köhler 1924, 97–98). Cf. Augustine's *Homilies on the Gospel of John* (PL 35, 1379–1977), especially tractate 27, paragraphs 8 and 11 (PL 35, 1619–20). Another possible source was the Bohemian Brethren. We know that Schwenckfeld was acquainted with some of their teachings, though which particular ones has not been established. Most scholars identify the document that Schwenckfeld brought to Wittenberg in December 1525 (CS II, 272:19–22) as the *Excusatio fratrum Waldensium contra binas literas Doctoris Augustini* (1508); see Urner 1948, 335; Preger 1859, 300; Weigelt 1973, 52. However, it has been suggested that is was a later 1524 confession (Schneider 1857, 21 n. 2). Certain similarities exist, but the fact that the Brethren denied the applicability of John 6:54 to the Eucharist establishes Schwenckfeld's independence of them, as Weigelt 1973, 52, has already pointed out. Schwenckfeld himself equated the Bohemian position with that of Zwingli (CS II, 122:11–125).

30. See McLaughlin 1985a: "Schwenckfeld and the South German Eucharistic Controversy, 1525–1529," in Erb 1985.

31. CS III, 370:14–18.

32. CS II, 242:14–16, 280:6–13; CS III, 358:3–7.

33. Crautwald was born to a peasant family in the episcopal center of Neisse and probably attended school there. He attended the University of Krakow in 1506, began teaching at St. Jakob's school in Neisse in 1507, and would later be its rector. In 1514 he became secretary and notary to Bishop Turzo; in 1517 he held two positions as an altar priest; and in 1520 he was made a canon in Neisse and episcopal protonotary, in which function he wrote up the account of Jakob Salza's election. He had joined the reform movement by 1522. Already before that he

ment of the Liegnitz theology, and Schwenckfeld consulted with him until Crautwald's death.[34] Crautwald was that common figure, an academic who was personally retiring but whose lectures and books contained explosive material disguised only by prolixity and a lack of fanfare. One senses that he was abashed and not a little frightened when his recondite views were made public and efforts were made to draw all too concrete conclusions from rather theoretical propositions. Though actually a year younger than Schwenckfeld, he conveyed the air of declining old age, partly because of his chronic ill health, but also because of his awareness that he, unlike Schwenckfeld, was a pensioner, dependent on the goodwill of the prince.[35]

When Schwenckfeld had first written to share his findings with the clergy in Liegnitz and other friends, Crautwald had heatedly rejected them.[36] But in September Schwenckfeld approached Crautwald again, hoping to win him over in private conversation. This time Crautwald consented to reconsider the matter.[37] The result was a personal revelation (September 16–17) based upon his knowledge of Hebrew.[38] Crautwald argued that when Christ had said, "This is my body," he had meant to express the same thing as John 6:54–57, that is, "My body is this, a bread for the soul," a word reversal which according to Crautwald was consonant with common Hebrew usage. With this philological interpretation Crautwald had provided a perfect exegetical counterpart for Schwenckfeld's own eucharistic theology.

---

had been a firm supporter of Reuchlin. In the fall of 1523 he was made a canon in Liegnitz with duties as lecturer for the younger clergy. By early 1524 he was lecturing on the Pauline Epistles in German. Schwenckfeld may well have attended. For biographical information on Crautwald see Weigelt 1973, 7–11, 64–65; also G. Eberlein 1900, 6–16, and G. Eberlein 1903, 268–86. A near-contemporary biography is Adam Reissner's "Vita beati Valentini Crautuualdi Silesij Theologi" (CLM 718, 549r–552r). Cf. Otto 1872, 318–27, and F. Bahlow 1908, 140–75.

34. Weigelt 1983 is a laudable attempt to give the figure of Crautwald a deservedly greater prominence in the Schwenckfelder tradition. In pleading his case Weigelt overestimates Crautwald's contribution to the initial eucharistic "discovery" and Schwenckfeld's later Christology.

35. It may well be that Crautwald was considerably older than has been believed. Douglas Shantz, who is writing a dissertation on Crautwald at the University of Waterloo, suspects that Crautwald may have been born a full twenty years earlier than 1490.

36. CS XIV, 803:32–35. Crautwald seems to have held somewhat conservative views on the sacrament. He absented himself from Liegnitz on the day of the first non-Catholic celebration of the Eucharist in 1524 in order to oversee the publication of his translation of a late medieval *ars moriendi* (Konrad 1917, 80–81). The title of the work published was "Ein nuczbar Edell / Buchlein von be- / reytunge zum sterben. . . ."

37. CS XIV, 803:28–804:3.

38. Crautwald described his revelation in some detail in a letter probably written in October (CS II, 173–209).

Nonetheless, though he was certain that the real presence was an error and that his own approach was correct, Schwenckfeld was not immediately convinced of the validity of Crautwald's solution.[39] It was in this frame of mind that Schwenckfeld set out for Wittenberg in December 1525.[40]

To one who had looked with confidence to Luther and Wittenberg for years, his visit there must have been a frustrating disappointment. Melanchthon was out of town, and Luther could spare only a little time. It fell to Bugenhagen (who had many strengths and virtues, but theology unfortunately not among them) to thrash out the issues with Schwenckfeld and defend the real presence. With a little prompting from Schwenckfeld, Bugenhagen discovered all of the traps and failings of the (as yet undeveloped) Lutheran eucharistic theology. An almost taciturn Luther held to the "clear simple word" of Scripture and demanded proof that John 6:54–56 applied to the words of institution,[41] which surely must have irritated Schwenckfeld, for whom, as we have seen, the exegetical issue was secondary. The four days were spent in warm, calm conversation, but Schwenckfeld had not convinced Wittenberg, nor had he heard any useful counterarguments.[42] As Schwenckfeld was about to depart Luther whispered to him, "Hold still for a while. The Lord will be with you."[43] Luther, however, had come to a decision. Some twenty years later he commented in the *Tischreden*:

When he [Schwenckfeld] came from Silesia, he wanted to convince Doctor Pomeranus [Bugenhagen] and I that his opinion of the sacrament was correct. And because he could not hear well [a reference to Schwenckfeld's impaired hearing], he asked us to pray for him. Yes, I wanted to pray—that he would also become dumb.[44]

39. Schwenckfeld admitted to Luther that he was becoming more convinced every day that Crautwald's interpretation must be the right one, but that he was not yet absolutely certain (CS II, 280:6–13). Schwenckfeld finally came to a decision sometime in the first half of 1526 (Crautwald to Moibanus, June 24, 1526, CLM 718, 384r).

40. Our source for this event comes in the form of a letter written in 1540 by Schwenckfeld to his uncle (CS II, 235–82). From its style and detail it must have been based on a diary written at the time of the visit. See Pietz 1959.

41. CS II, 277:11–13, 278:1–3.

42. CS II, 264:29–265:2.

43. CS II, 282:3–6.

44. WA Tischreden 5, 300:1–8.

Beginning at the end of December and continuing through the early months of 1526 Luther sounded the alarm against the new heretics in Liegnitz.[45]

Schwenckfeld returned to Liegnitz not knowing that Luther had already written him off as just one more *Schwärmer*. In the months that followed, the Liegnitz circle produced a corpus of apologetic treatises to persuade Luther.[46] In the process they also developed the wider theological implications of their eucharistic position. But they did not yet appeal to a wider audience by publishing their results, partly out of uncertainty of the validity of their own position, partly out of prudence and caution.[47] It is hard to escape the conclusion that in all of this Crautwald, since he wrote most of the letters and all of the treatises, came to play the dominant role. The fact that nothing survives of Schwenckfeld's writing from before June probably indicates that nothing substantial was written.[48] After having provided the original impulse and direction with his twelve *Questiones*, Schwenckfeld seems to have relinquished the theological leadership of the Liegnitz movement to the more learned, and more convinced, Crautwald.

Besides cultivating their contacts with Wittenberg,[49] Schwenckfeld and Crautwald canvassed their nearer neighbors in Breslau,[50] Woh-

45. Luther to Michael Stifel, December 31, 1525, WA Br 3, 653; to the Christians in Reutlingen, January 4, 1526, WA 19, 120:25–30; to Agricola, February 18, 1526, WA Br 4, 33:4–11; to Spalatin, March 27, 1526, WA Br 4, 42:34–48; "Vorrede zum Schwäbischen Syngramm," 1526, WA 19, 459:3.

46. Of these works we can be reasonably sure only of *De imagine et veritate* (CLM 718, 120r–147v), mentioned by Luther, WA Br 4, 53; *De sensu verborum coenae dominicae* (CLM 718, 188r–199v), mentioned by Crautwald in his letter to Schleupner (CLM 718, 289r–289v), and the *Collatio* (CS II, 343–408), also mentioned in the same passage to Schleupner.

47. Bugenhagen had warned Schwenckfeld about the possibility of misleading the people with a doctrine that rested upon someone else's (Crautwald's) personal revelation (CS II, 262:8–17). On Schwenckfeld's decision to remain quiet for a while, see CS II, 253:11–14.

48. For an indication of Schwenckfeld's letters known to have been lost, see CS II, passim.

49. Two letters survive, both written to an unknown theologian at Wittenberg, perhaps Justus Jonas. Crautwald had already been in touch with Jonas (CS II, 273:11–274:5). As for dating, we may have a reference to this correspondence in a letter to Dominicus Schleupner (CLM 718, 289r–289v). The Schleupner letter was written earlier than April 8; it is mentioned by Crautwald in a letter to Michael Wittiger of that date (CLM 718, 306v). The position of the letters to Wittenberg in the manuscript CLM 718 would also suggest this early date, since the compiler seems to have attempted a chronological ordering. The Wittenberg letters are found at CLM 718, 243r–270v, and are therefore presumably earlier than the letters to Schleupner and Wittiger.

50. Both Schwenckfeld and Crautwald wrote to Hess (before April 8). Only Crautwald's is extant (CLM 718, 271r–288v). It is mentioned by Crautwald in his letter to Wittiger, April 8 (CLM 718, 306v). Schwenckfeld and Crautwald also wrote Moibanus about the same time, but neither letter has survived. We do have one from Crautwald dated June 24, 1526 (CLM

lau,[51] and elsewhere in Silesia,[52] with mixed success. Efforts to recruit Nürnberg as an ally proved abortive,[53] but the successful mission of the Silesian Matthias Winkler to Strassburg, Basel, and Zurich,[54] combined with Luther's final rebuff (April 14, 1526),[55] abruptly shifted Liegnitz from the Lutheran to the developing Reformed camp. They broke their public silence on April 21 with an open letter presented to the *Fürstentag* in Breslau and posted elsewhere in Silesia.[56] In it they repeated Schwenckfeld's argument against the real presence, his dismay at the lack of popular improvement, and his condemnation of the new indulgence of the Eucharist. They called for mass catechization

718, 380r). Neither Hess nor Moibanus proved receptive. This letter is the last contact between Liegnitz and the Lutheran leadership in Silesia. But they had better luck with Michael Wittiger, notary and chancellor to the bishop in Breslau. See Crautwald's letters to Wittiger dated April 8, 1526 (CLM 718, 299r–307r), May 20, 1526 (CLM 718, 308r–313v), and May 27, 1526 (CLM 718, 314r–318v). The next two letters may have confused dating. They are lumped together with a date at the end, "Dominica Trinitatis." The next letter is dated the second Sunday after Trinity (CLM 718, 322r–349v). I believe it likely that the first of the two letters was dated "Dominica Trinitatis" (CLM 718, 314r–318v), and the second letter dated the first Sunday after Trinity (CLM 718, 318v–320v). It is of course possible that the second letter was added onto the first as an afterthought and that both were sent on Trinity Sunday. We know that Wittiger was finally convinced because he appears as head of a Schwenckfelder group in Breslau in 1534 (Weigelt 1973, 150–51).

51. See two letters to Egetius, the first dated December 10, 1525, and the second undated but obviously a follow-up of the first (CLM 718, 212r–221v). Egetius was one of the first men to whom Crautwald had spoken after having his revelation in the fall. The two men agreed to study Hilary of Poitiers's *De trinitate* together.

52. Letters to Matthias Funk and Adam Adamus, respectively pastor and preacher in Hainau, another of Friedrich's possessions, failed to win them from Catholicism. Crautwald to Adamus, June 17, 1526 (CLM 718, 222r–225v), and Crautwald to Funk (CLM 718, 226r–233v). The latter was later published by Schwenckfeld under the title *De coena dominica* (CS II, 409–38).

53. Crautwald to Dominicus Schleupner, preacher at St. Sebald's, Nürnberg, written before April 8, 1526 (CLM 718, 289r–298r). This letter is mentioned in Crautwald's letter to Wittiger dated April 8, 1526 (CLM 718, 306v). Schleupner, who was from Silesia and was a personal friend of Crautwald, had sent a copy of the 1525 "Ratschlag" addressed to the city council by Nürnberg's Protestant preachers. For the "Nürnberger Ratschlag" of 1525 see Osiander 1975, 319–45.

54. On Silesian contacts with the South, see Weigelt 1973, 77–93. Weigelt does not cite Wolfgang Capito's letter mentioning Winkler's visit to Strassburg, (April 4, 1526, CR 95, 465). See also McLaughlin 1985a. Zwingli wrote Crautwald and Schwenckfeld (April 17, 1526), welcoming them as allies in the battle against the real presence (CR 95, 567–70).

55. Bugenhagen sent a letter addressed to both Schwenckfeld and Crautwald on April 13, 1526 (Bugenhagen 1966, 61–62). Luther wrote separate letters on April 14, 1526 (WA Br 4, 52–53). Schwenckfeld claimed in his letter to Zimmerman (CS XIV, 804:16–17) that Luther had written about two months after his visit, i.e., in February. No such letter survives. But Schwenckfeld's description of the contents reads like a slightly confused combination of the two letters in April.

56. CS II, 325–33. It was issued under Schwenckfeld's private seal and signed by "Valentin Crautwald, Caspar Schwenckfeld, along with the pastors and preachers of Liegnitz." Concerning its public posting, see CS II, 644:14–645:12.

of the populace followed by the institution of a ban. Finally they announced that they had ceased to celebrate the Eucharist and would continue their nonobservance until these things were accomplished; the cessation was known as the *Stillstand*.

This document represents a decisive moment in the Silesian Reformation and the career of Schwenckfeld. It made public their disagreement with Wittenberg, and marked them all as *Schwärmer* and heretics. As a result the hesitant Silesian Lutherans finally and irrevocably broke with them. Responding to their own increasing isolation, the Liegnitz circle arranged for the publication of three of Crautwald's works, one of them in German, in order to reach a broader audience.[57] The umbilical cord to Wittenberg was cut and they were now on their own, to develop a theology and a reform program as they saw fit.

Schwenckfeld and Crautwald were the dominant figures, and they worked in tandem. Letters addressed to one were frequently answered by the other. Occasionally both would answer, each dealing only with the topics which interested him.[58] Schwenckfeld normally wrote in the vernacular, Crautwald in Latin.[59] Crautwald's area of expertise was his knowledge of Greek and Hebrew. When it came to questions concerning these languages—what Schwenckfeld termed problems of grammar—Crautwald was the authority.[60] Schwenckfeld's specialty was the battle against the real presence. The rest of their theology, however, is not so easily divided into Crautwaldian and Schwenckfeldian components.

Eucharist and Stillstand

The study of Schwenckfeld's personal appropriation of the formative Liegnitz theology of the Eucharist must rely on his single major work datable to 1526, a letter to the otherwise unknown N. Holstenius.[61]

57. Two Latin works were published in fall 1526, *Collatio et consensus verborum coenae dominicae* (CS II, 383–408) and *De coena dominica* (CS II, 409–38), which was originally the letter to Matthias Funk. The untitled German work is in CS II, 297–323.

58. An example of both men answering one letter, each according to his talents, is found in Crautwald's letter to Hess, CLM 718, 271r–271v. Crautwald answered Moibanus in Schwenckfeld's stead in CLM 718, 380r.

59. "Also haben wir hernach Crautwald Latine, C.S. Germanice von diesem Mysterio iuxta datam nobis gratiam, geschrieben" (CS XIV, 804:31–32).

60. ". . . quanquam ego grammaticae judicium alijs committam, haec ex cratoaldo meo partim accepi, per quem nobis Dominus ista & alia dedit" (CS II, 350:17–18).

61. CS II, 337–60 (after June 3, 1526). Schwenckfeld refers to Crautwald's June 3 letter to Wittiger (CS II, 354:26–29). Holstenius probably lived in or near Breslau because Schwenckfeld assumed that he could easily consult Crautwald's letter to Wittiger (CS II, 354:26–29).

To begin where he would not have wanted us to—with the words of institution—Schwenckfeld accepted Crautwald's interpretation and continued to reject both Karlstadt's and Zwingli's for the same reason: while Crautwald's exegesis emphasized the reality and centrality of participation in the flesh of the glorified Christ, Karlstadt and Zwingli reduced the entire sacrament to a pure memorial and robbed the Eucharist of all but a symbolic significance.[62] Schwenckfeld's criticism of Karlstadt and Zwingli, and his acceptance of Crautwald, took no account of the intrinsic merit of the various grammatical and philological arguments. He sidestepped the entire technical scholarly debate.

His disagreement with both the Lutheran and Catholic interpretations concerned only the *mode* of distribution and not, as with Zwingli and Karlstadt, the objective reality of what was distributed in the sacrament. They agreed on what was given, the glorified body of Christ; Schwenckfeld simply refused to see it bound in any way to the elements of the sacrament.[63] Not that consubstantiation or transubstantiation were impossible (Zwingli's point), but rather that God had simply not ordained it, and for good reason.[64] Actually Schwenckfeld accepted the ubiquity of Christ, but carefully defined and distinguished it from Luther's notion.

As the word (*logos*), Christ can be considered under two aspects or offices:[65] the creative word which formed the world in eternity and maintained it in existence, and the word of restoration which was joined to the flesh in order to save fallen man.[66] The power of the creative word is ubiquitous; the essence of the word of restoration is found only in heaven (after the resurrection and ascension) and in the hearts of all believers. Confusing the two, as the Lutherans and Catholics do, would lead to inane results—following the Catholics, the bread of the sacrament would have eternal life; following the Lutherans, the entire physical universe would be "saved."[67]

While in the letter to Holstenius Schwenckfeld never denied the possibility of a physical ubiquity for the body of Christ (and in fact

62. On Karlstadt, CS II, 358:3–7; on Zwingli, CS II, 349:10–19.
63. CS II, 348:9–19.
64. CS II, 350:27–33.
65. Crautwald was probably the source for this distinction (CS II, 405:18–21). The editors date publication of this work to autumn 1526. However, in its original manuscript form it must have been circulating in early 1526, because Crautwald mentions it to Schleupner before April 8, 1526 (CLM 718, 289r–289v).
66. CS II, 351:8–352:3.
67. CS II, 345:3–7, 14–20; 348:4–8.

some of his arguments presuppose it), in the years following (1527–28) he tended to focus more on the metaphysical impossibility, the "scientific" impossibility, of physical ubiquity even to the exclusion of the earlier emphasis on the argument from Judas and the indivisibility of the incarnate Christ. This was but one sign of the attraction, the tidal pull, that Zwinglian ideas exerted upon the Liegnitz group.

Nonetheless, Schwenckfeld did not embrace Zwingli's reasoning. Instead he used the issue to provide a systematic undergirding for his own conceptions concerning the Eucharist. Starting, as had Zwingli, with the statement in the Apostles' Creed that Christ had "ascended into heaven . . . whence he shall come to judge the living and the dead," Schwenckfeld concluded, as had Zwingli, that Christ would remain in heaven until the final judgment and would therefore not be physically present on earth in the interim. But Schwenckfeld's characterization of heaven, drawing upon Augustine, Hilary of Poitiers, Cyril, and Fulgentius,[68] allowed him to argue that this was no barrier to the real participation in Christ's flesh by Christians still living on earth. Heaven is defined not as a place, but as a mode of existence, as the presence of God, outside time and space.[69] Because God according to his essence is ubiquitous, that is, nowhere and everywhere, and because Christ's body shares in that essential ubiquity, he is available to all who seek him. Here Schwenckfeld took up again his distinction between the creative word and the restorative word.[70]

In the true inner Eucharist the body of Christ does not come "down" to earth and into the bread. It is the believer who "ascends" (*sursum*

68. For his use of Hilary and Cyril on heaven and God's right hand, see CS III, 202:11–16; of Fulgentius and Hilary on the nature of God's omnipotence, CS III, 210:1–10; and of Augustine on the nature of God's ubiquity, CS III, 214:8–20.

69. Schwenckfeld often preferred to call heaven the heavenly, or superheavenly, existence (CS III, 202:1–9, 213:9–12). He departs here from Crautwald, who placed heaven outside the firmament. "Ascendit etiam localiter supra coeli firmamentum Actor. 1. Atque in coelo est. dum Corpus, in quo ascendit, extra coelum esse non potest" (CLM 718, 444r–444v). Schwenckfeld, under Crautwald's guidance, would later flirt with a Ptolemaic conception of hell, only to reject it again. But heaven was never so handled (Pietz 1956, 25–26 nn. 71, 75). Cf. Lashlee 1969, 166. On the nature of heaven, see also CS III, 20:32–36.

70. Or to use his other terminology, *praesentia potentiae* and *praesentia gratiae* (CS III, 209:8–17). The distinction also explains Schwenckfeld's charge that the Lutherans taught pantheism (CS II, 684:7–13). In Schwenckfeld's view, Luther taught that God and Christ were essentially present (*praesentia gratiae*) everywhere, whereas he himself taught that their power was ubiquitous (*praesentia potentiae*). Bornkamm 1925, 169, fails to grasp the distinction. Schwenckfeld was also careful to point out that it is improper, strictly speaking, to apply terms signifying time, place, and accidents to God and the ascended Christ, but that we all do so out of habit and for the sake of human weakness (CS III, 221:35–222:2; 250:19–23).

corda) into heaven.[71] In the Eucharist the believer partakes of Christ's essence, not merely his power. Neither the believer, nor the humanity of Christ for that matter, becomes part of the divine essence.[72] Both maintain their own identities, while dwelling in the divine essence and bathing in its glory.[73]

The objective power and importance of Christ's flesh made both the Catholic-Lutheran and the Zwinglian interpretations untenable for Schwenckfeld.

> The earthly and external bread is broken by the external man symbolically [*in imagine*]. The celestial bread, that is, the incarnate word of God is broken by the reborn internal man in truth [*in veritate*]. The living incarnate word is broken, I say, on the cross and distributed to all believers, and through it they are given life and nourished in eternity. But this is not done through the letter as we once dreamed, saying, this is done through faith when I believe. But rather the living word of God, Christ, the celestial bread, indeed truly [*vere vere*] feeds our souls, truly restores and consoles our despairing consciences. We truly drink the blood of Christ, the incarnate Word, the true wine, and we quench our eternal thirst.[74]

Schwenckfeld insisted on a real participation in Christ's body and blood against those who would limit the Eucharist to a purely symbolic memorial of Christ's salvific action on the cross. Faith was necessary for the reception of Christ's body, but the Eucharist was not merely a more graphic way of signifying that Christians receive the benefits of Christ's sacrifice.

Schwenckfeld's concentration on the inner reception of the Eucharist placed the value of the external liturgical event in question. Because Christ had clearly established it, ignoring it or doing away with it was impossible.[75] For Schwenckfeld the externalities in Christian-

---

71. CS II, 464:12–17, 510:37–511:6. Hence for Schwenckfeld it is not a question of ubiquity, but rather of accessibility. It is not that Christ is selectively ubiquitous (Maier 1959, 80–81), since he is not present in this world. Rather it is a question of believers going to Christ, as Maron 1961a, 66–68, has pointed out. As Schwenckfeld's Christology developed, his views on Christ's mode of presence also changed. Cf. Hirsch 1922, 165.

72. CS III, 215:11–14.
73. CS III, 215:11–14.
74. CS II, 354:34–355:8.
75. CS II, 343:5–8.

ity—the sacraments, the spoken and written word of God, and the visible church as a whole—served only to minister to the unregenerate remainder in each reborn Christian, the Old Man; they played no role in justification, or specifically in effecting the inner Eucharist.[76]

The exact relationship between the external ceremony and the internal eating, however, remains unclear in the letter to Holstenius. How spiritualistic was Schwenckfeld at this stage? The two "events" seem to be contemporaneous, but this may be because Schwenckfeld dealt with the relationship between the two eatings in a very theoretical way. The fact that Schwenckfeld in this same letter defended the Liegnitz *Stillstand* might suggest that the internal eating was not really bound to the external ceremony. But this need not be the case. Since Schwenckfeld still distinguished salvific faith from the reception of Christ's body and blood, it would seem that the inner Eucharist was not absolutely necessary for salvation.[77] The exact relationship of faith, the inner Eucharist, and justification, however, remained quite murky.[78] Schwenckfeld was still undecided how radically to separate the inner and outer Eucharists. His ambivalence is all the more striking in contrast to Crautwald's thoroughgoing divorce of the two.[79] But compared to the more positive evaluation of the external Eucharist in his own twelve *Questiones*, Schwenckfeld's reticence is clearly a step in the direction of a more radical spiritualism. Here Crautwald led and Schwenckfeld followed.

This incipient spiritualism made acceptable the suspension of the Eucharist. The first formal announcement of the *Stillstand* in the circular letter of the Liegnitz pastorate (April 21, 1526) was both a defense and a formalization of an already-established, spontaneous prac-

76. See CS II, 343:22–344:4, 358:10–16, on the application of this distinction to the Eucharist. The distinction ultimately derives from Crautwald's contrast of image and truth in *De imagine & veritate sive Umbra et Corpore* (CLM 718, 120r–147v).

77. Faith enabled a Christian to partake of Christ, but it was not itself that participation. See *Questiones*, CS III, 500:22–25, 504:37–505:7. In the letter to Holstenius Schwenckfeld states that only the just, i.e., the faithful, Christian could participate (CS II, 346:8; cf. 354:34–355:8).

78. Is faith alone sufficient for salvation and eternal life? Or is participation in Christ's body and blood also requisite? If so, do faithful Christians automatically commune by reason of their faith without regard to the external ceremony? These questions were left unanswered. Schwenckfeld wavered on the temporal relationship for some time (Maier 1959, 20; Loetscher 1906, 32). But in later years he was certain that the internal eating was independent of the external, although optimally the two coincided.

79. Letter to Hess, CLM 718, 278r. Cf. CS II, 307:26–308:11, 317:7–11. Crautwald argued that faith and a desire to partake of Christ's body and blood are sufficient to effect the same.

tice which had begun the previous autumn.[80] Initially, the *Stillstand* was caused by dissatisfaction with the Mass, both Catholic and Lutheran, Latin and German.[81] Both forms failed to comply with New Testament requirements, flying in the face of Paul's directions. Further, both celebrated the real presence with an elevation and adoration of the host.[82] But by the time Schwenckfeld wrote his letter to Holstenius in June 1526 the *Stillstand* had come to represent much more than a criticism of the Lutheran and Catholic liturgies. These were symptoms of a greater failing in the church. After all, why suspend the Eucharist? Why not merely reform it to apostolic standards?

> I hear you with many others saying: Why wasn't the true use of the supper instituted after the truth was perceived? I answer: Why aren't there yet any true Christians? Why aren't the dinner guests as yet gathered? Why aren't there yet any of the cleansed, who might eat worthily? Pray to the Lord with us that the Church might first be gathered through the catechism and built up upon the Rock, Christ. Then finally will it be easy to institute the symbols. However, this does not require our powers, but only the spirit of the Lord. We wait, therefore, eagerly and with sighs until Christ invites his guests through his spirit.[83]

Let us leave aside for the moment the nature of the gathered Church for which Schwenckfeld waited and the catechism which he hoped would be instrumental. Why didn't the Liegnitz clergy replace the Lutheran and Catholic services with one of their own devising? The conversion of the *Stillstand* from a spontaneous temporary stoppage to a long-term formal institutional measure was the result of an intense

80. CS II, 332:17–333:4, 329:5–11. Schwenckfeld admitted to Butzer in 1533 that he had already observed the *Stillstand* for eight years (CS IV, 820:1–2). Cf. Maron 1961a, 89. F. Bahlow 1918, 71; Kluge 1917, 237; and Rosenberg 1767, 65, are wrong in placing its inception in 1526. During Schwenckfeld's visit to Wittenberg he had admitted, "bey uns koendten wir keinen haben / der forthin Messe lesen wolte / denn sie beguenden den grewel zuvernemmen" (CS II, 279:26–280:5).

81. Crautwald, CLM 718, 301v–303v, 315r. Schwenckfeld, CS II, 358:27–30, 359:2–33.

82. In Breslau Ambrosius Moibanus rewrote parts of the Catholic Mass in 1525, eliminating its sacrificial nature while retaining the elevation of the host (Sabisch 1975, 61–62; Sabisch 1938; cf. Sanders 1937). Liegnitz complained about the retention of the elevation in Breslau (Crautwald to Moibanus, June 24, 1526, CLM 718, 380r–390r). A reference to an earlier letter of Schwenckfeld's on the same subject is found in 282r–282v. Crautwald also complained to Wittiger about it, on April 8 (CLM 718, 299r–307v), May 20 (308r–313v), and May 27 (314r–318v).

83. CS II, 359:2–33.

inner debate in which fear of idolatry and false worship contended with the principle of *Freedom of a Christian*.[84] The people must first be taught. They must be catechized before they could properly understand and use the symbols of the sacrament.

The *Stillstand*, therefore, was not based on a spiritualist contempt for all things external. Rather, the very importance of the symbols and the fearful consequences of their misuse were at the root of the decision to suspend the Eucharist until the community of Christians was sufficiently educated.[85] They were tarrying for the ignorant.

It is difficult to judge how widespread the acceptance of the *Stillstand* was. It was always voluntary, and in Liegnitz itself Catholics continued to celebrate the Mass for years. We know that the *Stillstand* extended out into the countryside, and one observer claimed in 1529 that the celebration of the Eucharist was totally neglected (*gantz nydder gelegt*).[86] Where the *Stillstand* was accepted it seems to have been taken up by the populace at large with some conviction; it proved very difficult for the Lutherans to reinstate it.[87]

While Schwenckfeld never again communed, even during his lifetime some of his followers in Silesia began to celebrate the Eucharist again.[88] Ostensibly they had succeeded in reestablishing a church community according to apostolic standards.

The Church

For we see in all of the German nation as yet no Christian community according to the example and form which Paul and Peter

---

84. Crautwald's letters to Wittiger allow us to glimpse the developing rationale for this decision (CLM 718, 301v). Crautwald's attack on the elevation of the host is quite similar to Karlstadt's (Sider 1978, 108–12). On the dangers of idolatry, see CLM 718, 310v; on the dangers of eucharistic abuse, CS II, 331:14–17. See also Crautwald's undated letter to Schwenckfeld, CLM 718, 362v–363r.

85. For the Liegnitz reformers themselves there was no indecision or doubt about the Eucharist. The *Stillstand* was not employed to discover the truth or to allow divisions among the Protestants to heal. Thus the suggestion that Luther had inspired the *Stillstand* can be true only in part. See F. Bahlow 1918, 71; Hampe 1882, 14; Kluge 1917, 237. In *Against the Heavenly Prophets*, Luther had advised staying away from the Eucharist until one was no longer in doubt and had a strong faith. The Liegnitz leaders were not in doubt, and they believed their faith to be strong. Although faith was an important problem, knowledge was more central to the *Stillstand*.

86. Schwenckfeld advised the pastor of Raudten, Simon Ruff, to maintain it a bit longer (April 26, 1527, CS II, 613–621). Quotation from Weigelt 1973, 128.

87. Friedrich ordered its reinstitution in 1534 and again in 1542 (Knörrlich 1959, 159; Rosenberg 1767, 444–54).

88. Michael Hiller (d. 1557), a Schwenckfelder in Silesia, wrote a communion service (Kriebel 1968, 20).

depicted. It is not all that common to be a Christian man, as can be seen today. Look at Acts. [89]

The Liegnitz program to reinstitute the apostolic Church bears close resemblance to the efforts and outlook of the South German and Swiss Reformation, the seedbed of reformed Protestantism. Here, even more clearly than with the Eucharist, Liegnitz shared in tendencies differentiating that stream of Protestantism from Lutheranism: vigorous use of the ban, intensive Christian instruction and examination, and a radically simplified form of worship.

The ban had been an important part of Schwenckfeld's program already in 1524, and during his visit to Wittenberg it had come up again, this time in conjunction with the problem of the future Church (*futura Ecclesia*). [90]

I spoke a great deal with him [Luther] about the future Church, and how this was the only way to separate the true from the false Christians. Otherwise there would be no hope. He knew full well that the ban must always accompany the gospel. Where it was not instituted there would never be any improvement, and the longer it was lacking the worse things would be. For one can easily see how things are going everywhere. Everyone wants to be thought evangelical and claim the name of Christ to his own advantage. [91]

The ban was also taken up in the Liegnitz circular letter, where it was directed against the moral lapses of "those who partake of the Eucharist and wish to be in such a Christian community." [92] Though the ban may have been used in individual congregations, it was not imposed on the principality as a whole, probably due to Friedrich's resistance. [93]

It was the catechism, however, which was the heart of the Liegnitz

---

89. CS II, 218:1–8.

90. CS I, 274:14–20. See Pietz 1959. Luther had proved to be surprisingly receptive, admitting that at one time he had considered setting up a register of true Christians. The difficulty was that he had not been able to find any true Christians (CS II, 280:21–281:6). Nevertheless, in the *Deutsche Messe* (January 1526) Luther had raised the possibility of a church within the church, or *ecclesiola*, for earnest Christians, and this proposal was incorporated into the Hessian church order that year (Williams 1962, 457; Pietz 1959, 3).

91. CS II, 280:14–21.

92. CS II, 331:27–332:9.

93. Later Hess spoke with Friedrich about setting up a ban, but without success (Rezek 1884, 292).

reform.[94] It addressed what they viewed as the fundamental problem facing the reform and Christianity as a whole: the relationship of outer symbol and inner reality, Image and Truth, as applied to the whole church, but particularly to the Eucharist.[95]

Unlike the ambitious plans for a ban, those for the catechism became reality. The first Protestant catechism, the *Katechismus Lignicensis*, was written as early as autumn 1525,[96] followed slightly later by another, this one found among Crautwald's works.[97] They remained in manuscript. Both adults and children were to be instructed. The procedure was simple. On specified days of the week earnest Christians would gather and hear a sermon on one of a list of important topics, after which they were examined and encouraged to raise questions.[98]

94. It was first clearly mentioned in 1526 (Crautwald to Hess, before April 8, 1526, CLM 718, 272r, 280v). During his visit to Wittenberg Schwenckfeld had discussed what should be done with the children, but it is by no means certain that this concerned catechization: "Quid Ordinasset cum pueris" (CS II, 282:2). Since both Schwenckfeld and Crautwald would later insist on the catechization of all Christians, children and adults alike, it would seem unlikely. In a letter written sometime before April 8, Crautwald emphasized to Johannes Hess the necessity for catechization in order to collect the scattered Church. It was, after all, the way Christ had prepared his own disciples (CLM 718, 272r, 280v). Sometime later, but still before April 8, Crautwald wrote Dominicus Schleupner suggesting that the clergy of Nürnberg prepare a catechism. He also asked that they search their libraries for any old (patristic?) catechisms (CLM 718, 289v, 293r). Schleupner and the Nürnberg clergy seem not to have written a catechism, although they did perhaps search their libraries. In his extant catechisms Crautwald used Rabanus's *Liber institutionis clericorum*. Although he miscited it as being written by "Beda" (Bede), it is the same work cited by Schwenckfeld in CS III, 161:13–26. See also Cohrs 1902, 190. Cohrs knew only that Bede had not written a book of that title. But Crautwald's most persistent efforts were directed at Michael Wittiger of Breslau; see his letters of April 8, May 20, and June 3 (CLM 718, 304v, 309r–311r, 319r–320v). Wittiger originally agreed to write the Liegnitz catechism(s) and then reneged. Crautwald pressured him, but we do not know with what success. The Liegnitz circular letter also insisted upon the necessity of basic Christian instruction or catechization (CS II, 331:4–13).

95. CS II, 354:7–12, 359:2–33. In his letter to Schleupner Crautwald discussed the catechism in the context of the eucharistic controversy with Wittenberg, and the problem of images and the word of God (CLM 718, 289r–290v). In his letter to Hess the relationship is even clearer (CLM 718, 271v–272r). The *Stillstand* itself was meant to provide time for the people to be catechized (CLM 718, 332:17–333:4). The Liegnitz circular letter had also placed the catechism in a eucharistic context (CS II, 332:17–333:4).

96. This was first discovered and published by Wotschke 1911. It was later reprinted in CS XVIII, 6–10. Wotschke found the *Katechismus* in the Prussian Archives among other materials dated 1525. The document itself is undated. If written in 1525, it must have been after October since it contains Crautwald's exegesis of the words of institution.

97. There are three parts: "Catechesis" (CLM 718, 26r–37r); "Canon Generalis super his quae spectant ad Catechismus" (37v–55v); and "Institutiuncula de signis seu symbolis et sacramentis" (56r–63v). All three are printed in Cohrs 1902, 196–225. The "Catechesis" is also printed in G. Eberlein 1900. I would date the three as later than the *Katechismus Lignicensis* based solely on their length and comprehensive nature. The *Katechismus* is a very simple, unassuming document by comparison.

98. Crautwald reminds the teacher-minister to adapt his methods to the people that he is addressing according to level of education, civil status, wealth, age, and sex (Cohrs 1902, 198:1–3). Boredom was to be overcome by admonition and the telling of stories, presumably Bible

As to content, the catechisms reflected the Liegnitz doctrinal concerns, Christology[99] and the Eucharist.[100]

Liegnitz's concentration on the catechism betrayed a growing unease with the sacramentalization of the preached word among the Lutherans.[101] They feared the formal "intoned" word which threatened to replace the Catholic sacraments as the new indulgence, inculcating a false sense of security, a cheap grace.[102] The fundamental task of the church was to teach the word, not merely proclaim it.[103] Luther's argument that Christ's word of promise was somehow bound to the Eucharist, was somehow *in* the sacrament, fed Schwenckfeld's fears that Luther was succumbing to the dead letter, the dry formalism, which for him characterized Catholicism. As Schwenckfeld wrote about his visit to Wittenberg: "I disagreed with them all [Bugenhagen, Jonas, Luther] about the word of God and faith. It will be our task, and especially Valentin's [Crautwald's] to prove that the word of the Lord is not in the sacrament. We must show what the word of the Lord is, and that it is not the letter."[104]

Scripture (the letter) must always be distinguished from the living

stories (199:26–29). Crautwald even made a point of providing seating for his listeners (198:24). It is also clear that fairly basic instruction was to be meted out: Crautwald advised that the more learned be sent away with a list of recommended reading for their own study (199:30–37). Douglas Shantz has determined that Crautwald borrowed very extensively from Augustine with regard to catechetical method. See Shantz's contribution in Erb 1985.

99. CLM 718, 37v–55v.

100. CLM 718, 37v–55v. The *Katechismus* taught Crautwald's exegesis and the twofold nature of the sacrament (CS XVIII, 10:21–30). Interestingly, the later catechism cited only Augustine on the Eucharist (Cohrs 1902, 219:5–12; 220:5–7). This might lead one to suppose that these three documents were written earlier than the *Katechismus Lignicensis*. However, the position on the Eucharist in the "Institutiuncula" was already non-Lutheran: the real presence is rejected. This part would therefore have been written after Crautwald's revelation, because before that he had opposed Schwenckfeld's denial of the real presence. In Crautwald's thought the denial of the real presence and the development of his exegetical interpretation were simultaneous.

101. CLM 718, 319v. Crautwald tended increasingly to contrast preaching and the catechism ("Instructio Pii Concionatori V. C.," Cod. Aug. 37.27.2., 381–82). This document may well date from 1526 or 1527. It is placed in the manuscript before treatises dated 1527. The first section of the manuscript contains letters in chronological order, and the second half, treatises from an earlier period, among them this document.

102. "Predicamus omnes hodie publice et Evangelice intonamus" (CLM 718, 319v). The dangers of a preaching style which struck too high a note and thus misled the people is described in 319r–319v. Late Protestant catechisms fell into much the same trap: the words of the catechism were often only memorized by rote as another type of holy words (Strauss 1973, 223–24).

103. "Orandus est igitur Christus ut filios Dei, qui dispersi hodie sunt in Unum congregat. Preterea habendam duco rationem Ministerii nostri, hoc est De Christiano catechismo cogitandum" (Crautwald to Hess, CLM 718, 280v). Cf. the Liegnitz circular letter, CS II, 325–33, in which the catechism is emphasized to the exclusion of preaching.

104. CS II, 278:27–29.

word (Christ) who lies behind and beyond the written page and lends it authority and power. Those who celebrate the Eucharist, for instance, do so not because the Bible commanded it, but because Christ speaking through the Bible does so.

> They do it because they believe, and because they believe, they do not seize only upon the syllables of command, but rather they hold on to Christ, God, who is commanding them. And thus they take hold of this God through the symbols of the words, so that you might see the pious being led from the ministry of the word to the word itself. [105]

This was not to deny Scripture, but merely to make clear that it was incomplete when not grasped in and with the spirit of Christ to whom it pointed. [106] This statement would not have of itself served to distinguish Schwenckfeld from Luther, but Schwenckfeld went a bit further to credit God with a direct intervention which was not through externals, though it did give meaning and value to externals. In this he was very close to Zwingli's position on the relationship of spirit and Scripture. [107]

It is necessary to emphasize here that the inner working of God is not viewed as completely sufficient of itself; it does refer itself always and immediately to the written word. The difference between Wittenberg and Liegnitz was one of purpose. Luther sought to bind the spirit to the letter and the sacraments in order to endow them with its power, while Schwenckfeld worked to distinguish the two in order to avoid the sterility that too great a concentration on the visible elements of religion could bring. In 1526 the two men were bound on divergent courses, but passed within hailing distance of each other.

Crautwald plotted Liegnitz's course, providing the theoretical underpinnings for an increasingly spiritualistic theology. [108] The issues involved lay close to Crautwald's heart: inner versus outer, divine versus human, *veritas* versus *imago*. Like other German humanists he had suffered a crisis of conscience over his devotion to pagan classical literature, feeling himself another Jerome accused of being a Ciceronian

---

105. CS II, 343:8–12.
106. CS II, 345:3–5; ". . . qui non dijudicant verbum naturale spiritus, veritatis, Internum, a verbo prolative literali, imaginario, externo" (CS II, 345:8–13).
107. Gestrich 1967, 71, 91–92.
108. Not surprisingly his writings are clearer, and more radical. CS II, 406:7–10, 407:26–29.

rather than a Christian.[109] Given the choice of the outer word of human reason and pagan philosophy, or the inner word of God's revelation in Christ, he embraced the latter and consigned his writings in philosophy, poetry, and prose to the fire.[110] He was still grappling with the larger issue of the knowledge possible to natural and spiritual men when Schwenckfeld approached him about the Eucharist.[111] The result, alongside the narrower question of the words of institution, was an epistemology of *veritas et imago* or *res et symboles*.

Crautwald's position is a variation on Augustine's and similar to Zwingli's.[112] As does Augustine, Crautwald carefully distinguishes signs from things signified, for example, words from what the words represent, or the elements of the Eucharist from the body and blood of Christ. The signs merely point to what they signify. Augustine dealt with the problem in the context of his larger Neoplatonic epistemology.[113] In essence, he argued that external objects gave no true knowledge, but only directed the mind inward, where the truth was learned from Christ who illumined the mind directly with the "Ideas" that constitute true knowledge. Both Zwingli and Crautwald differed from Augustine in the temporal sequence of sign and knowledge.[114] Whereas for Augustine the sign pointed to a truth which one then grasped, for both sixteenth-century thinkers the signs only referred back to things already known. Augustine's signs served a real pedagogical function; Zwingli's and Crautwald's were mnemonic devices of questionable importance. They tended to become superfluous.

109. On the development of a religious crisis in German humanism in the decades before the Reformation, see Spitz 1963. Erasmus, who did not see classical culture and Christianity as necessarily opposed, took great pains to counteract the effects that this passage in his beloved Jerome might have (Bainton 1969, 131).

110. "Divinitus cognoscere cepit, omnia quae in Philosophia, et Prosa et carmine conscripserat in ignem coniecit" ("Vita," CLM 718, 549v).

111. See *De Cognitione Dei ex creaturis locus Rom:1. latius tractatur Invisibilia Dei ex creatione Mundi, dum per opera intelligentur, pervidentur* (CLM 718, 10r–17r), and *Observatio de spiritali cognitione Iudicio atque Sapientia. De Duplici ordine spetie & forma Rerum* (CLM 718, 18r–25r). Neither mentions the eucharistic controversy, which, given the subject matter, would suggest an early date. Their location before the treatises concerned with the eucharistic controversy, at the beginning of a manuscript which is in general chronologically arranged, would also point to a date before Crautwald's involvement with Schwenckfeld and the Eucharist.

112. Crautwald dealt with these issues at length in *De Imagine et veritate sive umbra et corpore De Duplici pane et potu in Coena Dominica* (CLM 718, 120r–147v). He opened the treatise by referring to the works of Augustine and Melanchthon that dealt with the same problem (120r–122r).

113. See Augustine's *De Magistro, PL* 32, 1193–1220. Cf. Strauss 1978, 181, on the impact these ideas had on sixteenth-century pedagogical theory.

114. Gestrich 1967, 138–39.

For both Schwenckfeld and Crautwald, then, religious commitment involved a retreat from the demands and allurements of the "external" world. For the nobleman it was united with his retirement from court and ducal politics to his estates and matters of high theology. For the humanist it entailed a rejection of pagan antiquity and human achievements in favor of pure Christianity and divine wisdom. And for both men it brought a deep suspicion and distrust of anything human, anything worldly, anything external, which claimed a role in Christianity.

One of the practical effects of this attitude is found in the Liegnitz catechisms. Later Lutheran efforts, beginning with Luther's *Large Catechism* and *Small Catechism* in 1529, were designed to produce good Christian subjects. The emphasis upon the duty of obedience to higher secular authority ran throughout the Lutheran catechetical tradition.[115] This was not so in the Liegnitz catechisms. The magistrate is conspicuous by his absence, and the instruction is purely religious. The Lutheran clergy insisted that it was the duty of the secular authorities to impose the catechism, if necessary by force, upon their subjects. In the Liegnitz catechisms and in the writings of Crautwald and Schwenckfeld there is no suggestion that the secular power had a role to play in the catechization of the people.

Abstract ecclesiology finds its concrete expression most often in the liturgy. It is known that the Liegnitz reformers were engaged in preparing a radically revised Mass, but if it was ever completed, it has not survived.[116] An interesting document which does survive is the *Confession of Sins* (1526).[117] Designed for prayer meetings, it contains no sacramental rite, although the Eucharist is explained in the Schwenckfeld-Crautwald manner.[118] The book contains communal

115. Strauss 1973 contains a persuasive treatment of this issue. Strauss argues that Luther and the Lutherans, when faced with the results of the 1528 visitations, finally gave up their reliance on voluntary individual self-indoctrination and came to rely on the coercive powers of the godly prince.

116. See Crautwald's letter to Moibanus, June 24, 1526, CLM 718, 380r–390r. Crautwald admitted having changed some things, but much remained (383r–383v). This is not to be confused with the minor, though unspecified, changes made in the usages of the collegiate church of the Holy Sepulcher, (Engelbert 1963, p. 180; F. Bahlow 1918, 70–71). The collegiate church at this time was still the center of Catholicism in Liegnitz. Might there be some connection between the missing Liegnitz liturgy and Michael Hiller's communion service (Kriebel 1968, p. 20)?

117. *Bekanntnus der Sünden*, CS V, 933–67. First published in 1538, it was originally prepared in 1526. See Weigelt 1974/75. Cf. Seltzer 1934, 98; Althaus 1914, 19–27.

118. CS V, 941:16–30; 949:1–2, 20–28.

prayers said before and after each day's work.[119] Special prayers were included for those suffering from illness or other problems, as were prayers for the end of the day. The general tenor is one of praise, thanksgiving, and penitence. One peculiarity is the emphasis upon trinitarian concerns, something which also occurs in the Liegnitz catechisms.[120] Often prayers were directed separately to the Father, Son, and Holy Spirit, evoking their different attributes and activities. The *Confession of Sins* was in effect the script for the weekday gathering of the faithful. The catechism may have been associated with the evening portion of the prayers, but this is by no means certain.[121]

While the Liegnitz position on the Mass and the Eucharist was clearly stated, their baptismal doctrine was not. This second sacrament received surprisingly short shrift in the writings of both Schwenckfeld and Crautwald. Claims that the *Stillstand* also affected baptism are incorrect insofar as the official Liegnitz stand was concerned. There is no mention of it in Crautwald, Schwenckfeld, or the Liegnitz circular letter.[122] Schwenckfeld mentioned baptism only twice, once in the twelve *Questiones* and once during his visit to Wittenberg, and both times he compared it to the Eucharist.[123] The *Katechismus Lignicensis* repeated the distinction of the inner and outer baptisms, the outer

119. For the end of the morning prayer and reference to the coming day's labor, see CS V, 949:31–950:6. For the end of the evening prayer, 960:1–4.

120. CLM 718, 37v–55v.

121. Weigelt 1974/75, 605–06, believes that the prayer book and catechism probably formed a whole which served conventicles of the Liegnitz group. But the prayer book has at least two parts, one for morning and one for evening. The doctrinal agreement of the prayer book and catechism on the Eucharist does not prove that the two works were parts of a single conventicle meeting. It proves only that the same group, the Liegnitz reformers, had a hand in both. It is of course possible, and probable, that on occasion catechism and prayer sessions were combined, but to posit a necessary connection would be going too far. The prayers appear to be daily, the catechism does not.

122. Sebastian Schubart, a onetime follower of Schwenckfeld and later an anti-Schwenckfeld Lutheran, maintained that baptism was avoided by some people even in 1526. Schubart's chronology, however, is sloppy, and his wish to tar the Liegnitz reformers with the Anabaptist brush is all too apparent (Kluge 1917, 237; Rosenberg 1767, 65). Both Kluge and Rosenberg rely on Schubart's account, given in Rosenberg 1767, 150–51. Schubart wrote this after returning to the Lutheran fold. His account jumps from Crautwald's 1525 revelation to the arrival of Sebastian Eisenmann and the ensuing spiritualist movement of 1527. He then returns to 1526 and the *Stillstand* of the Eucharist and baptism. He also portrays the Liegnitz reformers as seeking to hide their supposed Anabaptism. When Crautwald had occasion to remark upon the Anabaptists in Germany, he spoke of rebaptism as a problem which still lay in the future for Liegnitz. See Crautwald to Schleupner, before April 8, 1526, CLM 718, 293r–293v; to Wittiger, May 27, 317v; to Moibanus, June 24, 381v. Although there were Anabaptists in Silesia at that time, Crautwald was unaware of them (Weigelt 1973, 109, 114–115).

123. CS II, 278:9–17; 504:37–505:7.

lacking all efficacy without the inner.[124] Given the dualism which all
the Liegnitz reformers saw in the sacrament, the problem of infant
baptism was bound to occasion some concern. In 1526 the importance
of the issue had not yet made a deep impression upon Schwenckfeld
and the people around him. Crautwald showed signs of a certain sympathy for the Anabaptists, but in general, baptism was still not an issue.[125]

The Liegnitz position did develop, or at least became clearer, in
1527–28. There was never any attempt to institute rebaptism, though
neither Crautwald nor Schwenckfeld saw anything intrinsically wrong
with it if properly used and understood.[126] In Liegnitz they were unable to institute adult baptism because of stiff (and unspecified) opposition, but they did delay the baptism of children until they had
learned their catechism.[127] The children were not baptized into a separate community nor was a deep personal faith and calling a prerequisite. All children were baptized into the general church.[128]

From expressed intentions and their partial realizations it is possible
to reconstruct the church which Schwenckfeld and Crautwald hoped
eventually would be erected in Liegnitz. In effect, the population was
to be divided into three groups: those outside the church, the catechumens, and the initiated. Presumably the ban would be used to discipline the two latter groups. While both catechumens and initiated
would take part in the prayer sessions, only the advanced, the initiated,
would be allowed admittance to the mysteries, the Eucharist, because
only they would know how to distinguish the symbol of the Lord's Supper from the true eating of the body and blood of Christ. It is not clear
if these divisions were to remain permanent, or whether with time the
outsiders would dwindle and the catechumens merely become children studying their catechism.

Perhaps what is most striking is the absence of any mention of the
invisible church of the elect. Both Schwenckfeld and Crautwald were

124. CS XVIII, 9:29–10:3.
125. Writing to Wittiger (May 27, 1526) Crautwald referred to the controversy over rebaptism. His remarks are equivocal in the extreme (CLM 718, 317v).
126. TA 7, 167:14–38.
127. TA 7, 160:3–16; CS III, 81:20–24. Thus Schneider 1862, 12, is correct in denying
Rosenberg's assertion (1767, 65) that baptism was dismantled along with the Eucharist. At least
during his Silesian period, Schwenckfeld did not advocate a *Stillstand* for baptism as Maron
1961a, 94, and Ecke 1911, 135–36, have assumed.
128. Children were not assumed to be damned if they died unbaptized. Their fate was entrusted to God's judgment (CS III, 81:20–23).

still deeply committed to reconstructing a visible gathering of true Christians. There were to be (eventually) sacraments, communal prayer, and the discipline of an evangelical ban (as described in the New Testament), and leadership for the church was to be provided by ministers. The church which Schwenckfeld and Crautwald envisioned would not be a sect, but the established Church. Despite the strong spiritualistic overtones (which were not lacking in South German and Swiss Reformed circles), Liegnitz had embarked on a course which might ultimately have produced a Reformed church polity.

Christ and the New Man

> But, if you want to come to the root of the matter, you whould first consider why Christ came to earth in the flesh, and what in the final analysis his flesh and blood was to accomplish.[129]

During his visit to Wittenberg Schwenckfeld had glimpsed the key issue. Christology and the closely related problem of anthropology were at the heart of his disagreement with Luther. Schwenckfeld's comment bears repeating.

> I disagreed with them all about the word of the Lord and faith. It will be our task, especially Valentin's [Crautwald's] to prove that the word of the Lord is not in the sacrament. We must show what the word of the Lord is, and that it is not the letter.[130]

For Schwenckfeld, as for Luther, the word of God lay at the center of man's relationship to God. But unlike Luther, Schwenckfeld saw the word of God primarily as the second person of the Trinity, the consubstantial Son who had become flesh. The spoken or written word merely described this word and directed men to it.[131]

The nature and significance of that union of divinity and humanity in Christ was the touchstone of Schwenckfeld's theology. His teachings on the Eucharist, the Church, the New Man, and the outward ministry were all determined by his Christology. A desire to safeguard the

129. CS II, 422:12–423:2.
130. CS II, 278:27–29. Cf. Crautwald to Matthias Funk, June–August 1526, CS II, 422:12–423:2.
131. "Quod sola Fides in Verbum Dei vivum, naturale & coaternum, id est, Christum (non autem in prolativum aut literale, vel syllabarium) nos justificiet, clarum est" (CS II, 343:3–5). Cf. 343:8–12, 345:8–13.

unity of God and Man in Christ played a key role in Schwenckfeld's original rejection of the real presence. Luther had posited Christ's real presence in the Eucharist, but had specified that only worthy Christians would receive Christ's body and blood to their salvation, while the unworthy would partake of Christ to their damnation. In the twelve *Questiones* Schwenckfeld had objected that this was to separate the word from the flesh of Christ.[132] Schwenckfeld argued in this manner: It is possible for the word to be present without the flesh (in its role as creator), but it is not possible for the flesh to be present without the word. Thus, either the unworthy received the word in the real presence of the Lutheran Eucharist and were saved, or the body and blood of Christ were simply not there. Since it was obvious to Schwenckfeld that not all who received the Eucharist became good Christians, he found the first alternative impossible; hence, there could be no real presence.

Again, when the Lutheran preachers claimed that Christians were saved through hearing the word and having faith, or that faith arose from the word, Schwenckfeld was quite ready to agree. But for him the word was Christ himself, and not the Bible or the sermon. The conflict between these two uses of the term *word* was at the root of Schwenckfeld's distinction between the living word and the letter. Only later would this develop into a confrontation of spirit and letter. And only secondarily was it a conflict between inner word and outer word. The contrast was between the living word—incarnate Christ— and the word of Scripture. The nature of the union of word and flesh in Christ determined that the living word would also be the inner word, the spiritual word.

Schwenckfeld's anxious defense of the unity of the two natures in Christ enhanced the dignity and value of the glorified flesh of the risen Christ. It was the incarnate Logos who ruled in his Father's name, and it was the body and blood of Christ, by virtue of their union with the Logos, which granted eternal life in the Eucharist.[133] Schwenckfeld's concern for the unity of flesh and word in Christ was also behind his insistence that God suffered in the flesh. It was not merely Christ's

132. CS II, 344:29–345:2, for example. Schwenckfeld also took exception to Luther's repeated statement that the word was in the Eucharist. For Luther this meant that the promise of redemption through Christ, when joined with the elements, made the sacrament. Schwenckfeld would interpret it as saying that Christ, the Logos, was in the elements (CS III, 500:26–35, 501:4–8, 502:10).

133. Schwenckfeld argued that while Christ's body was in the sepulcher the Eucharist could not have been celebrated, since Christ's dead body could not grant life (CS II, 351:8–352:9.

humanity which endured the passion, but the word incarnate which suffered in his humanity.[134] Schwenckfeld's Christology completely overshadowed, one might say obviated, the preached word and the Eucharist: the word became flesh so that the flesh might enter into the word.[135]

> The word of God is God, it is divine, it is spirit, it is life and not just a letter. The word of Christ is not simply a human word. Why do we think of that word in the same way that we think of human words? The word was made flesh so that the flesh might enter into the word. What does this business of the bread have to do with the incarnate word? It was because of the flesh and not because of the bread that the word was incarnated. Indeed, the word incarnate was a heavenly bread before there was wheaten bread. These two breads are as different as heaven and earth, as soul and body.[136]

As a result, for Schwenckfeld it was the incarnation, not the passion, which really effected man's salvation. It was not what Christ endured in the flesh for man, but what the flesh became through the sufferings of the God-Man Christ.[137] The word had taken on human flesh not so much to stand in man's place and pay the price on the cross for man's sins, but rather, by assuming human flesh and undergoing pain and torment, the word had fashioned a new human flesh, which, given to Christians, made them a new race of spiritual men dwelling with God in heaven. To state this in traditional dogmatic terms, the righteousness of the reborn Christian would be alien (as with Luther and almost all Christian theologians), but it would not be merely forensic. The true Christian would become righteous in some large measure through rebirth, and not merely have Christ's righteousness imputed to him.[138]

---

134. CS II, 356:3–26. This particular formulation stems from Crautwald, who in turn was drawing upon Hilary of Poitiers, (Crautwald to Egetius, December 10, 1525) where Crautwald refers Egetius to Hilary on this problem (CLM 718, 219v).

135. The formulation itself is another of Crautwald's contributions (CLM 718, 247r). Cf. Augustine, *Homilies on the Gospel of John*, tractate 26, par. 10 on John 6:41–59. PL 35, 1610–11.

136. CS II, 345:14–20.

137. In these years Schwenckfeld never dealt with the passion as such. Crautwald mentioned the ransom theory of atonement only briefly. But according to Crautwald fallen man remains a sinner even after the ransom is paid. He requires the blood of Christ to cleanse and heal him. Only then can he enter into God's presence and receive the heavenly spiritual gifts which await him (CS II, 310:28–212:21).

138. Though Beachy 1977 may not do complete justice to the teachings of Luther and the other "Magisterial Reformers," it is true that the radicals developed the idea of ontological

But because no man in this life ever becomes fully righteous, each reborn Christian is in actuality two men. Like a Russian *Matryoshka* doll the new inner man nestled inside of the old outer man. But for Schwenckfeld the traditional distinction was no mere metaphor. "New Man" and "Old Man" were not simply more graphic ways of describing the psychological struggle between the will to be an earnest Christian and the tendency to backslide. That struggle was only a symptom of a contest between two real, metaphysically distinct natures, one spiritual and one material. This dichotomy within Christians explained the purpose of the outward sacraments, the outer word, the entire outward church.[139] The old man must be disciplined, harnessed to the work of Christ, and bent to the will of God. Controlling the old man was not easy, but it was possible because the new man possessed a real power and righteousness from Christ. The cry that all men were sinners and were too weak to overcome sin was therefore untrue, and merely an excuse for antinomianism.[140]

The inner new man was spiritual and, like Christ, was no longer of this world. The heart of the new man was a temple in which Christ dwelt; it was already in heaven.[141] Since the new man was spiritual in a metaphysical, and not just a metaphoric or psychological, sense, Christ really dwelt in his heart, and heaven was a real "place." As a result, it was impossible for any outward, material, this-worldly object, ceremony, or person to mediate between Christ and the Christian. Since both were in heaven, since both were spiritual, they were by definition in each other's presence, in intimate contact with each other. External "mediators" tended to become not bridges, but barriers which deflected away from Christ. As a result Schwenckfeld would view with an increasingly jaundiced eye the entire outward church, the sacraments, and the written and spoken word, and would limit their usefulness to sanctification.

Schwenckfeld's conclusions in the twelve *Questiones* concerning the nature of Christ, the purpose of the incarnation, and the nature of the new man had been the result of his own reading of the Bible, in particular the Gospel of John and the Pauline Epistles. But in the further

---

change much more thoroughly. It lay at the center of their beliefs, whereas with Luther it was more peripheral.

139. CS II, 343:22–344:4.
140. CS II, 120:3–122:11.
141. CS III, 503:10–13.

development of that insight both he and Crautwald bore the impress of the *De trinitate* of Hilary of Poitiers.[142]

De trinitate had been directed against the Arians, and its purpose was to defend the full equality of Christ, as God, with his Father. In the process Hilary emphasized the unity of the two natures in Christ, and the divinization of the flesh.[143] *De trinitate* shared certain key elements of the Liegnitz Christology, soteriology, and anthropology,[144] and though Crautwald and Schwenckfeld did not simply appropriate the theology of Hilary, they were greatly influenced by it in the formulation of their own teachings. But Hilary had also believed in some form of a real presence, a fact which Schwenckfeld and Crautwald had good reasons to overlook. Given the efficacy of the flesh as described by Hilary, to posit a real presence, in their opinion, would be to reintroduce works righteousness. The Silesians' rejection of "externals" as contributing to justification was based upon this most Protestant principle—man contributes nothing to his own salvation. Justification is by faith alone, and faith comes through the word.

During 1525 and 1526 the Liegnitz reformers, led by Schwenckfeld and Crautwald, broke with Wittenberg over the Eucharist and other issues. This was not a sectarian experiment. It was simply the way in

142. Crautwald himself was probably led to *De trinitate* by the lengthy citation found in Oecolampadius 1525, Hijv–Hiiijr. The passage from book 8 of *De trinitate* dealt with the nature of Christ's union with his Church. It is not merely a unity of will, but of the physical body. Christ unites his Church to him through his flesh in the sacrament. Hilary employed John 6:56–57 to prove his point (*PL* 10, 245–49, book 8, par. 13–16). The October 1525 letter describing Crautwald's revelation and his explanation of the words of institution also cited book 8 as support for the centrality of John 6:54–57, sending the reader to Oecolampadius and Zwingli for further citations (*CS* II, 208:20–29). In December Crautwald advised Egetius to review books 8 and 10 of *De trinitate* and promised that they would study Hilary together (CLM 718, 219r, 221v).

143. Hilary argued that faith does not divide Christ into Man and God (*PL* 10, 384). Cf. Schwenckfeld's emphasis in the twelve *Questiones* on not dividing the word from the flesh (*CS* III, 502:36–503:16).

144. According to Hilary there were three "moments" in the incarnation (*PL* 10, 284–85). (1) In the beginning the Word existed without the human nature. (2) Then it joined with the flesh in the virgin birth. (3) But the union was complete and perfect only with the resurrection and ascension. The purpose of the incarnation was to endow Christ's flesh with the glory of the Father and the word so that it in turn might confer this glory upon man (*PL* 10, 309–11). The glorified body is now in heaven, reigning with God, as God (*PL* 10, 425–26). It is this body which is distributed in the Eucharist (*PL* 10, 245–46). In fact the Last Supper explained the entire mystery of Christ's passion (*PL* 10, 372). The Christian, the new man, is made conformable to the glory of the body of Christ (*PL* 10, 432–33). Hilary also carefully distinguished the substantial word from the spoken word of Christ. Hilary accused the Arians of equating the Word with a mere voice (*PL* 10, 358–59).

which the events of the Liegnitz Reformation unfolded, and it bears comparison with the autonomous developments at Augsburg, Strassburg, Basel, and Zurich, especially in ecclesiology.

The Liegnitz eucharistic position was also less peculiar than it at first seems. Almost all the contending Protestant parties combined an emphasis on faith with a belief in some sort of real participation. The problem was both to define the relationship of the two and to specify the exact nature of the "presence" which real participation required. The sole exception seems to have been Zwingli (at least most of the time), and that explains the triumph in most Reformed churches of Calvin's teaching, which unlike Zwingli's emphasized a real participation. The short-lived University of Liegnitz, which opened its doors on September 26, 1526, might also have anticipated the Genevan academy had it survived[145] (although since there were already strong spiritualistic elements at work, this drift into what would be the Reformed camp might not have continued). Nonetheless, the entire tenor of Liegnitz's theology and program in 1525–26 had aspects of Reformed thought.

Interestingly, the results of Schwenckfeld's revelation seemed to diminish his own role in the Liegnitz reform. He became second in importance to Crautwald and was swept along by that scholar's speculations. Whether he was dissatisfied with his loss of autonomy is impossible to determine, but he did become conspicuously quiet, writing little. It is intriguing to wonder whether he would have become just another pious Junker had Crautwald and the other clerics been allowed to continue their program, since that program was based on the university and the presbytery. But they were not and he did not.

On August 26, 1526, the Hungarian king and much of his nobility were killed or captured by the Turks at the battle of Mohacs. After two unsuccessful *Fürstentage* the Silesian estates finally accepted Ferdinand of Austria as their overlord, on December 5, 1526.[146] Liegnitz was soon caught between Wittenberg and Vienna, and its fate determined by extrinsic factors.

145. F. Bahlow 1918, 82–88.
146. Knörrlich 1959, 118–19. Already in 1525 Karl of Münsterberg-Oels had placed himself solidly in the Catholic camp. In January and February the conservative Utraquists in Prague had formally allied themselves with the Church of Rome (Schimmelpfennig 1884, 130–31). The concessions won by the Czechs were sufficient to satisfy Karl. The Peasants' War was another factor. On December 14, 1525, Karl ordered all married clergy out of his lands (Engelbert 1963, 142).

4 Chief Teacher and Heretic of Liegnitz
(1527–May 1529)

In the recent past, powerful opposition has arisen concerning the gospel with regard to the article of the sacrament: Is the body of Christ in the bread or not? God (who ordains all things wisely) has withheld this from us perhaps until now so that having regained possession of Holy Scripture and the letter of his word through his grace, we might not suppose that all was finished. But rather that we should beseech him for the inner word that is spirit and life (and in which alone our salvation lies). — Schwenckfeld, 1527

Duke Friedrich's chief teacher and preacher has erected and preached and even had published by the Swiss at Zurich a new, unheard-of, and horrible heresy, which has offended many, and not only the pious old Christians in Silesia and elsewhere, but even the people at Wittenberg whose teaching has been condemned by His Majesty the Emperor and other Christian kings and potentates.—King Ferdinand's open letter to Friedrich, January 1529

Friedrich of Liegnitz led the stiff Protestant resistance to the election of the Habsburg archduke Ferdinand as Silesia's overlord. They had good reason to fear the new king of Bohemia who, in conformity with the Edict of Worms, had already executed Protestants in Austria.[1] But there was no real choice other than Ferdinand, because the other candidates were Catholic as well, and of them all Ferdinand seemed best fitted to meet the Turkish threat.[2]

Sparring between the Catholic king and his Protestant subjects began almost immediately. Deploring the religious division in Silesia, the estates petitioned the king to impose peace and uniformity "in accordance with the gospel and God's word." Ferdinand counseled negotiation and required that any agreements made between the bishop and the princes be ratified by him.[3] But in the meantime (March 27,

---

1. Friedrich's opposition to Ferdinand may well have cost him his post as *Oberlandeshauptmann* in May 1527 (Engelbert 1963, 146). Ferdinand had had Kaspar Tauber executed in Vienna, September 17, 1524.

2. Rosenberg 1767, 14.

3. On the instructions of the Silesian envoys to Ferdinand and his reply, see Rosenberg 1767, 407–08. Karl of Münsterberg-Oels was now clearly back in the Catholic camp. In January 1527 Johannes Hess reported Karl's definitive withdrawal from the Protestant party (F. Bahlow 1918, 93).

1527) he ordered Breslau to expel its Lutheran ministers and overturn its Protestant innovations.[4]

Ferdinand was to receive Silesia's formal homage during a visit in May. In preparation a *Fürstentag* was called for April, at which Friedrich of Liegnitz attempted to forge an alliance of the Protestant powers.[5] Agreement ran aground, as so often happened in the empire, on the Lutheran demand that any political alliance be based on doctrinal agreement as defined by a formal and precise set of articles.[6] As a result, Ferdinand faced a divided Protestant party, a situation that he and his advisors exploited. On May 16, 1527, during his stay in Breslau, Ferdinand issued a mandate which, had it been obeyed, would have destroyed the Protestant movement in Silesia and would have restored unchanged the pre-Reformation Catholic church.[7] Its prompt and unapologetic rejection by Breslau and Liegnitz persuaded Ferdinand that a change of tactics was in order.[8]

He left Breslau on May 18. Two days later, while the king was in Schweidnitz (a part of Royal Silesia and hence under direct royal control), he had a Protestant preacher, Johann Reichel, executed for denying the real presence.[9] Whether the man held a Schwenckfeldian, Zwinglian, or Karlstadtian doctrine of the Lord's Supper is unknown, but what is important is the new focus in Ferdinand's assault on the Protestants. Henceforth his efforts would be directed at those heretics

4. Engelbert 1963, 148–49. Ferdinand repeated his demand in May (F. Bahlow 1918, 94–95).

5. Part of Friedrich's strategy involved a printed *Apology*, probably drafted by Schwenckfeld, "Grund, Ursach und Entschuldigung auf etliche Verunglimpfung von wegen der Predigt des heiligen Evangelii," CS XVIII, 11–23. It was published by Adam Dyon in Breslau and was dated 1527. I agree with Knörrlich 1959, 125–26, that it was probably presented at the *Fürstentag*. For a comparison of passages in the *Apology* that reflect Schwenckfeld's influence, see CS XVIII, 11–12. See also Knörrlich 1959, 124. The entire structure of the *Apology* is strikingly similar to Schwenckfeld's letter to the bishop (1527, CS II, 671–99), his letter to Friedrich of Liegnitz (1528, CS III, 99–118), and Schwenckfeld's own first *Apology* (January 1529, CS III, 391–431). In each a framework is provided by a chronological narrative of developments.

6. Knörrlich 1959, 125–26. Schwenckfeld described the Lutheran demand for a detailed common confession of faith in his letter to Bishop Salza (1527, CS II, 645:13–28).

7. F. Bahlow 1918, 93–94. It was probably drafted by Johannes Faber, Ferdinand's chaplain and confessor, who later became bishop of Vienna (1530) and a leader of the Counter-Reformation. On July 11, 1527, Faber became a member of the Breslau chapter (F. Bahlow 1918, 93), and on April 1, 1528, he became archdeacon (Engelbert 1963, 157).

8. CS XVIII, 24–26; F. Bahlow 1918, 94. For the text of Ferdinand's reply, see Rosenberg 1767, 51. Ferdinand did issue a further mandate against the Protestants in May from Brunau. Its contents may have been the same as at Breslau, Knörrlich 1959, 129–30.

9. Weigelt (1973, 91) is correct in refusing to assume that Reichel was a follower of Schwenckfeld as F. Bahlow (1918, 94) had done.

who denied the real presence, and in Silesia this meant that he would concentrate on Liegnitz.[10]

Ferdinand and his chief religious advisor, Johannes Faber, were merely repeating the maneuver they had employed to divide the Protestants of southern Germany into Lutheran and Zwinglian camps.[11] And the Lutheran party quite cynically connived with the king to isolate Liegnitz.[12] As summer dragged on into autumn Schwenckfeld and the others in Liegnitz gradually gave up hope that the Lutherans would ever come to terms.[13] They felt increasingly vulnerable, as the eschatological overtones in their writings betray.[14] Friedrich's ability to protect them was considerably diminished in May when Ferdinand replaced him as *Oberlandeshauptmann* with Karl of Münsterberg-Oels.[15]

There was also a Lutheran opposition party within Liegnitz, based in the university.[16] Schwenckfeld's efforts to win over two professors[17] forced him to define his thought more precisely and to defend his conclusions more forcefully. His letters to them mark an important stage in his theological development.

It was in 1527 that Schwenckfeld clearly resumed the leading role in the Liegnitz Reformation. All of the public explanations issuing from Liegnitz (Friedrich's *Apology*, Friedrich's reply to the mandate of Ferdinand, and the second *Apology* of the Liegnitz clergy) bear

10. Ferdinand issued another mandate (June 28, 1527) against those who denied the sacraments. F. Bahlow 1918, 95.

11. Köhler 1924, 346–51. Faber had been vicar of Constance at the time.

12. Breslau emphasized the dangers of the *Schwärmer* to the bishop in 1528. Engelbert 1963, 155.

13. Schwenckfeld to Paul Speratus, July 2, 1527, CS II, 628:3–4. In CS II, 707–09, he was still sanguine, but the *Apology* (November 11, 1527) had to be published in Nürnberg because Breslau refused permission to have it printed there. Cf. F. Bahlow 1918, 100–01. Schwenckfeld's letter to the bishop in the fall was really directed against the Lutherans (CS II, 631–70). Both CS and F. Bahlow 1918, 101, date the letter to October 1527.

14. CS II, 646:2–32, 648:25–649:13, 654:29–31, 655:3–4, 661:1–22, 662:18–26, 664:6–19.

15. Engelbert 1963, 149. Karl was instructed by Ferdinand (December 13, 1527) to prevent Friedrich from levying the Turkish tax upon church subjects (Engelbert 1963, 154–55).

16. Valentin Trotzendorf, the famed pedagogue at Goldberg, led the intellectual opposition, Georg von Zedlitz the political (Weigelt 1973, 103; F. Bahlow 1918, 112). Trotzendorf also taught at the university. Both Bernhard Ziegler the Hebraist and Conrad Cordatus were sent from Wittenberg. Johann Rurer joined the faculty in April 1527 to replace Cordatus, who had finally received Luther's permission to flee *Schwärmer*-infested Liegnitz (F. Bahlow 1918, 82–88).

17. Conrad Cordatus and Johann Rurer. Schwenckfeld's letter to Cordatus is discussed below; he wrote to Johann Rurer on February 10, 1527 (CS III, 24–33) and in November 1528 (CS III, 120–236).

Schwenckfeld's stamp and were written in Schwenckfeld's German, not Crautwald's Latin. Crautwald was increasingly caught up in his duties as lecturer at the university and was perhaps reverting to the life of the quiet scholar he had led before Schwenckfeld had approached him in the autumn of 1525.[18] In any event, it was Schwenckfeld's works that circulated in manuscript and were published by Oecolampadius and Zwingli.[19] It was therefore Schwenckfeld who achieved notoriety and was exiled, while Crautwald remained free to study and write in Liegnitz right up to his death in 1545, notwithstanding the fact that the city became officially Lutheran in 1539.

Schwenckfeld had also begun to travel again. Though most of his writings from 1525 and 1526 were written at Ossig, the letters and treatises of 1527 most often came from Wohlau, where Schwenckfeld may have owned properties.[20] At Wohlau he organized the clergy into an outpost of the Liegnitz reform, and he used it as a base from which to tour the countryside, proselytizing and encouraging those who were tempted to backslide.[21] He also established a network along which his manuscript treatises circulated.[22] In an age in which printing made its

18. Most of Crautwald's works in 1527 were university lectures: "Annotationes aliae ex praelectione D. Valentini Craut: in eundem Episolam ad Corinth: I. Cap. X . . ." (CLM 718, 370r–379r); "In priorem ad Corinthos CAPUT III . . ." (Cod. Aug. 37.27.2, 447–56); "Collectanea in Epistola Pauli. Ad Romanos. Ex meditationibus et etiam ex praelection Cratoaldi . . ." (Cod. Aug. 37.27.2, 457–516); "In Epistola ad Galatas. V:C" (Cod. Aug. 37.27.2, 521–42). Crautwald also produced three works on the Eucharist: "D. Valen: Craut: Silesii Theologi: Annotata quaedam super Genuinum Dominicae Coenae Intellectum" (CLM 718, 170r–187r); "De Verborum Coenae Dominicae Simplicitate qua confunditur stulta simplicitas hominum Deque Corpore et Sanguine Verbi Dei" (CLM 718, 188r–199r) is conjecturally placed in 1527 as is "Argumenta causae et rationes Quamobrem Impanatio excelsa Hominibus sit Abominatio Coram Deo" (CLM 718, 200r–210v).

19. Oecolampadius published *De cursu verbi dei* at the end of May 1527. Zwingli published *Ein Anwysunge das die opinion der leyplichen gegenwertigkeyt unsers Herrns Jesu Christi im Brote . . . gericht ist* at the end of August 1528.

20. Friedrich of Liegnitz had become its lord in 1524 (S. Schultz 1946, 3). Perhaps Friedrich had rewarded Schwenckfeld. It is less likely that he held a ducal post there.

21. Schwenckfeld refers to this circle of friends in a letter to Butzer (July 3 and 7, 1528), where he writes, "VVolauiae (.oppido in quo mihi frequens est habitatio.)" CS III, 80:8–15). The letter to Simon Ruff, pastor of Raudten, April 26, 1527 (CS II, 613–21), provides a glimpse into Schwenckfeld's activities. In giving Ruff advice on how to maintain the *Stillstand*, Schwenckfeld nearly transcribes a sermon he had given at Raben, another village on Friedrich's lands (CS II, 620:16–18). The opening of the letter speaks of Schwenckfeld's visit to a minister in Liegnitz or Ossig (CS II, 618:1). He had also left books in Glogau (CS II, 618:7) and with a noble who may have been in residence in Raudten (CS II, 620:24–25).

22. In the letter to Ruff Schwenckfeld mentions the passing around of the treatises (CS II, 618:1–6, 620:24–25, 621:8–9). His manuscript letter to the bishop in 1527 was expressly directed at a larger audience (CS II, 637:23–638:1). Schwenckfeld also gave Friedrich permission to circulate his advice on the proper course to follow (CS III, 112:3–6). When Schwenckfeld

first great gains, the importance of handwritten communication is often overlooked. Although Schwenckfeld would make effective use of the printing press, manuscript transmission remained crucial: much of his corpus owes its preservation to a brisk trade in his unpublished works.

Schwenckfeld's renewed activity, and the bold clarity with which he now began to express the spiritualism latent in his earlier writings, signaled the decisive resolution of a personal crisis. This third *Heimsuchung* (the first in 1519 with his conversion, the second in 1525 with his rejection of the real presence) entailed his definitive break with Luther and his reformulation of the entire nature, purpose, and history of the Reformation along spiritualist lines.[23]

Schwenckfeld's spiritualist awakening was part of a larger phenomenon in Liegnitz and may in fact have been precipitated by it. The arrival of Sebastian Eisenmann in late 1526 or 1527 seemed to have had much the same effect in Liegnitz that the Zwickau prophets had had in Wittenberg six years earlier.[24] Soon there developed an atmosphere in which visions and prophecies were the order of the day, and Crautwald, Fabian Eckel, Johann Sigismund Werner, and the other Liegnitz clergy were caught up in it. Activity centered on the Lieb-

protested the publication of his *De cursu verbi dei*, he pointed out to Oecolampadius that he had intended it only as a private opinion (CS III, 62:7–14). He also warned Butzer not to publish his *Anwysunge* (CS III, 79:1–18).

23. There is much disagreement about the dates and causes of the various *Heimsuchungen*; see Pietz 1959, 23; Ecke 1911, 48–57; Hirsch 1922, 153; Kluge 1917, 232; Kriebel 1968, 9; Lashlee 1969, 73–74; Furcha 1970, 13; Maron 1961a, 114–15, 135; Sippel 1911, 927. Many of the difficulties can be obviated by assuming three such events instead of only two. Schwenckfeld referred to a visitation for the year 1527 (CS IX, 453:2–5). I agree with Lashlee 1969, 73–74, on the dating, but not on the significance. I believe with Sippel 1911, 927, that it represented the final working out of the ideas inherent in his eucharistic position. But since the conclusions which he drew were so dramatic and wide-reaching, and his break with Luther so traumatic, I disagree with Hirsch 1922, 153, who saw it as only an aftershock of the eucharistic decision. Hirsch was reacting to the importance which Ecke 1911, 48–57, had placed upon divine visitation as a third independent force alongside Luther and the Bible, in Schwenckfeld's thought. I, too, disagree with Ecke if he means that the *Heimsuchung* imparted doctrinal content. However, I disagree with Hirsch's attempt to downplay it as an inevitable, if delayed, movement of the will attendant upon the intellectual discovery of 1525. What makes 1527 crucial is Schwenckfeld's decision to continue his spiritualizing course despite opposition from Lutherans and Catholics and despite the consequences for the visible Church, consequences that deflected reformers like Luther and Zwingli from also consistently developing the elements of spiritualism in their own thought.

24. On the *Schwärmerei* in Liegnitz, see F. Bahlow 1918, 78–82, 149–54; Schneider 1862, 12–13; Weigelt 1973, 62–63; Rosenberg 1767, 65. The movement may be datable to as early as 1526 if the spirits referred to in Luther's letter to Cordatus are more than just a reference to Schwenckfeld's and Crautwald's appeal to the spirit in the Eucharist (November 28, 1526, Wa Br 4, 138).

frauenkirche, with whose cantor, Gregor Tag, Eisenmann lived when he first arrived in Liegnitz. Prepared by fasting, those seeking the spirit gathered for prayer in the school attached to the church. Tag recorded the resulting revelations, but unfortunately none of this material survives.[25] Schwenckfeld's involvement remains undocumented, but there can hardly be any question that he did participate in the meetings, since he later introduced similar ones in southern Germany.[26]

Given the pressure on Liegnitz from outside and the tension within, there was a supercharged atmosphere perfect for Eisenmann's spark. The experience of direct revelation jolted Schwenckfeld's spiritualism from the realm of speculation to that of reality, and his spiritual fervor was given no chance to cool. From 1527 until his departure from Silesia in 1529, the pressure and imminent danger never subsided.

The Reformation of the Spirit

The work in which we can trace the transformation of Schwenckfeld's spiritual experience into spiritualistic theology is one of the classics of radical Protestantism: Schwenckfeld's letter to Conrad Cordatus, a Wittenberg-trained professor at Liegnitz. Written on March 27, 1527, and later published by Oecolampadius (May 31, 1527) under the title De cursu verbi dei (The Course of the Word of God), it is an eloquent and elegantly simple outline of the spiritualist understanding of the word.[27] Drawing upon a thoroughgoing dualism, Schwenckfeld explicitly rejected Luther's conception of the spoken word as a vehicle for the spirit, not least because it condemned so many who had no

25. There is one hostile account by Sebastian Schubart, a former Schwenckfelder, in his *Against the Teachings of the Schwenckfelders* (1542), reprinted in Bahlow 1918, 149–54. On Schubart, see Knörrlich 1959, 139. Schubart's account is biased, but amusing.

26. In a letter which has been dated variously from February 1531 to August 1534, Schwenckfeld described the process of moderate fasting, prayer, and revelation in which he and the unknown addressees had taken part (CS IV, 78:14–28). On the problem of dating, see CS IV, 71–72, and CS XVIII, 51–52.

27. Dated at Wohlau, CS II 581–99. Schwenckfeld describes Cordatus's position on the relationship of the preached word and faith in classically Lutheran terms (CS II, 591:5–592:1). Cordatus had written in the autumn of 1526 to report Liegnitz's spiritualist excesses and to ask Luther's permission to leave his post at Liegnitz. Luther advised him to stay on (November 28, 1526, WA Br 4, 138). In a later letter (January 29, 1527), Luther urged Cordatus to leave as soon as possible. Cordatus finally left Leignitz in April 1527 shortly after receiving Schwenckfeld's letter (F. Bahlow 1918, 82–88).

opportunity to hear or read the word, and because it stripped God of his freedom.[28] It invited a return to works righteousness.

> If faith were through the word or from the outer word, preached or heard, then it would follow that justification is from or through the work of our hands. Or, at the very least, that it would not be possible without man's help. But who cannot see how absurd that would be? Abraham, who was the pattern and example of our justification, had faith in God, not in the preached word (for there weren't any preachers yet, or even the Law), and it was reputed to him as justification.[29]

Schwenckfeld conflated the concepts of spirit, inner word, predestination, and prevenient grace to describe the living faith which must precede any fruitful encounter with God's spoken or written word.[30] Without this divine gift the outer word could become a tool of wickedness, or at best an instrument of self-deception: "If you were to dun the ears of the unfaithful with the word of God a thousand times, they would receive nothing but sound. At the most they will report a short-lived carnal emotion of simulated faith produced by their own free will."[31]

When we compare Schwenckfeld to Zwingli, with whose position on word and spirit he had much in common, the radicalism of Schwenckfeld's spiritualism becomes apparent.[32] The Zurich reformer had also posited a preceding grace which he often called spirit and faith, but for Zwingli this "faith" was really only a necessary precon-

28. See CS II, 593:14–15; 594:15–18. On Schwenckfeld's fears for those outside the reach of the New Testament: pagans, CS II, 689:15–23; Old Testament fathers, 694:7–696:10; children and the deaf, 678:7–16; and those who lived before the Reformation, 682:31–683:11. Luther's belief in an oral tradition of Christ-oriented promises among the Old Testament patriarchs from Adam to Abraham struck Schwenckfeld as fanciful (CS II, 687:15–29). The word of promise which gave salvation throughout the ages is not the spoken word expressing a promise, but rather the promised word, Christ, the word incarnate (CS II, 688:9–12).

29. CS II, 594:1–7.

30. CS II, 595:14–20; 596:1–4.

31. CS II, 592:26–593:3. This faith is not a true living faith, but only a rational or historical faith, a belief that the events recounted in the Bible are factually true, not a trust in Christ as personal savior (CS II, 594:11).

32. Zwingli was emphatic in his denial that any external thing could produce faith (Gestrich 1967, 27, 29, 33, 50, 70, 77, 132, 143–44). He also distinguished the historical faith (*fides historica*) drawn from Scripture and the true living faith of the Spirit. Zwingli probably drew this distinction from Melanchthon's *Loci communes* of 1521 (Gestrich 1967, 26–31, n. 36). Cf. Grützmacher 1902, 168–69; Seeberg 1929, 50.

dition for true salvific faith.[33] Spirit, or grace, or faith was necessary to open fallen man's eyes, illumine his mind, and cleanse his heart. It gave man the *facility* for saving faith, *fides qua*. But that faith, the saving trust in Christ, really came only through contact with God's word in the Bible, which conveyed the content of belief, *fides quae*.

Schwenckfeld made no such distinction. The faith which God poured into the hearts of those he had chosen was complete and sufficient, granting knowledge and justification, because it served to join them to Christ, the living inner word incarnate. "Faith is truly a heavenly gift. It is justice coming down from heaven, purifying and changing the heart, which thus through this grace believes, but not merely in the written word. Rather it is carried outside of itself into the word of God to whom it clings through the Holy Spirit."[34] What some had viewed as exceptional divine intervention in the cases of Paul and Cornelius the centurion was for Schwenckfeld the one way to salvation. There was only one undivided faith for all men who

> are to be saved, and it is built upon Christ the eternal living word in heaven (who is there yesterday, today, and in eternity, Hebrews 13:8) and not upon these letters or external promises. For even if someone doesn't know or understand these external promises, he is already saved if he only knows in his heart him of whom the promises speak.[35]

Schwenckfeld also considered God's sovereignty. "The course of the living word of God is free. It does not hang upon visible things, nor is it bound to the minister, or ministry, or time, or place. But it abides

33. Gestrich 1967, 71 terms this preparatory faith *Vorgabe-Glaube* and distinguishes it from salvific *Vertrauensglaube*. The *Vorgabe-Glaube* drew the Christian to the word of God and brought him to believe what he understood there. The logical moment separating the two is *Erkenntnis*. This knowledge the elect receive from a reading or hearing of God's word after having been prepared by the *Vorgabe-Glaube*. Gestrich, however, is not totally successful in overcoming the difficulties involved in Zwingli's teachings on faith and Scripture. How, for instance, were the pious pagans like Socrates and Seneca saved? Although Seneca may have had the opportunity to hear the Christian message, what of Socrates? Gestrich 1967, 52 n. 123, cites Zwingli: "Potest enim deus infundere fidem in cor gentium, quam deinde operibus comprobant et ostendunt, qualiter non temere de Socrate,, Seneca aliisque multis sentio." How did Zwingli reconcile the *Vorgabe-Glaube/Vertrauensglaube* with his Augustinian epistemology?

34. CS II 594:17–21. Cf. 505:32–506:2.

35. CS II, 689:32–690:5. Cf. 503:6–27. For other examples of direct revelation, see CS II, 505:14–25, 596:16–597:7. Schwenckfeld also argued that the Hebrews had no essential advantage over the pagans (690:6–12).

totally in invisible things, although it is vaguely represented to us in visible things."[36]

Schwenckfeld excluded the outer word from the work of faith and justification and restricted it to the task of sanctification, the betterment of the outer man. Scripture also ceased to be self-interpreting.[37] And although Schwenckfeld would always appeal to Scripture to prove his positions, he knew that his efforts to convince were doomed if his audience was not informed directly by God. This would prove to be the underlying theoretical base for Schwenckfeld's thoroughgoing and consistent advocacy of religious toleration.[38]

The knowledge which faith brings, the *Erkenntnis Christi*, so central to Schwenckfeld's theology, was in part his answer to Luther's insistence that God was hidden, that certain mysteries like the Eucharist were to remain inaccessible to human understanding.[39] Schwenckfeld countered:

> But you know that our Christian faith is no darkness, but rather a bright light and knowledge of the things which we believe and hope. Nor is anything which helps us to salvation too high to investigate. For we have a reliable access to the holy things through Christ's blood, Hebrews 10. So don't let anyone lead you astray about knowledge [*erkenntnis*] of the truth, and pursue it as long as you do so in the fear of God and as far as the anointing [*Salbung*] which you have received allows. For the Lord says in John to his disciples [John 14:17]: you know the spirit of truth. What can that be but a true knowledge and living assurance and clarity concerning all those things which we believe? . . . Therefore, we cannot close our eyes when dealing with the Christian faith, because it comes from light and leads us to truth. The pagans close their eyes with their faith, for they may not investigate it. Christians on the contrary must be informed about what they

36. CS II, 596:7–11. Cf. 485:21–26.

37. Schwenckfeld had to agree with the Catholics: the Bible was not a clear self-interpreting document (CS III, 173:5–9).

38. The freedom of the spirit, combined with God's predestination, made coercion futile (Kühn 1923, 145, 149). Schwenckfeld saw a clear causal connection between what he considered undue reliance on the written word, and religious persecution (CS II, 496:37–497:7)

39. Luther charged that his opponents relied upon human reason in their treatment of the Eucharist (WA 23, 123–24, 161–62). Schwenckfeld defended himself by emphasizing fallen man's inability to discern divine truths. Most often reason is a tool used by the devil to lead men astray (CS II, 679:26–28; CS III, 228:33–38).

believe, and must know what the body of Christ is, and how they are to seek and find it. [40]

As we have seen, Schwenckfeld tended to combine many concepts into one and to transform ideas into experiences. He coalesced the "knowledge of Christ," the Eucharist, and the Christian's confrontation with the incarnate Logos, Christ glorified. [41] *Erkenntnis Christi* became a knowledge which comes from Christ: a knowledge about Christ, who he is, where he is to be found; but more important, it was knowing Christ, being as it were his personal acquaintance, living continuously in his presence.

(1) We come to Christ through the drawing of the Father. (2) We see Christ when we know him. (3) We believe in Christ when we are joined to his body. (4) We eat of Christ when we partake of his nature. [42]

Schwenckfeld on occasion listed doctrines which are learned from Christ the schoolmaster, but these were clearly secondary to the personal encounter with the redeemer. [43] Knowledge and faith were therefore combined differently in Schwenckfeld's thought than in Luther's. It was not so much a question of knowing that Christ was crucified and believing that he died for us (*pro nobis*), but rather a question of knowing the crucified and now-glorified Christ personally. By looking within and raising his heart (*sursum corda*) the Christian confronted Christ in heaven, came to know him, and studied with him. This was true knowledge, *Erkenntnis*.

The necessity that each earthbound soul know the glorified Christ made the chasm separating the spiritual and the earthly central to the Christian experience, and it gave the Holy Spirit a dominant role in the life of each believer.

But they [the Lutherans] can't recognize that [by crediting the outer word with producing faith] they fasten shut the Kingdom of Heaven, rob the Holy Spirit of his office, and credit the creature with what is proper to the creator. All of which proves that they haven't correctly considered Paul's remark in Romans [Rom.

40. CS II, 449:1–17.
41. To eat Christ is "Erkantnus Christ" (CS II, 552:12–20).
42. CS II, 571:23–31.
43. A list of subjects taught in the school of Christ is given in CS II, 639:8–30.

8:15] and the ministry of the spirit [*Ministerium Spiritus*]. As a result, they judge God's affairs superficially according to the flesh and the letter, and convince themselves that they have the judgment of the Holy Spirit [*Judicium der heilige Geist*]. The fruits, however, identify it for what it is. God forgive us our sins, Amen.[44]

It is the Holy Spirit who unites the believer with Christ, who feeds him the body and blood of Christ, who enlightens and instructs, and who brings forth the fruits, the good works which are the marks of a true Christian.[45] The Holy Spirit gave focus to all of the various spiritual entities which appear in Schwenckfeld's thought.[46] In his withdrawal from the cares and contaminations of the world of men, Schwenckfeld had finally entered into the holy of holies in the temple of theological contemplation—trinitarian speculation. By anchoring one pole of reality, the spiritual, in the Holy Spirit, Schwenckfeld guaranteed that his theological focus would be God and not man, his point of departure metaphysical and not social or psychological.[47] This was essentially an Augustinian world view and here Luther and Crautwald were Schwenckfeld's guides.[48]

44. CS II, 691:11–18. Cf. CS II, 682:14–30; CS III, 262:5–14.
45. CS II, 456:14–25, 506:3–9, 510:37–511:6, 594:17–21.
46. He also entered into the trinitarian speculation which, as he recognized, his contemporaries and especially Luther shunned (CS II, 456:7–13). Cf. CS III, 218:9–14, where Schwenckfeld sends his readers to the Athanasian Creed for instruction on the roles of the three persons; see also CS III, 257:8–16. The *Confession of Sins* (CS V, 933–67), discussed in chapter 3, is shot through with trinitarian motifs, including prayers directed separately to the Father, Son, and Holy Spirit. Gordon Rupp's claim that the Holy Spirit was not really in contention in the early years of the Reformation would therefore have to be somewhat modified, that is, if 1527 were granted to be "early" (Rupp 1958, 13). Knowledge of the various roles of the three persons of the Trinity formed part of the *Erkenntnis Christi*, and trinitarian formulas became increasingly important in Schwenckfeld's writings (CS II, 639:8–20). Although Maron (1961a, 60) may be right that later in Schwenckfeld's writings the Holy Spirit was in effect swallowed up by the body and blood of Christ, at this early stage such was not the case. Nor was it true in this early period (contrary to the view in Erbkam 1848, 468) that the Holy Spirit was for Schwenckfeld really only the spirit of the glorified humanity.
47. CS III, 410:8–11. Augustine was pivotal in developing the idea of spirit as an essence or substance. "Mens et spiritus non relative dicuntur, sed essentiam demonstrat" (cited in Rothe 1974). Augustine's work on the nature of spirit was done with reference to the nature of God.
48. Lashlee 1969, 62, claims Crautwald as the principal conduit for the "Neo-Platonic ontology and epistemology of Early Christian thought." I agree that Crautwald and the church fathers contributed to Schwenckfeld's conceptual framework. But during the period which Lashlee identifies as crucial (July 1525–December 1525), Schwenckfeld could also have been influenced by the writings of Zwingli, Oecolampadius, and the early fathers directly. Maier 1959, 99–100, singles out Tauler as Schwenckfeld's principal source, although he admits that Schwenckfeld did not read Tauler with any intensity until after 1531. Maier points out the

God had divided all things into two orders: "the heavenly, spiritual, invisible, eternal and . . . the earthly, physical, visible, transitory things."[49] For Schwenckfeld, these two orders were mutually exclusive; the spiritual did not work through the physical. However, it was possible for some physical objects to become spiritual, for example, Christ's body, which had been physical on earth and was now spiritual and in heaven. It was this profound metaphysical dualism that made unacceptable the claims of the spoken and written word to bridge the gap separating man and God. Not the word which men spoke, but the only-begotten word of God who became flesh could reconcile fleshly man with his spiritual God.

Spiritual things distinguished themselves from fleshly in that they were invisible, eternal, and divine.[50] Through Christ's incarnation, passion, death, resurrection, and glorification the spiritual God was joined with the fleshly man, producing the *tertium quid*, the spiritual man.[51] Christ's spiritual flesh shared with believers made Christians participants in his glorified humanity. It allowed them to overcome the hurdle of their fleshly flesh and to bridge the chasm from earthly to

amazing similarities and concludes a direct lineage. But certainly by the sixteenth century Tauler's ideas had become elements of the common intellectual heritage of the literate segments of European society. The most detailed analysis of the sources of Schwenckfeld's Neoplatonism is found in Pietz 1956, 27–29, 56–58. Pietz argues for an ultimately Augustinian source for Schwenckfeld, which was mediated by Luther and then by Crautwald. He values Crautwald's contribution as more important and ties it to the concept of "spiritual judgment." Although the importance of that point should not be downplayed, it is noteworthy that in the twelve *Questiones* Schwenckfeld (contrary to the analysis in Lashlee 1969, 62) already shows signs of accepting a dualism of spirit and matter, of inner and outer.

49. CS II, 454:12–14.

50. Faith *is* the Holy Spirit (CS II, 506:3–9). Spiritual judgment is the Holy Spirit judging in the new man. Heaven is spiritual because God dwells there. Or, to be more precise, heaven is the presence of God (CS III, 202:27–34). The spiritual flesh of God is spiritual because in it dwells the fullness of the Godhead in the second person, the Logos. Although Schwenckfeld writes of various spiritual entities, there is really only one, God. Not surprisingly, angels and demons, not least the devil, seldom appear in Schwenckfeld's writings. In this early period Schwenckfeld mentions angels only once, where he discusses God's dealings with the Old Testament fathers which were conducted "durch die Engel und durch sich selbst mit den seinen, den predigte Er selbst in jhren Hertzen . . ." (CS II, 693:35–38). The question of man's spirit is also left unclear. Is it truly man's or is it God?

51. Baur's conclusion (1843, 342) that Schwenckfeld in effect made flesh into spirit reflects nineteenth-century German philosophical preoccupations more than sixteenth-century religious problems. Sciegienny's contention (1975, 92) that spiritual flesh was merely flesh which was obedient to the spirit misses the point. Schwenckfeld's thought demanded an ontological base for all moral and religious values. Obedient flesh would be ontologically different from disobedient flesh. Seyppel (1961, 82) is correct to point out that *wesen* had assumed a more psychological connotation since Eckhardt. And at times Schwenckfeld seems to be using the term in that sense. But underlying all actions and qualities is an ontological base. One is spiritual and therefore lives and thinks spiritually.

spiritual. This true inner Eucharist was depicted in the liturgical Lord's Supper. Hence Schwenckfeld's oft-repeated assertion that a proper understanding of the Eucharist was absolutely necessary and not *adiaphora*. To know where Christ was, what sort of body he had, and how Christians might participate in it were all parts of *Erkenntnis Christi*, and they formed the very core of Christian belief. They answered the two most important questions posed by believers: Why did God become man (*Cur deus homo*)? And how may men be saved?

Schwenckfeld's identification of spirit with the Holy Spirit, and his views on the new spiritual man, allowed him to address his major practical concern: the visible improvement of individual Christians. For Schwenckfeld, reform of the individual Christian was the goal, and for this the Reformation was but a means. That is to say, Schwenckfeld was primarily concerned that individual Christians have a true living faith which expressed itself in works of love, and that the reform of doctrine and of church practice and structure be directed to that end.[52] The emphasis on individual improvement and the optimistic reevaluation of the abilities of the new spiritual man led Schwenckfeld to reconsider and redefine a whole series of concepts central to Luther's original impulse and message: original sin, works righteousness, free will, and predestination.

Schwenckfeld continued to stand with Luther in opposing the semi-Pelagianism found in some late medieval theologians; he rejected the teaching that man could initiate his own salvation by doing the very little that he was capable of in his fallen state (*Facere quod in se est*).[53] In Schwenckfeld's opinion, as in Luther's, fallen man was simply incapable of that autonomous first step.[54] Of necessity, it was only by God's unprovoked grace and prodding that man changed, since fallen man was by his very nature incapable of anything but sin. It was im-

52. Contrast this with Luther who was primarily concerned with the Truth, that is, God's truth, and who maintained that if the whole world must be forfeit to maintain the truth, so be it (Ozment 1973a). Ozment argued that here we see "scholastic" Luther rejecting the humanist overemphasis on Christian living as the goal of true religion.

53. CS III, 454:24–26. On the problem of the "Facere quod in se est," see Oberman 1967, 131–46; McSorley 1969, 183–217. Theologians such as William of Ockham and Gabriel Biel had taught that God would recognize man's pitiful efforts and give man grace in order to proceed further on the path of repentance, faith, and good works. At no point were man's efforts commensurate with the help and rewards which God bestowed, but man's free turning to God was a *sine qua non*.

54. In fact, Schwenckfeld saw in Luther's insistence on the clarity of the written word and the mediatory role of Scripture in producing justifying faith the danger of a revived semi-Pelagianism. CS II, 598:12–14, 599:10–11.

mediately clear, however, that Luther's teaching on sin and conversion was also incompatible with the doctrine of free will. Luther himself readily admitted this.[55]

Schwenckfeld had already rejected in 1524 similar teachings in Melanchthon's 1521 *Loci communes* because Schwenckfeld believed they made God in some sense the author of sin. But it was not until 1528 that he presented a thorough criticism of Luther's handling of the same issue.[56]

Luther's position disturbed Schwenckfeld because, in Schwenckfeld's opinion, it too made God the author of sin and tended to have untoward effects among the populace at large.[57] The fatalism it produced had resulted in unbridled living, especially among the nobility. Coupled with the misunderstanding of justification by faith alone, it gave the licentious yet another excuse for their sinfulness. According to Schwenckfeld, Luther failed to understand Augustine and the significance of the dualism of old man and new man.[58] While it was true

55. In *Bondage of the Will* Luther argued that man possessed no free will, that he sinned by necessity and was saved against his will. For an analysis of Luther's work in the larger context of Christian tradition, see McSorley 1969, 297–353. How this could be without convicting God of horrible injustice, Luther continues, is a mystery which human reason, even human reason enlightened by grace, cannot penetrate.

56. Letter to Johann Rurer, professor at Liegnitz, February 10, 1528, CS III, 24–33. The letter is in reply to a now lost letter from Rurer. Perhaps Rurer had taken exception to remarks in the appendix to *De cursu verbi dei*, CS III, 683:31–684:13. CS dates the appendix to the autumn of 1527. In *De cursu verbi dei* (March 1527), there was as yet no sign (CS II, 581–99). Schwenckfeld was much more concerned there to combat the freedom of the will against Luther's use of Scripture in producing salvific faith. He does emphasize the freedom of the spirit and inner word (CS II, 596:7–11). In May 1527 Johannes Faber had delivered a series of sermons in Breslau attacking Luther's teaching on justification and free will (Engelbert 1963, 151), and in the same month Balthasar Hubmaier published a treatise on free will. Hubmaier had dedicated a first treatise, *Von der Freiheit des Willens* (April 1, 1527), to Markgraf Georg von Brandenburg-Ansbach. The second treatise, *Das andere Buchlein von der Freiwilligkeit*, dated May 20, 1527, was dedicated to Friedrich of Liegnitz. Both works were printed by Simprecht Sorge who left Nikolsburg and took up residence in Liegnitz after Hubmaier's execution. Sorge also printed Schwenckfeld's first *Apology* in January 1529 (CS III, 391). For Hubmaier's work consult Hubmaier 1962, 379–431. Some of Hubmaier's statements bear resemblance to Schwenckfeld's. A distinction must be made between the two treatises. In the first, Hubmaier elaborated his first theory that the spirit in man was free, and free from sin, even after the Fall. After rebirth the soul also partook of this freedom (Hubmaier 1962, 384–86, 390). In the second treatise, Hubmaier did not go into the status of the spirit after the Fall, but merely said that through the word man was reborn, and that reborn man had free will (although the flesh did not) (p. 405). The format of the second treatise determined the content. Hubmaier limited himself to a discussion of various biblical citations pro and con drawn from Erasmus, although he neither mentioned the humanist nor in fact agreed with him. Hubmaier instead appealed to Augustine's *Contra Julianum* (p. 429), as did Crautwald (Cod. Aug. 37.27.2, 475).

57. CS III, 32:32–33:3; 28:32–29:7.

58. CS III, 26:10–25. See also CS II, 683:31–684:6. Schwenckfeld claimed he advocated a middle way between Erasmus and Luther (CS III, 25:24–27), though in fact he ignored Erasmus and set his sights on Luther.

that the old man was in bondage to Satan by reason of his sinful nature, the new man was free to do good.[59] The battle between flesh and spirit, old man and new, would have been meaningless if both old and new, flesh and spirit, were sinful. In effect, Schwenckfeld took Luther's graphic analogy of the human will as a beast with two possible riders—God and the devil—and developed it, expanding the significance of God's intervention. The indwelling of Christ through the Holy Spirit produced not only faith, but also generated good works pleasing to God.[60] Schwenckfeld so emphasized Christ and the spirit that man's role, that is, the new man's role, seemed limited to pure instrumentality. To the extent that Christ was present, man was good and his works acceptable.

The will of the new man was therefore free in the sense that Augustine would have accepted—to the extent that the spirit controlled, the new man was free from the trammels of sin, doing good works by necessity and not free to do good or evil.[61] This suited Schwenckfeld's purpose well, since his concern was to exhort the new man to lead a Christian life, not, as with Luther, to abash the old man with the blame for his own sins.

The capstone of Schwenckfeld's teaching on sin and redemption was predestination, or, as he sometimes labeled it, preordination. Although he progressed no further than single predestination, it sufficed to replace Luther's concept of grace in explaining God's acceptance of sinful man.[62] With Schwenckfeld, as with the Reformed tradition, the emphasis upon the unfailing execution of God's eternal decree tended to overshadow the existential crisis of the terrified sinner who faced a wrathful God and possessed nothing but God's promise in Christ. Far from consoling oppressed consciences, it spurred the Christian to seek anxiously signs of God's election in the good works which the Holy Spirit effected in those who were chosen.[63] Only in these works was there consolation.

59. CS III, 30:24–39. Beachy 1963, 17–18, is correct to emphasize the impaired ontological status of fallen man in Schwenckfeld's thought, but that corruption includes the will. Sciegienny 1975, 60–61, is wrong in asserting Schwenckfeld's rejection of a bondage of the will.

60. CS III, 26:1–25, 481:29–32. Schwenckfeld is probably relying on Wessel Gansfort (CS III, 370:37–371:3).

61. For a discussion of the complex distinctions concerning freedom with regard to the will, see McSorley 1969, 25–31.

62. CS III, 457:14–19.

63. CS III, 26:26–27:18. Schwenckfeld maintains the possibility, however, that the new man can fall. Here Koyré 1955, 12, errs, at least for this period. It is an inconsistency in Schwenckfeld's teaching (CS III, 354:29–37, 462:29–463:5). Maron 1961a, 76, is also wrong in asserting that the ability of the reborn to fall is found only in Schwenckfeld's later writings.

The entire thrust of Schwenckfeld's theological development in 1527, its emphasis on the spirit's role in faith and the possibilities for individual regeneration, redefined the relationship between inner renewal and outer reform. He had subtly changed his insistence that a powerful, heartfelt, living faith among Christians was a necessary precondition for the reform of external elements of the visible church. No longer merely a prerequisite, inner spiritual reform tended to become the goal itself, and the church, its sacraments, and its offices increasingly seemed to be hindrances and obstacles rather than instruments.

Tracing influences is a dangerous and usually unremunerative activity. But the combination that we find in Schwenckfeld of spiritualism and a proto-Calvinist emphasis on works as marks of election fairly begs after "influences." Both Andreas Karlstadt and Thomas Müntzer seem likely candidates, but prove not to have had much impact.[64] Erasmus may have exercised a general indirect influence, but surely no more than that.[65] Of those whose thought fed Schwenckfeld's spiritualism, aside from Crautwald and Zwingli, Luther must hold a

---

64. He read some of Karlstadt's tracts on the Eucharist, but from Schwenckfeld's own statements it is clear that he valued Zwingli much more than Karlstadt. On Karlstadt's early Orlamuende theology, see Sider 1974. Although Karlstadt had a much more obvious tie to late medieval mysticism, there are points of strong similarity with Schwenckfeld. Most recent scholars agree, however, that Karlstadt was not an important source for Schwenckfeld (Weigelt 1973, 52–53; Ecke 1911, 47–48. Maron 1961a, 155–56.) Furcha 1970, 107, wrongly associates Schwenckfeld with Karlstadt on the Eucharist: Karlstadt rejected the notion of participation in Christ's glorified body. On May 17, 1528, Karlstadt attempted to send a letter to the Silesians, but it was intercepted by Luther (WA Br 4, 571–73). The letter revealed that Karlstadt had attempted to contact the Silesians earlier, but had always failed; it would seem that Karlstadt was planning to seek refuge among them. The letter never reached Silesia, and we know of no attempt on the Silesians' part to contact him. Schwenckfeld would later become quite friendly with Karlstadt during their exiles in southern Germany (CS IV, 899).

It is true that many of Schwenckfeld's positions resemble Müntzer's, and that there is often a common vocabulary. Maron 1961a, 156, catalogues the similarities but concludes that a relationship of dependence cannot be proved. As Urner 1948, 331, points out, Schwenckfeld did not share Müntzer's doctrine of the inner word. Nor did he consider contemporary revelations as normative (Maier 1959, 103). Müntzer is nowhere mentioned in Schwenckfeld's early writings. Crautwald identified Müntzer with sedition (Cog. Aug. 37.27.2, 450), glossing the word *seditionibus* in 2 Cor. 6:5.

65. The thesis of Sciegienny 1975, 60–61, that Schwenckfeld was an erring disciple of Erasmus rather than of Luther is not in itself improbable. But the selection of the *Enchiridion* as representative of Erasmus's thought presents difficulties because Schwenckfeld never cites that work. We do have references to Erasmus in Schwenckfeld's works, but they are limited to Erasmus the philologist, grammarian, and biblical scholar. Cf. his references to Erasmus's *Greek New Testament* (CS II, 472:4–11) and *Annotations* (CS III, 184:4–6; 189:2). He may also have read one of Erasmus's works on free will (CS III, 25:16–27). If Schwenckfeld did indeed owe much to Erasmus, it probably came indirectly through Crautwald or Adam Reissner. Sciegienny has restated his thesis in a lecture entitled "Schwenckfeld and Christian Humanism," in Erb 1985.

preeminent position.[66] Luther's spiritualism, hammered by Zwingli, refined by Crautwald, and made molten by the heat of events, was ready to take on the distinctive form which Schwenckfeld's personality and interests would give it.

Schwenckfeld's new perspective forced him to reevaluate and to recast his vision of the course of church history and the significance of the Reformation itself. Two themes, the role of spiritual judgment and the gradualness of both decline and reform, ran throughout his reconstruction and determined his personal decisions and behavior in the months leading up to his exile from Silesia.

Unlike Luther or the Anabaptists, Schwenckfeld did not link the fall of the Catholic church to any political or ecclesiastical event or trend.[67] Rather, the loss of spiritual understanding of both Scripture and the sacraments, a process whose stages were marked by the neglect of the catechism and the invention of transubstantiation, had led to confusion, ignorance, superstition, and works righteousness.[68] The result was the Catholic church, with its clear "literal" word of God and its "real" sacraments.[69] Schwenckfeld set no firm date for the fall of the

66. Sciegienny 1975, 57; Maron 1961a, 42–43; Furcha 1970, 80. It has long been recognized that many of the spiritualist positions espoused by Schwenckfeld and other radicals can be found in the early Luther. Cf. H. Gerdes 1955, 20; H. Gerdes 1958, 50, 54; Grützmacher 1902, 10, 161; Hirsch 1922, 146, 154, passim; Jones 1959, 6; Pietz 1956, 72, 116. Seeberg 1929, 66, 69, 70, 76; Steck 1955, 12, 15, 17. As Bornkamm 1932, 92, points out, Luther's love of contradiction and use of ambiguous terminology make Luther's own views difficult to establish. Maron's criticism (1961a, 157) of Hirsch's effort to prove Schwenckfeld's reliance on Luther is questionable. Even if it is granted that Schwenckfeld read Luther in a "vulgärmystischen" sense, it would be necessary to prove that Luther had not meant to convey it. Luther's thought with regard to the spirit and its relationship to the word, and his treatment of the dualism of inner and outer, both show growth and change in this early period. Cf. Bornkamm 1932, 85–109; Grützmacher 1902, 15–42.

67. The Anabaptists tied the fall to the Constantinian settlement (Garrett 1958), while Luther associated it with the recognition of the pope as head of the Church (Haaugaard 1979, 46).

68. CS II, 500:32–501:24, 640:10–16. Schwenckfeld outlined nine steps in the decline of the sacrament (CS II, 457:22–459:1). (1) After the loss of spiritual judgment, reason and philosophy stepped in. The result was the doctrine of transubstantiation. (2) The Eucharist was then made into a sacrifice. (3) Because the catechism was also neglected, Christian congregations disappeared. The Mass resulted, with the priest alone handling the elements. (4) The priests began to offer the sacrifice of the Mass for the living and the dead in private masses. (5) The laity lost the use of the cup. (6) Worship of the sacrament began. (7) Reservation of the sacrament started. (8) The feast of Corpus Christi was instituted in 1264. (9) Abuses such as using the sacrament for curing animals began. The idolatrous misuse of the Eucharist and the historical faith which resulted from a literal reading of Scripture left the people dissatisfied. Feeling that God must surely require more, they were led to works righteousness (CS II, 459:17–461:15).

69. CS III, 171:36–172:13.

church, in part because the true spiritual Church had always carried on despite these external trappings.[70]

Since the decline of the church had been gradual and the errors and abuses were so deep-rooted, the reform of the church would be a long, slow business, a fact which too many reformers failed to realize.[71] There were to be two stages.[72] The first had been negative, the Reformation of the letter. Man-made laws, doctrines, and customs which had grown up in the church had been dismantled, and here Luther had played the leading role. The Protestant literal word had been used against the Catholic literal word.

> Doctor Martin Luther's teaching was designed to tear out the errors which in times past had taken root in the papacy alongside the pure word of life of our Christian faith. It was the means through which the conscience was once again freed from the papal laws and unbearable burdens with which it had been weighted down. To do this, Doctor Luther used the dead letter to so identify and refute the man-made laws and tyranny which had usurped a place in God's affairs that everyone could grasp and understand it.[73]

The Lutherans were satisfied, and in their eyes the Reformation was complete.[74] But according to Schwenckfeld, it was plain that the reform of the church had only just begun. As Schwenckfeld described it, Luther had led the people out of Egypt into the desert and had left them there, calling it the Promised Land.[75] The Lutherans had gone too far, but yet not far enough. In their attack on man-made laws they had also brought divine law into disrepute, and as a result antinomianism was rife.

> It is as if someone coming upon a madman in chains freed him without curing the poor man, thus letting him run around to his own detriment and the detriment of others. Freeing the man would not be bad in itself. But if the situation doesn't allow one

70. CS II, 459:2–7.
71. CS II, 446:14–20. Crautwald also felt that the Reformation was only just beginning. Letter to Butzer, July 5, 1528, TA 7, 174:32–175:3.
72. CS II, 447:5–14.
73. CS III, 102:37–103:6. Cf. CS II, 680:11–681:1, 683:31–684:6.
74. CS II, 446:20–447:4, 683:14–30.
75. CS III, 105:27–30.

to help further, it might be better to have left the imprisoned mad-
man in bonds. Such is the case now. Formerly, the conscience
was generally too burdened and bound up. Now, after the dismantling of the prison, it has become insolent, wild, and negli-
gent. Since an outwardly pious life would result (and also to some
degree an accompanying fear of God), the earlier bearable burden
would be better than the insolence, wildness, and disobedience
from which nothing good can come. With Luther's present teaching, therefore, it is impossible for any improvement to take place.
Indeed, it is to be feared that the destruction of all discipline, wisdom, and honorableness will become ever worse.[76]

Schwenckfeld criticized Luther and his followers both for being too
hasty and zealous in their work of destruction and for tarrying for the
weak brethren.[77] Where the truth was known, church practice must
be made to conform without delay, especially with regard to the Mass.
But in many areas God's truth was not yet fully revealed. What the
Lutherans took to be the whole truth was in reality only the beginning
of God's revelation.[78] The fullness thereof would be achieved in the
second stage, the Reformation of the spirit, which was now at hand.[79]
The church was again to be endowed with spiritual judgment and to
assume visible form as in the early church, the church of the fathers.
The time of Luther and the Protestant literalists, servants of the letter,
was past; yet they refused to yield.[80]

And so he [Luther] opposes the true knowledge of Christ according to the spirit [*waren erkantnus Christi nach dem Geist*], erects
a new tyranny, and wants to bind men to his teaching. And to say
it right out, he has gone so far as to oppose the office of the Holy
Spirit, who, it is clear, plans to erect a Christian church [*christliche gemeine*] with the correct use of the sacraments, brotherly
admonition, ban, and consequent betterment of Christian living.[81]

76. CS II, 107:1–15.
77. CS III, 38:26–39:16; CS II, 533:28–534:17.
78. CS II, 640:17–24; CS III, 62:7–14. As Schwenckfeld admitted, he himself was not yet
informed on certain important issues (CS III, 62:7–14).
79. The new stage was based on the "innerliche Wort / das Geist und leben ist" (CS II,
447:5–14).
80. CS III, 103:14–35.
81. CS III, 103:26–35.

Luther, caught up in the letter of the Scripture, had fallen into the same error as the Catholics: employing force to bind men to externals. What had been torn down as transubstantiation had been rebuilt in the doctrine of a real presence.[82] The new spiritual Church, whose members were already scattered everywhere, even among the Catholics, was already heralded by disasters and *Heimsuchungen*. One cannot miss in Schwenckfeld's reconstruction the apocalyptic overtones whose urgency was fueled by Schwenckfeld's increasingly endangered position in Silesia.[83]

The brooding figure of Luther hovered over Schwenckfeld's efforts to formulate his own changing perception of the reform. It was far easier to write off Luther's teachings that it was to exorcise the man himself. The best that Schwenckfeld could do was to cast him as a fallen prophet, a man who had possessed a good part of the truth but had fallen again into error through pride and reliance on the secular powers.[84] "Such things began everywhere when they took over the government and would rather stand under its protection in security than under the cross of Christ."[85] The example of Luther was to serve Schwenckfeld well during his coming ordeal. The career of Luther represented to Schwenckfeld how the righteous may fall by doubting God's ability to achieve his aims without human assistance or even in the face of seemingly irresistible human opposition.

Isolation and Exile

Since the election of Duke Ferdinand as king of the Bohemians, the course of the truth has encountered obstacles, and under that king the Papists have grown in hope that shortly they will once again possess things as they did before Luther. Nor is their hope vain if the Lord does not overthrow their plan. They press hard

82. CS III, 105:34–106:4, 111:9–12.

83. CS II, 464:35–465:4, 650:25–30, 663:33–664:19; CS III, 103:26–35. In one passage Schwenckfeld ties the real presence to the last judgment, the devastation in the holy places, and divine visitations (CS II, 527:2–7).

84. CS III, 29:33–30:2, 106:18–20. On the relationship between Luther and his erstwhile followers, see Edwards 1975. According to Schwenckfeld, Luther had held spiritualist views but had later dropped them (CS II, 675:3–676:7, 677:19–30).

85. CS II, 677:27–30.

upon our prince [Friedrich]. They wish us to be exiled, or if possible, to be burned at the stake.[86]

Crautwald's evaluation of Liegnitz's position in April 1528 was for the
most part accurate and reflects the growing fear and uncertainty among
the Liegnitz clergy. The tacit alliance of Lutherans and Catholics was
beginning to bear fruit. Breslau and Ferdinand had come to an understanding, united in their enmity toward the radicals in Silesia.[87] Under
the pressure, the solidarity of the Liegnitz group began to show signs
of strain, and some defections occurred.[88] Luther contributed directly
with his Confession concerning Christ's Supper (February 1528), which
launched a lengthy attack on the Liegnitz theology of the Eucharist.[89]
By June Crautwald was making provisions for the event of a Lutheran
triumph; in particular he sought a place of refuge for the Liegnitz reformers in the empire, with their allies in Strassburg.[90]

The choice of that city shows that Crautwald, Schwenckfeld, and
the others were not totally isolated on the religious landscape. Since
1526 they had worked with success to strengthen and expand their ties
to the urban reformers of Switzerland and Southern Germany.[91] This
alliance, based on a common opposition to the real presence and, with
the exception of Zwingli, the acceptance of a middle position
on the Eucharist, was advertised by Oecolampadius's publication of
Schwenckfeld's Course of the Word of God (May 1527) and Zwingli's
edition of Schwenckfeld's Instruction (Anwysunge) (August 1528),
both done without Liegnitz's permission and over its objections.[92]

Schwenckfeld became increasingly less sanguine about the chances
of the success or survival of the Liegnitz reform. He viewed the
struggle then being waged primarily as a competition to win the loyalty
and services of the clergy. Compared to the violence, the "sword" of
the Catholics, and the soft life and security of the Lutherans, Liegnitz
had nothing to offer. The teaching of the Liegnitz school threatened
to obviate the necessity of a clergy altogether; clerics who agreed with

86. CLM 718, 392r–392v.
87. Engelbert 1963, 155; Meyer 1903, 146.
88. Konrad 1917, 87.
89. WA 26, 433–37.
90. TA 7, 171:32–36.
91. For a detailed discussion of Schwenckfeld's relationship with the southern theologians,
see McLaughlin 1985a.
92. On the latter work see Weigelt 1973, 95–97.

them ipso facto tended to cease being clerics.[93] As a result, even before the final blows, Schwenckfeld himself had ceased to rely on a reform of the clergy and had begun to look more and more for direct divine intervention.

The final act of Schwenckfeld's Silesian career began on August 1, 1528. The new royal mandate issued on that day was aimed at Liegnitz and the Anabaptists, with the former taking pride of place.[94] Upholders of the "new heresy against the holy sacrament of the real body and blood of our Lord Jesus Christ" were now to be handled in the same manner that the heretics against baptism (the Anabaptists) had always been—they were to be executed. All assemblies of the eucharistic heretics were also forbidden. Ferdinand followed up his decree by expelling or executing Protestant preachers in the upper Silesian districts of Glatz and Sprottau.[95] Friedrich of Liegnitz rejected the mandate, denying the necessity for it and questioning Ferdinand's right to interfere.[96] Nonetheless, Liegnitz no longer had the support of the other Silesian Protestants, and it was clear that Liegnitz could not face down the Catholic challenge alone.

For Schwenckfeld Liegnitz's untenable position created a political and personal crisis whose resolution completed his transformation from *homo politicus* to *homo religiosus*.[97] In long discussions with Friedrich their options had been reduced to two: they could either reestablish political ties with the Lutheran powers in Silesia and elsewhere through religious compromise, or they could hold firmly to the course already chosen and suffer the consequences. Although Friedrich would eventually choose the former, Schwenckfeld advised the latter. He suggested that Friedrich make preparations for the clergy who would suffer. Then Schwenckfeld wrapped himself in a fervent, excited resignation, placing his trust in God's purpose and power.

> God now gives the proper medicine. He stirs up the tyrants, allows persecution to oppress us in order to root out the abuses of the gospel among us and in order to punish us, and drive us into

93. TA 7, 159:7–28; CS III, 11:2–6, 109:7–20.
94. Engelbert 1963, 157; F. Bahlow 1918, 104; Knörrlich 1959, 144–45; Rosenberg 1767, 418–26.
95. Engelbert 1963, 158.
96. Rosenberg 1767, 85–88; CS XVIII, 34–38. It is possible that this reply, along with Breslau's, may have been submitted at a *Fürstentag* (CS III, 119).
97. For the following see Schwenckfeld's "Ratschlag" to Friedrich, ca. October 1528, CS III, 99–118.

corners to pray, so that the true gospel which is a word of the cross and a folly to the wise of the world may proceed powerfully in its proper way. And thus we must take heed that in this we not resist God, and we yield and make way for his well-deserved wrath and for Satan, until we grow stronger. We read in Acts that Paul let himself be lowered in a basket over the wall, and that in the first churches the gospel was not further preached than it was accepted. Where it is not accepted, that is a sure sign that God does not want it to be such a common thing.[98]

Schwenckfeld drew concrete and practical conclusions from his spiritualistic views. The Reformation should not be and was not in fact dependent on the support and protection of the secular authorities. God could take care of his own. The true Church, still lacking any visible institutions, was not vulnerable to attack or persecution. But the Lutheran church was, and Schwenckfeld fully expected that the Catholics would crush it. The Catholics in their turn would simply pass away, having already lost all credibility, especially among the young. After Armageddon, as it were, the faithful could gather again openly.[99]

Schwenckfeld's fatalism extended to his own future. "My heart is still happy and unafraid. I know that it can be worse at the end. But I will imitate [nachfolgen] Christ my Lord so that it goes for me in this world as it went for him."[100] The prospect of total defeat and personal martyrdom tested and annealed Schwenckfeld's convictions. Though he remained politically and socially adroit, there would always be a hard core of principle and expectation that refused to compromise, to dissemble, or to accommodate. He was like some sixteenth-century Bartleby: his obstinacy—for all its lack of aggressiveness, or perhaps precisely because of this lack—irritated, infuriated, and drove his opponents to distraction.

The campaign against Liegnitz continued unabated. In the middle of January 1529 Ferdinand rebuked Friedrich in a public letter.[101] He charged Schwenckfeld by name (he is styled Friedrich's "highest teacher and preacher") with holding heretical eucharistic views and,

98. CS III, 111:15–26. On the fate of the clergy: CS III, 112:16–22.
99. CS III, 108:4–109:25.
100. CS III, 112:7–10.
101. For the text see Rosenberg 1767, 434–38. The Breslau chapter received their copy on January 18 (Rosenberg 1767, 92).

referring to the Zurich edition of Schwenckfeld's *Instruction*, accused him of being a Swiss adherent and of holding erroneous and condemned christological doctrines. Schwenckfeld and his followers were to be punished with death in accordance with provisions of the August mandate. Schwenckfeld wrote an *Apology* in response, but it was quite unapologetic.[102]

It was clear to both Schwenckfeld and Friedrich that it was no longer safe or politic for Schwenckfeld to remain in Liegnitz. And so, on February 14, 1529, he left.[103] Friedrich dutifully reported this to Ferdinand on the fifteenth.[104] But Schwenckfeld did not leave Silesia, not just yet. Friedrich was careful to specify that Schwenckfeld had left *his* lands. Schwenckfeld remained in Silesia for two months, perhaps awaiting developments, but certainly making financial arrangements.[105] Having committed himself, it was difficult for him to flee his own "crucifixion," until he received a sign releasing him from his martyr's post. He reported that a divine voice ordered him to "Get up and out of the fire!" He fled Silesia on April 19, 1529.[106]

---

102. CS III, 391–431. The chronology of this document is confused. There was an edition published in June 1529 at Augsburg with a laudatory preface by Capito. It may have been published already at Liegnitz or personally submitted by Schwenckfeld at a *Fürstentag*. Cf. CS III, 617:27–618:8.

103. There was some confusion on the date since the *Corpus Schwenckfeldianorum* miscalculated Invocavit Sunday as February 16 (CS III, 440, 442, 469:20). F. Bahlow 1918, 113, 184 n. 200, corrected this error. The correction was adopted by S. Schultz 1946, 160, and Weigelt 1973, 63.

104. CS XVIII, 41–43; Rosenberg 1767, 441–42. Kadelbach 1860, 3, is wrong. Friedrich did not exile Schwenckfeld.

105. He lived off the income of his estates for the rest of his life (S. Schultz 1946, 3, 161). In 1554 Schwenckfeld recounted a financial "transaction" from this period which shows him in a more humorous light. "Many years ago while I was a member of the court of Duke George of holy memory at Brieg, I was called in confidence to a good friend. An adventurer credibly revealed to us with a divining rod where a treasure of 900 Hungarian gulden, as he said, was hidden in an old wall. But then he [the adventurer] said that it had not been given him to retrieve the treasure, and that it belonged to whomever God gave possession. Now, it remained there for many years. I felt as little temptation as the nobleman on its account. Later, when I had to emigrate, I was inspired by Satan: Say, the treasure has been preserved and given to you for provisions. I joined with two trusted companions (I was to receive half of the treasure) who hacked at the spot in the wall where the divining rod years before had dipped. That day they made a large hole. They decided to continue the next day. Around midnight Satan came, tore the treasure out, and threw down the walls into a pile right on our chamber. God wonderfully protected us. The innkeeper lost three horses which were below in the stalls. The bells were rung and all the peasants came running in the night. They had to run a ladder up to us so that we could climb down, since the stairs had collapsed." CS XIV, 282:34–283:18.

106. Thirty-two years later on his deathbed the same voice assured him that his name was written in the Book of Life (CS XVII, 1014:15–21).

Silesian Aftermath

The Catholics were distracted from their campaign in Silesia by the Turkish threat.[107] As a result of both Schwenckfeld's departure and the increased Turkish pressure Friedrich's stock rose again with Ferdinand, and he was even able to begin reordering the church in his lands.[108] Despite Schwenckfeld's advice, Friedrich II of Liegnitz pursued a steady, careful policy of *rapprochement* with the Lutherans. In 1529 he borrowed the services of another nobleman, Friedrich von Heydeck, from Albrecht of Prussia. Heydeck's task was to consolidate the church in Liegnitz. Instead of mastering the Schwenckfelder movement, however, Heydeck became a convert. When he returned to Prussia he was instrumental in spreading the Schwenckfelder message. Even the Prussian duke seemed favorably inclined. But the continuing pressure of the Lutheran clergy, the debacle at Münster (1535), and the death of Heydeck (1536) sealed the movement's fate in Prussia.

In Liegnitz, after the false start with Heydeck, Friedrich proceeded against the more radical Schwenckfelders. In the years after Schwenckfeld's departure Friedrich discharged a number of key Schwenckfelder ministers. This was a prelude to the introduction in 1533–35 of a new compromise Lutheran-Schwenckfelder church order. In 1537 Friedrich also began negotiations with the Schmalkaldic League. As a result the league extended its protection over Liegnitz in 1539, though Friedrich never actually joined the league. A few months later the last Schwenckfelder pastor, Johann Sigismund Werner, was relieved of his duties. The new church order (1542) enjoined adherence to the Augsburg Confession. Efforts to suppress the Schwenckfelders were not immediately successful, and strong Schwenckfelder communities were found in Silesia long after Schwenckfeld's death. After many vicissitudes a large group emigrated to America in 1734.

Schwenckfeld maintained close ties with the Liegnitz reformers, particularly Crautwald, and Friedrich, despite the latter's obvious shift toward Lutheranism.[109] In 1534 Friedrich asked Schwenckfeld's ad-

107. F. Bahlow 1918, 114.
108. The indispensable guide to the history of the Silesian Schwenckfelders is Weigelt 1973. For what follows see pp. 126–95.
109. He performed occasional errands for Friedrich. A cryptic remark dated July 18, 1531,

vice on the *Stillstand* and the various ministers in Liegnitz, and he invited Schwenckfeld to return.[110] Schwenckfeld made plans to go to Silesia in the early 1540s, only to have his hopes dashed in 1542.[111] His failure to integrate himself into the urban society of southern Germany was in part due to his expectation of eventually returning to Silesia.

In his first few years in Strassburg Schwenckfeld tried to influence events back in Silesia and prepare the way for his own return. In 1529 he republished his first *Apology*, now provided with an introductory letter from Wolfgang Capito. In January 1530 he published a second *Apology* in response to attacks by Johannes Faber. It was dedicated to Bernhard of Cles, bishop of Trent (1485–1539), Ferdinand's court chancellor and president of the king's privy council (*Geheim Rat*).[112] With this work Schwenckfeld attempted to split the Catholic party at the royal court, turning Cles against Faber, and to defuse the threat to himself and Liegnitz.[113] In effect he charged Faber with a kind of in-

---

in the Strassburg archives suggests that Schwenckfeld may have served as an intermediary for Friedrich with the city of Cologne (TA 7, 333:24–334:3). On July 1, 1529, Schwenckfeld sent Friedrich by way of Georg of Brandenburg a copy of the first treaty of Kappel (June 24, 1529), which he had gotten from the Strassburg Chancellory (CS III, 491:6–12, 27–29). Might Schwenckfeld have been the source of Friedrich's information about the Augsburg *Abschied* in December 1530 (Krämer 1977, 315)? Friedrich may have sent Popschütz his *Hofmarschall* as an observer, but not as a representative, because Silesian dukes were not princes of the empire (Weigelt 1973, 170).

110. Schiess I, 505–06 (Frecht to Blaurer, June 28, 1534) and Th.B. 7, 136 (Frecht to Butzer, June 26, 1534). Capito wrote on May 21, 1534, that Friedrich had often called on Schwenckfeld to return, but that he refused for fear of losing his religious freedom (TA 1, 992).

111. CS VII, 11; CS VIII, 231–33. The undated imperial passport in the Vienna archives may have been made out during negotiations after the Schmalkaldic War, rather than in 1542 as CS suggests.

112. "Vom waren und falschen verstandt unnd Glauben . . . Caspar Schwenckfelds andrer Apologia," CS III, 612–710. The dedicatory letter was signed January 1, 1530, but printing was not completed till February 24, 1530. On Cles see "Bernhard von Cles," *Allgemeine Deutsche Biographie* 4 (1876), 324–25; Jedin 1963, 251, 294, 373, 394–96, 561–62. Cles had placed the Bohemian crown on Ferdinand's head in 1527. In 1530 he was granted the cardinal's hat during the imperial coronation of Charles V in Bologna. Even the papal tiara seemed within Cles's grasp. He was the leading political and religious adviser to Ferdinand until his death in 1539. Faber inherited his mantle. Though a staunch Catholic, Cles enjoyed a reputation for Erasmian reasonableness and was associated with Catholics like Vergerio and Morone, who hoped for a peaceful reuniting of Christendom (Jedin 1963, 251; CS III, 613–14). Faber's attack ("*Doctor Johann Fabri. Christenliche ableynung des erschroecklichen yrrsal / so Caspar Schwenckfelder in der Schlesy / wyder die warheyt des hochwirdigenn sacraments leibs und bluts Christi / auffzurichten understandenn hat. M.D.XXIX.*") was published in Vienna by Johann Singriener on February 8, 1529 (Weigelt 1973, 102). On the controversy between the two men, see Vorburger 1983.

113. Schwenckfeld admitted as much (CS III, 618:9–22, 624:21–27). Cles had sat on a commission examining Breslau's religious reforms and was well acquainted with Silesian affairs

competent Lutheranism and claimed the role of Catholic defender for himself. Though the attempt failed, it showed Schwenckfeld's daring and pointed up his excellent intelligence concerning the royal court. He seemed always to have friends and informants in the camps of his enemies.[114]

He also sought to neutralize Lutheran enmity. He argued that mutual toleration and negotiation were the only proper ways to organize relations between competing religious factions.[115] This did not prevent sharp criticism. In his unpublished "Judgment" (*Judicium*) on the Augsburg Confession (circa 1530–31) and in other works he outlined the three areas in which he differed with the Lutherans.[116] He dis-

---

(CS III, 614). He also seems to have had little love for Faber. Johan von Kampen had sarcastically referred to Eck, Cochlaeus, Faber, and Nausea as Aleander's four evangelists. Cles agreed with this uncomplimentary assessment (Jedin 1963, 394). Schwenckfeld appealed to Cles to enter the middle way between papal fanatics and Lutherans. On Faber as an obstacle to reform, see CS III, 622:3–18; on good men among Catholics seeking the middle way: 622:26–39, 649:34–650:10, 654:21–29.

114. He was reported to have been entertained by nobles during a 1541 visit to Vienna. Frecht to Vadian, November 25, 1541, *Vad. Br.* 6, 87. Schwenckfeld also had an admirer in Dr. Johann Kneller, a lawyer and imperial counselor of Weil der Stadt CS VII, 63.

115. Schwenckfeld sent a copy of his second *Apology* to Georg, Markgraf of Brandenburg (July 1, 1529, CS III, 490–91). Georg was the most influential Lutheran prince in Silesia and was Friedrich's brother-in-law. With the *Apology* and a letter he also forwarded a copy of the first Swiss Treaty of Kappel (June 24, 1529). Schwenckfeld touted it as a model for all Christians. CS III, 491:6–12, 23–27. The Kappel "Landfrid" granted individual freedom but limited institutional reform. It was by no means as one-sided as Zwingli would have liked (Locher 1979, 362–63). Johannes Brenz, Georg's spiritual adviser, was quick to defend against Schwenckfeld and his spiritualism ("Brenz an Markgraf Georg zu Brandenburg," December 31, 1529, and "Brentii Depulsio eorum, quae Schuuenckfeldius in exegesin Brentii supra Johannem de sacramento adnotavit," Brenz 1868, 70–88). See also "Praefatio in Explanationem Amos Prophetaei" (1529–30?), Brenz 1974, 460–71. The "Depulsio" resulted when an unnamed subject of Georg requested Schwenckfeld's views on Brenz's 1527 commentary on John. Schwenckfeld's annotations were then shown to the Markgraf, who in turn passed them on to Brenz for comment. The unnamed friend of Schwenckfeld may have been Pastor Johann Hechtlein (TA 2, 160, 163f., 208). Cf. Brecht 1966, 260–64.

116. CS III, 859–940. On the mistaken belief that Schwenckfeld did not use the first printed German edition, CS tries to give a more precise dating of late 1530 or early 1531. That edition, according to CS, had 22 articles. But Schwenckfeld cites only 21, and the first German edition actually had only 21 articles. Schwenckfeld accurately (with allowances for different orthography and two scribal errors) transcribed the text. He also cited the catalogue of abuses which followed (CS III, 876). For the German edition of the confession, see Reu 1930, vol. 2, pp. 167–304, col. 4. CS also misinterpreted "sein Judicium uber die Augspurgischen Confession und derselbigen eingeleibte Artikul mitzutheilen" as meaning that Schwenckfeld's correspondents wanted a copy of the Confession in addition to his opinion of it. As I read it, they wanted his opinion of the Confession as a whole and also of its individual articles, which is precisely what Schwenckfeld gave them. On the "Judicium" see P. Eberlein 1955, 58–68. See also Schwenckfeld's reworking of Lazarus Spengler's "Eyn kurtzer ausszug / aus dem Bepstlichen rechten / . . . 1530" CS III, 757–811. Aside from the internal evidence which points to Schwenckfeld's authorship, both catalogues of Schwenckfeld's works (1561, 1595) list it. It was published by Schwenckfeld's printers, Schoefer and Schweintzer, in Strassburg. On the use of

agreed with the Lutheran teaching concerning the sacraments, the eucharistic real presence, and what he considered to be an *opus operatum* baptism. Second, he found fault with the Lutheran reliance on the secular authority and infringement on Christian freedom. Binding these two objections together was his uneasiness with the increasing Lutheran emphasis on the visible church. His rejection of the Augsburg Confession rested as much on his general belief that such documents were both useless and dangerous, as upon his detailed criticism of its contents. Because in Schwenckfeld's opinion these developments within the Lutheran community were never reversed, chances for a *rapprochement* remained small. Despite his efforts to mold Catholic and Lutheran opinion, Schwenckfeld was not sanguine. He advised his friends in Silesia to withdraw from the new Protestant tyranny, just as they had from the old Catholic tyranny. [117]

Although Schwenckfeld maintained his ties to Silesia, his letters, treatises, and books could not influence events in the same way that his personal presence in Silesia and at Friedrich's court had. Schwenckfeld's exile was a great loss for the Schwenckfelder movement. But his contributions to the struggle against Lutheranism and Catholicism had already won him enduring enmity and notoriety. His position on the Eucharist was specifically condemned by the Catholic *Confutation* of the Augsburg Confession, and all his writings were prohibited in the Council of Trent's *Index*, an honor shared only by Luther, Calvin, and Balthasar Hubmaier. [118] Not to be outdone by the Catholics, the Lutherans enshrined his name and teachings in the *Formula* and *Book of Concord*. [119]

Despite Schwenckfeld's close contacts with Silesia, and especially

---

secular authority compare Spengler, fol. F., lines 10–17, Fb 26–Fii 1; Fii 17–24, and Schwenckfeld, CS III, 783:20–23; 785:17–19, 786:15–17. On the sacraments: Spengler, Giii 18–Giiib 1, Giiib 6–11, Giiib 21–Giiii 11, and Schwenckfeld, CS III, 792:29–793:3, 793:14–794:11, 794:19–795:22. On the outward church: Spengler, Ciiii, Eb 25–26, and Schwenckfeld, CS III 770:14–771:35, 777:36–778:2.

117. Schwenckfeld wrote a confidential short treatise, "What the True Christian Church Is" (CS IV, 50–60). It is undated but a reference to Johannes Faber would seem to place it around 1530 (CS IV, 55:3–4). The fact that Faber is only identified in the margin as bishop of Vienna suggests that he may not yet have held that post when the treatise was written. Faber was made bishop in 1530. Though there is no explicit reference to Silesia, the mention of Faber and the concentration on Catholics and Lutherans applies to Silesia, not southern Germany. See especially CS IV, 54:1–22, 58:22–60:8.

118. Ficker 1891, 40–42. Schroeder 1978, 273.

119. Tappert 1959, 499, 632, 635.

Liegnitz, for many years, his fate in the 1530s was determined by events in southern Germany and Switzerland. His path had separated from that of his friends and colleagues. His future lay in the West of Germany, and he never returned to Silesia.

5 *Champion of Christian Freedom* (1529–1533)

Therefore, before everything else in religion, that Christian freedom must be preserved through which God the almighty in his mercy freed us from the tyrannical yoke of the papacy.—Schwenckfeld, 1530

For me, not a little in the things of faith is laid on the Christian freedom which the Lord wished to acquire for us with his blood.—Schwenckfeld to Butzer, June 8, 1535

Nothing good will ever be accomplished so long as faith and its consequences, as it should stand before God, are not left free.—Schwenckfeld to Leo Jud, September 10, 1533

The events leading up to his exile and the exile itself had a profound and enduring impact upon Schwenckfeld's character and position. Faced with suppression and personal catastrophe, he had rejected the allures of both popular uprising and state intervention to rescue the reform.[1] Exile set the seal on Schwenckfeld's dualism. It was the psychological moment around which he was to organize his life. It marked him as a true confessor of the faith, something which he never let his judges and opponents forget.[2] It gave him a certain advantage over those reformers like Butzer, Blaurer, and Frecht who had not yet tasted the bitter fruits of faith. Nonetheless, he never really forgave the Strassburg reformers for their role in causing his exile.[3] Their initial warm reception of him may have had an element of guilt in it. He had given up his homeland, his own house and castle, his social position

---

1. Cf. Schwenckfeld's "Bedencken" to Friedrich, CS III, 99–118, and "Von guten und boesen gewissen / anzeigunge auss heiliger Schrifft," February 16, 1929, CS III, 440–69. This would appear to be a letter-treatise on matters of practical ethics, probably addressed to the Liegnitz reformers on the occasion of Schwenckfeld's exile. On obedience to authority as a matter of conscience, 451:30–452:5; on the vagaries of God's economic and social ordinance, 460:26–463:5, 467:32–468:3.

2. See Schwenckfeld's "Protestacion" before the council at the Strassburg synod (June 12, 1533), CS IV, 789:15–18, which is repeated almost word for word in "Ain schrifft an die Burgermeister und Rhat zu Augsburg" (before May 23, 1534), CS V, 106:1–4; and in "Protestacion" to the Ulm council (November 3, 1536), CS V, 535:13–21. See also CS IX, 651:16–21; CS VII, 44:65sq; CS VIII, 608:24sqq; CS XV, 184:15–17.

3. See the Strassburg preachers' "Gegenantwurt" to Schwenckfeld's "Schutzschrift" (between October 10 and 19, 1533), TA 8, 159:32–160:13. Butzer and the others resented Schwenckfeld's repeated reminders on the matter. The sharpness of their comment also betrays a lingering sense of guilt.

and status in order to become a pilgrim. He was a foreigner on earth; his true homeland was heaven.[4]

The concrete result of this attitude was Schwenckfeld's lack of effort to become part of the society of southern Germany. He never sought citizenship or permission to dwell permanently in any of the cities in which he stayed.[5] He never bought a house or even leased one; instead he invariably stayed as a guest in the houses of friends, acquaintances, and relatives. It was his standing as a good "guest" that he defended before the city councils of Strassburg, Augsburg, and Ulm.[6] Except for the first four years at Strassburg (1529–33), for which we lack evidence,[7] Schwenckfeld spent his first eleven years in southern Germany constantly on the move. Since no more than a fraction of his travel was due to local government insistence, his wanderlust must have had its source in his own restlessness.

He faced city life with a measure of unease and incomprehension. The twin foci of his life in Silesia had been his own estate at Ossig and the ducal court just outside the walls of Liegnitz. His Silesian writings were peopled by priests, princes, nobles, and peasants, not burghers or merchants. He had even used the market economy as an earthly analog to God's inscrutable providence.[8] Schwenckfeld would never feel completely at home in an urban setting.

Initially he claimed no special call from God as prophet or pastor, insisting that he was a simple Christian confessing his faith, no more.[9] His adamant refusal to join any church and his desire to remain free to worship Christ as he saw fit must be placed in the context of his refusal to find a place in secular society. Given the communal ethos of

4. CS III, 460: 10–17, 651:16–21; CS IV, 40:36–41:24. In 1529 Zwingli recognized that Schwenckfeld's exile affected the way in which he dealt with others (TA 7, 282:10–15).

5. CS V, 148:20–28; CS VI, 546:28–30.

6. CS IV, 789:9–14; CS V, 105:24–29, 537:21–22, 540:24–26.

7. There is one intriguing document, a letter dated February 13, 1532, addressed to N.N. (CS IV, 519–56). A manuscript source says that it was written to "Etliche Guthertzige zu Strassburg" (CS IV, 519), thus assuming that Schwenckfeld was not in the city on that date. Document 128, a letter dated March 1532 and addressed to a young wife, does not indicate Schwenckfeld's absence from Strassburg. CS suggested it was for the wife of Graf Wilhelm von Fürstenberg. More likely it was to Margareta Scher, who married Klaus von Grafeneck in 1530 (Bernhardt 1972, vol. 1, p. 323). The three daughters of Peter Scher von Schwarzenberg, a Strassburg *Schirmburger*, were all Schwenckfelders (Bernays 1901, 47–52). In his letter of September 24, 1531, to Johann Bader, pastor of Landau, Schwenckfeld expressed the wish to discuss matters in person (CS IV, 243:4–35). Perhaps he did.

8. Schwenckfeld compared the mystery of God's inequitable distribution of wealth to the inexplicable mechanics of the yearly market (CS III, 420:29–421:24).

9. CS IV, 789:33–790:10; CS V, 106:22–52, 536:7–17, 29–34.

the southern German cities, his attitude was bound to meet a lack of understanding and hostility. That this was not universally the case, that he found adherents and protectors in the urban milieu, casts light on the inner life of those very closely knit societies.

In large part his noble status made it possible for him to stand outside the normal bonds of urban life. Though the nobility had been politically domesticated as patricians in the cities in which Schwenckfeld moved, social distinctions were jealously maintained. Schwenckfeld thought of himself as a noble and in dress and behavior he was easily identifiable as such. He was quick to claim the legal privileges and social precedence which were his due.[10] Many, perhaps most, of his friends and acquaintances were landed nobles or urban patricians. Non-nobles like Butzer and Frecht made much of Schwenckfeld's nobility; the guildsman Frecht could barely conceal his class consciousness, envy, and, one might go so far as to say, hatred. As a result social tension played a role in Schwenckfeld's problems with the clergy.[11]

Schwenckfeld's independence had a strong economic base. He was able to maintain the style of a nobleman and pursue his various activities because of the income that he continued to draw from his estates in Silesia.[12] He also received support for his numerous printing ventures and occasionally travel expenses from wealthy backers.[13] There is some evidence that he supplemented his income through business or investment.[14] At least until the Schmalkaldic War Schwenckfeld suffered no want and was able to indulge in two expensive pastimes— the purchase and the publishing of books.

The Schwenckfeld who arrived in Strassburg in 1529, however, was also a man left shocked and uncertain by his sudden exile. He feared

10. CS V, 107:11–14, 146:3–18, 147:1–13; CS VI, 546:16–27.

11. Wolfgang Capito complained that Schwenckfeld as a noble was used to being taken seriously and having adulators (Capito to Jakob Truchsess von Rheinfelden, May 21, 1534, TA 1, 992).

12. CS VIII, 608:7–19.

13. S. Schultz, pp. 306–07.

14. In his dealings with the councils of Strassburg, Augsburg, and Ulm he constantly referred to his "Geschäften" (CS V, 106:35–107:2, 146:9–22; CS VI, 546:28–30). An intriguing hint is found in Schwenckfeld's August 1535 letter to Butzer (CS V, 361). He informed Butzer that he was riding off to Augsburg to look after his affairs because Lucas Meuting had died. The Meutings were smaller-scale Fuggers. Did Schwenckfeld invest with them? Was he an agent for bankers? This would explain some of his traveling if true. In a letter of June 25, 1534, Gervasius Schuler of Memmingen warned Butzer that Schwenckfeld was returning to Strassburg in order to attack the ministers and "nonnullis laturus illic aliquot pecunias" (Th. B. 7, 133).

that he had spoken for himself and not for Christ. Had he left the Lord's school too soon? Should he choose confidants more carefully? Should he not wait for God's gifts to drive him forward again?[15] With the unauthorized publication of his works by Oecolampadius and Zwingli still rankling, Schwenckfeld decided to hold himself "in der Still[e]."[16] For the duration of his stay in Strassburg he limited his printed output to uncontroversial edificatory works and books against the Catholics and Lutherans in Silesia.

Nonetheless, it was impossible for Schwenckfeld to avoid attention. The fact that he was at once an exile for conscience' sake, a pious nobleman and active reformer, a published theologian and controversialist did not allow for anonymity. But even beyond that, his powerful personal presence compounded of tact, reserve, humility, thoughtfulness, and a muted enthusiasm, which were like glowing coals beneath the ashes, gave off real warmth.

He was attracted and attractive to Strassburg's radical community.[17] Because of a rare policy of consistent religious tolerance in the late 1520s, Strassburg had become the refuge for a rich variety of dissidents. Anabaptism, Spiritualism, and apocalypticism were rife in the city. Leading radical figures like Pilgram Marbeck, Melchior Hoffmann, and Sebastian Franck lived in the city or passed through Strassburg during Schwenckfeld's stay, and he got to know most of them. This heady theological potpourri nourished Schwenckfeld's own thought. Still shaken by his experience in Silesia, he was open and vulnerable to the beckoning fellowship of the Anabaptist communities. He in turn was woven into their eschatological expectations as one of the two prophets of the endtime, playing Enoch to Melchior Hoffmann's Elias.[18] Having found Catholicism and Lutheranism wanting, he now measured the worth of the Anabaptists.

15. Schwenckfeld to Jakob Kautz, July 19, 1529, TA 7, 242:25–244:24.

16. CS V, 148:5–6.

17. See McLaughlin 1985d: "Schwenckfeld and the Strassburg Radicals." Sixteenth-century Strassburg has received more attention from scholars than its importance merits. As a result there are many good works on the radical community there. Gerbert 1889 is still fundamental. Williams 1962 is also essential. But the best treatment of Strassburg's radicals is to be found in Deppermann 1979.

18. TA 8, 15–37. Interestingly Schwenckfeld once complained to Johann Bader that Elias wouldn't be heard if he appeared in their day (CS IV, 252:12–253:4, 254:8–25). It was also prophesied that Schwenckfeld, who had pleased the Lord greatly, would be granted an early death so that he might escape the coming time of tribulation. Johannes Baptista Italus, known as Venturinus, a Sienese and wandering prophet, stayed with Capito at the end of February

His relationship to the radicals was anomalous from the very first. It is hard to believe that he would ever have felt completely at home among the common people who tended to fill the Anabaptist ranks. But his position was made even more ambiguous by his close ties to the clerical and secular regimes. He served them as both an observer and in a sense a moderator of the radical scene.[19] He had standing in each camp but belonged to neither.

The Anabaptists presented a congenial and comforting companionship to a man who had been shaken loose from his supportive friends and like-thinking colleagues. They too had suffered for their faith, embracing exile and martyrdom, holding firm in the face of threats and blandishments. The fevered prophesying, the secret conventicles, the earnest pious conversation over meals—all this must have drawn Schwenckfeld to them. But he couldn't suppress a condescension toward their childlike credulity and hasty acceptance of self-proclaimed saints and prophets, their evanescent loyalties and groupings, their discreditable associations.[20] And as much as he praised them for their willingness to suffer and be scorned for the Lord, Schwenckfeld couldn't help suspecting that some of that scorn was well deserved and had little to do with Christ and his gospel. He must have asked himself if true Christians could not also be respectable; need they be bizarre? His sober formality must have made him stand out like a blackbird among peacocks.

There were substantive theological reasons as well for his decision, reached within a year of his arrival in Strassburg, to remain aloof but friendly with the other radicals. He had no taste for the apocalyptic fantasies of the Melchiorites. For him the Antichrist was not an individual, not even a conspiracy, but merely an ever-present temptation to rely on the material and the external, at the cost of the spiritual and internal.[21] The Anabaptists themselves fell under suspicion for their unwise obsession with water baptism. Schwenckfeld also found that

---

1530. After prophesying about Schwenckfeld he left Strassburg to visit Luther. The council provided him with some money to help defray expenses, TA 7, 254:9–17, 256:25–27.

19. On Schwenckfeld's conferences with Jakob Kautz, see TA 7, 242–46; 249:1–13. He also argued with the reconverted Nicolaus Guldi in January 1530 (TA 7, 252:7–13). And of course there were his conversations with Hoffmann. In an early draft of a letter to Simon Grynaeus (April 11, 1535), Schwenckfeld pointed out that "sovil ann mir weer den gemeynen man helffen Stillenn/wie ich auch offt gethan hab" (CS V, 293:11–19).

20. On Schwenckfeld's view of the Strassburg Anabaptists, see "Judicium de Anabaptistis," CS III, 830–34.

21. On these themes consult the articles by Walter Klaasen and Werner Packull in Erb 1985.

they accorded fallen human nature too much credit and failed to realize the extent of the disaster that the Fall had occasioned. But most
distressing for Schwenckfeld personally were their separatist impulses
and uncharitable treatment of nonmembers of their peculiar sects.
Schwenckfeld's refusal to join their ranks and to subordinate his beliefs
and actions to the demands of the community eventually led the Anabaptists, or at least those under the leadership of Pilgram Marbeck, to
shun him. This was a bitter experience for Schwenckfeld, and he
never forgave Marbeck. Their rejection only ratified his own decision:
Schwenckfeld would not be absorbed into any sect that he could not
lead. The movement that he did eventually found maintained a surprising autonomy vis-à-vis its progenitor—a fact which reflects
Schwenckfeld's personality.

There were others in Strassburg whose station in life and whose
manner would be more to Schwenckfeld's taste. In Wolfgang Capito,
a courtly figure and scholarly humanist, he almost found a worthy
substitute for Crautwald. Schwenckfeld lived in Capito's house for his
first two years in exile, but theological and ecclesiological differences
would deprive him of Capito's friendship along with that of most of the
other Strassburg clergy. His Strassburg residence brought him face to
face with the developing Reformed tradition. Having rejected the ex-
clusivistic church discipline of the Anabaptists, he was simply not
ready to accept Strassburg's state church. Because of religious principle
he lacked those with whom he would have felt most comfortable on a
personal and social level. Those who were attractive as religious
kindred were socially and personally distasteful. It was a formula for
isolation.

Judaic Tyranny and Christian Freedom

Schwenckfeld's first clash with his South German allies came in September 1529, when Ulrich Zwingli and Johannes Oecolampadius
passed through Strassburg on their way to the Marburg Colloquy with
Luther and Melanchthon.[22] Schwenckfeld and Zwingli came to words
over Schwenckfeld's Christology of the glorified Christ. But Christol-

---

22. Köhler 1953, 63. For Schwenckfeld's description, see CS XIV, 108:2–26; for Zwingli's
description, TA 7, 282:5–18. The two men stayed at the house of Matthaeus and Katharina
Zell, close friends of Schwenckfeld.

ogy would not again play an important part in Schwenckfeld's battle with his hosts until the end of the 1530s.

The real stone of offense was baptism and the related but larger issue of the nature and purpose of the church. Schwenckfeld's development had carried him from Lutheranism by way of a Reformed-style ecclesiology to an increasingly trenchant spiritualism. He might have been able to find a niche in Strassburg, however, if Martin Butzer, increasingly the leader among the Protestant clergy, had not pursued a diametrically opposed course toward greater institutionalization. The real cause of Schwenckfeld's alienation was Martin Butzer's drive for order, uniformity, and concord.[23] Quite different from the tolerant, moderate, irenic Butzer pictured by some historians was the Butzer who emerges from his dealings with dissidents and colleagues alike during the 1530s. A devious, none too scrupulous manipulator of men and ideas, who threatened the weak and fawned on the powerful, the Butzer with whom Schwenckfeld clashed was more the consummate political churchman and ecclesiastical statesman than pastor or theologian.[24] Schwenckfeld eventually found it impossible to forgive Butzer's theological wanderings.

> From this alone one might easily recognize that with him [Butzer] it is nothing but deceit and falsehood, that he pretends one thing outwardly and believes something else in his heart. For if he should fully explain himself and give an accounting, then an entire community [gemaind] could easily judge that he either understands nothing of this matter or he is acting against his own conscience.[25]

Butzer was driven by the desire to erect, maintain, and defend a disciplined body of Christians bound together by charity. It was this

23. Maron 1961a, 161, puts the beginning of the split between Schwenckfeld and Butzer too early, in 1525. It was only in 1525 that Schwenckfeld came to hold generally the same eucharistic views as Butzer, and it was from this common spiritualistic interpretation that Butzer later departed.

24. For a standard depiction of the "tolerant" Butzer see Chrisman 1967, 83–88. Abray 1978, 73–75, points out that the tolerant Butzer was the product of the later Sturm-Marbach debates. Sturm wished to brand Marbach's orthodox intolerance an innovation by emphasizing Butzer's tolerance. In fact, as Abray quite rightly insists, Butzer's move toward Lutheranism was from the beginning bound up with his taking a hard line against dissenters; see also Mitchell 1960, 254 n. 2, 382. His fawning on Luther at Wittenberg in 1536 disturbed Musculus and even the rabid Lutheran Johann Forster (Germann 1894, 140). Gerbert 1889, 40, had portrayed Butzer as a "Kirchenmann."

25. CS V, 157:16–25.

corpus christianorum itself rather than any particular doctrines which it might hold that commanded Butzer's allegiance.[26] Unity and concord were the lifeblood of the Christian community, and Butzer was determined that those who threatened it must be either placated or expelled.[27] From this viewpoint Butzer's unbending opposition to the Strassburg dissidents and his conciliatory overtures toward Luther are parts of one campaign and not contradictory elements in an uncoordinated theological personality.

Already in 1527, two years before Schwenckfeld's arrival, there was evidence of change in Butzer's attitude toward the Anabaptists. The arrival of Hans Denck, Michael Sattler, and Ludwig Haetzer in the preceding year had awakened Butzer to the danger which they and others like them posed for the church.[28] But it was the close friendship between Wolfgang Capito and one of his houseguests, Martin Cellarius, that provoked Butzer's abrupt about-face. Until 1527 the Strassburg reformers, faced by a still-potent Catholic party, were agreed on a basically spiritualistic interpretation of the sacraments.[29] They wanted to counteract the tendency to place too great a weight upon the external sacraments to the detriment of God's internal action. Specifically, they denied baptism and the Eucharist any role as means of grace. Instead, they described them as signs announcing the internal reception of God's gifts, an internal reception determined not by any outward ceremony, but by God's eternal predestination.[30] Since Capito and Butzer were quite certain that neither baptism nor the Eucharist were *sine qua non* for salvation, they allowed a measure of freedom in their use. In 1524 Butzer even suggested a *Stillstand* for those confused about the Eucharist. With regard to baptism, both he and Capito admitted that infant baptism should not be imposed upon unwilling

26. The best treatment of Butzer's view of the church is Courvoisier 1933. "Ce n'est pas sans raison que l'on a pu dire de Bucer qu'il n'avait pas à proprement parler un système théologique (ce que est exagéré) mais qu'il avait surtout une ecclésiologie" (Courvoisier 1933, 69).

27. Cf. Kittelson 1973.

28. Denck was only driven out after a disputation with Butzer (Deppermann 1979, 163). The disputation was held against the council's wishes, and Denck's expulsion afterward was at Butzer's suggestion. It was Butzer who first appreciated the danger which the Anabaptists might pose (Chrisman 1967, 181).

29. Chrisman 1967, 180; Courvoisier 1933, 54–56, 74–75; Deppermann 1979, 152–54; Krüger 1970, passim; Gerbert 1889, xi; Williams 1962, 249–50.

30. Still the best treatment of Butzer's early theology is Lang 1900. For his sacramental teachings, see pp. 207–88.

parents and that charity and Christian freedom called for tolerance in the matter.[31]

In 1527, however, just at the time Schwenckfeld was entering his own more spiritualistic phase, Capito and Butzer began to go their separate ways. In July Capito provided an introduction for Martin Cellarius's *The Works of God (De operibus Dei)*, a work which Schwenckfeld and Crautwald praised warmly, and which had a thoroughgoing spiritualistic interpretation of the church and the sacraments.[32] Butzer, who had begun to agree with Zwingli about the danger of the Anabaptists and the necessity of infant baptism, was particularly worried by what he interpreted as Capito's drift toward Anabaptism.

> It seems scriptural to us to baptize infants. But out of charity, if a church has become accustomed to baptizing adults, it is possible to bear postponement of baptism for a while. The contrary appears scriptural to him [Cellarius], that is to baptize adults, but that it is possible for infant baptism to be dispensed until the churches are better informed.[33]

Since Cellarius's position was also that of Capito and Schwenckfeld, Butzer in rejecting it strained his friendship with Capito and foredoomed his relationship with Schwenckfeld. Through 1527 and 1528 Butzer became increasingly convinced of the validity of Zwingli's equation of baptism and circumcision. This in turn made Butzer's attitude toward the Anabaptists more rigid. The need to unite the "orthodox" against the Anabaptist menace also lay behind Butzer's attempts at agreement on the Eucharist with Luther.[34]

Butzer's position within the city, and that of the Protestant clergy as a whole, was also undergoing change just as Schwenckfeld came to

31. On *Stillstand*, Mitchell 1960, 17. On baptism, Lang 1900, 220–21; Röhrich 1831, vol. 1, p. 328; Usteri 1884, 456–525.

32. For Capito's introduction, see TA 7, 116–21. Crautwald wrote Bucer (April 28, 1528) of his approval of Cellarius's work (TA 7, 156:8–16). On Cellarius see Gerbert 1889, 64–72; Deppermann 1979, 169–70.

33. Butzer to Zwingli, September 26, 1527, Lang 1900, 233 n. 1.

34. On Butzer against the Anabaptists: TA 7, 126:23–127:35, 149:14–151:5. On Butzer's agreement with Zwingli: Lang 1900, 224–32. On Crautwald's and Schwenckfeld's appalled reaction: CLM 718, 393r–393v, 394v; TA 7, 167:14–169:11, 175:25–176:22; CS III, 79:19–33, 80:19–82:9. On Butzer's shift on the Eucharist: McLaughlin 1985a and Köhler 1924, 791. In later years Butzer also touted eucharistic concord as the best weapon against the "Epicureans" (Lienhard 1981, 39).

Strassburg. On February 20, 1529, the city council finally succumbed to clerical pressure and popular agitation and abolished the Catholic Mass in Strassburg.[35] This was the last popular success the Protestant reformers enjoyed in that city. The preachers and pastors of Strassburg began to shift their locus of power and support and to become increasingly identified with the council. Until this event Butzer, Capito, and Matthaeus Zell had been insurgents relying upon popular support to force the pace of reform against a cautious and divided council. The identification of preachers and magistracy was not achieved immediately; only with the synod of 1533 and the decrees of 1534–35 would it come close to completion. But almost immediately the Protestant reformers began behaving as members of an established church, acting as servants and consultants to the magistrate, cooperating and working with the secular authorities rather than agitating from without.[36] The co-opting of the reformers allowed—and required—their reliance upon the magistrate in order to proceed against the Anabaptists and to construct a new church order. This goal was neither popular nor unpopular. There would be no street disturbances or mass petitions, no threat of civic unrest if the preachers' demands were not met. Most of the population would accept, but not rejoice in, these measures. There remained many fervent nondissident Protestants in Strassburg, but the enthusiasm of the early popular reform movement quickly dissipated. The development of the church thus mirrored that of the state—an uneasy, unhappy, and in some ways ineffective transition from *Gemeinde* (community) to *Obrigkeit* (lordship).[37] The battle between Butzer and Schwenckfeld would be fought in the salons and council chambers, not in the streets.

Strassburg's abolition of the Mass also affected the city's political standing in Germany. As a consequence its representatives received a frosty welcome at the second Diet of Speyer (1529).[38] Strassburg, more than any of the other Protestant states who had to face a revived Catholic party and a determined Charles V, must have felt increasingly iso-

35. Chrisman 1967, 172, 176.
36. In the wake of the Schmalkaldic War and the imposition of the Interim, Butzer and other pastors became involved in a popular movement to oppose the Interim and to erect a more Christian community (Bellardi 1934). See also Brady 1978, 259–90.
37. The best treatment of the general issue of shifting urban constitutional powers is Naujoks 1958.
38. King Ferdinand refused to allow Daniel Mieg, Strassburg's representative, to take his seat on the Council of Regency (Ranke 1847, vol. 3, p. 176).

lated. An alliance of Protestants, which at Saxony's insistence had to be based upon common doctrine, had become a political necessity. Butzer's and Strassburg's quest for concord, therefore, was fueled in large part by fear of the emperor. Schwenckfeld was very much aware of this fact.[39]

The Speyer diet also passed a decree (April 23, 1529) against the Anabaptists which revived imperial laws prescribing death. It was accepted by the Lutherans.[40] Though the decree had no immediate practical effect upon Strassburg's treatment of the Anabaptists, it clearly marked the boundary of prudent religious experimentation. Strassburg would strive to remain within the pale of orthodoxy and to distance itself from the taint of Anabaptism.

When Schwenckfeld arrived in Strassburg in May 1529, therefore, the political and religious climate was deteriorating for the radicals. Having immediately grasped the situation, he was pleased when the Marburg Colloquy (October 2–4, 1529) failed to build bridges to the safety and security of Lutheran respectability.[41] By 1530 Butzer's fears for Capito and suspicions of Schwenckfeld were aroused. He undoubtedly saw Schwenckfeld succeeding Cellarius as Capito's evil genius.[42] Because Schwenckfeld maintained a careful public silence, Butzer was forced to draw Schwenckfeld out on the issue of baptism and compel him to take sides.[43] Perhaps Butzer hoped to win him over; more likely he wished to expose Schwenckfeld as an Anabaptist.

The resulting controversy, which involved a number of Zwinglian reformers and even Zwingli himself, made clear the unbridgeable gap separating Schwenckfeld and the developing Reformed consensus of

39. "Ich besorg warlich (Mein Leo) Ir wurden heute vil sein die es in solchem falle villieber mit seynem gegenteill denn mit jhm hillten das nur die kirche gros wurde und dz man frid hett und einig weer (Ich wil itzt nicht sagen das man das creutze vermitte) Denn Ich hab wol gesehenn wie es sider des Keysers bejwesen Inn dem hohen herrlichen Artickel vom sacrament is ergangen." Schwenckfeld to Leo Jud, July 5, 1533, CS IV, 808:11–19.

40. Williams 1962, 238.

41. CS IV, 45:30–46:13. The passage also suggests that Schwenckfeld was accused of disturbing the unity of the Strassburg preachers by pointing out contradictions between past doctrinal statements and the present policy of achieving concord. Capito had not been an enthusiastic supporter of the effort either. Kittelson 1975, 153.

42. Schwenckfeld's criticism of Butzer's Confessio Tetrapolitana probably did not help. On March 23, 1556, Johann Schweintzer, at one time Schwenckfeld's printer in Strassburg, confessed that he had gotten to know Schwenckfeld at Capito's house in 1531, and because of Schwenckfeld's disapproval of the Confessio Tetrapolitana, he, Schweintzer, had suspended his observance of the sacrament, which suspension he had maintained from that time on (CS IV, 643).

43. CS IV, 242:36–246:9. Cf. CS V, 317:25–27, 320:4–8.

southern Germany and Switzerland.[44] Schwenckfeld rejected infant baptism as an abuse equivalent to that of the Catholic Mass. Water baptism conveyed no benefits and was not an initiation; it was an individual profession of faith and a confession of benefits (the inner baptism) already received.[45] In baptism, as in the Eucharist, inner must precede outer if the outer form is to have any meaning. Rebirth, penitence, and faith had to occur before the outward sacrament; otherwise it was a vain and empty thing.

Had infant baptism stood alone, Schwenckfeld might well have remained silent. But the arguments which Zwingli, Butzer, and others used to defend the practice threatened, in Schwenckfeld's opinion, to corrupt the very nature of the church and robbed Christ of his unique role in salvation. In response to Schwenckfeld's insistence that baptism must be accompanied by present faith, Zwingli had argued that the mystery of predestination, when properly understood, overcame the objection. Baptism was a pledge to raise a child in the knowledge of Christ, a knowledge which the church possessed and dispensed. Only the elect would accept that message unto faith and salvation. Predestination obviated the necessity of present faith among Christians, as it had among the Israelites, whose circumcision was the equivalent of the Christian sacrament. In the New Testament, as in the Old, the church was allowed and required to use coercion if necessary so that all of "Israel" became part of the covenant.

As for parents, they are compelled to educate their children according to the teaching of the church [magisterium ecclesiae], as it was formerly said in Deuteronomy 31, in order that among all Christians the custom of educating and teaching might be preserved. For who does not see that the Catabaptists nowadays seduce many? And that unless the teaching of the church opposed it, many would not offer their children to the public teaching of

44. "Questiones de baptismi sacramento," CS III, 846–58. CS dates it ca. October 1530. He had sent another set of eighteen articles to the pastor of nearby Landau, Johann Bader (CS IV, 70). The articles are lost. Schwenckfeld later wrote a very long letter (September 24, 1531) taking issue with Bader and by implication Zwingli and Butzer (CS IV, 240–61). On Schwenckfeld's baptismal teaching, see Knoke 1959; Kriebel 1968; Urner 1948. Zwingli wrote a "Responsio" which was not published until after Zwingli's death, and even then without mentioning Schwenckfeld by name. "Questiones de sacramento baptismi a Docto quodam propositae Huldrico Zuinglio," Schuler and Schulthess, vol. 3, pp. 563–88.

45. CS III, 849:8–11, margin; 849:19–27.

the church. And thus would arise as many disagreements as there were insolent smatterers [*contumaces scioli*].[46]

The Church of God was the people of God, the army of God, and its members had to be uniformly trained and disciplined.[47]

In his defense of infant baptism, Zwingli brought together the three elements which, for Schwenckfeld, branded reformed Protestantism as an attempt to "erect a new Judaism under the appearance of the gospel, and bring a new yoke of servitude for the consciences that Christ had freed with his blood."[48] It abrogated Christian freedom, it reestablished the Old Testament law which Christ had overturned, and through the use of predestination and the identification of circumcision and baptism it threatened to make the life, suffering, and resurrection of Christ superfluous.

Had the Jews along with their children generally possessed the Holy Spirit, rebirth, grace, and justification, why should Christ have suffered? For what reason was Christ's suffering? What had it accomplished? Again, if forgiveness of sin was in the Law and in John's baptism, why must Christ shed his blood? You come with your predestination, climb so high in the hidden judgment of God that you lose Christ, his passion, his Holy Spirit, indeed his entire dispensation, and the fullness of time as well. As if he had accomplished nothing more with his coming in the flesh than to preach, etc. That makes a mere prophet out of Christ. You can't deny it since you consider the office, preaching, baptism, and the entire career of Christ as equal to John's.[49]

They had made the Christian church into a Jewish synagogue.[50] By equating baptism with circumcision they had imposed a new law and abrogated Christian freedom. "They [the Zwinglians] say: Infant baptism is free, but we will not suffer anyone who does not baptize them

46. Schuler and Schulthess, vol. 3, p. 587. Interestingly, though Zwingli here defends coercion of the parents, he bypassed Schwenckfeld's earlier objections that no coercion or legal force should be used to force individual belief (p. 579).

47. Schuler and Schulthess, vol. 3, p. 587.

48. CS IV, 244:29–245:2.

49. CS IV 245:7–20. See also 246:3–12, 249:12–37.

50. CS IV, 246:27–28. It should be noted that despite Schwenckfeld's fears of Judaizing, there seems to be no animosity toward the Jews, either biblical or contemporary. One must assume that Schwenckfeld shared in the common prejudices against the Jews, but nowhere in his writings do I find him commenting upon them favorably or unfavorably. On Schwenckfeld's views concerning the two Testaments see Gottfried Seebass's lecture in Erb 1985.

[i.e., infants]. That is a pretty freedom. God help that your charity and faith be better."[51]

The harsh treatment meted out to the Anabaptists in Zurich and the violent rhetoric directed at them elsewhere also helped convince Schwenckfeld that the South German and Swiss reformers erred. For shedding innocent blood David had been forbidden to build the temple; could the reformers expect anything different from God?[52]

Having rejected infant baptism, Schwenckfeld proceeded to refuse rebaptism.[53] Though clearly less dangerous than the Zwinglian baptism, the Anabaptist sacrament also made too much of the outer symbol. Instead Schwenckfeld extended the eucharistic *Stillstand* to baptism and conducted some discreet advertising for this alternative.[54] This, more than his position itself, made him a threat to the new order.

At the heart of the problem, for Schwenckfeld, was Zwingli's and Butzer's vision of the church. For Zwingli the church had precedence over the individual believer both ontologically and chronologically.[55] Individual Christians were Christians by virtue of their membership in either the visible or invisible churches. For Schwenckfeld the church was merely a gathering of believers; the individual preceded the church. Schwenckfeld's focus was on individual faith, individual self-discipline, and individual salvation. He simply lacked any sympathy for the ideal of *corpus christianorum* which ran throughout Zwingli's and Butzer's thought. Schwenckfeld was an ecclesiological nominalist; he thought the Church should be collected, not built.[56]

Since his time in Silesia, Schwenckfeld's teaching on the baptism had achieved a new clarity and concreteness. Infant baptism was an error. Adult baptism, or much more accurately, believer's baptism was the norm.[57] But even believer's baptism was not necessary or even

51. CS IV, 252:8–15, margin.
52. CS IV, 258:34–259:17.
53. CS IV, 257:13–18.
54. On the *Stillstand*, see CS III, 815:38–816:3. He prepared a German treatise that provided his friends and followers with a detailed explanation and defense of their reservations concerning the sacrament ("Von der kindertauff," CS III, 812–24). It must have been written after May 1, 1530, because it cites a work by Justus Menius of that date, but a more precise dating than 1530–31 is not possible. The use of the first-person singular when referring to "mein kind" would exclude the childless Schwenckfeld (CS IV, 815:9–25). Perhaps it was written for Jakob Held von Tieffenau, who was eventually expelled for refusing to baptize his children (TA 8, 473:2–6; CS V, 359).
55. "Ordinem, ut antea dictum est, sic servamus ut, ubi nulla est ecclesia, nulla sunt membra Christi . . ." (Schuler and Schulthess, vol. 3, p. 586).
56. See, for instance, CS III, 854:19–20.
57. Schwenckfeld's opposition to infant baptism waxed and waned, but it was intensified

helpful in achieving salvation. It played no role at all in justification.[58] Concentration on water baptism, be it Catholic, Lutheran, Reformed, or Anabaptist, was misleading. It was inner baptism which was constitutive. Even though in the context of the baptismal controversy Schwenckfeld would emphasize inner *baptism*, he preferred terms like rebirth, regeneration, or the indwelling Christ.[59] In a sense there was only one inner sacrament, one inner event: spiritual rebirth. The other ways of envisioning that event, the symbols of baptism and eucharist, tended to divert attention from the unique ongoing spiritual process.

Schwenckfeld's denial of any salvific role for baptism was based, as was his criticism of the Lutheran and Catholic Eucharists, on *sola fide* justification. Biblicistic arguments about the actions and words of Christ and the Apostles—whether they had in fact baptized children or ordered it done—were clearly secondary to Schwenckfeld's belief that *sola fide* justification made infant baptism senseless. But unlike the Anabaptists and the Zwinglians, he did not discover a new raison d'être for baptism in the construction or reinstitution of the church. Schwenckfeld never viewed baptism, infant or adult, as either an initiation or a ticket of admission into the visible church. Baptism was an individual confession of one's faith in Christ. It had no ecclesiological goal.

All of the contending parties from Catholics to Anabaptists fell into the same error in one way or another. By seeking to defend infant baptism or by lending too much importance to water baptism they were all thinking like the Jews of the Old Testament. Particularly alarming to Schwenckfeld were the South German developments in this regard. More than any others, reformers like Butzer and Zwingli were Judaizing.[60] Their use of predestination diminished and demeaned the role

during his visit to Augsburg, 1533–34, because of Lutheran insistence on infant baptism. But in 1554 he went so far as to admit that infant baptism was unforbidden patristic usage (Urner 1948, 333). Though adult baptism was preferable, infant baptism was tolerable if, and only if, a clear understanding of the real inner baptism was emphasized.

58. Kriebel 1968, 19, makes this clear.

59. Maier 1959, 25.

60. Friedman 1983 argues that reliance on rabbinic exegetes like Kimchi and Ibn Ezra did tend to "Judaize" Protestant theologians like Butzer to an extent not normally admitted in the literature. Already in 1528 Crautwald was quite concerned with the Strassburger's use of rabbinic commentaries (Crautwald to Capito, June 29, 1528, TA 7, 170:15–171:23). Crautwald was probably responsible for crystallizing Schwenckfeld's distrust of Judaizing trends in Butzer and Zwingli. As a Hebraist himself Crautwald had had to make a decision on the use of the Old Testament. It was he, not Schwenckfeld, who first rejected the identification of circumcision and baptism (TA 7, 168:25–36). Both Schwenckfeld and Crautwald had also disputed with Sabbatarian Anabaptists in 1528 (Hasel 1972; Weigelt 1973, 113–119, 124–26). Schwenckfeld's

and majesty of Christ. In time their Christology would reveal itself to Schwenckfeld as not merely Nestorian, but even Arian. Their identification of baptism and circumcision showed their intentions. Their "church" would be a Judaic tyranny. In defending the freedom of a Christian, Schwenckfeld was defending the Christian character of the Reformation itself.

Schwenckfeld's own views on the proper form and organization of the Christian church were less clear, less developed, than was his criticism of others. This has occasioned a sharp disagreement among scholars. Did he truly and effectively deny the validity and usefulness of an external church, thus paving the way for individualism, separatism, quietism, and indifference or passivity?[61] Or did he retain a vision of the visible church however much deemphasized?[62] Had he been consistent and drawn the logical conclusions from his own principles, he perhaps would have agreed with Sebastian Franck that Christians had matured and outgrown the visible church of the Apostles.[63] But in fact he did not. He eagerly awaited God's intervention and the reinstitution of the apostolic forms. Schwenckfeld's distinction between contemporary reality and future hopes is essential for understanding his vision of the church, albeit a vision which never achieved full clarity and detail.[64]

The future church would be voluntary, but composed of believers and hypocrites alike, with the eucharistic ban used to exclude the manifestly sinful.[65] The Eucharist and baptism would of course be properly understood and used. Leadership would be provided by two

---

letter to Leonhard von Liechtenstein of Nikolsburg (January 1, 1532), though ostensibly directed at the Sabbatarians, seems in fact to be only a veiled attack on those reformers who would use the secular authority to impose a Judaic church order (CS IV, 444–518). Crautwald's contribution to Schwenckfeld's outlook on baptism is less easily determined. Schwenckfeld seems to have solicited his opinion. CS III, 835–44, contains a short treatise on the subject from Crautwald's pen. Nevertheless, Crautwald was considerably more hostile to the Anabaptists and even contributed to Friedrich's decision to expel the Anabaptists from Liegnitz (Weigelt 1973, 125). Schwenckfeld's personal experience in Strassburg played a determining role in his attitude. Schwenckfeld also accused his Catholic opponent Faber of relying on Jewish commentators (CS III, 682:5–683:5).

61. Maron 1961a, 140, 169; E. Gerdes 1967, 131–32; Köhler 1913a, 211.
62. Ecke, 1911, 252; Friedmann 1949, 83–84; Holl 1923, 459–60; Sippel 1911, 966.
63. Sippel 1911, 957, noted Schwenckfeld's inconsistency.
64. Ecke 1911, 235–36, 323; Heyer 1939, 45; Williams 1962, xxviii. An important reason Schwenckfeld's ecclesiology remained undeveloped was that he never had the chance actually to organize and run his own church.
65. Schwenckfeld denied that the church was a "Platonic city" (CS III, 909:23–910:9, 913:19–915:25). Cf. CS III, 825:4–11, 829:18–34; CS IV, 767:11–768:12; CS V, 139:18–26.

types of ministers: apostles or ministers of the word, and ministers of Scripture.[66] The latter would be men like the church fathers and saintly figures throughout history who expounded the Bible for the benefit of Christians. The former, the apostles, would be called of God, and like the various authors of Scripture, would enjoy direct divine inspiration. They, like the first Apostles, would receive an increase, that is, a marked visible improvement in doctrine, church order, and morals, all of which would invariably accompany their efforts. This charismatic, pneumatic leadership was absolutely essential to a truly apostolic church order; God must grant his spirit.

Schwenckfeld expected that the day was not far off when such apostles and such churches would arise, because Luther had been a sign of things to come.[67] But that was still in the future. Though there were ministers of Scripture, there were no apostles. Nor did Schwenckfeld claim that vocation for himself. In the meantime true Christians remained scattered throughout the world awaiting God's pleasure. Where individual Christians were known to each other they should form conventicles, consoling, exhorting, instructing each other. The conventicles were not to be churches or sects. While denying that the Lutherans, Reformed, and Anabaptists embodied the true visible church, Schwenckfeld could not yet present an alternative to which Christians could adhere. As a result he did not usually advise separatism. One remained a part of the local church order while maintaining one's freedom.[68] The *Stillstand* on baptism and Eucharist, the decision neither to accept nor to reject formal confessions of faith did not constitute separatism. Schwenckfeld's refusal to accept Butzer's either/or—either accept the church of Strassburg or condemn it—was based on his sense of expectation. The church of Strassburg was not *yet* Christian; no church was. Schwenckfeld was willing to wait on the Lord.

For all of Schwenckfeld's expectation, what he awaited was not eschatological, and this explains his patience.[69] The history of God's church was cyclical, with periods of ignorance punctuated by divine

---

66. CS V, 129:32–131:5. Lashlee 1969, 182–83, 186, 190. Crautwald may have been the source for this distinction (CS VI, 204:17–34, 212:33–36; CLM 718, 488r–488v). The relationship to Melchior Hoffmann's concern for apostolic messengers of the end time is undecipherable, but the similarity is strong.
67. Ecke 1911, 323, 326–34; CS V, 110:7–9.
68. Ecke 1911, 228–33.
69. Ecke 1911, 75–76; P. Eberlein 1955, 60; Furcha 1972, 254.

visitation (*Heimsuchung*) and knowledge.[70] Nor was there any political or social element. The worldly status quo would not change, only the church. The apocalypticism of Müntzer and Münster was completely foreign to Schwenckfeld's thought. The actual form that Schwenckfelder conventicles took reflected Schwenckfeld's convictions. The sacraments were not reinstituted nor was the ban exercised. Believers met in small prayer, prophecy, and Bible study sessions, awaiting a new Pentecost.[71] Both the expectant conventicles and the future church had no use for a Christian magistrate, the secular sword in the service of the church. During Schwenckfeld's years in Strassburg, his views on church and state developed and were clarified. The efforts of the reformers to suppress dissent and the appeals and arguments of the suppressed dissenters lent Schwenckfeld's position both theoretical sophistication and the concreteness and piquancy of personal experience. His vision of tolerance was more radically Augustinian than the Lutheran idea from which it had grown. It would bear important fruit later in the sixteenth century both in Holland and in Brandenburg.[72] Schwenckfeld's teachings constituted the most thoroughgoing specifically Christian ideal of religious toleration produced by the Reformation.

Schwenckfeld's voice was but one in a chorus raised against the theory and practice of Strassburg's budding state church.[73] Butzer and his colleagues had constructed a bold rationale for their actions, and Schwenckfeld's response can be understood only against the background of its unyielding militancy.[74] Butzer and company insisted that

---

70. CS III, 659:14–18.

71. The Schwenckfelders in Strassburg seem to have fasted and then gathered for prayer and prophesying (CS IV, 78:14–28). The *Confession of Sins* was probably published while Schwenckfeld was in Strassburg (Weigelt 1974/75, 606–08. Capito to Jakob Truchsess von Rheinfelden (May 21, 1534), TA 1, 990: ". . . und also warten mit zweien oder dreien, so seins verstands sich auch anmassen, bis der h. geist wider keme wie am pfingstag zu Hierusalem."

72. Kühn 1923, 140–41. Cf. Wiebe Bergsma, "Schwenckfeld in the Netherlands: Aggaeus van Albada (c. 1525–1587)," in Erb 1985 and Bergsma 1983.

73. In 1529 the Dutch humanist Gerhard Geldenhauser published at Strassburg two editions of an Erasmus work against the execution of heretics (TA 7, 123–24). Wolfgang Schultheiss, pastor of Schiltingheim and a leading "Epicurean" opponent of Butzer's efforts to organize the church, published in 1531 a rhymed German tract on toleration which contained views on the subject similar to Schwenckfeld's. "Ermanung zum geistlichen urteyl inn gottlichen sachen und wie man zur waren eynigkeit des glaubens diser zeyt kommen muege" (TA 7, 291–97). On Schultheiss, see Bellardi 1976. At the beginning of February 1531 Sebastian Franck wrote to Johann Campanus denouncing the efforts to reinstitute Judaic tyranny (TA 7, 308:10–309:22). In December Pilgram Marbeck also argued publicly against the intrusion of secular coercion into the Christian church (TA 7, 505–12). See also Ziegler 1971.

74. The clergy's position was argued in a letter to the council, February 25, 1531 (TA 7, 327–30).

it was the duty of the magistrate (*Oberkeyt*) to insure the establishment of God's kingdom.[75] Christian rulers were obliged to arrange for sufficient instruction in divine doctrine and the holy gospel, and to keep Sunday holy, just as the Sabbath was enforced in the Old Testament. No lukewarm believers or blasphemers were to have a place in government. Because so few people, of any age, attended, the people were to be driven to sermons.[76]

The magistrates were not to listen to those who claimed that the secular authority had no role to play in the church. God had instituted secular authority primarily to maintain worship and faith.

> Therefore St. Paul says in Romans 12 [vs. 7]: "whoever is placed in authority [*furgesetztt*] let him discharge his duties with zeal." And at 1 Cor. 12 [vs. 28] he numbers governance along with doctrine, prophecy, and other gifts of the spirit of Christ. And although at that time those who presided among the Christians had no sword, one knows well that St. Paul would have wished—as he had ordered to be prayed at 1 Tim. 2 [vs. 1f.]—that either all power be with the believers, or the powerful become believers.[77]

The exercise of civil authority in the church was an act of duty and Christian charity.[78]

> No one, however, will be forced to believe, . . . consciences always remain free under Christ. For where the authorities [*Oberkeit*] wish to act against the word, each one can say with Peter: "One must be more obedient to God than man" [Acts 5:29]. . . .[In Strassburg] it has always been taught that the authorities were responsible for abolishing false doctrine and ceremonies. Why should they then not have the power [to maintain and further] sound doctrines and ceremonies?[79]

No one who was against the gospel was to be allowed on the council. Everyone was to hear sermons once on Sunday. All children were to attend catechism instruction. No one was to receive the Eucharist until his faith was examined.[80] To counter those who spoke against infant baptism and left their children unbaptized,

75. TA 7, 327:12.
76. TA 7, 327:13–26.
77. TA 7, 327:27–328:4.
78. TA 7, 328:5–15.
79. TA 7, 328:17–23.
80. TA 7, 328:24–38.

necessity demands it not be allowed that infant baptism be deferred, and no one should be permitted to leave it undone. All Christians, who are lords over all external things and who know that above all else divine unity must be striven for, should serve this church by themselves and with others in a satisfactory and convenient manner. Also, no one should be permitted to scorn Christ's supper.[81]

This shaft was undoubtedly aimed at Schwenckfeld and his followers.

All these ideas distressed Schwenckfeld: the appeal to the Old Testament, the vision of a ruling, governing ministry, the abuse of unity and charity, and the insistence on a Christian magistracy. Nonetheless, Schwenckfeld refused to make public his no less bold vision of church-state relations and religious toleration. He was acutely aware that his views were unwelcome and that censorship made it impossible to have them published.[82] He recorded them only in a series of four letters to Zurich's Leo Jud.[83] They remain his most remarkable works and are without equal during the Reformation.

The Protestant reliance on the secular magistrate was for Schwenckfeld part of a clerical conspiracy, a self-serving effort to seize power within the church and to erect a new papacy, a new Judaism.[84] It was not that the magistrates desired to interfere in the church, but rather that the clergy misled the magistrates by appealing to the Old Testament and misinterpreting it.[85] If one compared the treatment accorded the learned with that meted out to the simple Christian, the clerical conspiracy was immediately obvious. They imprisoned and executed laymen while among themselves they dueled with feathers.[86] Why was Melchior Hoffmann so harshly treated and Luther so assiduously wooed? Hoffmann merely wished to glorify Christ, to be sure incorrectly, but nonetheless in good conscience,[87] whereas Luther con-

---

81. TA 7, 329:1–15.
82. CS IV, 755:23–37.
83. CS IV, 747–71 (March 3, 1533); CS IV 801–11 (July 5, 1533); CS IV, 824–43 (September 10, 1533); CS V, 3–10 (March 2, 1534). For a later (1548) version of the same arguments, see CS XI, 599–625. On this correspondence with Jud see Klaus Deppermann's lecture in Erb 1985.
84. CS IV, 751:19–28, 754:9–30, 804:17–20, 805:12–17, 838:4–10.
85. CS IV, 751:29–752:11, 754:9–30, 807:11–15.
86. CS IV, 835:33–836:13. Schwenckfeld was also aware that he was himself receiving special treatment. Others were exposed to naked force, whereas he was worth convincing (CS IV, 833:18–25).
87. CS IV, 835:17–32, 836:14–17.

demned Butzer and Zwingli with hatred and contempt.[88] For Schwenckfeld it was clear that the entire drive for concord was part of a plan to reestablish clerical hegemony over a docile, passive, and disenfranchised laity.[89] Butzer and the others were always touting love and charity to cover their innovations just as the papists had claimed the inspiration of the Holy Spirit to justify theirs.[90]

In Schwenckfeld's view, the worldly magistrate (there was no specifically Christian one) had absolutely no authority within the church.[91] Christians could be magistrates—the vocation was a noble one—but people went too far in making gods out of them.[92] The magistracy was instituted by God to serve his purposes. It was to maintain peace, order, and harmony, and it was to rule according to natural law.[93] The goal was human righteousness and civic order.[94]

> Thus you have my opinion . . . that neither clergy nor the magistrate [Oberkeit] may coerce anyone with regard to faith. But the magistrate is responsible to see to it that no one, be it the pope or others, employs force against their [the magistrates'] subjects by reason of faith, so long as they hold themselves suitably obedient in temporal things, live and work without insult, rebuke, and injury toward each other, just as it was at the beginning with the church in Rome, Athens, Corinth, and almost all of Asia. Of which we have a fine example in Gallio, Acts 18 [vss. 12–17], which shows clearly what it is fitting for a magistrate to judge.[95]

Schwenckfeld looked to the experience of the apostolic church as a guide to proper church-state relations. The church had prospered under a pagan government while it had decayed under the Constantinian settlement (which he identified with the Arians).[96]

The Protestant clergy feared that the church would dissolve and the simple be seduced. That was because they wanted more people in heaven than God had chosen. Those who truly belonged to the

88. CS IV, 837:11–20.
89. CS IV, 840:14–842:11. See also CS III, 906:12–13; CS IV, 130:1–15.
90. CS IV, 839:18–28.
91. CS IV, 752:12–20.
92. CS IV, 769:39–770:36, 804:20–28.
93. By *natural law* Schwenckfeld meant local and imperial secular law and custom. CS XI, 607:30–37.
94. CS IV, 752:20–37.
95. CS IV, 754:38–755:8.
96. CS IV, 756:5–22.

Church could not be misled, and those who were misled were already outside the Church.[97]

But what of civil discord and unrest?

Even if faith and its consequences were left free, one need not fear any rebellion, revolt, or conspiracy. One could arrange matters with suitable care, sufficient earnestness, and sound reason. And even if something verminous should infiltrate, it could be rooted out easily, just as happened with the Jews through Roman power. Similarly, the pagans had not worried when Paul held gatherings under their rule and placed bishops here and there in the cities.[98]

And again,

How might peace be maintained when every fool [leczkoppff] is allowed to publicly chatter what he will? Answer: It is incumbent upon the magistrate to prevent [zuweren] anyone who wants to prevail by force [mit der faust wolt zugreiffen]. But because with faith, doctrine, and ceremonies it remains with God, the magistrate has nothing to prevent. I might also ask, how was peace maintained in Athens? Whether the magistrate had immediately ordered Paul to be still and to depart?[99]

Schwenckfeld cited examples of states which had flourished with religious diversity from ancient Corinth to contemporary Venice. It was not Christian tolerance that was dangerous, but Judaic zeal. If one obeyed the Law of Moses,

then one should not spare one's own wife if she is seduced by the gods, but rather one should put her to death, and the same for his son, daughter, brother, and so on, exactly as in the case of the false prophet who should be killed, Deuteronomy 13 [vss. 5–9]. Think on that, because you say that it was as little an allegory [figur] as Thou shalt not lust . . . What misery you would cause if you should teach and depict God's word in this way.[100]

97. CS IV, 834:16–31, 836:14–30.
98. CS IV, 755:16–22.
99. CS IV, 837:25–838:4.
100. CS IV, 804:2–8. Schwenckfeld also thought that replacing secular law with the New Testament was just as impractical (CS XI, 607:30–37).

Such thinking would lead only to disaster, both religious and civil. For Schwenckfeld, Münster was the logical outcome not of separatist Anabaptism, but of theocratic Protestantism.[101] The road to Münster did lead from Strassburg, but more from Butzer's pulpit than from Hoffmann's cell.

Schwenckfeld's views on church and state derived from Martin Luther's *Two Kingdoms*, but they were a more radical version.[102] In large part their differences were rooted in personal experience. Luther became the theological guiding light of an officially sponsored and protected Lutheran Church, while Schwenckfeld remained in the vulnerable position of the younger Luther who had written *Secular Authority: To What Extent It Should Be Obeyed* (1523).[103] But there was also an important theological difference. Luther had insisted on the Christian's freedom from human innovation and imposition in order to yoke him more firmly to true doctrine and the Bible. Schwenckfeld acknowledged only the sovereignty of the Holy Spirit, the inner Christ.[104] This spirit was to be proven by Scripture, but not ruled by it. The freedom of a Christian was the freedom of Christ to choose and regenerate whom he willed, when and where he willed.[105] Attempts to impose belief, coercion, persecution of manifest heretics, and even the forcible dismantling of Catholicism constituted *lèse-majesté*. It was human presumption every bit as bad as the pope's, and it was inherently useless.[106] Human beings could neither grant faith nor dislodge it; they could only inflict pain.

Complementary to Schwenckfeld's strictures on the limits of secular authority was his high opinion of its function and its autonomy in its

101. Schwenckfeld blamed the Münster uprising on a too literal reading of the Prophets and the attempt to erect Christ's kingdom in the flesh, and both apply to Butzer as well (CS V, 420:20–36). Because the Protestants persecuted and spilled blood, Schwenckfeld personally could not think of joining their churches (CS IV, 830:30–831:6, 832:27–32). No real Christian could, he felt; by definition, a persecuting church is not the Church.

102. Kühn 1923, 146–47. In the fourfold classification of Stayer 1972, 2–3, Schwenckfeld would fall among the "apolitical moderates" with Luther. Schwenckfeld also owed a great deal to Luther with regard to the *lex naturalis* and his notions of civic righteousness (Pietz 1956, 110, 113, 139–51).

103. WA 11, 229ff.

104. Kühn 1923, 144–45; Lecler 1955a, 57, 78.

105. Kühn's conclusion (1923, 149) that for Schwenckfeld predestination made coercion useless is substantially correct. But in this period *predestination* as a concept was in bad favor with Schwenckfeld. God's intervention is more immediate and personal in his thought.

106. In 1533 Schwenckfeld taunted the Reformers for their actions against the papists (CS IV, 833:26–834:3). In 1548 he declared that they simply had no right to oppress the Catholic church (CS XI, 607:31–608:6).

own realm. By disengaging it from entanglement in the life of the Church Schwenckfeld had left it free to pursue its divine vocation according to the dictates of natural law. His catalogue of successful pagan and Christian governments that had ruled over religiously diverse populations found no counterpart in the more purely evangelical Marbeck, Luther, or Brenz.[107] We may detect here some borrowing from the humanists and Sebastian Franck, though the unalloyed favor with which Schwenckfeld viewed the secular authorities would seem to be lacking in them.[108] Perhaps what is most striking is his insistence that state churches, persecution, and religious coercion were disastrously dangerous to both church and state, and that tolerance was the only practical and practicable approach.

Schwenckfeld felt that history bore him out. In 1548 he described the chaos of the Schmalkaldic War and the humbling of the Protestant churches as the direct and unavoidable result of their provocative, violent, and utopian efforts to unite church and state.[109] The eventual establishment of authoritarian state churches was not viewed as a necessary or desirable result of the Reformation by many of those who presided over its inception. This is very clear not only because a well-informed, widely traveled, and politically experienced member of the upper class could feel this way, but also because he found an audience and a following among both the clergy and the ruling classes of city, court, and countryside. Only with this in mind can we make sense of Schwenckfeld's experiences in Strassburg, Augsburg, Ulm, and Württemberg.

Strassburg Synod

By the end of 1530 Butzer had identified Schwenckfeld as a threat, and he had begun to broadcast his suspicions to correspondents in the other South German cities.[110] As would become clear later in Augs-

---

107. Schwenckfeld praised Johannes Brenz's "Ob ein weltliche oberkeyt, mit gotlichem und billichem rechten moege die wiederteuffer durch feuer oder schwert vom leben zu dem tod richten lassen." Brenz 1974, 480–98.

108. Mitchell 1960, 306–07; Röhrich 1932, pt. 2, 75; Weigelt 1972, 40–42.

109. CS XI, 611:5–8.

110. In January 1531 some of Schwenckfeld's admirers in Augsburg anxiously wrote to determine if it was true that he was an Anabaptist (Geryon Sailer to Butzer, January 25, 1531, TA 7, 300:8–20). Sailer reported the concern of Wolfgang Rehlinger. Since Schwenckfeld had himself not published anything on the subject, one must suspect Butzer of starting the rumor. Johann Bader of Landau was being fed information from Strassburg as well (CS IV, 40:36–

burg, Ulm, and Württemberg, Butzer's effort to discredit Schwenck-feld often hurt his reputation as well as Schwenckfeld's.

The campaign against Schwenckfeld and the other radicals began within Strassburg about the same time. In December 1531 the preach-ers complained to the council that "it was said" that they did not have the gospel, that they did not have Christ's sacraments, that they were "Scripture- and soul-murderers," and that they should not be listened to.[111] Eleven months later the preachers charged "again" that Schwenckfeld was drawing many people away from the sermons.[112] Because of cooling fervor or outright opposition, nonattendance at ser-mons was a widespread problem for the ministers, but Schwenckfeld himself never called for avoidance of sermons. Nonetheless there was some truth to the charge. Given Schwenckfeld's criticism of Butzer and the other Strassburg clergy, his friends and followers would find the sermons increasingly superfluous or offensive.[113]

But it was not Schwenckfeld's appeal to the simple laity which Butzer feared. Schwenckfeld's subsequent career in southern Germany would show time and again how great his impact was among two groups whose support made the Reformation possible and whose con-tinued adherence was vital to its success: the clergy and the ruling elite.

It is surprising that so many ministers should find Schwenckfeld per-suasive, given the generally anticlerical cast of his theology. But these same ministers had also turned their backs on the Catholic hierarchy in order to embrace the comparatively anticlerical Protestant reform. There were many who hesitated, rejected, or accepted with great mis-givings the new orthodoxy. The initial euphoria of liberation gave way

---

41:24, 44:13–23, 46:26–47:31, 48:28–34). In September Oecolampadius wrote to Capito to warn against his guests (September 17, 1531, TA 7, 344:19). Oecolampadius did not name the "contubernales." In October Wolfgang Musculus of Augsburg advised Butzer not to rupture "fraternal concord" with Schwenckfeld and Schultheiss, but rather to embrace them as brothers (October 3, 1531, TA 7, 346:24–347:3). In the same month Berthold Haller of Bern wrote to Butzer and requested more information about Schwenckfeld, Servetus, and "other men of this sort" (October 4, 1531, TA 7, 347:11–13). At the end of the year Butzer chided Ambrosius Blaurer of Constance for having publicly approved Schwenckfeld's newly published *Catechism*, and declared, "He is totally different from us" (December 29, 1531, TA 7, 306–07). *Catechis-mus von ettlichen Hauptartickeln des Christlichen glaubens*, CS IV, 208–38. It was published in Augsburg (TA 7, 337:23–338:5). Nicolaus Thomae of Bergzabern was also warned off the *Catechism* by Konrad Hubert, Butzer's "famulus." Like Musculus in Augsburg, Thomae was not convinced (TA 4, 250:20–33; TA 7, 394:1–6, 543:1–15).

111. TA 7, 358:4–10 (ca. December 16, 1531). Marbeck was exiled on December 20, 1531 (TA 7, 362:14–363:10).

112. TA 7, 563:10–15 (November 18, 1532, and later).

113. Cf. Katharina Streicher's apology to the Ulm city council in 1544–45 (Fritz 1934, 186).

only slowly and regretfully to the concern for consolidation. In Strassburg, pastors such as Wolfgang Schultheiss and Anton Engelbrecht
were eventually deposed for their opposition.[114] Wolfgang Capito and
Matthaeus Zell, two of the architects of the Strassburg Reformation,
were just barely reclaimed by Butzer from Schwenckfeld for the new
church.

Capito, a humanist Hebrew scholar and advisor to the archbishop
of Mainz, had joined the Protestants and come to Strassburg in
1522.[115] His presence lent authority and respectability to the Reform.
By virtue of his learning and his association with high ecclesiastics,
Capito was the leading figure among the Reformers until Martin Butzer's rise to power during Schwenckfeld's stay in Strassburg. But Capito
was also closely aligned with the dissidents. His friendship and respect
for Schwenckfeld, and his own doubts about Butzer's program, proved
formidable. It was only at the end of January 1534, months after
Schwenckfeld had left Strassburg, that Butzer claimed to have won
Capito over.[116] It was a protracted struggle whose decisive turn came
in 1531 when the deaths of Zwingli, Oecolampadius, and Capito's
own wife left Capito shaken in body and spirit.[117] He himself was bed-
ridden for months with the plague that had claimed his wife. Butzer
seized the psychological moment to win Capito over, removing him
from the Strassburg dissident climate by sending him on a trip to various Swiss and South German cities, and arranging for Capito's participation at the Bern and Basel synods. Butzer also promoted Capito's
remarriage to the widow of Oecolampadius, Wibrandis Rosenblatt.[118]
Nonetheless, it took Capito more than a year after his return to overcome his scruples.

Matthaeus Zell was a different matter. It was his thunderous ser-

114. Cf. Bellardi 1976; Bellardi 1973; Bellardi 1974; Van den Berg 1981. By all accounts
Engelbrecht was a troublesome, wayward character. He was fired on March 3, 1534 (TA 8,
284:10–13).
115. Kittelson 1975.
116. Butzer to Ambrosius Blaurer, January 30, 1934, TA 8 270:1–9. On November 27,
1533, Butzer described to Musculus the division among the Strassburg ministers: Engelbrecht
and Zell vs. Butzer and Hedio with Capito coming around to Butzer's way of thinking (TA 8,
210:1–8). At the October synod Capito had argued that in all the major issues Schwenckfeld
agreed with the Strassburg ministers (TA 8, 211:15–21). Capito still used and acknowledged
Schwenckfelder prayers and devotions in his 1536 *Precationes christianae* (Althaus 1914, 23–
25).
117. Kittelson, 1975, 188. The death of Capito's wife was probably also the occasion for
Schwenckfeld's departure from the Capito household.
118. Kittelson 1975, 190–93.

mons that had fueled the popular movement in the early years of the Reform. And he alone of the ministers seemed to retain his influence with the common people. Butzer was very keen to get Zell's support in defense of "the ministry and the unity of the Church" before both the people and the magistracy.[119] There were two obstacles: Zell's wife and Zell himself. Katharina Zell, one of those imposing women whom the early Reformation seemed to produce, was a member of Schwenckfeld's circle and a vocal opponent of clerical intolerance.[120] Butzer believed Matthaeus Zell's reluctance to support him resulted from Katharina's influence.[121] In large part it no doubt did. But Zell's own career of reformation provides an additional explanation. He was a preacher of the word in a time when that constituted revolt against the Catholic hierarchy. He was even less likely than Capito to become an institutional man. Though he gave in to Butzer's demands in 1534 (and an illness at the time may help explain this), Zell was conspicuous by his absence in the actual administration of the new church order and in the suppression of the sects. Till the end, he remained a simple, forthright preacher.[122]

Resistance among the Protestant clergy to the ties binding church and state was not limited to Strassburg. Leo Jud, Zwingli's closest lieutenant, himself questioned the close cooperation of ministry and magistracy in Zurich and showed signs of attraction to the earnestness and zeal of the Anabaptists, although this may have been the product of his dismay at the failure of the Zurich church to instill real piety in the Christian community, and his deep shock at Zwingli's battlefield death.[123] Impressed by one of Schwenckfeld's manuscript treatises, Jud wrote Schwenckfeld to urge that he publish his views on the secular magistrates' role in the church.[124] Despite the fact that Jud remained in substantial doctrinal agreement with Schwenckfeld, Butzer and Bullinger were able to recapture their straying colleague.[125]

119. Butzer to Blaurer, January 8, 1534, Schiess 1, 459.
120. See Bainton 1971, 55–76, and Klaustermeyer 1965.
121. Klaustermeyer 1965, 171–75.
122. On his deathbed Matthaeus advised Katharina to maintain close ties with Schwenckfeld (Klaustermeyer 1965, 209–11.
123. Pestalozzi 1860, 36–53; Morita 1975, 145–47; Pollet 1962, 307–08. See the lecture by Klaus Deppermann in Erb. 1985.
124. "Underschaid des Alten and Newen Testaments / der Figur and waarheit," CS IV, 414–43. It could have reached Jud through either Karlstadt or Wilhelm von Zell (CS IV, 749). Schwenckfeld's four letters to Jud resulted.
125. In the process Bullinger produced his ground-breaking work on the two Testaments,

They were able to do so by playing upon Jud's desire for a church unity embodied and guaranteed by ministerial collegiality and clerical solidarity. He and many others in southern Germany came to believe that for the church to survive and flourish, the clergy had to close ranks; differences of opinion were to be kept private. From Jud in Zurich to Capito and Zell in Strassburg to Bader in Landau and Bonifacius Wolfhart in Augsburg, a semblance of harmony was maintained by the personal decision of each not to publicize disagreements. A classic example of this approach was the outcome of the Marburg Colloquy: the promise to refrain from mutual recrimination. During Schwenckfeld's stay in Strassburg and again after the 1535 Tübingen Colloquy, he himself followed this path and maintained a politic science. But he was bound to fail in this resolution because he was not a member of the guild. He remained a layman, an outsider.

The second obstacle to Butzer's plans for the church was the magistracy. The government of Strassburg was a complex congeries of committees and councils, all of whose members were drawn from a limited pool of eligible candidates.[126] This political—and social—elite was composed of two "fractions," the patricians of the old nobility and the wealthier guildsmen.[127] It was among such people, and especially among the patricians, that Schwenckfeld circulated, lending his books,[128] discussing religion at the dinner table, in the clubs (*Stuben*), on street corners, and at family prayer gatherings. He had direct personal access to the masters of the city in a way that Butzer and the others did not.

The Protestants, who held the preponderance of seats in the various councils, were divided into "zealots" and "politiques."[129] The zealots

---

The Testament or Covenant of the One and Eternal God (De testamento seu foedere dei unico et aeterno), Morita 1975, 147–48. Jud to Butzer, February 9, 1534, TA 8, 279:1–12; April 27, 1534, TA 8, 305:25–308:36; April 1534, TA 8, 311:4–7. Jud held views similar to Schwenckfeld's on the Eucharist and baptism. He also scolded Butzer over his efforts at concord with Luther. Why court Luther and condemn Schwenckfeld? Of the two, Schwenckfeld was the more Christian, Jud felt.

126. For a good description of the organization of the Strassburg government see Chrisman 1967, 14–32; Brady 1978, 163–95.

127. On the social structure of Strassburg's ruling class, see Brady 1978, 53–162. Other helpful treatments of urban upper classes in southern Germany are Rieber 1968, 299–351; Eitel 1970; Naujoks 1958.

128. Significantly, the first evidence of Schwenckfeld's activity in Strassburg is his loan of a copy of the *Anweysung* to Hans von Gültingen, a Württemberg noble. (July 19, 1529, TA 7, 244:32–245:7).

129. These are Brady's terms. For what follows consult Brady 1978, 241–45. Events in Ulm and Augsburg confirm Brady's conclusions.

supported a policy of thorough reform without delay along Zwinglian lines. By and large they seem to have come from among the lesser merchants and simple guildsmen. The politiques, on the other hand, were drawn from the patricians and wealthier guildsmen, and generally they were better educated, more widely traveled, and more cosmopolitan than the zealots. They favored a slower pace with more consideration given to Strassburg's political position within the empire. It was among the zealots and their supporters in the streets and guildhalls that the Zwinglian vision of the city as a *corpus christianorum* flourished.[130] Republicanism, parochialism, and the desire to maintain broader political participation coalesced in support of a rigorously disciplined and doctrinally defined church order. The politiques and the aristocracy, for the most part, were not as republican as the zealots. Often holding fiefs from princes, and socializing with other nonurban nobles who were part of the growing system of territorial principalities, they lacked the instinctive social antagonism that gave republicanism its bitter edge. To be sure they feared princely encroachment upon their own sovereignty, but that was a political matter. Because of their wealth, education, and involvement (both economic and political) outside the city, the politiques' horizons were broader. Imperial policy and politics weighed more heavily in their thinking. They were less inclined to view Strassburg as a self-sufficient island or as the apple of God's eye. This also was reflected in their attitude toward the church. Order, harmony, and decorum were the goals of their internal ecclesiastical policy. They did not seek to erect God's kingdom on earth. They sought a larger consensus outside the city in the empire as a whole. In a sense, the politiques and the aristocracy whom they represented never really saw themselves as part of the urban community at all. The relationship of ruler and subject is quite different from that of leader and community. As has already been noted, Strassburg's governors were well on the way from community (*Gemeinde*) to lordship (*Obrigkeit*), in both politics and religion.[131]

Schwenckfeld, and the others who preached toleration, found a

130. See Moeller 1972.
131. Thus while I agree with Moeller 1972, 92, that the Zwinglian movements in the South German cities were lay in origin, not all sections of the laity were equally supportive of the Zwinglian program. Those elements which Moeller 1972, 110–11, sees triumphing after the Schmalkaldic War and undermining the communal nature of urban government were already present in the city councils. They resisted the unwanted corollaries of conceptions of *corpus christianorum*. They also found Schwenckfeld's views quite congenial.

ready audience among the politiques and even to some extent among the zealots. Neither faction was eager to purge the dissidents, nor did they look with favor on a new church order dominated by the clergy.[132] The Reformation had fed upon anticlericalism, and the distrust of clerics had not disappeared with the expulsion of Catholic priests and monks. The arrogance and appetite for power of the new Protestant clergy, as seen by the secular authorities, did nothing to allay their suspicions.[133] When the Strassburg council finally moved to expel the radicals and to install the new church order, their reasons were pragmatic, not programmatic.[134] In the end, events and their own sense of responsibility to maintain peace and order forced them to assume reluctantly duties which they found extremely distasteful.

A central figure in all of this was Jakob Sturm—patrician, *Stettmeister*, chairman of the special commission for religion, and leading politique.[135] Sturm was particularly opposed to the political involvement of the Protestant preachers. The eventual church settlement, which gave the clergy far less power than they wished, was in many ways his work.[136] His exact relationship to Schwenckfeld is suspiciously difficult to define. He may well have been Schwenckfeld's principal defender in the government, and he certainly thwarted Butzer's attempt to have the city publicly condemn Schwenckfeld.[137]

132. Brady 1978, 247. The policy of toleration for which Strassburg was so justly famous owed far more to the common sense and broad-mindedness of the magistrates than it did to the principles of the preachers (Dollinger 1953, 241–69).

133. For an interesting expression of this distrust, see Scribner 1975.

134. Abray 1978, 97–98; Brady 1978, 246–47; Chrisman 1967, 202–03.

135. Brady 1978, 241–42. As Strassburg's perennial diplomatic representative at the *Reichstag*, regional urban negotiations, and the courts of princes and emperors, Sturm was concerned for Strassburg's political survival. He had scotched an earlier attempt to abolish the Mass (1526), and the eventual abolition in 1529 came over his strenuous objections.

136. Brady 1978, 247.

137. Most scholars credit some tie between the two but are hampered by lack of evidence; see Abray 1978, 255; Brady 1978, 241–42. Ficker 1941, 152, 155–57. In 1530 Sturm favored Schwenckfeld's eucharistic formulation in place of Butzer's for Strassburg's statement of faith at Augsburg (Ficker 1941, 152:44–47, 157). He may have tried to block the preachers' attempt to call Schwenckfeld before the synod for examination. In the preachers' plan for the synod handed in on May 31, 1533, a prominent place was given to the examination of Schwenckfeld and Alexander Berner, his disciple (TA 8, 23:16–35). However, at the synod Schwenckfeld is represented not as having been "called," but as having appeared voluntarily (TA 8, 79:32–33). This complicated and confused issue is discussed below. After Schwenckfeld's departure from Strassburg in 1534, Sturm gave him his personal assurance that the city would have no further comment on the matter (CS V, 320:16–21). This undermined Butzer's efforts to portray Schwenckfeld as an exile and a potential threat to other city magistrates in southern Germany. Sturm may in fact have provided Schwenckfeld with introductions to two of Schwenckfeld's other patrons, Bernhard Besserer and Wolfgang Rehlinger, *Bürgermeister* of Ulm and Augsburg

Whatever the exact nature of Sturm's relationship to Schwenckfeld, it is clear (and it was clear to Butzer) that the core of the opposition to his plans for the church was found among the patricians both in the council and outside it. Butzer was also convinced that Schwenckfeld played an important role in that opposition.[138] Because of Schwenckfeld's insidious and baleful influence upon both the clergy and magistracy of Strassburg, he became one of Butzer's key targets. The Strassburg synod in June 1533 was in large measure designed to unmask Schwenckfeld and to convict him out of his own mouth, much as Eck had done to Luther in 1519 at Leipzig.[139]

The Council had put off the preachers and the synod for the better part of a year.[140] For their part, the clergy, and in particular Butzer, concealed the full extent of their plans "in order to counter those who say that through this a new papacy is being prepared."[141]

The synod was divided into two parts, the preliminary synod (June 3–6, 1533) and the main synod (June 10–14). Both were presided over by the four members of the council's special religion commission (Ja-

---

respectively. Sturm and Besserer were colleagues from many *Reichstage* and other meetings. Wolfgang Rehlinger was Sturm's relative (Brady 1978, 85). In 1543 Rehlinger left Augsburg and moved to Strassburg, where Sturm nominated him for citizenship in 1545 (Brady 1978, 273.) Schwenckfeld was known to Rehlinger as early as 1531 (TA 7, 300:8–20). There is also a letter from Schwenckfeld to an unnamed *Bürgermeister* in 1548 (July 18, 1548, CS XI, 619–25). The editors of CS believe it was written to Sturm. The citation of the "Buechlin / Grund and Ursach / rc der Prediger von Strassburg newerung . . ." would seem pointless if the letter was not addressed to a Strassburg magistrate (CS XI, 625). Another possibility is Hans Walter Ehinger, *Bürgermeister* of Ulm. But a letter addressed to Ehinger by name was published in the same 1570 edition of Schwenckfeld's works (CS XI, 62–69). Why would the editors delete his name in one place and include it in another? The fact that Sturm was *Stettmeister* and not *Bürgermeister* should occasion no problem, because to have identified the recipient as *Stettmeister*, a title peculiar to Strassburg, would have given away his identity. If it was written to Sturm, and that seems likely, then Sturm had written to Schwenckfeld asking his opinion on the role of the secular authority in the church in the post-Schmalkaldic world.

138. TA 8, 209:24–34. Myconius of Basel wrote to Capito (June 27, 1533) that a visiting noble claimed Schwenckfeld had strong support among the "senatores" (TA 8, 99:34–100:3). Butzer also complained to Frecht of Ulm that he was being criticized by certain nobles (May 8, 1535, TA 8, 450:20–24).

139. Unfortunately Schwenckfeld had been very careful not to publish any of his more inflammatory views, as the Strassburg preachers admitted (ca. October 1533, TA 8, 156:19–27). In preparation Butzer tried to enlist Bader of Landau as an informant; see Bader to Butzer, January 24, 1533, TA 8, 1:14–16. He was also made privy to the contents of Schwenckfeld's letters to Jud (Pestalozzi 1860, 49–50; CS V, 6:7–23).

140. The Peace of Nürnberg (July 23, 1532) made it possible (Wendel 1942, 51). But the council didn't set up a commission to plan it until November 30, 1532 (TA 7, 578:8–17). The commission, headed by Sturm, reported on April 12, 1533 (TA 8, 3:9–21). After further consultations the council finally ordered the synod convened on May 24, 1533 (TA 8, 15:20–16:2). Further instructions were given on May 28, 1533 (TA 8, 16:20–26).

141. TA 8, 5:17–20.

kob Sturm, Martin Herlin, Andreas Mieg, and Sebastian Erb).[142] Though Schwenckfeld claimed that the council had granted immunity for all statements made at the synod, in point of fact the synod was not designed, as Capito also suggested, to allow a free and open discussion of doctrine.[143] The structure and chronology of the synod makes this clear. The council closely controlled the preliminary synod (*Vorsynod*), which excluded the sectarians, the guild representatives, and the rural clergy.[144] During its sessions sixteen Articles of faith were propounded, and the city clergy were invited to criticize and approve.[145] This was followed by formal, mutual criticism among the ministers. A united front having been established, the rural clergy and parish representatives were called in for the main synod in order to rubber-stamp the articles. Only at the end of the main synod were the dissidents admitted. They were confronted by the fait accompli of a united church and an established doctrine. Schwenckfeld, Clemens Ziegler, Melchior Hoffmann, and the others who were called could accept it or criticize it, but they could not change it. Their criticism, however, served to identify them as enemies of the church and made their eventual purge all the easier. The clergy's intentions concerning Schwenckfeld were made manifest by the tenth article, which was directed specifically at Schwenckfeld.[146]

Most of the other dissidents clearly were ordered to attend the synod (Hoffmann, for example, was brought from prison), but it is less clear whether Schwenckfeld was summoned or was present of his own volition. Butzer and Capito would claim that Schwenckfeld came unbidden and had launched an unprovoked attack on them and their teachings. Schwenckfeld for his part insisted that he had been ordered to appear and had only engaged in criticism when pressed by Butzer.[147]

142. The most thorough discussion of the synod is found in Wendel 1942, 51–89. But see also Deppermann 1979, 248–58, for an interesting corrective.

143. CS V, 320:8–11; Chrisman 1967, 57–59.

144. The laity simply outnumbered the clergy. Sturm played the major role in organizing the synod (Chrisman 1967, 211; Wendel 1942, 57–59, 61).

145. TA 8, 25–32. The articles were composed by a committee (Butzer, Capito, and two *Kirchenpfleger*—Conrat and Lindenfels). It was based on Butzer's private letter of April 1533 (Deppermann 1979, 250–51).

146. TA 8, 28:4–12. The article was directed against Schwenckfeld's *Stillstand* for the Eucharist. It did not mention him by name.

147. CS V, 323:18–29. Wendel 1942, 88, believed Schwenckfeld's appearance was voluntary. Deppermann 1979, 249, assumed that he was summoned. Capito claimed Schwenckfeld had approached a member of the council, Hans Sturm (a distant relative of Jakob), and asked permission to participate (Capito to Jakob Truchsess von Rheinfelden, May 21, 1534, TA 1,

The discrepancy is important since it was because of Schwenckfeld's supposedly unbrotherly, uncharitable, and unwarranted action, and not because of any specific doctrinal difference, that Butzer and the other clergy urged the council to expel Schwenckfeld from the city.[148] Two solutions to the mystery suggest themselves: either there was an honest misunderstanding about who was and was not to be called, or Martin Butzer manipulated both Schwenckfeld and the council. Schwenckfeld probably suspected the latter; he certainly believed that Capito lied after the fact.[149]

Butzer's own account of the synod—the only account that survives—insinuated that Schwenckfeld intruded upon the proceedings, but it also made clear that Schwenckfeld thought himself summoned, and it belied the characterization of Schwenckfeld's performance as an unprovoked attack; if anything Schwenckfeld's reserve and reluctance were quite evident.[150] Intriguingly, Schwenckfeld's name had figured prominently in the clergy's original proposal to the council, but it had been dropped either by the commission headed by Sturm, or by the council as a whole. Coincidentally, Sturm was out of town on diplomatic business at the end of the synod when Schwenckfeld spoke.[151] Had Schwenckfeld learned of the original proposal but not its subsequent modification? Did Butzer take advantage of Sturm's absence to use the synod against Schwenckfeld? With the evidence available it is impossible to decide. Nonetheless, Schwenckfeld's suspicions added a new bitterness to his rivalry with Butzer.

The preliminary synod had revealed the deep divisions within the clerical ranks. Objections had been raised to the sixteen articles with regard to infant baptism, the Eucharist, and the role of the secular magistrate, issues which also disturbed Schwenckfeld.[152] It is a mea-

---

991). Butzer, Capito, and the other ministers would insist that Schwenckfeld had attacked them and their teaching without provocation (TA 1, 991; TA 8, 145:7–10.)

148. TA 8, 146:7–11, 155:31–156:6, 165:23–166:24. These citations are from a "Gegenantwort" (between October 10 and 19, 1533) to Schwenckfeld's "Schutzschrift," CS IV, 814–24 (TA 8, 145–69).

149. CS V, 323:1–5, 18–22.

150. Butzer's protocols are found in TA 8, 79:31–90:15, and CS IV, 790–99. "Nach gethanen gebett is Schwenckfeldt auff sein begehren uffgestanden / und begert . . ." (CS IV, 790:26–27). "Bedenkte sich Schwenckfeldt zu dem synodo berueffen . . ." (CS IV, 799:23).

151. On the clergy's proposal, see TA 8, 23:16–24. On Sturm's absence, see TA 8, 79:23. Sturm was probably on his way to Schmalkald.

152. TA 8, 35:29–63:3. Deppermann 1979, 251–52. The opposition was led by the "Epicureans"—Schultheiss, Engelbrecht, and Sapidus. Jakob Ziegler, a renowned humanist on the city payroll, left the city rather than participate in the synod. He later published a blistering

sure of Butzer's skill and the council's determination to impose order that, despite the failure to achieve agreement even among the city clergy, the articles were used as the de facto formula of doctrine for the rest of the synod.[153]

On June 10, 1533, the main synod began. The rural congregations and their ministers were examined and were offered the sixteen articles. They were accepted without demur.[154] On the following day, Wednesday, both Clemens Ziegler and Melchior Hoffmann were questioned.[155]

On Thursday it was Schwenckfeld's turn. He and Butzer sparred throughout the morning. In the afternoon and the following morning Schwenckfeld was absent due to illness. They resumed Friday afternoon (June 13) and concluded on Saturday morning. The men clashed over two problems: Schwenckfeld's relationship to the clergy and Church of Strassburg, and his evaluation of the sixteen articles. Schwenckfeld broached the first when he challenged anyone to prove that he was an offensive or unpeaceful guest, or in any way opposed to the clergy, as some (read Butzer) had bruited about. This whole tack put Butzer on the defensive because he could only reply that they had this all on hearsay evidence.[156] Schwenckfeld denied all their complaints and asked simply to be left alone to pursue the truth, his conscience untrammeled. As the protocols of the synod recorded his claim: "He was not here to disparage anyone, to set up or to pull down. He has no command from God. He will not put forth anything to change. Rather he will only present what he thinks and what he still lacks."[157] And as his own written "Protestacion" submitted to the synod reiterated:

> In short, I don't give myself out here as a teacher or leader, but only as a poor student of Jesus Christ. I have not come here in

attack on the proceeding (*Jakobi Ziegleri Landavi Synodus*, TA 8, 234:15–241:25). Otto Brunfels, another important scholar and teacher, also chose to leave Strassburg shortly thereafter. Both Engelbrecht and Schultheiss were eventually fired, and they returned to Catholicism. On the fate of the "Epicureans," see Deppermann 1979, 252–53. On the "Epicureans" generally, see Lienhard 1981.

153. The status of the suggested revised forms of articles 14–16 remains unclear. TA 8, 61:38–63:3.

154. TA 8, 70:21–75:20.

155. TA 8, 75:21–79:20.

156. CS IV, 790:26–791:14. Schwenckfeld submitted a "Protestacion" to the council (CS IV, 788–90).

157. CS IV, 791:15–21.

order to reform, depose, or oppose the preachers, or in order to make a congregation dependent upon me. It is, to sum up, not my intention to afflict anyone, but instead to confer about Christ, his heavenly riches, and his kingdom, and to talk of divine righteousness, be it at table or otherwise with good friends. I hope that no Christian could complain, especially where it is not against public order [gemein ordenung], but rather in the fear of God.[158]

Schwenckfeld went through the articles one by one, but really disagreed with Butzer on only three points: baptism, the Eucharist, and the role of the secular authority. Schwenckfeld repeated his criticism of infant baptism and rejected the argument from the Old Testament. But Schwenckfeld was careful to point out that for him the issue was hypothetical, he being neither a parent nor a minister.[159]

The Eucharist was a different case. Butzer accused Schwenckfeld of setting too high a standard for communicants—a personal experience of rebirth. As a result of Schwenckfeld's example and, if Butzer's informants were to be believed, Schwenckfeld's harsh criticism of the Strassburg practice, members of the church were refusing to partake.[160] For his part Schwenckfeld pointed out the inconsistencies of Butzer's attempts to achieve an agreement with Luther on the sacrament, and he requested at the very least that the ban be established.[161]

When it came to discussing the final issue, the role of the secular authority, Schwenckfeld displayed exemplary prudence. Rather than argue the case viva voce, he submitted a very carefully worded and, in comparison to what was found in his letters to Jud, a very conservative written statement.[162] The most forceful part was an exhortation to the clergy to rely on God, not the secular authority, to suffer meekly as Saint Paul and Christ had done, and not to seek vengeance.

His ill health notwithstanding, Schwenckfeld acquitted himself well at the synod, exercising caution but making clear his dissatisfaction with the direction of Butzer's remodeling of the church. Clearly the issue here was not so much individual theological positions, but rather the right of private citizens to hold and discuss views at variance with those of the established church. Set more broadly, it was a question of

158. CS IV, 789:33–790:10.
159. CS IV, 794:12–797:22.
160. CS IV, 790:26–791:25, TA 8, 28:4–12.
161. CS IV, 798:8–12, 799:15–16; article 9, TA 8, 27:13–28:3.
162. "Auff den Artickell von der Oberkeit," CS IV, 800.

the limits to be placed on the autonomy and activity of a religiously active laity.

Butzer and his supporters claimed victory and reported that Schwenckfeld had lost some of his following as a result of the synod. In particular, Katharina Zell and some of the clergy were supposed to have become disenchanted.[163] But as Myconius wrote from Basel (June 27, 1533), the reaction of the Strassburg council in general was quite different.

> I hear that certain among the senators, although they have be- come sick of everyone, feel and speak so magnificently about Schwenckfeld that they not only present him to honest men, they commend before all what he has argued so learnedly and cleverly from your own books against you, so that it is easily seen what sort of talent lies hidden in this man. And if he has the strength [si vires suppeterent] they do not doubt his victory. A certain noble has reported this to us. I did not want to hide it from you.[164]

Butzer therefore misjudged the situation when, shortly after the synod, he tried to force Schwenckfeld to give written assurance of his agreement with the Strassburg clergy or face expulsion from the city.[165] The council had no intention of proceeding any further with the mat- ter. With Melchior Hoffmann and Claus Frey, considered the most dangerous of the dissidents, already in prison, there seemed little else to do. Butzer's unauthorized publication of Hoffmann's interrogation at the synod earned him a sharp rebuke, and despite the ardent wishes of Butzer's friends elsewhere, the council never allowed him to make public the transcript of Schwenckfeld's part in the synod.[166] Still badly divided among themselves and lacking the support of the city council, the clergy's efforts to come to terms with Schwenckfeld after the synod

163. Butzer to M. Blaurer, June 17, 1533, TA 8 93:17–23, and July 9, 1533, TA 8, 119:30– 120:3; Schwarz to Musculus, July 8, 1533, TA 8, 118:1–13. Butzer described Schwenckfeld's proud, critical, and self-sufficient attitude toward the clergy as a disturbing revelation for Schwenckfeld's supporters, an attitude which would discomfort primarily the clergy (TA 8, 118:26–36). Wendel 1942, 93, dates Schwenckfeld's break with Capito and other clerics to the day following the synod.

164. TA 8, 99:34–100:3.

165. CS IV, 886:6–21. Wendel 1942, 93, specifies the day after the synod, but the evidence is not so precise. See also TA 8, 187:9–11.

166. Butzer's rebuke, July 7, 1533, TA 8, 117:5–10. Phrygio of Basel urged Butzer to publish the Schwenckfeld material (August 19, 1533, TA 8, 123:19–28). Another reason that Butzer did not heed Phrygio's call may be that the surviving protocols do not convey the impression of Butzer's victory.

were confused and ineffectual.[167] Schwenckfeld dismissed them with a reference to the synod, at which he had not been condemned or even warned by the presiding officers.[168] Relying upon Capito and Caspar Hedio, another Strassburg pastor, to mend his fences with Butzer, Schwenckfeld left the city for a visit to Augsburg.[169] He was in Speyer by September 10.[170]

Schwenckfeld's departure was not occasioned by the results of the synod. There were none. He had successfully fought Butzer to a standstill. His decision to leave shows, rather, that he was confident of his position within Strassburg. Two months after the synod there had been no further efforts to construct a new church order or to move against dissidents. The council was content with the status quo, and the clergy was still not united. Hedio and Capito were serving as mediators between Schwenckfeld and Butzer, and Zell was on Schwenckfeld's side. The synod had proved abortive. It was safe enough for Schwenckfeld to spend a few weeks in Augsburg.[171]

167. See the "Scriptum," August 1533, TA 8, 124:22–129:36. In it the clergy promulgated, among other things, a new rule of faith: A Christian had to recognize and publicly confess other true Christians, ministers, or churches wherever he met them. It was not permissible to withhold one's testimony. It was also "unchristian" to await better ministers (TA 8, 126:6–14, 127:33–35, 128:21–35).

168. For Schwenckfeld's response to the "Scriptum" (end of August 1533), see CS IV, 812–24.

169. CS IV, 886:26–32. Schwenckfeld's visit to Augsburg had been discussed as early as January 25, 1531 (TA 8, 300:8–20). He was invited by Bonifacius Wolfhart (CS V, 106:14–24).

170. His third letter to Jud is dated "Speier 10 September 1533" (CS IV, 843:22).

171. He wrote Jud (September 10, 1533) that he was on his way to Augsburg, "villeicht ettliche wochen da bleiben" (CS IV, 843:8).

6 Knight Errant of Discord
(September 1533–December 1536)

I thank our Lord Jesus Christ, who has tempered your trial so that you ar‿ thus dissatisfied with your wavering. Who would not wish to be certain in all things? And you remain firm in the unity of your fellow priests.—Martin Butzer to Leo Jud, November 30, 1533

It is good when one speaks much about unity, but only so far as such unity agrees with Christ and his divine doctrine and truth. But all unity is cursed which strives against Christ, against God's word, and [against] his truth.—Schwenckfeld, after August 2, 1534

Something else occurs to me: if you should confer [contuleritis] with Schwenckfeld, do so very cautiously and, if possible, in a friendly way, constantly remembering this: "He is with me who is not against me." From the obstinacy and errors of others [the Lutherans] learn to forgive these [those who are not against us] certain things in certain questions. Apply [conferte] yourself to the chief points of Christianity about which there is no controversy so far among the pious.—Thomas Blaurer to Ambrosius Blaurer, May 28, 1535

Landau, Speyer, Esslingen, Württemberg, Ulm, Augsburg, and Swabia

Though Schwenckfeld could not know it, his short trip to Augsburg would last ten months, and his departure from Strassburg would mark the beginning of a period of extensive travel throughout southern Germany that continued for the rest of the decade. During that time he laid the groundwork for his network of friends, patrons, and disciples—the Schwenckfelders.[1]

Initially all that made the South German Schwenckfelders a group were their close personal ties to Schwenckfeld, and the nature of those ties varied considerably. In Ulm he seems to have "adopted" the family of the widow Helena Streicher by playing the role of a distinguished and benevolent uncle to her young children. For others he was a much-sought-after dinner guest whose tastefulness and pious conversation lent distinction to the family table. In Augsburg there must have been a veritable competition among the society hostesses who were religiously inclined. Many of the political leaders recognized a kindred

1. See McLaughlin 1985b.

spirit, albeit more spiritually intense. His measured words and digni-
fied gestures must have made an attractive contrast to the strident tones
of his clerical competitors. This was a man whom one could consult
without conceding one's own autonomy. Schwenckfeld's teachings
complemented his personality. They appealed especially to those lay-
people who chafed at the pretentions of the new Protestant clergy. The
total effect of his views on the church, the sacraments, and the word
was to shift the focus of religion from the church to the home, from
the altar to the family table. At least initially, Schwenckfelder meetings
had less the air of conventicles than of family evenings of prayer. One
can sympathize with a frustrated pastor like Martin Frecht of Ulm,
who was excluded from the family quarters of the socially prominent
families only to watch Schwenckfeld ushered in and solicitously
cared for.

The return of religion to the hearth and the liberation of the laity
from the often unpleasant tutelage of a professional male clergy was
especially attractive to women, and the Schwenckfelder movement in
southern Germany was always marked by strong female leadership. In
part this was surely the result of Schwenckfeld's own personality.
Alongside his courtliness and nobility was a genuine respect for the
women with whom he corresponded; he took them very seriously, a
rarity in the age of paternalism. Perhaps what set him apart from many
of his clerical opponents was his ability not only to speak well, but to
listen carefully to men and women alike.

Schwenckfeld's tour of the South combined proselytization with a
running firefight against Butzer and the forces which Butzer inspired.
His first stop was probably at Landau, whose pastor, Johann Bader,
Schwenckfeld had won over from Zwinglianism in the baptismal debate.[2] Landau and the neighboring area would be a center for
Schwenckfeldianism well into the seventeenth century. From Landau
he went to Speyer, where he developed a coterie of admirers among
the judges and lawyers of the imperial court. The high point of the
movement's success there was undoubtedly under the Schwenckfelder
bishop Marquard (1560–1681).[3]

---

2. On Bader, see Gelbert 1868; Usteri 1883; CS IV, 70, 240–61. Bader's later views on
baptism combine a spiritualistic distinction of inner and outer to the disadvantage of the latter,
with a refusal to baptize the impious (Gelbert 1868, 246, 248, 255–56; Schiess 2, 272–73). He
advised Butzer to get Schwenckfeld's works on the two Testaments from Leo Jud and read them
before criticizing them (Bader to Butzer, July 31, 1533, Th. B. 6).

3. Schwenckfeld was in Speyer on September 10 (CS IV, 843:22). On the Schwenckfelders

The next stop on Schwenckfeld's journey was the imperial city of Esslingen. Here Schwenckfeld gave Martin Butzer and Ambrosius Blaurer, the reformer from Constance, a taste of the troubles he would cause them in years to come. Bordering on Catholic Württemberg, the city had been slow to reform, and as a result it was badly divided and lacked any central religious control.[4] In 1526–28 it became the center of a large and potentially violent Anabaptist conspiracy which was forcibly suppressed. Finally in 1531 the city council joined the Schmalkaldic League and, taking courage from this political prop, they began calling Protestant preachers. In September 1531 Ambrosius Blaurer, the "Apostle of Swabia," was invited to come and organize the new church, which he proceeded to do along Zwinglian lines. After his departure in June 1532 the council appointed Jakob Otter as chief pastor, making him independent from and superior to the other clerics.[5] Otter proved to be a difficult and arrogant colleague. It did not help matters that Otter supported the council's plan to transform Blaurer's ideal of a church discipline dominated by clerics into one controlled by the council.[6] Opposition to Otter gathered around the preacher Martin Fuchs, while Otter found an ally in the preacher Jakob Ringlin. In this charged atmosphere Schwenckfeld's arrival caused an explosion. Schwenckfeld was immediately adopted by Otter, who gave him lodging and invited him to dinner with Ringlin and Hans Sachs, the *Bügermeister*. Sebastian Franck, who was already living in Esslingen and seems to have had ties with Otter, may also have been at the dinner.[7] Schwenckfeld's message found approval with Otter in large part because both men shared the early Strassburg theology. But Ringlin went even further and became quite enamored of Schwenckfeld's spiritualism.[8] Despite Fuchs's efforts to tar his two opponents with the stigma of unorthodoxy, it was he and not Otter or Ringlin who was forced to leave. All of this provoked fears in Strassburg and Constance for the future of the Reformation in Esslingen.[9]

---

there, see CS VI, 428–44. On Marquard, see Mielke 1976; Mielke 1977, 312–15. See also Wiebe Bergsma's lecture on Aggaeus van Albada in Erb 1985 and Bergsma 1983.

4. On Esslingen's church in this period, see Keim 1860.

5. Keim 1860, 68, 95–96.

6. On the Otter-Fuchs battle, see Keim 1860, 68, 95–96, 101–07, and the pertinent letters in TA 8 and Schiess 1.

7. Weigelt 1970, 8. There is no exact date given for this meeting. It was between September 10 (Speyer) and September 19 (Ulm).

8. Keim 1860, 101–07.

9. Schiess 1, 430, 432, 434. Rumor had it that Schwenckfeld wanted to settle in Esslingen (p. 441).

The prospect of a Schwenckfelder church there was quite real. Butzer's and Blaurer's initial efforts to warn Otter of the danger which Schwenckfeld posed had been met with incredulity, in part because Otter was receiving contradictory, favorable advice about Schwenckfeld from Katharina Zell, Pastor Bonifacius Wolfhart of Augsburg, and others.[10] Exactly when Otter did break his ties with Schwenckfeld is unknown, but it was probably early, and it was certainly accomplished by 1544.[11] Nonetheless, Schwenckfeld's influence remained considerable. Nearby Stetten im Remstal, the home of a Schwenckfelder preacher, was constantly visited by Esslingers, as were Schorndorff and Cannstatt, which were also Schwenckfelder centers. Schwenckfeld came to Esslingen often, and he seems to have spent much of the 1540s just outside it at the "Bruderhoff im Wald." It was also his refuge during the Schmalkaldic War (1547–1549).[12] Schwenckfeld's most important friend in Esslingen was Hans Sachs, one of a string of officials whose patronage Schwenckfeld enjoyed.[13]

From Esslingen Schwenckfeld along with Sebastian Franck and another unknown "Fanatiker" went to nearby Koengen, the *Schloss* and village of Hans Friedrich Thumb von Neuburg, a friend and correspondent of Ambrosius Blaurer and the leading Protestant nobleman in Württemberg.[14] They also visited Hans Konrad Thumb and his sister Ursula at Stetten.[15] Here also, as in the case of the Esslingen clergy, Blaurer's efforts to warn Hans Friedrich Thumb had little or no effect. The Thumbs refused to listen to complaints against Schwenckfeld and pointed out that Schwenckfeld taught only what Blaurer himself had preached some years earlier. Unlike the Esslingen clergy, Hans Friedrich and Hans Konrad would remain Schwenckfeld's patrons, friends, and disciples. As we will see, the fate of Schwenckfeld and the Schwenckfelder movement in Württemberg was determined by that relationship.

10. Otter to Butzer, January 1, 1534, TA 8, 248–49. Schwenckfeld was Wolfhart's houseguest (CS IV, 844–45).

11. Keim 1860, 112. Otter threatened to resign if the council did not take steps to prevent Esslingers from visiting the Schwenckfelder and Anabaptist services in Stetten. Keim's idea (1860, 98–99) that Otter had refused the Stetten preacher Konrad Binder's participation in Esslinger clerical convents because Binder was a Schwenckfelder is inaccurate. This occurred before Schwenckfeld's arrival in the area; cf. Schiess 1, p. 391. Binder was an Anabaptist (TA 1, 72, 1010).

12. Keim 1860, 112. CS VII, 3–4. F. Weber 1962, 41.

13. Sachs served as *poste restante* for Schwenckfeld. CS VII, 94, 96.

14. Blaurer is our source for this (Blaurer to Machtolf, October 19, 1533, Schiess 1, 428–29; Blaurer to Butzer, October 19, 1533, Schiess 1, 434).

15. CS IV, 850, 859:1–25.

Franck and Schwenckfeld went on together to Ulm, where they stayed with an acquaintance of Franck.[16] Schwenckfeld was met there by Hans Heinrich Held von Tieffenau, one of the Strassburg contingent serving as pastors in troubled Augsburg. Both Hans Heinrich and his brother Jakob remained close friends of Schwenckfeld throughout their lives. Before conducting Schwenckfeld back to Augsburg, Held arranged a meeting with Martin Frecht and the Ulm clergy (September 29, 1533). Schwenckfeld, aware that Butzer's complaints had preceded him, was very careful not to get drawn into controversial areas.[17] Frecht, who had also been forewarned, was cautious, but he was impressed despite himself. The suspicion and reserve of this beginning was carefully tended by Butzer, and distrust grew into hatred. Frecht became Butzer's most important stalking-horse, and Schwenckfeld became Frecht's *bête noire*. But that still lay in the future

Schwenckfeld finally arrived in Augsburg on October 2, 1533, and took up residence with Bonifacius Wolfhart, who had invited him to the city.[18] Augsburg provided a perfect opportunity for Schwenckfeld. Because the city council resisted efforts to impose a church *Ordnung* (they would only begin during Schwenckfeld's stay), it was a divided city. There were four religious factions: Zwinglians of a Butzerian stripe, a strong though chastened Anabaptist community, an embittered Lutheran minority, and a struggling Catholic rearguard. A shortage of qualified Protestant pastors, exacerbated by the resignation of two Lutherans, had been remedied in 1531 through reinforcements from Strassburg: Bonifacius Wolfhart, Wolfgang Musculus, Sebastian Meyer, and Theobald Nigri (Schwarz). Nigri had resigned in 1532 and had been replaced by another Strassburg recruit, Hans Heinrich Held von Tieffenau.[19] They joined Michael Keller, a "pure" Zwinglian. Given this state of affairs, the Lutherans in the city, on the advice of Luther, avoided the Augsburg Eucharist, baptism, and wedding ceremonies—a Lutheran *Stillstand* as it were.[20] The Anabaptists, whose millennial hopes had been dashed by municipal repression in 1527–

---

16. On this our only source is Frecht to Butzer, October 30, 1533, Th. B. 6. TA 8, 202:31–203:13, is only an excerpt.

17. TA 8, 203:8–10.

18. TA 8, 132:26–29. Schwenckfeld hoped to continue his study of Hebrew with Wolfhart, whom he had known in Strassburg (CS IV, 847; Wolfart 1902, 102). Schwenckfeld also had some undefined business with members of the royal court (CS IV, 88:2–7).

19. Roth 1902, 11–12, 18, 20.

20. Roth 1902, 51–52.

28 and imperial repression in 1530, had begun to recover by 1531, this time emphasizing an earnest piety and moral improvement.[21] This religious diversity and practical toleration of nonviolent dissent must have been very attractive to Schwenckfeld, especially considering the drift of events in Strassburg.

Butzer, who kept close watch on developments in the wealthy and powerful Augsburg, was alarmed by the prospect of Schwenckfeld's presence in the city. In the middle of October 1533 he wrote to warn the Augsburg clergy and enclosed a copy of the latest round in his epistolary debate with Schwenckfeld.[22] Butzer praised Schwenckfeld as a good man filled with godly zeal, intelligent if a bit too subtle. Conceding that they agreed on most issues, he condemned Schwenckfeld for having unrealistic expectations for the church; the purity and the "spiritual powers" (virtutes spiritus) of the primitive church would simply never come again. Though Schwenckfeld himself could not be called an enemy of the church, there were others who would take advantage of him to disturb the church.

Augsburg's response must have had a chilling effect on Butzer.[23] The clergy there refused to be drawn into Butzer's battle. Rebuking him for having sent the treatise to them rather than to Schwenckfeld directly, they returned it and advised Butzer to suppress it altogether. It was clear that Butzer, not Schwenckfeld, was considered the problem.[24]

After their initial reaction, the Augsburg clerical corps quickly divided into pro- and anti-Schwenckfeld (or pro- and anti-Butzer) camps. Wolfhart was the most important Schwenckfeld supporter. He had gotten to know Schwenckfeld in 1529 at Strassburg, where they had both lived with Capito. From the moment of his arrival in Augsburg Wolfhart had preached on the sacraments in a Schwenckfeldian vein.[25] Hans Heinrich Held was also a loyal, if unobtrusive, sup-

---

21. Roth 1902, 399–400.

22. TA 8, 145–70. CS V, 814–24. TA dates it ca. October 10–19, 1533.

23. Written by Wolfhart, TA 8, 173–74. TA dates it to the second half of October 1533.

24. An even more forceful expression of Butzer's loss of credibility in Augsburg and evidence of divisions among the preachers in Strassburg itself was a response to Butzer written by the newly arrived Bartholomaeus Fontius (November 25, 1533, TA 8, 210–12). Fontius had signed the Strassburg "Gegenantwort," the treatise sent to Augsburg. But despite that, he berated Butzer (Wolfart 1902, 105–06). "I think first of all you must decide what you want this man to be: two-legged or four-legged, man or beast, Jew or Greek, pious or impious" (TA 8, 211:21–36). He urged Butzer to stop dividing the church with his Lutheran willfulness and aggressiveness (TA 8, 211:35–212:13). For Butzer's comment on this letter, see TA 8, 231:4–8.

25. In 1531 he preached on baptism and the distinction of inner and outer word in phrases

porter.[26] Bartholomaeus Fontius, a Venetian who had lectured on the Old Testament in Strassburg before coming to Augsburg, and Jakob Dachser, a reconverted Anabaptist, were considered Schwenckfelders.[27] Opposing them were Butzer's correspondents Wolfgang Musculus, the physician Geryon Sailer, and the Strassburger Sebastian Meyer.[28] Michael Keller's position was anomalous. Though he may have supported early efforts to have Schwenckfeld expelled, his eucharistic position was so close to Schwenckfeld's that in time they became allies in the opposition to Butzer's efforts at concord with the Saxons.[29] The Lutherans within the city were unremittingly hostile to Schwenckfeld and his followers.

Through Wolfhart, who enjoyed socializing with the upper classes in Augsburg, Schwenckfeld came to know many of the leading political figures, among them Wolfgang Rehlinger, *Bürgermeister* during Augsburg's Reformation year 1534.[30]

Schwenckfeld's arrival in Augsburg could not have come at a worse time, at least from Butzer's point of view. In January 1534 Wolfgang Rehlinger and Hieronymus Imhof were elected *Bürgermeister*.[31] The *Altbürgermeister* were Ulrich Rehlinger and Mang Seitz, both Zwinglians. Three of the four leading figures then, were Protestant (Imhof was considered a papist). The council as a whole also had a Protestant coloring.[32] The opportunity to carry out the Reformation seemed at last to be at hand, but the Protestant ranks were sorely divided by com-

very reminiscent of Schwenckfeld (Roth 1902, 56–57, 94–96). Wolfhart so deemphasized and spiritualized baptism that many Anabaptists felt reconciled with the Augsburg church. The Lutheran Agricola complained, but with no success. On Wolfhart, see Wolfart 1902; Pollet 1958, 80–105; Pollet 1962, 254–64.

26. Roth 1902, 46; Clasen 1972, 65; Pollet 1962, 227 n. 9.

27. Clasen 1972, 65–66, Roth 1902, 60.

28. Roth 1902, 60. On Musculus, see Pollet 1962, 226 n. 5.

29. Roth 1902, 60, believes that Keller joined forces with Meyer and Musculus in seeking Schwenckfeld's ouster in 1534. Pollet 1962, 241 n.6, used a June 7, 1534, letter from Geryon Sailer to Butzer to argue that Keller had joined forces with Wolfhart to defend Schwenckfeld; cf. TA 8, 344:15–20. As Köhler 1924, 265, 719–21, recognized, Keller's eucharistic theology was quite close to Schwenckfeld's. See also Roth 1902, 14–15, 70. In 1536 Keller joined with the Schwenckfelders Georg von Stetten and Wolfhart against the Lutheran Johann Forster and the Butzerian Musculus (Germann 1894, 167–69). Keller also supported Wolfhart's efforts to get another Schwenckfelder minister, Johannes Baumgartner, hired in 1537 (Germann 1894, 225–26). Keller had also agreed with Wolfhart's views on baptism in 1531 (Germann 1894, 126–27).

30. See Roth 1902, 41, 159–61, for Schwenckfeld's patrician or upper-class supporters. On the Schwenckfelder movement in Augsburg as a whole, see Clasen 1972, 62–66.

31. Roth 1902, 149–51.

32. Ulrich Welser, another Schwenckfelder, was also elected to the council. Roth 1902, 151.

peting religious, social, and political concerns. Although the Catholics were hopelessly outnumbered, they still had imperial support, Fugger wealth, and the political power of the very wealthy and noble cathedral canons. Opposed to the Catholics were the Lutherans and the Zwinglians who were themselves divided by two main issues: the Eucharist and the limits of legitimate church-state relations.

The Lutherans defended the real presence and opposed the forcible Reformation of the city by the secular authority.[33] The Zwinglians rejected the real presence and demanded immediate and thoroughgoing reform including confiscation of the revenues of the cathedral canons.[34] In order to achieve their goals during the election, the Zwinglian preachers spoke from the pulpit for "godly" magistrates and against unreliable ones. Their success showed the power that the preachers possessed, especially among the guilds. Given the social tension which was endemic in Augsburg and which the preachers exploited, and given the threat of imperial intervention should the city move against the cathedral canons, the council was in a most uncongenial situation. The mass of the population and a majority of the council preferred Zwinglianism, whereas the political conditions required a Lutheran moderation.

Schwenckfeld's ideas offered the perfect mix, and this explains his popularity and success. Many of Schwenckfeld's closest friends and followers in Augsburg were former Anabaptists. They were attracted to his near-Zwinglian eucharistic position, his opposition to state churches, and his spiritualistic emphasis. During his stay in Augsburg conventicles flourished once again.[35] In addition, his conservative social outlook and his anticlericalism were attractive to the city councillors caught in the cross fire of Lutheran sacramental dogmatism, Zwinglian political-social radicalism, and the Catholic imperial threat. Here one could be a good Zwinglian without paying the political price. In fact, the Schwenckfelder faction, with Wolfgang Rehlinger at its head, resisted efforts to establish a new Protestant church order.[36] The Schwenckfelders were wise to resist. When a church or-

33. This is very clear from Johann Forster's account (Germann 1894, 147–50, 241). Forster agreed with Schwenckfeld that giving preachers control of the sword could lead to a new Münster (Germann 1894, 245, 248, 254).

34. Germann 1894, 129–30, 152–59, 177–78.

35. Roth 1902, 60–61.

36. Wolfart 1901, 91. Many patricians, even Protestant ones, were made uneasy by the ministers' efforts to impose a Reformation by force (Wolfart 1901, 104).

der was pushed through in July 1534, a month after Schwenckfeld's departure, it still fell far short of the thorough Reformation that its supporters had hoped for. Sacraments and liturgy were Zwinglian, to be sure, but discipline was neglected.[37] Religious toleration continued de facto.

Butzer kept in close contact with supporters in Augsburg and dedicated to the Augsburg council his book against the Münsterites, the *Report out of Holy Scripture on the Correct Godly Establishment and Administration of the Christian Community [gemeyn], the Appointment of Ministers of the Word, the Maintenance and Use of the Sacraments.*[38] With this work Butzer set out his vision of the proper church order and tried to associate Schwenckfeld's opposition to it with the Münster debacle, in order to promote eucharistic concord between Lutherans and Zwinglians. Butzer's supporters in the city, perhaps with the help of the Lutherans, sought twice in May 1534 to have Schwenckfeld and Wolfhart expelled, but with no success.[39] Having mastered the opposition, Schwenckfeld felt free to leave Augsburg. In early June 1534 he returned to Strassburg to meet Butzer's challenge head-on.[40]

Schwenckfeld's departure by no means weakened his supporters' position within Augsburg. It may in fact have strengthened them by giving them a lower profile. It was harder to mobilize opposition to the Schwenckfelders when there was no Schwenckfeld upon whom to focus.[41] Their strength was clear in a number of ways. Butzer's credibility had suffered irreparable damage, and on the occasions when he visited the city, his reception by council and clergy alike was distinctly cool.[42] He was, and was made to feel, distinctly unwelcome.

37. The eventual liturgical changes undertaken in 1537 were very Zwinglian and were produced by Keller and Wolfhart revising a Musculus proposal. Germann 1894, 193–98.

38. Sailer to Butzer, December 21, 1533, TA 8, 231:4–8; Sailer to Butzer (January 15, 1534, 264:12); Sailer to Butzer, January 19, 1534, 264:16–18; Sailer to Butzer, February 18, 1534, Th. B. 7; Sailer to Capito and Butzer, April 24, 1534, TA 8, 305:16–21. Roth 1902, 59–60, speculates that Butzer may also have written to members of the council. For the *Report*, see Butzer 1960, vol. 5, pp. 109–258. Though originally intended to influence events in Münster, by the time it was published in early March 1534 Butzer had decided to dedicate it to the Augsburg council. As Ambrosius Blaurer was quick to recognize, the introduction was aimed at Schwenckfeld even if it did not mention him by name (Schiess 1, p. 486).

39. CS V, 103–07. Sailer to Butzer, May 23, 1534, TA 8, 342:24–27. The attempts were foiled by the other preachers.

40. CS V, 111.

41. Schwenckfeld's absence may have made effective cooperation possible between Keller and Wolfhart, as Sailer's letter to Butzer (June 7, 1534) suggests (TA 8, 344:15–20).

42. Butzer came to Augsburg on May 18, 1537, and was there three or four days before the

Opposition to Butzer did not prevent the city from accepting the Wittenberg Concord in 1536. Bonifacius Wolfhart took part at Wittenberg and personally signed the document.[43] But as with many South German cities this was a political decision intended to assure the city of the support of the Lutheran powers in the Schmalkaldic League. Wolfhart and Keller paid only lip service to it and soon returned to the Schwenckfeld-Zwinglian position.[44] The protests of the Lutheran pastor Johann Forster fell on deaf ears. Throughout the century, through the Schmalkaldic War, the Interim, and the Lutheranism of the *Hasenrat*, Zwinglianism and Schwenckfeldianism (often difficult to distinguish in this setting) continued to hold the allegiance of most Augsburgers.[45]

One of the reasons for the Schwenckfelders' success was their access to the printing press. During the 1530s and probably also the early 1540s there was no effort to prevent Schwenckfelder publication in Augsburg.[46] Augsburg remained open to the Schwenckfelders and to Schwenckfeld himself until 1553, and perhaps even later.[47] As a result,

---

Bürgermeister even received him. They complained that no one had invited him. He maintained that they had called him to help with the formulation of the new church order (Germann 1894, 193). Butzer tried to combat Schwenckfeld indirectly as well. He dedicated a second book to the Augsburg council, *Dialogi oder Gesprech von der gemainsame, unnd der kirchenubungen der cristen, und was yeder oberkait von ampts wegen, auss goettlichen bevelch an denselbigen zuversehen und zubessern gebuere* (1535). It too was directed against Schwenckfeld, at least in part (Roth 1902, 412).

43. Köhler 1953, 454. Wolfhart persuaded the *Bürgermeister* to send him to Wittenberg despite Butzer's grave misgivings (Germann 1894, 135).

44. Keller openly acknowledged that he had only accepted the concord because it was the will of the "Oberkeyt" (Germann 1894, 156–57). On Palm Sunday 1537 Wolfhart once again preached a Schwenckfeld version of the Eucharist (Germann 1894, 190).

45. Locher 1979, 468–69.

46. One of the first things that Schwenckfeld did upon arriving in 1533 was to publish a work dedicated to the family Thumb von Neuburg in Württemberg, *Von der Erbawung des Gewissens*, CS IV, 850–82. In the years that followed, other Schwenckfeld or Schwenckfelder works were also published (Germann 1894, 162–65, 220–21, 243–44, 255–56; Roth 1902, 412–14). The Lutheran Forster complained. But as he knew, the magistrates supported it (Germann 1894, 255). From 1536 to 1538 Bonifacius Wolfhart himself was in charge of book censorship (Wolfart 1902, 150). Members of the council and the church administration financed publication of Schwenckfelder works (Germann 1894, 166). Jakob Rehlinger, *Kirchenprobst* and the son of Wolfgang, arranged for the publication of Franck's *Guldene Arche* in 1538 (Germann 1894, 255–56). A feud between Forster and Georg von Stetten, Schwenckfelder and church provost, occasioned by one of these publications eventually caused Forster's dismissal (Germann 1894, 162–78). The two church provosts, von Stetten and Max Oham, and others refused to attend convents for some sixteen weeks in 1536 before being forced to return by the council. Roth 1902, 413, sees this as the real cause of Forster's eventual dismissal.

47. He posted a letter to Wilhelm von Zell from Augsburg on March 10, 1535 (CS V, 281:10–11). In 1539 Schwenckfeld returned briefly to Augsburg in the company of Bünderlin (Wolfart 1902, 147). There were probably other unrecorded visits. In 1553, during the only real

it was perhaps the largest center of Schwenckfeldianism in southern Germany.

Schwenckfeld's eight-month stay in Augsburg was broken by at least one trip. In early March 1534 Schwenckfeld traveled to Memmingen and neighboring Mindelheim to visit two close friends, Adam Reissner, the Mindelheim city clerk, and Wilhelm von Zell, an elderly patrician of the same city.[48] It was through von Zell, who had contacts in Zwinglian circles everywhere in southern Germany, that Schwenckfeld first learned that Ambrosius Blaurer had written against him to correspondents in Lindau, Isny, Kempten, Ulm, Esslingen, Reutlingen, and perhaps Memmingen.[49] Schwenckfeld responded with an "Apology" to Kempten, a letter to Blaurer, and a visit to Memmingen, where he defended himself against Blaurer's charges.[50] He was invited to preach publicly and in the houses of the city clerk and of both *Bürgermeister*. Neither Gervasius Schuler nor Simprecht Schenk, the two leading ministers, objected. Schuler seems to have

attempt to control them, only three Schwenckfelders were punished, and not too severely at that (Clasen 1972, 62).

48. Schwenckfeld's fourth letter to Jud (March 2, 1534) is dated from Mindelheim (CS V, 10:13). On Reissner see Erb 1980; Schottenloher 1908; Bücher 1950. He had probably made Schwenckfeld's acquaintance in Strassburg where Reissner had stayed with the humanist Jakob Ziegler, one of the four leading "Epicurean" opponents of Butzer's new order (CS V, 5; Erb 1980, 34). Schottenloher 1908, 20, dates Reissner's stay to 1533–34. But this is unlikely because he assumed the post in Mindelheim March 18, 1532 (CS V, 5). He remained city clerk until the Catholics finally removed him from office in 1548. He lived in Mindelheim until his death (between 1576 and 1582), spending his time gathering and copying the works of Schwenckfeld and Crautwald. Given von Zell's extensive travels, he and Schwenckfeld may already have met in Strassburg. Blaurer wrote Butzer (December 23, 1533) that von Zell had sought out (*ausgesucht*) Schwenckfeld in Augsburg a month and a half earlier (Schiess 1, 451. Cf. Butzer to Blaurer, November 5, 1533, TA 8, 438–39). Von Zell was an old and respected patrician, a close friend of Zwingli and his chief agent in southern Germany, and a frequent visitor in the Swiss cities, especially Constance and Zurich. CR names him "Haupt-Mittelmann Zwingli's fuer Suddeutschland" (CR 96, 327 n. 1). He would play an important if unwitting role in the Swiss-Schwenckfeld christological controversies of the 1540s. Johannes Zwick of Constance unbeknownst to von Zell sent von Zell's copies of Schwenckfeld works to Joachim Vadian of St. Gall (December 2, 1539, Vad. Br. 5, 579). Interestingly, Blaurer had pulled the same trick on von Zell almost exactly six years earlier, Blaurer to Butzer, December 23, 1533, Schiess 1, 451–52.

49. Such at least is the implication of Blaurer's letter of February 23, 1534, to Butzer (Schiess 1, 471–72). Here he defended having warned six cities immediately after mentioning a letter from von Zell. He seems to be responding indirectly to von Zell's criticism of this action. Though Blaurer names only six other cities, von Zell's involvement suggests that Blaurer had also written to Memmingen.

50. The Kempteners had immediately sent Blaurer's letter on to Schwenckfeld for comment (Schiess 1, 484). Schwenckfeld wrote a now lost "Apology" (CS V, 2). Blaurer claimed never to have received the letter (CS V, 11). On the Memmingen trip, see CS V, 12. See Blaurer's description to Butzer (March 11, 1534, Schiess 1, 477–78, and April 7, 1534, Schiess 1, 484).

been neutral while Schenk may actually have been won over for a time.[51] All of this had a decisive effect upon Memmingen's relationship to Blaurer in Constance and Butzer in Strassburg.[52] Both men were accused of uncharitable behavior toward Schwenckfeld, and Blaurer was warned to change his ways. Schwenckfeld may also have visited Kempten, and he seems to have had much the same effect there as in Memmingen.[53] It must have seemed as though Schwenckfeld was undermining Butzer's and Blaurer's position throughout southern Germany. In fact he was. The Allgäu—Memmingen, Kempten, Isny, Ravensburg, Lindau, and the surrounding countryside—quietly remained a haven for upper-class Schwenckfelders throughout the century.[54]

Having left Augsburg in early June Schwenckfeld once again went to Memmingen, where he openly criticized Butzer's book against Münster and circulated a treatise on baptism. Wilhelm von Zell joined Schwenckfeld in Memmingen,[55] and they arrived on the eighteenth in Ulm, where Bonifacius Wolfhart met them.[56] The three men stayed in the house of the *Bürgermeister* of Ulm, Bernhard Besserer, whom Schwenckfeld had met in Augsburg the preceding January. At the time Schwenckfeld had had quite an impact on Besserer, as Frecht had nervously reported to Butzer.[57] Bernhard Besserer was still

51. Schiess 1, 485. On Butzer's and Blaurer's fears for Schuler, who seems to have needed some coaxing to break with Schwenckfeld, see Blaurer to Butzer, March 3, 1534, Schiess 1, 480; Butzer to Blaurer, April 30, 1534, Schiess 1, 492; Butzer to Blaurer, June 8, 1534, Schiess 1, 502. Schuler's letter to Butzer (June 25, 1534, Th. B. 7) strikes a very careful balance. He reports Schwenckfeld's criticism of Butzer and Butzer's book against Münster, regrets Schwenckfeld's attacks on Butzer, and asks for books and a public disputation with Schwenckfeld. What really determined Schuler's attitude toward Schwenckfeld was Schuler's desire for peace and charity. There was already revelation enough. As with Butzer, so with Schuler: it was not Schwenckfeld's doctrine per se, but his divisive impact that made him unwelcome.

52. Musculus to Blaurer, March 29, 1534, Schiess 1, 479; Blaurer to Butzer, April 7, 1534, pp. 484–85; Butzer to Blaurer, April 30, 1534, p. 492; Butzer to Blaurer, May 29, 1534, p. 501; Butzer to Blaurer, June 8, 1534, p. 502. Part of the reason for Schwenckfeld's success was the support he got from Wolfhart in Augsburg (Blaurer to Butzer, April 20, 1534, Schiess 1, 488–89). The *Stadtschreiber* Maurer seems to have been the most fervent convert (CS V, 14).

53. Frecht to Blaurer, April 5, 1534, Schiess 1, 452; Blaurer to Butzer, April 7, 1534, p. 454; Butzer to Blaurer, April 30, 1534, p. 497. The Kempteners delayed sending a copy of Schwenckfeld's "Apology" to Blaurer (Schiess 1, 484).

54. See McLaughlin 1985b.

55. Schuler to Butzer, June 25, 1534, Th. B. 7.

56. Frecht to Butzer, June 26, 1534, Th. B. 7; Frecht to Blaurer, June 28, 1534, Schiess 1, 504–06.

57. Wolfart 1902, 104–05; Frecht to Butzer, January 8, 1534, Th. B. 7; Frecht to Blaurer, January 14, 1534, Schiess 1, 462–63. Wolfart mistakenly believes that Schwenckfeld had visited Besserer in Ulm in January.

or once again in Augsburg, so his son Georg played host for Schwenck-
feld and his companions. Over meals they discussed theology with
Frecht. The city clerk, Sebastian Aitinger, who would remain an im-
portant friend of Schwenckfeld throughout the years, also invited them
to dinner.[58] On the twentieth Wolfhart returned to Augsburg, and
Schwenckfeld went on to visit the Thumbs at Stetten and Koengen.[59]
From there he proceeded to Strassburg, arriving at the beginning of
July.[60]

During Schwenckfeld's ten-month absence important developments
in Strassburg had radically changed the religious situation there.
When Schwenckfeld had left the preceding September, Butzer's efforts
to impose a new, more restrictive church order had been frustrated,
although Butzer was still working to get the council to force Schwenckfeld to "spend his penny elsewhere."[61] In October 1533 the preachers
submitted a proposal which would have outlawed those who spoke
against the "truth" and attempted to withdraw others from it. A commission would have been established to examine dissidents, and citizens would have been called upon to report deviations to the commission. All children were to be baptized in their parish churches within
a prescribed period.[62] The preachers also asked that a final meeting of
the synod be held to pass judgment on those charged earlier. Because
of the council's inaction, the preachers complained, "some are more
impudent than before, as if error had been victorious."[63] On October
13 the council ordered a reconvening of the synod in ten days' time.[64]
On the day before the synod met, the council decided to limit the
synod to the examination of those who had made their opposition public.[65] At the synod itself (October 23, 29) there was discussion of practical measures to be taken.[66] A commission which had been given

58. Cf. Schwenckfeld to Sebastian Aitinger, February 10, 1539, CS XVIII, 208–20.
59. Schiess 1, 506. See also Hans Konrad Thumb to Jakob Sturm, June 26, 1534, TA 8,
363:6–364:2.
60. Butzer complained to Blaurer of Schwenckfeld's presence in the city (July 10, 1534,
Schiess 1, 508). Schwenckfeld must have arrived around July 1. He later stated that he stayed
seven whole weeks in Strassburg (CS V, 542:1–7). Our first report of his departure from Strassburg came in a letter from Butzer to Blaurer (August 17, 1534, Schiess 1, 522).
61. TA 8, 165:23–166:11.
62. TA 8, 135:21–141:20, submitted before October 13, 1533.
63. TA 8, 143:11–144:7, also before October 13, 1533.
64. TA 8, 144:24–33.
65. TA 8, 176:14–21.
66. TA 8, 177:24–181:17.

Hoffmann's and Schwenckfeld's books to examine in the previous spring was ordered to present a written report.[67] They presented their findings, Butzer's letter to Schwenckfeld, Schwenckfeld's reply, and Butzer's response to Schwenckfeld's reply.[68] The council also took the occasion of the synod to warn the preachers to come to some agreement among themselves and to refrain from squabbling publicly in their sermons. The synodal commission finally reported back to the council on November 11, 1533, but made no recommendations.[69] No decisions were taken, no actions commanded.

Informed by his sources in Strassburg of Butzer's machinations, Schwenckfeld wrote to the four presidents of the synod,[70] and, in effect, accused Butzer of deceit, libel, and attempted extortion. He also sent the presidents a copy of his most recent letter to Butzer, which Butzer had failed to present at the October synod, and explained that he couldn't return immediately to defend himself because he had business with his friends at the royal court. This letter could not have improved Butzer's position in Strassburg.

Strassburg's allies began to worry about the situation in the city.[71] There was still deep division among the preachers.[72] Engelbrecht, Schultheiss, and Matthaeus Zell were firmly opposed to any hint of coercion in matters of religion. Capito had become more amenable, but that did not help much. Butzer and Hedio were by now unpopular in the city, and without Zell's support there was no hope of achieving their goals through popular action. This meant they would have to rely on the council, but unfortunately the council was also divided. A clear majority opposed the new "Papism," and argued that the planned changes were against the liberties of the city. They also objected that "force is not to be used on the conscience unless external insolence disturbs the republic."[73] Between this opposition and the disinclination of others to waste time on religion,[74] the council took no action on the preachers' proposals.

On December 26 the council admitted that, because of the press of

67. TA 8, 178:23–32.
68. TA 8, 182:30–193:12.
69. TA 8, 204:28–206:38.
70. On November 16, 1533. CS IV, 883–88.
71. E.g., Myconius to Capito and Butzer, November 23, 1533, TA 8, 209:13–18.
72. Butzer to Myconius, after November 23, 1533, TA 8, 210:1–8.
73. TA 8, 209:24–34.
74. Butzer to Bullinger, October 29, 1533, TA 8, 201:23–37.

business, the synod's work was not proceeding as quickly as it might, but the council ordered the preachers to refrain in the interim from stirring up the people with their sermons.[75] On January 14, 1534, Caspar Hedio gave the traditional election sermon to the council.[76] In it he emphasized the duty of the "Oberkeyt" to order and control religion, and the dangers to both church and state if they failed to do so. Shortly thereafter the preachers submitted a long and detailed demand that the synodal decrees be accepted and enforced, and they threatened to resign if their demand was not met.[77] On February 16 the council capitulated.[78] Finally on March 4, 1534, the council voted to accept both the *Tetrapolitana* and Butzer's sixteen articles.[79] This marked the turning point and was a victory for Butzer, who had put unrelenting pressure upon both the council and his fellow ministers.

Events had also played into Butzer's hands. The deterioration of the situation in Münster and the establishment of the Anabaptist kingdom were skillfully used by Butzer to discredit his opponents and stampede the council. In November he had spread the rumor that Bernhard Rothmann, the leading clerical figure of the radicals in Münster, was the disciple of both Hoffmann and Schwenckfeld.[80] Butzer was convinced that the idea of religious toleration, "satanic license," was merely an Anabaptist plot which would enable them to seize power.[81] By late December the council was beginning to show signs of concern.[82] Hedio's January sermon to the council raised the spectre once again of the "new people" in the city.[83] But it was the reading of a sensitive political barometer that probably determined the council and sealed the fate of Butzer's opponents: On March 2, it was reported that the women bath attendants were calling the council members fools for

75. TA 8, 332:6–34.

76. TA 8, 262:14–263:39.

77. Between January 28 and February 2, TA 8, 265:20–269:8. It was signed by all but Engelbrecht and Schultheiss, who were reckoned among the opponents. Wendel 1942, 108–10.

78. TA 8, 279:15–280:19.

79. TA 8, 285:32–286:24.

80. Butzer to Blaurer, November 16, 1533, Schiess 1, 442–43.

81. Butzer to Blaurer, October 23, 1533, TA 8, 181:29–37; Butzer to Bullinger, October 29, 1533, TA 8, 202:1–11; Butzer to Bullinger, October 30, 1533, TA 8, 202:17–24.

82. Butzer to Blaurer, December 18, 1533, TA 8, 222:5–8. "Cum vident nun senatores Hoffmani furorem hic corripuisse tamen multos, ut de motu rerum timendum sit, volunt manum admovere; sed sero est."

83. TA 8, 263:11–18.

not realizing that the Anabaptists were getting the upper hand in the city.[84]

Butzer had also had success with his own colleagues. Engelbrecht was dismissed the day after Christmas, supposedly because attendance at his church did not warrant a minister. But when Engelbrecht offered to continue his services at his own expense, the council refused.[85] By January 30 Butzer had also won over Matthaeus Zell, at least partly.[86] In March Schultheiss was threatened with dismissal.[87] The united front which the clergy presented to the council undoubtedly had an effect.

On April 13, 1534, the council ordered all Anabaptists, with their families, to leave the city within eight days. The order was repeated in June.[88] Schwenckfeld was not personally affected by these decrees. His fate was finally brought up on June 19 during the council's discussion of the preachers' demands. It was decided to advise Schwenckfeld not to return to the city.[89] Intriguingly, this notice was to be informal and was to be conveyed by Schwenckfeld's own disciples in Strassburg back to their master in Augsburg. This is interesting for two reasons. First, because of the informality of the action, Schwenckfeld was not legally banned from the city. He would never be legally banned from any city in southern Germany, a fact which he was quick to point out to his opponents. Second, the council knew of and accepted the presence of his followers in the city, and instead of proceeding against them, chose to employ them as intermediaries. The Schwenckfelders in Strassburg suffered little more suppression in Strassburg than they did elsewhere.

The council's decision caused Schwenckfeld to return to Strassburg. He came at the invitation of his followers and well-wishers, and with the encouragement of members of the council, perhaps even of a *Bürgermeister*.[90] Schwenckfeld did not plan to return permanently. He had business there and wanted to secure his right to visit the city as he

84. "Ratsprotokoll," March 2, 1534, TA 8, 281:20–21. "Die widertaeufer ueberhand nehmen, dass die badermaegd sagen, sie, m.h.h., seien narren, dass sie solches nicht merken."
85. TA 8, 233:4–20.
86. Butzer to Blaurer, January 30, 1533, TA 8, 270:12–19. In Butzer's opinion Zell, because of his advanced years, was not as easily molded or manipulated as Capito. But they got Zell to appear before the council in support of their position.
87. March 23, 1534, TA 8, 295:1–2.
88. TA 8, 301:11–18, 359:21–23. Cf. Wendel 1942, 115.
89. TA 8, 356:30–33. Note that this was decided in discussion. There was no formal decree.
90. CS V, 146:3–18. The Schwenckfelders were claiming that Schwenckfeld went to Strassburg "favore consulum vestrorum," in order to debate with the preachers (TA 8, 364:11–17).

chose.[91] He came prepared for battle, bearing letters of support and recommendations from Augsburg, Bernhard Besserer, and Hans Konrad Thumb.[92]

On July 15 he submitted a "Supplication."[93] In it he complained that he had lived peaceably and had not been charged with anything. He also argued that it ill befit the council to do anything that would reflect badly on him or them. It is an impressive letter, impressive for its secular tone and content, impressive for its appeal to rank and privilege and its implied threats if that rank and privilege were not respected.

The council forwarded the "Supplication" to the preachers for comment and remarked that Schwenckfeld was claiming the religious freedom guaranteed by the "Nürnberger Abschied" (1532).[94] The preachers requested a new public hearing in order to clear *their* names.[95] Schwenckfeld's complaints had found a receptive audience outside the city, and the preachers found themselves accused of having treated him unfairly at the synod, of failing to meet his objections publicly, and of working behind his back and in his absence to place him in physical danger. The council rejected the preachers' request, fearing further division among the preachers and between the preachers and the council.[96] And

> because he [Schwenckfeld] can't come to an agreement with the Church, so may he go away and leave the Council in peace [*unbekummert*]. The presidents [of the synod] shall tell him in a friendly way that the Council doesn't want to mete out any dis-

91. Business is mentioned by Schwenckfeld (CS V, 146:19–22) and Thumb (TA 8, 363:19–31). Schuler (Schuler to Butzer, June 25, 1534, Th. B. 7) stated that Schwenckfeld was transporting money for people in Strassburg. On his plans not to remain permanently, see CS V, 148:20–28. Hans Konrad Thumb also said much the same thing (TA 8, 363:19–31). According to Frecht (Frecht to Blaurer, June 28, 1534, Schiess 1, 506), Schwenckfeld wanted to go to Strassburg and "live inconspicuously for a while" (*eine zeitlang verborgen leben*). Afterward he planned to return "here" (*hieher*). Whether that meant Ulm or its environs is not clear.

92. Wolfhart's decision to accompany Schwenckfeld to Ulm and to urge that Frecht write to Butzer on Schwenckfeld's behalf suggests that Wolfhart and the other Augsburg ministers may well have written in Schwenckfeld's support (Frecht to Blaurer, June 28, 1534, Schiess 1, 505). On Besserer's letter, addressed to Sturm and no longer extant, see Frecht to Butzer, August 3, 1534, Th. B. 7. For Thumb's letter to Sturm, see TA 8, 363:6–364:2.

93. CS V, 143–49. The exact date of Schwenckfeld's arrival is unknown, but it was prior to July 10 (Butzer to Blaurer, July 10, 1534, Schiess 1, 508.

94. July 15, 1534, TA 8, 366:8–26.

95. July 22, 1534, TA 8, 367:1–36.

96. TA 8, 367:39–368:9.

honor to him. Therefore, let him be told in all the more friendly way.[97]

This decision was taken on July 22, but Schwenckfeld managed to stay on in Strassburg for almost another month. Finally, shortly before August 19, 1534, he left the city.[98]

The council's treatment of Schwenckfeld shows that he was not expelled on doctrinal grounds, but because of his personal differences with Butzer and the other ministers. He was asked to leave in order to preserve peace and harmony. Given a choice between one man and the corps of ministers, the council made a sensible decision. It was not Schwenckfeld who posed a threat. The ministers threatened disruption if Schwenckfeld stayed. The council may have been willing to pay this price for peace, but it was careful not to go any further. Schwenckfeld was not officially banned. He even received a promise from Jakob Sturm that the city would observe an official silence on the whole matter.[99] This hampered Butzer's attempts to discredit Schwenckfeld elsewhere in Germany. The council also took no steps against his followers until the following year, and then for other reasons.[100] Overall, despite its irritation with Schwenckfeld, the council showed itself tolerant, sympathetic, one might even say indulgent toward him. One senses that on a personal level they preferred him to the preachers.

Schwenckfeld's departure was at best only a qualified victory for Butzer. His attack on the dissidents lost Butzer whatever popularity he had enjoyed within the city.[101] In fact, Butzer's harshness and that of his post-Interim Lutheran successors recruited followers for Schwenckfeld.[102] In a longer perspective Schwenckfeld may be considered even to have won the duel with Butzer. There was a sturdy

97. TA 8, 368:9–13.

98. Between August 9 (Butzer to Blaurer, TA 8, 369:20–23) and August 17 (Butzer to Blaurer, TA 8, 371:11–16), but closer to the seventeenth.

99. Schwenckfeld to Hans Konrad Thumb, after May 1, 1535, CS V, 320:16–21.

100. Both Alexander Berner and Jakob Held von Tieffenau were expelled under a law designed for the Anabaptists (TA 8, 438:16–18, 449:25–28). See Butzer to Blaurer, June 2, 1535, TA 8, 458:17–24, on the reasons for Berner's continuing exile. The matter of an oath also barred Schwenckfeld's return (Butzer to Blaurer, July 25, 1535, TA 8, 472:14–19).

101. Johann Sturm explained Butzer's unpopularity in the city to Queen Elizabeth's minister Walingham (February 23, 1577) as resulting from the "ejection" of Ziegler, Schwenckfeld, Engelbrecht, and others (Röhrich 1830–32, vol. 2, p. 121). It is of course possible that Sturm, who was involved in his own battle for toleration, may have been swayed in this statement by other considerations.

102. According to Katharina Zell in her Brieff an die gantze Burgerschafft der Statt Strassburg (1557), cited in Abray 1978, 72 n. 52.

Schwenckfelder congregation in Strassburg long after Butzer's church order had been replaced by a rigorously Lutheran one, and Schwenckfeld himself was able to visit the city long after Butzer's own definitive exile.[103]

Württemberg

After finally leaving Strassburg in mid-August 1534, Schwenckfeld headed north by way of Speyer to Frankfurt.[104] His whereabouts for the next six months (September 4, 1534–March 10, 1535) remain unknown, but he may simply have gone to ground with the Thumb family at Koengen or Stetten near Esslingen, to lick his wounds and to reconsider his position.[105] Badly shaken by his expulsion from Strassburg, he was embittered and fatalistic.[106] The temptation to retire from the field no doubt warred with his sense of outrage and his desire for vindication. He reappeared in Augsburg in March and immediately served notice that he had found a new cause—the battle against Butzer's effort at concord—and a new arena—Württemberg.[107] If Butzer had thought that Schwenckfeld's expulsion from Strassburg would eliminate him as a threat, he was soon to see that he was badly mistaken.

Once again Schwenckfeld had placed himself at the center of events in the South German Reformation. Duke Ulrich of Württemberg had only recently reconquered his lands.[108] Driven from Württemberg in 1519 by the Swabian League for his personal misconduct and political

103. Schwenckfeld returned to Strassburg secretly in 1558 (Husser 1977, 521). He may well have visited at other times, but there is no evidence.

104. CS V, 165:14–16. Frecht to Butzer, September 25, 1534, Th. B. 7 and Frecht to Capito, September 30, 1534, Th. B. 7 reported Schwenckfeld's presence in Speyer and Frankfurt.

105. Schultz 1946, 230, presumes that Stetten was his refuge. By a process of elimination this seems probable. Frecht would have reported if Schwenckfeld were at Ulm. Schwenckfeld's letter (CS V, 164–65) to the Zolls, who lived in Augsburg, clearly conveys the impression he was not going there. His letter to Wilhelm von Zell on March 10, 1535, implies by its length and treatment of recent events that Schwenckfeld had not been to Memmingen or Mindelheim recently. Schwenckfeld's presence in Württemberg may also be inferred from the fact that Duke Ulrich wrote Luther asking his opinion of Schwenckfeld in December 1534 (Heyd 1838, 32–33). Would he have written then if Schwenckfeld had not been present in the duchy?

106. CS V, 165:14–16. His criticism of the Stuttgart Concord (CS V, 247–61) was uncharacteristically blunt and harsh.

107. Letter to Wilhelm von Zell, March 10, 1535, CS V, 275–81.

108. On Ulrich see L. Heyd 1841–44, esp. vols. 2 and 3. On the Reformation in Württemberg, see Rauscher 1934.

misrule, Ulrich had long tried to regain his duchy. The league had handed Württemberg over to the Habsburgs, at first for them to administer, and after 1530 as their permanent possession. Though in most respects an improvement over Ulrich's reign, the Austrian administration was Catholic in a land which was increasingly Protestant. Austrian severity created a party in Württemberg for Ulrich's return, especially after Ulrich became a Protestant. In May 1534, with French money, with the discreet support of the Protestant imperial cities, with the indirect aid of the Bavarians, and with the army of Philip of Hesse, the Austrian regime was driven from Stuttgart.[109] Elector Johann Friedrich of Saxony mediated the treaties of Kaaden (June 1534) and Vienna (August 1535), in which the Habsburgs granted Ulrich and his heirs Württemberg as a fief. Ulrich was allowed a limited right to reform the church in his lands, but Anabaptists and "Sacramentarians" (read Zwinglians) were to be suppressed. One sees the fine hand of Lutheran Saxony in this stipulation.[110]

The Sacramentarians remained powerful in the duchy despite the treaties' ban. The Zwinglian camp boasted most of the nobility, a large proportion of the new clergy, and the populations of the cities within the duchy and the imperial cities on its borders.[111] Ulrich himself held views of the Eucharist similar to those of Schwenckfeld and the early Butzer.[112] But political considerations carried more weight. Philip of Hesse, though moderate and somewhat tolerant, was nonetheless a Lutheran. Ulrich owed him a vast sum of money for his military support and was dependent upon him for political backing. It was Philip who arranged Württemberg's entry into the Schmalkaldic League in 1536. And Saxony, which had also arranged and guaranteed the treaties, stood behind Philip and the league. In effect, the treaties mandated that the duchy be Lutheran. In the contest to control the church in Württemberg the Lutherans had the advantage, but final victory would come only with the death of Ulrich and the accession of his son Christoph, who was thoroughly Lutheran.[113]

Ulrich, however, was careful to maintain a balance between the two

109. The Austrians were easily overcome at Nordheim (May 12, 1534) and Lauffen (May 13, 1534). Rauscher 1934, 111.
110. Rauscher 1934, 112–13.
111. L. Heyd 1841–44, vol. 3, p. 43. See also Jakob Sturm's letter to Philip of Hesse, August 26, 1534, Beilage 14, in Sattler 1771, 114.
112. Rauscher 1934, 40–41; Butzer to Blaurer, end of July 1534, Schiess 1, 510.
113. Rauscher 1934, 177–94. Cf. Estes 1982.

parties. He called two reformers, Erhard Schnepf, a Lutheran in Philip's service, and Ambrosius Blaurer.[114] While Schnepf was given the northern part of Württemberg and was based in Stuttgart, Blaurer was given the southern part and was based in the university town Tübingen. The appointment of two reformers with widely differing views guaranteed that the battle between Lutherans and Zwinglians would continue to be fought at Ulrich's court, because in the court were made the decisions that affected the entire range of ecclesiastical affairs. There were three levers by which outside forces could hope to influence events: Ulrich himself, Philip of Hesse, and the handful of counselors and officials who ran the government of Württemberg. As Ulrich's decision to appoint two fundamentally opposed reformers shows, the duke hoped to achieve some sort of compromise which would obviate the clashes that the situation in Württemberg seemed destined to produce. Though Schnepf, Blaurer, and others assiduously courted and counseled the duke, their efforts never promised great success. As a result the Sacramentarians also courted Philip of Hesse, and both sides built parties in the newly reestablished court.

There were three figures of primary importance in the court and in the early years of the Württemberg Reformation: Johann Knoder, Georg von Ow zu Zimmern, and Hans Konrad Thumb von Neuburg.[115] Knoder served as chancellor (1534–35), then court chancellor (1535–50). Supported by lower officials drawn from Hessian service, Knoder, along with Schnepf, was the pillar of Lutheranism in the court.[116] Georg von Ow, though titled *Statthalter*, was in reality head of the *Rentkammer*, the ducal exchequer which also oversaw the Church.[117] Von Ow was a conscientious and loyal servant, a treacherous court infighter, and, like his duke, essentially neutral in the religious struggles, at least at first.[118]

---

114. Rauscher 1934, 114–15; A. Heyd 1838. On Blaurer's activities in Württemberg, see Brecht 1964 and Held 1965.

115. Rauscher 1934, 123.

116. On Knoder, see Bernhardt 1972, vol. 1, pp. 213–14. See also L. Heyd 1841–44, vol. 3, p. 64; cf. Butzer to Blaurer, end of July 1534, Schiess 1, 511–12. G. d. J. Bossert 1944–48, 281, claimed Knoder was "zwinglich [sic] gesinnte." But given Butzer's view and Knoder's position in the Lutheran duke Christoph's service, this is highly unlikely. On the Hessian contingent at court, see L. Heyd 1841–44, vol. 3, p. 187.

117. Bernhardt 1972, vol. 1, p. 25; vol. 2, pp. 532–33.

118. He seems to have engineered Hans Konrad Thumb's demise (Bernhardt 1972, vol. 2, p. 532). Butzer described him as reputedly good, but of unknown religious proclivities (Schiess 1, 511–12).

The third personage, Hans Konrad Thumb von Neuberg, was the hereditary court marshal (*Erbhofmarschall*) and the most powerful individual at court until his fall from favor in 1544.[119] He and his brother Hans Friedrich the *Obervogt* of Kirchheim unter Teck were cast by Butzer and Blaurer as the court advocates for the Sacramentarians.[120] Hans Konrad played an important role in the early phases of the Reformation. He directed the extensive confiscations of church property, a process which enabled Ulrich to repay his war debts and to set the state's finances on a sound footing.[121] Although Thumb benefited personally from the confiscations, his devotion to the Reformation was unfeigned and antedated Ulrich's return.[122] He and his brother had been the first nobles in Württemberg to introduce the Reform on their estates, and in 1532 the two had joined the Schmalkaldic League.[123] The two brothers were firmly and openly committed to the Reformation in its Zwinglian or Swiss form, and Blaurer was often their guest during his years of service in Württemberg.[124]

Nonetheless, Butzer's and Blaurer's hopes for the Thumbs were never realized. The *Erbhofmarschall* and his brother did remain the heart of the Sacramentarian faction at court, but they represented the Schwenckfeldian and not the Butzerian or even the Swiss variation on that theme. As we have seen, Schwenckfeld visited the Thumbs in 1533, and again in 1534.

Schwenckfeld's ties to the Thumbs alerted Butzer and the other

119. On the Thumbs, see Bernhardt 1972, vol. 2., p. 675; Boger 1885. On the *Erbhofmarschall's* importance at court, L. Heyd 1841–44, vol. 3, p. 67. The family fortune had been made by the father of these two Thumbs, Konrad the first hereditary marshal. On Konrad Thumb, see Boger 1885, 69–93; Bernhardt 1972, vol. 2, pp. 677–78. He was the leading regent during Ulrich's minority and the man in charge of finances thereafter. The Thumbs remained loyal to Ulrich in 1519, and both Konrad and his eldest son, Hans Konrad, who was the duke's contemporary and boon companion, went into exile with the duke. On Hans Konrad Thumb, see Boger 1885, 101–17; Bernhardt 1972, vol. 2, pp. 675–77. The elder Thumb returned to Württemberg in 1520 and the younger in 1521, both having fallen out of favor with Ulrich. They served the Austrian administration, the elder Konrad once again in control of finances. After his father's death in 1525 Hans Konrad was granted the hereditary marshalship (1527). The speed and ease with which Hans Konrad returned to favor after Ulrich's return suggests that he may already have intrigued with the exiled duke before the reconquest.

120. Schiess 1, 512.

121. Rauscher 1934, 123; Boger 1885, 108–09; Bernhardt 1972, vol. 2, pp. 675–77.

122. Both Hans Konrad and Hans Friedrich were later accused of despoiling church property for their own gain (Boger 1885, 116–17; G. d. J. Bossert 1944–48, 283).

123. Reform was introduced at Koengen in 1527 and at Stetten in 1528. On the Thumbs' early reform activity, see Boger 1885, 105–06; L. Heyd 1841–44, vol. 2, pp. 311–12; Rauscher 1934, 49, 109.

124. On Blaurer's ties to the Thumbs, see Schiess 1, 360, 371, and passim.

Strassburg reformers to the danger which Schwenckfeld posed in Württemberg. Within days of the decisive battle of Lauffen which won Württemberg for Duke Ulrich, Butzer, Capito, and the Strassburg clergy had written to Philip of Hesse, Ulrich, Johann Knoder, and Johann Jakob Truchsess von Rheinfelden, another member of Ulrich's council, to press their own vision of an irenic Reformation embracing Lutherans and Zwinglians, and to warn against Caspar Schwenckfeld.[125] Schwenckfeld, however, was not defenseless. The Schwenckfelders at court were joined by Graf Wilhelm von Fürstenberg, who had commanded the infantry during the battle for Württemberg. Aided by certain Strassburg nobles, they set out to destroy Butzer's standing with both Philip of Hesse and Ulrich.[126] They succeeded at Stuttgart. Butzer played no important direct role there. He had to rely on Blaurer and others to influence the court and to effect whatever plans he had.

The Schwenckfelder response to Butzer was not limited to personal attacks. Much more important was Schwenckfeld's concerted campaign against Butzer's policy of eucharistic concord. The need for such a campaign was first made clear by the Stuttgart Concord (August 2, 1534) between Schnepf and Blaurer, which was an apparent success for Butzer.[127] Blaurer was no theologian; he was a pastor and practical reformer. He shared with Butzer the fear of division and disunity which would negate the concrete results of the Reform. In an effort to end the disagreements with Schnepf, at Butzer's suggestion Blaurer accepted a formulation which the Lutherans had submitted at Marburg in 1529, but which, unbeknownst to Blaurer, had been rejected by the Swiss.[128] Blaurer was caught in the middle. The Swiss rejected it out-

125. Capito wrote to von Rheinfelden on May 21, 1534 (TA 1, 990–93). On von Rheinfelden, see Bernhardt 1972, vol. 2, p. 561. Butzer wrote on the following day to Chancellor Johann Knoder (TA 1, 993). The Strassburg clergy as a whole wrote to Philip of Hesse and Ulrich on May 18, 1534, with the same message (Lenz, 36–37). But the passage dealing with Schwenckfeld specifically was deleted before posting. Either the clerics themselves or the council considered it impolitic to impugn a friend of the Thumbs by name. Ulrich consulted Luther and Philip of Hesse about Schwenckfeld in December (A. Heyd 1838, 32–33).

126. Butzer to Blaurer, January 18, 1535, Schiess 1, 632; Butzer to Frecht, May 8, 1535, TA 8, 450:20–24. Fürstenberg may well have been influenced by Schwenckfeld, but his religiosity was not very deep (Wagner 1966, 182).

127. On the concord, see Köhler 1953, 320–58.

128. Schiess 1, 528. Butzer had sent it to Blaurer, but had neglected to explain its exact provenance and its unacceptability to the Swiss. Köhler 1953, vol. 2, pp. 337–38, has uncovered the course of events. He himself asks, "Aber hat Bucer mit dieser Urkunde ein ehrliches Spiel getrieben?" Butzer let Blaurer believe that Oecolampadius had accepted the articles. In Switzerland it was well understood that Butzer was behind it all.

right, while the South German preachers were much disturbed, and the Lutherans spoke openly of Blaurer's recantation.

Schwenckfeld wasted no time in condemning the agreement.[129] His attack concentrated on Butzer. He accused Butzer of being a fraud and a fool,[130] who had turned his back on his own teachings in order to embrace an illusory agreement with the Lutherans. Butzer had sacrificed the truth and his integrity and had gained nothing, because he and Luther still disagreed. Schwenckfeld insisted that concord and agreement were only possible when based on acceptance of truth. *Stillstand* and mutual tolerance, not a foolish and ill-considered concord, were the real remedies. Schwenckfeld's criticism of Butzer's "agreement" with Luther was perceptive and embarrassing, and it did nothing to calm the waters in Stuttgart.[131]

The Lutheran faction at court hastened to take advantage of the mutual recrimination among the Sacramentarians. On April 1, 1535, the ducal council at Stuttgart reported to the duke that there were Anabaptists in and about Schorndorff, a town on the river Rems some twenty kilometers from Esslingen, and that Schwenckfeld, who was still a guest of Hans Konrad Thumb in nearby Stetten, was a frequent visitor to their gatherings. The *Obervogt* of Schorndorff was ordered to keep close watch and to arrest any participants. Five days later Ulrich issued a decree against the Anabaptists and "other such sects."[132] Though Schwenckfeld was not mentioned, the decree was clearly directed against him. After receiving the report, Ulrich had in fact consulted Blaurer about Schwenckfeld, and Blaurer had pronounced Schwenckfeld to be a dangerous man.[133] However accurately it expressed his own

129. He was heard to attack it in Speyer and Frankfurt (Frecht to Butzer, September 25, 1534 and Frecht to Capito, September 30, 1534, Th. B. 7). Sometime that fall he reissued his *Confession of the Lord's Supper*, to combat this tendency to fall back into Lutheranism (*Bekanntnuss vom hailigen Sacrament dess Leibs und Bluts Christi / auf frag und Antwort gestellt*, CS V, 166–209). CS dates it ca. October 1534. This is a revised version of Doc. 100, CS III, 712–52, published in 1530. Schwenckfeld explained his motives to Wilhelm von Zell, (March 10, 1535, CS V, 277:1–18). He also circulated at least two manuscript works: "Wider den newen irrsall und concordiam Butzerj und Lutherj vom, sacrament" and "Judicium von Butzers und Luthers Concordia jm artickel des .h. sacraments. 1535. Auf den vertrag zu Stutgarten von des herrn nachtmal wegen 1534" (CS V, 150–162 and CS V, 247–61). The first treatise bore a date of 1534, the second, 1535. There were perhaps two other treatises: "Ursach warumb etliche nit beim sacrament Lutrisch sein werden" (CS V, 272–74) and "Zwelff Fragstuck von sacrament zu ain Christlichen bedenckhen gstellt" (CS V, 262–65). Neither bears a date.

130. CS V, 157:16–25.

131. Köhler 1953, vol. 2, pp. 355–56.

132. TA 1, 38, 994.

133. As Blaurer confessed to Hans Konrad Thumb (ca. April 20, 1525, Schiess 1, 686).

opinion, Blaurer's admission was a foolish and shortsighted move. It successfully split the Württemberg Sacramentarians into two factions. Had Blaurer seen the original report to the duke, he perhaps would have recognized the danger. While the second part of the document dealt with Schwenckfeld and the Anabaptists, the first section described the failure to establish religious uniformity in Württemberg and blamed that on the Zwinglians. The council's report was an effort by the Lutheran party to cripple Blaurer and the Zwinglians along with Schwenckfeld and the Anabaptists. It may also have been an attempt to discredit Hans Konrad Thumb.

In any event, the *Erbhofmarschall* intervened and imposed a ceasefire on the feuding Sacramentarians. He wrote in April to Butzer, Capito, and Zell in Strassburg, and to Blaurer in Tübingen.[134] He demanded to know what they had against his "relative [*Schwager*] and friend," and declared that, if they believed Schwenckfeld had erred, they should prove it from Schwenckfeld's own writings.[135] Blaurer was once again caught in the middle. He did not know Schwenckfeld personally, and he could not point to anything which Schwenckfeld had published that proved Schwenckfeld in error. He was wholly dependent on what others, particularly Butzer, had told him.

Blaurer's Zwinglian colleague in Tübingen, Simon Grynaeus, was drawn into the fray. Thumb and Schwenckfeld both carefully wooed Grynaeus, with some measure of success.[136] Though Grynaeus was chary of the impact which Schwenckfeld's views could have on the visible church, both men agreed in their opposition to the doctrine of the real presence. A pure Zwinglian, Grynaeus had had doubts about the Stuttgart Concord and immediately after his arrival in Württem-

134. Schiess 1, 683; CS V, 314.
135. They all replied, but only Blaurer's response has been found (Blaurer to Hans Konrad Thumb, ca. April 20, 1535 and April 25, 1535, Schiess 1, 686–87). Butzer and Capito must have also replied. Schwenckfeld responded to them in his sixth letter to Thumb (CS V, 322:4–9, 323:1–5). Matthaeus Zell also responded. Schwenckfeld wrote Zell to thank him for his "friendly, brotherly" letter (June 8, 1535, CS V, 348–51). Boger 1885, 107, has speculated that Schwenckfeld may have been related to the Thumbs through the Silesian Christoph von Axleben. Lee Hopple in his lecture in Erb 1985 suggests that "Schwager" may mean nothing more than a companion in arms.
136. On Grynaeus see Pollet 1962, 372–92. CS contains two preliminary drafts and the final version of a letter from Schwenckfeld to Grynaeus: first draft, April 11, 1535 (CS V, 282–95); second draft, April 19, 1535 (CS V, 304–06); final version, April 28, 1535 (CS V, 306–10). Schwenckfeld submitted them to Thumb for comment and correction. Each of the three successive versions was less vehement than the preceding. Thumb must have counseled calm and restraint.

berg had clashed with Schnepf and the other Lutherans.[137] He was considered neutral with a strong inclination to favor Schwenckfeld.[138]

Matters came to a head in late May. It is not clear whose idea it was—Schwenckfeld's or Thumb's or Grynaeus's—but on May 28, 1535, the Tübingen Colloquy convened.[139] Three presidents had been appointed by the duke: Hans Härter von Gärtringen, *Obervogt* at Tübingen; Hans Friedrich Thumb; and Simon Grynaeus. All three were Sacramentarians. Blaurer, fearful of facing Schwenckfeld alone, had as seconds Martin Frecht and Martin Butzer.[140] Butzer dominated the discussion for his side. Schwenckfeld was accompanied by Jakob Held von Tieffenau.

Blaurer's initial reluctance to take part was well-founded. Both from the choice of presidents and from the opening comments which Grynaeus made on their behalf, it was clear that this was by no means a hearing or trial of Schwenckfeld.[141] It was an attempt to mediate among the quarreling Sacramentarians, allowing the two sides to ar-

137. On Grynaeus's doubts on the concord (September 30, 1534) see Schiess 1, 557–58. On the clash with Schnepf (October 27, 1534), see Schiess 1, 596–98. Cf. Held 1965, 184. His friendship with Karlstadt in Basel may also have prepared him to accept Schwenckfeld (Pollet 1962, pp. 377–79). Grynaeus had also shared Leo Jud's doubts on state churches and Christian freedom. He seems to have been interested, too, in the christological speculation of Denck, Servetus, and others.

138. Rauscher 1934, 140–41. Grynaeus wrote to Blaurer (ca. May 25, 1535, Schiess 1, 695), informing him of an upcoming visit with Schwenckfeld and assuring him that his (Grynaeus's) heart was in the right place. That he should seek to reassure Blaurer in such unconvincing terms and that he should show such curiosity to hear Schwenckfeld may indicate an inclination toward Schwenckfeld.

139. Schwenckfeld had always requested an opportunity to confront his opponents. See CS V, 318:4–7, 312:3–19, 310:23–38. Pollet 1962, 386–87, sees Grynaeus as prime mover. Given the structure, purpose, and outcome of the meeting, I tend to see the hand of Hans Konrad Thumb or even Duke Ulrich.

140. Extract of a letter from Grynaeus to Thumb in Arnold 1703, 163.

141. I have already discussed Grynaeus and Hans Friedrich Thumb. Hans Härter was considered violently anti-Lutheran and opposed to the Stuttgart Concord (Butzer to Blaurer, August 26, 1535, Schiess 1, 733–34). On Grynaeus's statement, see CS V, 330:13–19. The only account of the course of discussions comes from Jakob Held von Tieffenau, "Bericht vom Gesprech C.S. mit Blaurer / Butzer and Frechten / zu Tuebingen uffem Schlos" (CS V, 326–42). As an outline of what was treated, and as an exposition of Schwenckfeld's views on those topics, it is reliable. But as an accurate record of what was actually said it leaves much to be desired. As Held explained, he wrote this account based on notes written up soon after the event. He also drew on unspecified "Protocollen und Acten," CS V, 342:21–24. One of these sources must have been Doc. 170, "Judicium von den jetzigen bestelten Predicanten / wie weit sich yhr ampt erstreckt / was auch an ihnen sey zubegeren / Auff Frag und Antwort Gestellet" (CS V, 122–42). CS V, 331:25–334:32, is almost a transcription of CS V, 129:33–133:7, as remarked in CS V, 328. Also, Held's version of the actual formula of concord differs from that of all the other surviving exemplars. Cf. CS V, 341:31–342:14 with footnotes on variants. This is a partisan document written by a participant for the edification of Schwenckfeld's supporters.

gue out their differences and achieve substantive agreement. By staging the meeting, the duke implicitly recognized Schwenckfeld and his theology as legally acceptable and just as valid as Blaurer and his teaching. The entire colloquy must be reckoned a coup for the *Erbhofmarschall*.

All the participants, but primarily Schwenckfeld and Butzer, argued about the church, infant baptism, the Eucharist, Christology, Schwenckfeld's behavior, and the preachers' treatment of him. Eventually, tiring of the endless debate and convinced of the impossibility of bringing the opponents to theological harmony, the presidents imposed a formula of concord which commanded all to maintain Christian love and to cease mutual recrimination.[142] Schwenckfeld was to cease slandering the church and its ministry "insofar as that ministry is performed in a true and Christian manner."[143] In return the preachers Butzer, Blaurer, and Frecht promised to stop their attacks on Schwenckfeld so long as he held to his side of the agreement.

Since the heart of Schwenckfeld's criticism of the preachers had been that they had been unchristian, Schwenckfeld's concession did not really amount to much.[144] Schwenckfeld refused to sign a testimonial to the legitimacy of the preachers' ministry, and the ministers' attempt to include Schwenckfeld's acceptance of the Stuttgart Concord in the Tübingen agreement failed.[145] Further, Schwenckfeld got promises that Butzer and Blaurer would undo the damage they had done to his reputation in Strassburg, Memmingen, Augsburg, and elsewhere.[146]

Of the three opponents who signed the Tübingen Concord, Martin Frecht was the most grudging in his acceptance of the document and its implications. He, unlike Butzer and Blaurer, was concerned by Schwenckfeld's christological views and worried about the impression

142. CS V, 341:18–21, 31–34. It was a somewhat imprecise and curiously one-sided document in Schwenckfeld's favor. Held's version of the formula varies from the other four extant. I have relied on the other four which are in substantial agreement. Held's version tends to make the document even more one-sided than in fact it was. The other four versions make the mutuality of the agreement clearer. CS V, 341:31–342:14.

143. CS V, 342:2–5, variant.

144. He even remarked upon it at the time. CS V, 342:2–5, variant.

145. On the written testimonial, see CS V, 331:10–31. On the Stuttgart Concord, see Schwenckfeld's reminder to Frecht in 1536 (CS V, 541:1–6).

146. Schwenckfeld to Butzer, June 8, 1535, CS V, 346:19–22; Schwenckfeld to Blaurer, June 13, 1535, CS V, 358:14–15; Butzer to Blaurer, June 11, 1535, Schiess 1, 705.

that the Tübingen Concord would have on the Lutherans.[147] In participating at Tübingen and signing the document, Frecht was playing the
role of Butzer's faithful shieldbearer. He would honor the agreement
as long as Butzer did.

Whatever misgivings Butzer may have had, he tried to live by the
agreement, at least initially, because he wished to retain the good opinion of Hans Friedrich Thumb.[148] But his efforts to have the Schwenckfelder Alexander Berner recalled from exile and to have Schwenckfeld
readmitted to Strassburg foundered on Berner's imprudence and the
council's refusal to bend the rules for Schwenckfeld.[149] Butzer's new
tolerance for Schwenckfeld lasted only a year, however, and it lapsed
with Schwenckfeld's opposition to the Wittenberg Concord.

Blaurer was the only opponent never to depart from the agreement,
and he disapproved strongly when Butzer resumed his attacks on
Schwenckfeld in 1536.[150] That is not to say that he was sympathetic toward Schwenckfeld, because he was consistently critical of
Schwenckfeld's ecclesiological views, his Christology, and his negative
impact on the Reform's process of organization in southern Germany.[151] Two factors, however, determined his fidelity to the Tübingen Concord. First, Schwenckfeld's friends and supporters had the upper hand within the Zwinglian party in Württemberg, and the leading
Zwinglian political figures at court were Schwenckfelders. In order to
continue to work in the duchy and to be effective Blaurer had to maintain amicable relations with the Schwenckfelders. Second, the issue
over which Butzer and Frecht broke with Schwenckfeld, the Wittenberg Concord, proved to be another bond uniting Schwenckfeld,
Blaurer, and the rest of the Zwinglians in Württemberg. Blaurer's acceptance of the Stuttgart Concord had left him isolated and unsure.[152]

147. Frecht to Blaurer, June 5, 1535, Schiess 1, 700; Frecht to Blaurer, July 28, 1535,
Schiess 1, 727.

148. Butzer to Blaurer, June 3, 1535, Schiess 1, 705; Butzer to Blaurer, July 12, 1535,
Schiess 1, 713.

149. After having been expelled from the city, Berner had publicly attacked the Strassburg
ministry while visiting in the neighborhood of the city. He also refused the oath condemning
sects and supporting the city's church required by the council (Butzer to Blaurer, June 3, 1535,
Schiess 1, 705). Schwenckfeld's case was slightly different. The council seemed to favor
Schwenckfeld, but they felt they couldn't make an exception for him on the oath without
opening a Pandora's box (Butzer to Blaurer, July 25, 1535, Schiess 1, 725).

150. A. Blaurer to Thomas Blaurer, November 15, 1536, Schiess 1, 828.

151. Cf. Schiess 2, 332, 394-95.

152. Karlstadt, Leo Jud, Myconius, Grynaeus, Katharina Zell, Pellikan, Bullinger, and Jo-

Thomas and Margaret Blaurer, Ambrosius's brother and sister, turned against Butzer and became two of his staunchest and bitterest opponents.[153] Pressure from his family and his own doubts finally brought Ambrosius to the realization that he too disagreed with Butzer, and for this reason he refused to sign the Wittenberg Concord.[154] The eucharistic issue provided common ground for an alliance with Schwenckfeld, which Thomas Blaurer urged upon Ambrosius. Grynaeus, the other Zwinglian leader in Württemberg, had drawn the same conclusion.[155] The Tübingen Concord was thus decisive for the church in Württemberg for the rest of the decade. The Sacramentarians had banded together against the Lutherans and Butzer.[156] The defection of the Sacramentarians, combined with the disapproval of the Swiss, left Butzer in a no-man's-land between the two parties and made his *approche* to the Lutherans all the more pressing.[157]

Schwenckfeld was elated by his success at Tübingen.[158] He had got-

hannes Zwick all rejected the agreement and warned Blaurer of its dangers. Schiess 1, 537–38, 540, 543, 555–58, 559, 588–89, 636, 639.

153. They were disturbed by Butzer's frantic efforts in January and February 1535 to conjure an agreement between Lutherans and Zwinglians, and outraged by his attempt at reconciliation with the Catholics in France. Schiess, vol. 1, 657, 660, 695–97, 716–23, 723–24, 742, 752, 753, 760–61, 763, 768, 805; vol. 2, 813–16, 819, 821–27. Cf. Eells 1971, 170, 179.

154. Already in September and August 1534 Blaurer expressed doubts about the Lutherans and their interpretation of the Eucharist (Schiess 1, 549, 559). On his inability to accept the Wittenberg Concord, see Schiess 1, 804. His recommendation to Constance (Schiess 1, 828–31) would have been accepted by Schwenckfeld as an accurate description of the Eucharist and the problems with the concord.

155. By chance, Thomas Blaurer visited Hans Friedrich Thumb at Koengen during Thomas's period of growing disenchantment with Butzer (Schiess 1, 661). He would have found congenial Thumb's views on the Eucharist and his distrust of arrogant and ambitious clerics. Thomas Blaurer and Butzer had disagreed since 1533 on the extensiveness and propriety of the use of coercion in religion (Schiess 1, 413, 657–58, 660–61). See Keim 1851, 325–26. In any event, he advised his brother to ally himself with Schwenckfeld against Butzer (Thomas Blaurer to Ambrosius Blaurer, May 28, 1535, Schiess 1, 695–97). The letter begins with a long attack on Butzer's "delirium," then proceeds to advise on dealing with Schwenckfeld. Grynaeus's opposition to concord was unwavering in 1534 and 1535 (Schiess 1, 555–58, 596–97, 601–02, 603–04, 657, 736). Butzer was inclined to see Karlstadt's influence there (Schiess 1, 605). Schwenckfeld's correspondence makes clear his agreement with Grynaeus on the Eucharist. They disagreed over Schwenckfeld's spiritualistic emphasis and his "separatism" (CS V, 282–95, 354–55).

156. The Schwenckfeld faction may also have been responsible for turning Ulrich in April 1535 against the efforts to achieve a eucharistic concord (Ambrosius Blaurer to Thomas Blaurer, April 30, 1535, Schiess 1, 689). A "certain nobleman" (a Schwenckfelder?) had given Ulrich a copy of the articles worked out with the French by Melanchthon and Butzer. Ulrich was incensed and his distrust of the concord efforts kindled. This may explain his decision to stage the Tübingen Colloquy.

157. Eells 1971, 190.

158. See his letters to Butzer, June 8, 1535, CS V, 343–47, and ca. August 1, 1535, CS V, 359–61; to Matthaeus Zell, June 8, 1535, CS V, 348–51; to Hans Härter von Gärtringen, June

ten a public hearing and official recognition. His clerical opponents were muzzled and all of Protestant southern Germany lay open to him. In Württemberg the Tübingen agreement conferred a quasi-legal status on the Schwenckfelders, which, along with their powerful connections at court, produced an unofficial tolerance for the better part of a decade. They would remain firmly entrenched among the landed nobility for the rest of the century.[159] Schwenckfeld himself was officially tolerated under Duke Ulrich, and was banned only in 1554 by Ulrich's Lutheran successor Christoph.[160]

Having secured his position in Württemberg, at least for the moment, Schwenckfeld set his sights on Philip of Hesse, the most forceful of the Protestant princes and arguably the most important. After spending June with the Thumbs, Schwenckfeld traveled to Hesse to meet with Philip, probably at Marburg, and probably in July.[161] This began a correspondence which continued on and off until Schwenckfeld's death.[162] Throughout the years Philip maintained a friendly, re-

---

10, 1535, CS V, 352–54; to Simon Grynaeus, June 10, 1535, CS V, 354–55; to Ambrosius Blaurer, June 13, 1535, CS V, 356–58. Schwenckfeld was effusive, but careful to remind Butzer and Blaurer of their obligations. No letter to Frecht has survived.

159. On the Schwenckfelders in Württemberg, see McLaughlin 1985b; TA 1, 88–106 and passim; G. Bossert 1921; G. Bossert 1929; Rauscher 1934, 153–55; Boger 1885, 1–117; F. Weber 1962, 6–8, 11–18, 23, 44–45.

160. L. Heyd 1841–44, vol. 3, pp. 74–75. On the toleration of Schwenckfeld, see TA 1, 100:3–9. In 1554 and again in 1558 Christoph forbade Schwenckfeld to enter the duchy and threatened him with arrest should he do so (TA 1, 129:32–39, 1036:22–37).

161. In a letter to Butzer (June 8, 1535, CS V, 347:25–28), he told Butzer to forward any reply to the Erbhofmarschall. According to CS his first letter to Philip (CS V, 385–400) written after their meeting was from the same hand as Hans Friedrich Thumb's letter to Paul Speratus (May 4, 1537, CS V, 661–84). CS speculates that either Veit Kappeler, pastor in Kirchheim unter Teck, or Konrad Gwynnant, pastor in Koengen, served as scribe in both instances. In any event Schwenckfeld was with the Thumbs. On the dating of the visit to Hesse, see CS V, 359–60. The Erbhofmarschall had suggested that Schwenckfeld go directly to Strassburg (CS V, 355:7–9). Philip, who was embroiled in the Münster affair, insisted that they discuss baptism, but Schwenckfeld was loathe to take up the issue (CS V, 387:1–11). On his return to Württemberg he wrote Philip, giving a fuller presentation of his views on baptism and rebaptism (before September 26, 1535, CS V, 385–400). It constitutes a little primer in spiritualism. In both his conversation and letter to Hesse, Schwenckfeld displayed remarkable caution. He omitted the date and place from which he wrote and failed to give any sign of his own authorship. He also asked Philip not to mention it to anyone. With the Tübingen agreement in mind he wanted to avoid any trouble with the "learned" (CS V, 387:14–19).

162. See French 1908. Philip tried to consult Schwenckfeld on his bigamy. Geryon Sailer was deputed by Philip to seek out both Schwenckfeld and Butzer on the question of his bigamy (Geryon Sailer to Philip, November 11, 1539, Lenz vol. 1, p. 348). There is no evidence that Sailer ever succeeded in contacting Schwenckfeld. He may not have tried. It was the Schwenckfelders in Strassburg who later pilloried Butzer for his involvement in Hesse's bigamy (Lenz, vol. 2, pp. 65, 72, 73ff., 80f.; cf. CS VI, 177–79). Schwenckfeld sent the Landgraf copies of his works and they argued Schwenckfeld's Christology in the 1540s and 1550s (French 1908,

spectful, and tolerant attitude toward Schwenckfeld, but it is difficult to judge how important Schwenckfeld's acquaintance with Philip really was. Schwenckfeld himself was convinced that "had he [Philip] not prevented it [*rigell fuergesteckt*] the preachers would have driven me out of Germany long ago."[163] The immediate effect in 1535 was to counter Butzer's earlier reports to Philip and to remove the Landgraf as a force against Schwenckfeld in Württemberg.

Ulm

When his Augsburg banker died, Schwenckfeld left Württemberg and went to Augsburg in August 1535 to arrange his business affairs. He left instructions that any letters be forwarded to Augsburg's *Bürger-meister*.[164] In early September he was in Ulm staying with *Bürgermeis-ter* Bernhard Besserer.[165] Though often absent from the city for extended periods, Schwenckfeld made Ulm his main base of operations for the next four years, and he built a numerous and influential following there. Initially, however, he kept a very low profile, in accordance with the Tübingen agreement.[166] Schwenckfeld maintained this self-restraint until 1538.[167] Both his followers and his opponents were suspicious and not particularly sanguine about Schwenckfeld's adherence

---

11–73). Convinced that Schwenckfeld was not totally wrong and had actually made some good points concerning the nature of Christ, Philip tried to arrange a settlement between Schwenckfeld and Melanchthon. On Hesse's attitude, see especially his letter to Duke Johann Friedrich of Saxony (March 7, 1559, French 1908, 84–86). Melanchthon's indifference and Schwenckfeld's death barred success.

163. CS X, 924:21–25.

164. CS V, 361:1–8.

165. Johannes Zwick to Vadian, September 16, 1535, *Vad. Br.* 5, 250; CS V, 401–03, esp. 402:7–11. Cf. CS V, 404–05.

166. *Vad. Br.* 5, 250. In the negotiations leading up to the Tübingen Colloquy Schwenckfeld had threatened to publicize his complaints against Butzer and the others and his criticism of their ministry (second draft of letter to Simon Grynaeus, April 19, 1535, CS V, 306:11–22). As his contribution to the peace he had agreed not to do so (Schwenckfeld to Martin Butzer, June 8, 1535, CS V, 344:9–345:6). In all likelihood the work which he intended to publish was the "Judicium von der jetzigen bestellten predicanten / wie weit sich jhr ampt erstreckt / was auch an jhren sey zu begeren / Auff frag und Antwort gestellet" (CS V, 122–42). Basically it was a reply to the Strassburg "Gegenantwort" (Oct. 1533), TA 8, 145–72. The "Judicium" was forceful, harsh, and uncompromising. Though there were rumors that it had been printed in early 1535, it was only published in 1570 (TA 8, 413:4–9).

167. See the preface to doc. 253, CS V, 809:2–810:2, where Valentine Ickelsamer explained that Schwenckfeld still had no desire to publish. CS dates this preface to 1536–37 (CS V, 798–806).

to the Tübingen Concord,[168] but Schwenckfeld had his reasons. He feared that no matter how justified, he had offended against Christian charity in his dealings with the clergy. And he hoped that, given time, his opponents would advance in truth and understanding.[169] In any event, he tried to avoid giving offense.

This was difficult for him to do since Martin Frecht, the leader among Ulm's ministers, was decidedly unhappy about Schwenckfeld's presence in the city. Frecht's initial meetings with Schwenckfeld in 1533 and 1534 had not been unfriendly, but Frecht, stung by Butzer's criticism, steadily developed into Schwenckfeld's bitter enemy.[170] It was Frecht who repeatedly raised the issue of Schwenckfeld's Christology and labeled it heresy. Within a few months of Schwenckfeld's return to Ulm in 1535 Frecht and the other preachers began to criticize Schwenckfeld's views (though not mentioning him by name) and to pressure Schwenckfeld's friends.[171]

Fortunately for Schwenckfeld, the situation of the church in Ulm, and the course of the Reformation there, favored him. He also had the protection and patronage of Bernhard Besserer and the other leaders in the city.[172] More clearly than anywhere else, Schwenckfeld's experience in Ulm casts a revealing light on the tensions between the Protestant clergy and the Protestant secular authorities in southern Germany. Ministers and magistrates held profoundly differing views on the church, its authority, and its relationship to the state. Schwenckfeld, whose opinions on the matter more nearly agreed with the magis-

168. There is a grudging tone in his opponents' letters. See Johannes Zwick to Vadian, September 1, 1535, *Vad. Br.* 5, 250; Frecht to Blaurer, June 5, 1535, Schiess 1, 700. Doc. 230, *CS* V, 604–08, is a letter from Schwenckfeld to an unidentified correspondent. The editors of *CS* think it was written to Jakob Held and date it January 1537. More likely is a date of January 1536. The reference to "concordia" (*CS* V, 607:2–3) is not to the Wittenberg Concord, but to the Tübingen Concord, which Schwenckfeld takes care to defend in the rest of the letter. The mention of a work "vom geistlichen stand" would also place it in late 1535 or early 1536; see doc. 205, *CS* V, 401. Schwenckfeld had sent it to Philip of Hesse on September 26, 1535 (*CS* V, 403:2–9). The recipient of the letter is unlikely to have been Held, who was present at Tübingen. It may have been someone in Strassburg or perhaps even Silesia.

169. *CS* V, 607:13–608:14.

170. For his initial reaction, see the letters from Frecht to Butzer on June 26, 1534, and August 3, 1534, Th. B. 7. Cf. Pollet 1962, 211–12. As Pollet 1962, 210–13, observed, Frecht became even more obsessed with Schwenckfeld than did Butzer.

171. In his letters to Helena Streicher in Ulm in early 1536 Schwenckfeld consoled and encouraged her to face the criticism which she was exposed to because of her relationship to Schwenckfeld. See esp. *CS* V, 478:26–479:2, 481:21–482:14, 483:6–9, 486:15–19, 505:11–26, 506:1–14.

172. On the Reformation in Ulm see Keim 1851 and Endriss 1931. On Bernhard Besserer, see Ernst 1941 and Walther 1929.

trates', relied upon and supported the magistrates' stance. They, in turn, used him as a cat's-paw or a counterbalance to the professional clergy.

Besserer was already the leading political figure in Ulm at the coming of the Reformation, and he dominated the special committee for religion when that was organized.[173] Besserer's position within the city and his impact on its Reformation might be compared to Jakob Sturm's in Strassburg, but Besserer had far greater control than Sturm ever achieved.[174]

Besserer's personal outlook found wide support among the patricians and left a lasting stamp on Ulm's religious development.[175] Firmly convinced of the truth of the evangelical teachings, Besserer was cautious in their application. This brought him into conflict with the first reformer in Ulm, Conrad Sam. Sam mobilized the guilds and the "common man" to pressure the patrician Besserer and his colleagues.[176] Though Besserer was often forced to give way to their demands, he never lost control, and he never ceased to dislike and distrust the clergy. His greatest fear was not of a Münster-like upheaval, but that clerical intolerance would lead to persecution and full-scale religious war.[177]

Nonetheless, action by the council could not be put off indefinitely. In 1531 a new *Ordnung* was promulgated for Ulm's church, and despite Besserer's misgivings, Butzer, Capito, and Blaurer were called in to consult.[178] Almost immediately they too started to agitate the common man against the government. This left an indelible impression

173. On Besserer's career and the structure of Ulm's government, see Walther 1929, 2, 6, 12, 57; Rieber 1968, 302.

174. Not that an opposition was lacking. The patriciate split over religion, and there was a sizable Catholic minority (Walther 1929, 20 n. 30, 53). In 1530 a third of the patricians wanted to accept the Augsburg *Abschied*, (Walther 1929, 36). But Besserer had a majority on his side in the inner ruling committee of the Five. His position became unassailable in 1529 when his son Georg joined the committee. Georg also served as *Bürgermeister* every three years from 1531 at least until 1546 (Walther 1929, 2, 20). The Besserer faction could count on Konrad Aitinger, the city's secretary (*Stadtschreiber*). Aitinger attended almost all meetings of the council and recorded the minutes and conducted all correspondence (Walther 1929, 2, 20, 55). Though not a voting member, he was a person of great influence because he was the one enduring figure among the constantly changing roster of elected officials.

175. Fortunately we are better informed of Besserer's religious convictions than of most other leading political figures in the South German Reformation. Our knowledge of Besserer's views comes from his "Gutachten" for the 1531 Reformation (Walther 1929, 59–63) and his letter of June 20, 1538, to Philip of Hesse (Walther 1929, 64–68). See also Walther 1929, 41, 46–48; Keim 1851, 226–27; Pollet 1962, 166–67.

176. Walther 1929, 65.

177. Walther 1929, 65–68; Naujoks 1958, 83.

178. Endriss 1931, 57.

on Besserer; he never liked or trusted Butzer again.[179] In the negotiations on the *Ordnung* Besserer personally thwarted the preachers' efforts to establish a clerically dominated system of discipline to control both morals and doctrine.[180] The church was allowed to oversee morals, but was not empowered to enforce doctrinal unity among the population. Eventually even this proved ineffective, and the city returned to completely secular legislation and enforcement of morals.

Besserer's opposition to the forcible imposition of new beliefs and practices on the population as a whole also had legal and political motives. He did not believe that the city had the right to intervene in questions of doctrine and faith.[181] Magistrates were to maintain peace and order, protect the weak, be impartial in dispensing a justice that punished the evil and rewarded the good. A Christian magistrate could further true religion by personal example and the careful instruction of his family and household, but he had neither the duty nor the right to suppress false religion and to impose true religion. During the years of Besserer's dominance, Ulm, for the most part, adhered to these principles, much to the dismay of its preachers.

The Eucharist was another issue that divided the clergy and the government of Ulm. The eighteen articles of faith formulated by Sam, Blaurer, Butzer, and Capito in 1531 had contained an exposition of the middle position on the Eucharist.[182] This formulation, and the consensus of the Protestant population which it expressed, hindered the later efforts of Butzer and Frecht to draw Ulm into the Wittenberg Concord. Further, Besserer showed personal preference for a spiritualism which flowed naturally from this position on the Eucharist. He did not place much value on externals in religion however much they might be useful in maintaining civic peace and order.[183] The immediate and mutual attraction between Schwenckfeld and Besserer was based on these shared values.

Besserer opposed a political alliance with the Swiss cities, despite his

179. Seven years later in his letter to Philip of Hesse he was still incensed against Butzer (Walther 1929, 65).

180. Keim 1851, 226–27, 242, 245; Endriss 1931, 59–61, 76–79; Naujoks 1958, 77–82, 86.

181. Walther 1929, 59–63. On Besserer's views on the powers of a Christian magistrate, see Frecht to Blaurer, December 14, 1533, Schiess 1, 447–48.

182. That is, that in the Eucharist there is a real spiritual participation but absolutely no real presence in the bread and wine. Keim 1851, 231, article 6 on the Eucharist. See Endriss 1931, 85, 116.

183. Walther 1929, 67. In 1529 Besserer's wife died without receiving the sacrament (Walther 1929, 41).

eucharistic views. He looked instead to Philip of Hesse and the Lutheran powers of the North.[184] This contradiction of religious and political policies was common to most South German cities and explains to a large extent their appearance of wavering and inconstancy. The desire for Lutheran political and military support made them vulnerable to Lutheran religious demands.

All of these factors played a role in Schwenckfeld's experience at Ulm. He was caught once again between the clergy and the magistrates; the government was more concerned to control its own clergy than any suppositious dissident influence.[185] This was made very clear when the council granted citizenship to Sebastian Franck, rejected the clergy's demand that Franck accept a set of articles of belief, and allowed him to set up his own printing press.[186] Schwenckfeld's presence as a guest in the *Bürgermeister's* house and his welcome by the highest classes of society also disturbed Frecht and his colleagues. In July 1536 the preachers complained that people were beginning to avoid their sermons and were not receiving communion.[187]

But by then the Wittenberg Concord (May 28, 1536) had radically altered the religious climate of Ulm.[188] A group of Lutheran and South German theologians and preachers, Martin Frecht among them, had accepted this ambiguous formula.[189] The South Germans foresaw difficulties and agreed not to publish the concord until they had had an opportunity to prepare their congregations. For their part, Luther and the Lutherans viewed acceptance of the concord as the acid test of the South's good intentions; the price of political and military support was its public acceptance.

Fears for the concord were well-founded. In July 1535 Besserer had expressed grave reservations concerning Melanchthon's attempt to negotiate a concord with the Catholics. It was this, as we have seen, that turned Thomas and Margaret Blaurer against efforts at eucharistic concord.[190] Both at Constance and at Ulm there had been misgivings

184. Keim 1851, 171–74. Besserer became a close confidant of Philip.

185. Naujoks 1958, 82–83.

186. Weigelt 1970, 10–11; Keim 1851, 272. Frecht thought Besserer had arranged Franck's acceptance just to spite the clergy (Frecht to Blaurer, November 4, 1534, Schiess 1, 595). Frecht also reported to Blaurer (March 3, 1535, Schiess 1, 668) that Franck's press had been financed by backers in Augsburg.

187. Frecht to Blaurer, July 29, 1536, Schiess 1, 811.

188. On the Wittenberg Concord, Köhler 1953, 432–55.

189. The Wittenberg Concord, CR 3, 75–78.

190. Frecht to Blaurer, July 28, 1535, Schiess 2, 811.

concerning the planned Wittenberg meeting, and Frecht was given careful instructions not to enter into any agreement that would appear to bind Ulm.[191] There was fear that the clergy conspired to settle the issue among themselves and then to impose it on the various secular authorities.

The magistrates were not alone in their anger at Butzer's stratagem at Wittenberg. News of the agreement leaked even before Frecht reached Ulm. The populace was incensed at the betrayal; Frecht's life was threatened, and he was publicly abused and ridiculed.[192] On July 11, 1536, Schwenckfeld returned to Ulm, took up residence again with Besserer, and plunged directly into the controversy.[193] The Swiss cities had rejected the concord out of hand. Of the major cities in southern Germany only Constance and Ulm refused to accept it, and upon Ulm's decision hung those of a number of smaller cities in the region. Frecht, Capito, and Butzer blamed Schwenckfeld's interference for Ulm's resistance.[194]

Schwenckfeld did criticize the agreement. He provided a detailed analysis of it for the magistrates and an enchiridion of arguments against it for the laity.[195] He charged that Butzer had conceded the real

191. Keim 1851, 325–28. Both Constance and Ulm felt that private individuals (i.e., the clergy) had no right to make such agreements.

192. Keim 1851, 355–36, 348, 350; Schiess 2, 809. The news may also have decided some of Schwenckfeld's followers and others to avoid the Eucharist. Frecht only complained about the Streicher family in July after the concord and Schwenckfeld's arrival (Schiess 2, 811).

193. After spending a few months in Ulm in the fall of 1535 Schwenckfeld had left for Memmingen or Mindelheim. Schwenckfeld wrote a letter to Philip of Hesse from Ulm (September 26, 1535, CS V, 402:7–11). See also Zwick to Vadian (September 16, 1535, Vad. Br. 5, 259). Frecht wrote Bullinger that Schwenckfeld was still there on October 14, 1535 (CS V, 404). Schwenckfeld's letter to Helena Streicher (February 20, 1536) was written at the suggestion of Wilhelm von Zell (CS V, 478:20–25). Whether he remained there for the entire time he was absent from Ulm is not known. Frecht to Blaurer, July 19, 1536 (Schiess 2, 809), states that Schwenckfeld had been staying with Besserer for eight days.

194. Schiess 2, 809; Capito to Luther, September 4, 1536, Th. B. 9; Butzer to Luther, September 6, 1536, Th. B. 9; Butzer to Zwick, October 25, 1536, Th. B. 9; Capito to Jodocus Neobolus December 26, 1536, Th. B. 9; Butzer and Capito to Luther, January 19, 1537, Th. B. 10.

195. Documents 218–220, CS V, 507–16. They are not dated and were never published. Doc. 218, "Artikel der Concordj vom Nachtmal 1536," consists of a running commentary on the Wittenberg Concord. By its tone and structure it was probably written for Besserer or some other official. Doc. 219, "Argument ains layen ad Concordiam Predicatorum," was obviously written for one of Schwenckfeld's followers. Doc. 220, "Fragstuck uff die Concordj," is a series of leading questions on the concord. It may represent Schwenckfeld's notes for some conversation or argument. Schwenckfeld also asked Crautwald to write on the issue. The result was "De concordia et unione sacramentali. Quae facta est Wittemberga Mense Maio Anno Salutis M.D. XXXVI. Epistola. Item Explicatio loci 1 Corinth XI. De Dignitate et proba manducantium. D. Valent. Craut: Silesij Theologi," CLM 718, 512–24, dated December 1, 1536.

presence to Luther, and he pointed out that because Butzer tried to reconcile the Zwinglian and Lutheran positions on the participation of the impious, Butzer had created a *tertium quid*—the unworthy—whose relationship to the sacrament was no longer determined by faith. For Schwenckfeld *sola fide* was endangered in this agreement.[196]

On the other hand, the necessity, expressed in the concord itself, to achieve a political consensus in the cities of the South encouraged Schwenckfeld: "If it had been a concord of truth and if the Holy Spirit had been present, then two or three gathered in the name of the Lord could have concluded it. But since it was a human concord against all Scripture and divine truth, the Holy Spirit has hindered it."[197] For his part, Schwenckfeld once again advised that a *Stillstand* be instituted, and there is evidence that some in Ulm ceased to participate in the Eucharist.[198]

The debate about the concord continued through the summer and fall. The Ulm council discussed it and could see only two ways to interpret the concord. [199] Either the two sides still disagreed, or the South German preachers, Frecht included, had departed from Ulm's official "approved doctrine." The fact that the preachers disagreed among themselves as to how to understand the document was not a good sign. The council also feared public unrest if the actual wording of the agreement were ever made public. But a broader issue also disturbed the council.

> It is also well to consider whether by signing [the concord] a snaring or coercion is sought; whether perhaps one might be prevented from receiving further future enlightenment which God through his spirit might graciously grant (since no one can achieve it himself) because of the impediment of this signing, which must be a burden to all the good-hearted [*gutherzigen*] and the conscience.[200]

196. On the real presence conceded, see CS V, 511:20–26. On Christ's institution of the sacrament as a remembrance only, not as a "power," see CS V, 511:14–19, 27–32. On "unworthy" and *sola fide*, see CS V, 511:33–513:14, 514:26–515:7, 516:5–16. Blaurer also attacked this aspect of the concord (Frecht to Blaurer, July 29, 1536, Schiess 1, 810–11). This passage also contains a very clear exposition of Butzer's position by Frecht. Though Schwenckfeld did not pursue the thought, Butzer's position was a partial step toward the Catholic doctrine of "faith formed by love" (*fides caritate formata*).

197. CS V, 513:24–31.

198. CS V, 514:1–8. On its effect, see Schiess 2, 811.

199. The two interpretations appear in a letter to the other Upper German cities (August 6, 1536, Keim 1851, 338–39).

200. Keim 1851, 339. One wonders if Schwenckfeld had a hand in writing this. Certainly

The political pressure applied by the Lutherans through Butzer proved too powerful to resist.[201] Finally on October 30 the council wrote to Luther accepting the Wittenberg Concord *insofar* as it agreed with the Augsburg Confession and its Apology, the Schweinfurt agreement (1532), and Ulm's own Reformation Order (1531).[202] They had chosen a very diplomatic way of handling the problem. In reality and in daily practice they rejected the concord; it was never published in the city.[203] On the same day that the letter to Luther went out, the council ordered the preachers to reaffirm from the chancel Ulm's true position: denial of a real presence, the Eucharist as remembrance, and spiritual participation.[204] They also had Conrad Sam's catechism reprinted, and the Zwinglian interpretation of the Eucharist in it was not only retained but actually expanded.[205] The council prevented Frecht from sending to Luther a letter signed by the clergy of Ulm which expressed unreserved agreement with the concord. Frecht was himself reprimanded for the effort.[206]

The council's acceptance of the Wittenberg Concord, therefore, did not mark its triumph, but its effective rejection. Nonetheless, because Ulm gave the appearance of having accepted the concord, there was still ground upon which Butzer and Frecht could maneuver. This was especially true with regard to Schwenckfeld, whom they continued to view as the major obstacle to real acceptance.[207] Schwenckfeld, having learned from his experience in Strassburg and Württemberg, anticipated them and asked for a hearing by the council. There he accused the clergy of breaking the Tübingen agreement by attacking him and spreading rumors against him.[208] Speaking for the clergy, Frecht

---

the content and the use of the term *gutherzigen* suggest it. Constance agreed completely with Ulm.

201. Köhler 1953, 475–76.

202. Ulm's political intent can be seen in its decision to send this "deceptive" letter. They had a more theologically informed draft which would have scuttled the agreement. They chose instead the ambiguous version and reserved their real opinions for internal consumption (Köhler 1953, 476).

203. Keim 1851, 344; Köhler 1953, 477.

204. Köhler 1953, 476; Keim 1851, 346.

205. Köhler 1953, 477; Keim 1851, 349.

206. Köhler 1953, 476.

207. Capito to Jodocus Neobolus, December 26, 1536, Th. B. 9; Butzer and Capito to Luther, January 19, 1537, Th. B. 10.

208. Having just returned from a trip to Württemberg, Schwenckfeld immediately confronted Frecht and the other preachers before the Committee of Five, on November 3, 1536. Schwenckfeld was not in Ulm on September 21, 1536, when he wrote to Helena Streicher (CS V, 528–30). During Schwenckfeld's hearing Frecht accused him of attacking the concord in Albeck, Kirchheim unter Teck, and Geislingen, all in Württemberg (CS V, 540:13–15, 542:8–

claimed that Schwenckfeld's rejection of the Wittenberg Concord constituted a breach of the Tübingen agreement, and that, in addition,
Schwenckfeld was opposed to Ulm's religious settlement of 1531.
Schwenckfeld countered by pointing out that the Stuttgart Concord
had been specifically excluded from the Tübingen agreement, and
that he could hardly be expected to accept or reject a document (the
Wittenberg Concord) which he had never seen—that was a particularly effective blow since the council had refused to publish it. For his
part, he accepted the Ulm church order as Christian.[209] It was the
clergy who had contravened it by resorting to rumors and gossip instead of taking their complaints to him or to the council.

    After both sides had aired their grievances, the Committee of Five
charged them to be satisfied. If one side learned of something against
the other they should settle it in a friendly way among themselves.
With that the committee departed. Schwenckfeld shook the hands of
the preachers to seal the agreement and left.[210] This first open clash
between Schwenkfeld and the preachers, staged and dominated by
Schwenckfeld, proved that Ulm's clergy could not count on the support of the council to dislodge or tame Schwenckfeld. It was also clear
that the council would do nothing to impose or defend the Wittenberg
Concord within the city. Schwenckfeld thus gained almost two full

---

12). Schwenckfeld rejected the charge, but did not deny his presence in those places. The five
members were Georg Besserer, Weiprecht Ehinger, Hieronymus Schleicher, Veit Fingerlin,
and Georg Schelling. Our record is from the Ulm archives and was made by the city clerk,
Sebastian Aitinger. Schwenckfeld was accompanied by Jakob von Rammingen. Von Rammingen had served in the Stuttgart Chancellory from 1533 to 1535. He fled Württemberg because
records of expenses for the Austrian defense of the duchy in his keeping were lost at Lauffen.
Fearful of proceedings regarding sums spent but no longer recorded, he fled. He remained in
Ulm from 1535 to 1553. The Besserers of Ulm tried to intercede for him with the duke. He
also married into the Besserer family in 1536 (Bernhardt 1972, vol. 2, pp. 543–44). It is clear
from the record that Schwenckfeld brought the complaint against the preachers and not vice
versa. The title of the document is "Verhoer Herr Caspar Schwenckfelds contra Die predicann-
ten" (CS V, 538:1–4). The form of the hearing had Schwenckfeld complaining about the
preachers' attacks on him and requesting proof of their charges. On the hearing see Endriss
1936, 20, 23–36.
    209. He also claimed to restrict himself to visiting two or three houses where he discussed
religion over dinner with friends (CS V, 540:20–26, 541:9–13, 18–25). This was another clever
tack. Three of the houses he visited were those of Bernhard Besserer, Hans Walther Ehinger,
another Bürgermeister, and Sebastian Aitinger, the secretary recording the proceedings.
Schwenckfeld had visited with Aitinger already during his brief stay in 1534 (Frecht to Blaurer,
June 28, 1534, Schiess 1, 505). Hans Walther Ehinger became a close friend of Schwenckfeld
and defended him before the imperial commissioners in 1547, (S. Schultz 1946, 299). Cf.
Keim 1851, 280.
    210. CS V, 544:31–36.

years of undisturbed peace in the city, and when Frecht and Schwenckfeld appeared before the council in 1538 and 1539, Frecht's complaint had nothing to do with the Wittenberg Concord. Schwenckfeld used those years to great advantage. Into the seventeenth century Ulm and its surrounding areas could boast one of the most numerous and public Schwenckfelder movements.[211]

211. On the Ulm Schwenckfelders, see my forthcoming article "Schwenckfeld and the South German Schwenckfelders" in Erb 1985; Fritz 1934, 145–46, 185–86, 192–209; Keim 1851, 271–72, 280, 307–10; F. Weber 1962, 9, 13, 26–27.

Minister of the Glorified Christ
(1537–1540)

After they had conceived a hatred and envy against this admonisher or
superattendant as some call him [Schwenckfeld], and against his faith and doctrine
of the spiritual Lord Christ and his kingdom, for years they have cried against him
especially on this point [the noncreaturehood of Christ] and they portrayed the
glorified Christ as a creature to the common man, indeed to all and sundry. They
also were heard to say that there were some who wanted to give Christ too much
honor.—Schwenckfeld to Hans Konrad Thumb, September 13, 1539

Through all of 1537 and the first half of 1538 Schwenckfeld enjoyed a
period of relative peace. His stock was high with Ulm's *Bürgermeister*
and city council. He was even employed by them in the attempt to
convert the obstinately Catholic nuns of the monastery at Söflingen.[1]
His extended absences from Ulm made him less a target and an irritant
for the preachers, which, of course, may have been why he made these
trips; they made him more an infrequent visitor than a guest.[2] He also
published little. Instead, he traveled widely and conducted an exten-

1. Schwenckfeld to Abbess Cordula von Reischach, ca. end of January 1537, CS V, 609–
31. As Schwenckfeld explained, he had spoken with the abbess in the presence of the *Bürger-*
meister and other caretakers (CS V, 612:30–613:10). The letter was written as a follow-up.
Söflingen was a constant thorn in Ulm's side because it left its services open to the population
of Ulm and the neighborhood. It was never reformed. Schwenckfeld's name was also thought
to lend dignity and acceptability to books in the city, at least according to the publisher Hans
Varnier. See the preface to Crautwald's *Catechismus Christi*, published in early 1537 (CS V,
569:11–20).
2. After his confrontation with the preachers on November 3, 1536, he probably left the
city again in late November or early December (CS V, 546, 547:1–4, 549:22–23). He returned,
probably at the end of December, when he provided the preface to Varnier's edition
of Crautwald's *Catechismus Christi* (CS V, 569:21–25). He was at Frankfurt for the *Messe* in
mid-March 1537 (CS V, 656:19–20). He was still not in Ulm on April 10, 1537 (Frecht to
Blaurer, Schiess 1, 843). Frecht thought he might be visiting the Thumbs. On May 4, 1537,
Hans Friedrich Thumb sent a letter to Paul Speratus which appears to have been written by
Schwenckfeld at Kirchheim (CS V, 661–64). The following day he wrote to Barbara Roelin of
Ulm promising to return soon (CS V, 689:28–37). He may still have been with the Thumbs in
June (CS V, 690). He eventually did return to Ulm that summer, but left again on August 15,
1537 (Frecht to Blaurer, August 23, 1537, Schiess 1, 855). He visited Stetten before going to
Esslingen, where he wrote a letter to Ursula Thumb (September 25, 1537, CS V, 710–18, esp.
718:32). He seems to have been away from Ulm through the winter and spring of 1538. He
may have been in Augsburg publishing books ca. December 1537–January 1538 (CS V, 840).
He may also have been in Speyer and Esslingen during that time (CS VI, 428). Schwenckfeld
was not in Ulm on May 14, 1538 (Schiess 1, 877) or on July 17, 1538 (CS VI, 120). See also
CS V, 689:28–37.

sive correspondence in an effort to instruct and encourage his adherents. He quite consciously reserved his peculiar doctrines and personal speculations for his unpublished works.[3] In this period Schwenckfeld began the process of knitting together the various groups in southern Germany and Silesia.[4]

Schwenckfeld's letters to Strassburg were addressed to his committed group of followers, who were under increasing pressure, and his message was usually one of consolation. The lines had been drawn in Strassburg and a steadfast resignation (*Gelassenheit*) was required. The situation in Ulm was still much more fluid. The preachers vied with Schwenckfeld for his followers and protectors. The Streichers bore the brunt of clerical pressure, while other Schwenckfelders were wooed by the preachers with some measure of success.[5] Frecht tried to move the council to act on both Schwenckfeld and the concord, but to little effect. Frecht even suspected that his too frequent complaints against Schwenckfeld engendered further antagonism, especially with the Besserers.[6]

During this relative lull Schwenckfeld and his followers were caught up in the swirl of christological speculation and controversy that seized the dissident movement in the South as a whole. The result was a new Christology that distinguished Schwenckfeld and his followers from their South German neighbors and marked them as a separate and identifiable movement. Schwenckfeld's dedication to the glory of Christ forced him to abandon his aloof independence and made him an actor with a personal mission and a new message.

3. ". . . dass jhr alles wol urtheilet / sonderlich / was ich nicht im Truck lasse aussgehen" (CS V, 736:6–10).

4. Crautwald began corresponding with the Schwenckfelders in Strassburg and Ulm. Crautwald to Jakob Held von Tieffenau, June 24, 1537, Cod. Aug. 37.27.2, fols. 9–13. The title gives the date 1538, the colophon, 1537. See Crautwald to Althansen, November 15, 1537, Cod. Aug. 37.27.2, fols. 1–7; Crautwald to Margareta Engelmann and Jakob Held von Tieffenau, ca. September 1538, CS VI, 140–41; Crautwald to Held, September 30, 1538, Cod. Aug. 37.27.2, fols. 14–24 and Cod. Aug. 45.9.2, fols. 62r (123)–73v (146); Crautwald to Althansen, February 24, 1538, Cod. Aug. 37.27.2, fols. 25–31; Crautwald to Alexander Berner, November 14, 1538, CS VI, 251–69. In 1539 Crautwald wrote to Katharina Streicher of Ulm (Cod. Aug. 37.27.2, fols. 33–45, 49–57). Schwenckfeld's own correspondence in the period covered all of southern Germany and Silesia.

5. On the Streichers, see CS V, 546–49, 657–60, 697–709, 719–36. See Schwenckfeld's letter to Barbara Roelin, May 5, 1537, CS V, 685–89.

6. Frecht to Blaurer, August 23, 1537, Schiess 1, 855–56; August 26, 1537, Schiess 1, 856–57; August 27, 1537, Schiess 1, 857. From these letters it would appear that Frecht appealed to the council against Schwenckfeld sometime in August. This may have had something to do with Frecht's appointment as "Oberster Prediger" on August 1 (CS V, 697).

As we have seen, there were strong christological motives in Schwenckfeld's theology from the beginning.[7] In the twelve *Questiones* (1525) he had rejected the Lutheran doctrine of the real presence in part because, in his opinion, it threatened to divide the word from the body of Christ.[8] After his visit in December 1525, Schwenckfeld had concluded that the root of the problem between Liegnitz and Wittenberg was in their different understandings of the word and the Incarnation.[9] Schwenckfeld's position on the Eucharist made the glorified Christ's heavenly, spiritual body the sole means of salvation. It eclipsed the rest of the Christian experience, the visible church, and the Bible. The eucharistic context focused the issue on the nature of the heavenly flesh in the glorified postresurrection Christ. That the flesh was heavenly, spiritual, and divine precluded its conveyance through earthly, material, creaturely means. The linchpin was Schwenckfeld's insistence on the closest of unions between Christ's two natures after the resurrection. Though stressing the personal union of the two natures in the glorified Christ, Schwenckfeld rejected the Lutheran doctrine of ubiquity because he believed that it threatened the integrity of Christ's manhood.[10]

Crautwald, who relied to a great extent on Hilary of Poitiers, dominated the early christological discussions.[11] It was also Crautwald who began to consider Christ's status during the period of "humiliation" on earth. Caught in the Lutheran-Zwinglian cross fire, Crautwald worked toward a christological overview which would support his eucharistic position. After a few tentative steps in 1527, Crautwald produced the first "Schwenckfeldian" treatment in 1529.[12] Criticism had it that Crautwald and Schwenckfeld actually held to two bodies of Christ— one in humiliation and one in glory (a Zwinglian one during Christ's

7. See chapter 3, the section "Christ and the New Man." Schwenckfeld's Christology is much discussed in the literature: Baur 1843; Ecke 1911, 124–28, 201–03; Erbkam 1848, 357–475; Hahn 1847; Hirsch 1922, 60–66; Loetscher 1906, 357–86, 454–500; Maier 1959; Maron 1961a, 35–66; Schoeps 1951, 25–36; Sciegienny 1975; Weigelt 1973, 160–68. On Schwenckfeld's christological debate with Vadian, see McLaughlin 1985c.

8. CS III, 500:26–35, 502:36–503:10.

9. CS II, 250:7–11; 278:23–29.

10. See CS III, 214:31–216:7–34.

11. As Weigelt 1973, 162–64, correctly observes.

12. The "first tentative steps" are found in Crautwald's "Collectanea in Epistola Pauli Ad Romanos . . . ," Cod. Aug. 37.27.2, fols. 476, 479, where Crautwald briefly discusses the nature and manner of the conception of Christ's flesh. But the first truly extensive treatment of the issues was taken up in Crautwald's "De cognitione christi seu diiudicatione corporis et sanguinis domini" (1529), CLM 718, 422v–458r. Cf. "In tria priora capitula libri Geneseos annotata," CS III, 580–611. Weigelt 1973, 162, dates the change to 1528, but cites works from 1529.

earthly life and a Lutheran one after his resurrection). Crautwald responded by positing one human body that was transformed by Christ's life and death.[13] Christ, born of the virgin and sinless, gradually was deified. This did not abolish Christ's humanity, but rather it bathed the flesh in God's glory; it lived from his grace and essence.[14]

Schwenckfeld's arrival in Strassburg in 1529 brought him into the center of christological speculation in Europe. There the early waves of Anabaptists included men like Haetzer, Denck, and Cellarius, all of whom were suspected of christological deviancy. In 1527 one Thomas Salzmann was executed for denying the divinity of Christ.[15] Michael Servetus stayed in Strassburg for a short time in 1531 while he was having one of his christological works published in nearby Hagenau.[16] Clemens Ziegler, the native Strassburger radical, produced a variation on the idea of a heavenly or celestial flesh.[17] Melchior Hoffmann, drawing on Schwenckfeld's ideas, developed his own views on Christ during his Strassburg years.[18] Schwenckfeld and Hoffmann, however, quickly disagreed concerning Christ's humanity. Schwenckfeld came to view himself as the middle way between Hoffmann's denial of Christ's true humanity and Butzer's "Judaic" diminution of Christ's divinity.

Schwenckfeld's arguments with the Strassburg clergy over the validity and applicability to the Christian church of the Old Testament had convinced him that Butzer and the other South German and Swiss theologians did not fully appreciate the break between the Old and New Testaments, and by implication had failed to grasp the uniqueness and significance of Christ's incarnation. They treated Christ as if he were just another prophet. As a result, Schwenckfeld suspected them of Arianism or Nestorianism.[19] Schwenckfeld's reaction was to place even greater emphasis upon Christ's divinity.

But Christ's divinity posed problems for Schwenckfeld's dualism.

13. CLM 718, 425r–426v.
14. CLM 718, 430v–433r.
15. Röhrich 1830–32, vol. 1, pp. 344–47. See also TA 7, 133–37.
16. Butzer eventually conducted a disputation against Servetus's christological views (TA 7, 336:24–337:18). See also the "Confutatio" by Butzer of Servetus's "De trinitatis erroribus," TA 7, 592:15–599:20.
17. Deppermann 1979, 157–58.
18. Since Hoffmann's first published work on Christology only appeared in 1530, Deppermann 1979, 191, concluded that Hoffmann had received the initial impulse from Schwenckfeld. He is also correct in stating that Schwenckfeld and Hoffmann developed their views in constant exchange with one another.
19. CS IV, 245:7–20, 551:23–552:5, 791:26–31. He even suspected Crautwald at one time (CS V, 766:16–33).

How was material, worldly, sinful flesh joined with spiritual, heavenly, pure divinity? The initial response, provided by Crautwald, argued that Christ's flesh was similar to ordinary human flesh, but not exactly the same, because it was sinless. Through the power of the Holy Spirit and the faith of the Virgin, Christ's flesh was pure and free from sin. During Christ's life, passion, and death this sinless flesh was spiritualized, bereft of its earthly qualities, and divinized.[20]

Schwenckfeld gave this explanation to Melchior Hoffmann when they met in Strassburg, but Hoffmann was not satisfied with it. He simply could not believe that a flesh which had come from the sinful humanity of Mary could atone for and save mankind. Instead, he posited a heavenly flesh which came from heaven and merely passed through the Virgin as if through a pipe or tube. Christ drew nothing from Mary. A new, heavenly man had won salvation for fallen mankind, and in that Hoffmann found consolation.[21]

In Schwenckfeld's eyes Hoffmann had gone too far, even though Schwenckfeld preferred Hoffmann's error to Butzer's.[22]

Melchior Hoffmann errs in that he ascribes to Christ and his flesh according to [after (?); German *nach*] the first birth what he had only after the second [birth] and he applies to the first birth the passage 1 Cor. 15 [vs. 47] about the heavenly man where it speaks of the man Christ after the resurrection, after he was glorified in God and finally had become a totally heavenly man.[23]

The problem was that Hoffmann's position denied Christ's true humanity.[24] Schwenckfeld's concern was not so much for the act of atonement as for its application to the individual Christian. Christ had grown in strength, wisdom, and grace on earth before he was deified at his death. Each Christian had to follow in his Master's footsteps on his way to heaven, and that was only possible by participation in Christ's glorified flesh. If there was no point of contact, no initial sim-

20. Although Schwenckfeld hints at this doctrine at the Strassburg synod in 1533 (CS IV, 792:22–793:19), his first full exposition is in a letter to Jakob Held which CS dates to 1534, but which could be earlier or later (CS XVIII, 134:15–149:23). However, suggestions of divinization of Christ's flesh are found in Schwenckfeld's writings as early as 1527–28 (Maier 1959, 32).

21. On Hoffmann's teaching, see Deppermann 1979, 189–91; Schoeps 1951, 37–46; Keeney 1968, 89–91, 214.

22. See his third letter to Leo Jud (September 10, 1533, CS IV, 835:17–32).

23. CS XVIII, 157:22–158:3.

24. Cf. a fragment of a letter (doc. 116) defending Christ's humanity against Hoffmann (CS IV, 112–14). CS dates it to 1531. See also CS V, 496:19–24, 157:22–158:3.

ilarity between Christ and ordinary men, would it be possible for Christians to imitate Christ?[25] In any event, throughout the 1530s Schwenckfeld competed with Hoffmann for the christological loyalties of the Schwenckfelders, particularly in Strassburg, and of the dissident community as a whole.[26]

A third participant in the dissident christological debates, Sebastian Franck, also influenced the development of Schwenckfeld's theology. Franck taught that since creation the inner word, Christ, was present in all men from birth. The historical Christ had served merely as an outward manifestation or recapitulation of the birth, suffering, and glorification which Christ endured in all men's souls.[27] The historical human Christ lost almost all significance for Franck. It was the eternal Word, the second person of the Trinity alone that mattered. Schwenckfeld rejected Franck's teaching out of hand as Pelagianism and mere philosophy, but Franck's docetism forced Schwenckfeld to reconsider the nature of the "reality" of Christ's humanity.[28] Since the humanity of Christ suffered (it was necessary precisely because it could suffer),[29] how was the close union of divinity and humanity to be retained? Did God, the divinity, also suffer?

Schwenckfeld worked out his answer during 1537.[30] One of his followers in Strassburg, Margareta Engelmann, had been disturbed by the idea that the divinity had suffered in the incarnation and atonement. Schwenckfeld had written to her and had also suggested that she contact Valentin Crautwald. Crautwald's replies, however, seemed to Schwenckfeld to put too much stress on the distinction and separateness of Christ's two natures in the passion and death, to the detriment

25. CS IV, 1137–39; CS XVIII, 149:18–23, 157:22–158:3. It was during Schwenckfeld's Strassburg period that his fascination with the *Imitatio Christi* began (CS IV, 413).

26. Most of the christological discussion is found in letters to Jakob Held and Margareta Engelmann.

27. Peuckert 1943, 251–54.

28. Letter to Valentine Ickelsamer (?), December 17, 1535, CS V, 422:23–427:5; second letter to a zealous, God-fearing person, June 11, 1536, CS V, 499:1–502:2. Cf. Schoeps 1951, 54–55. This is not to say that Schwenckfeld did not also learn from Franck (Hirsch 1922, 163–64), but that Schwenckfeld defined himself over against Franck to some extent. In his letter to Valentine Ickelsamer (?), his discussion of Franck's Christology leads immediately to the problem of Christ's suffering and his divinity (CS V, 427:6–13).

29. CS V, 518:31–521:33.

30. He did this in a series of four letters to Alexander Berner in Strassburg dated simply 1537 (CS V, 750–55, 756–61, 761–68, 769–76). Cf. Crautwald to Margareta Engelmann (1538), Cod. Aug. 45.9.2, 74v (147)–95r (189). Schwenckfeld had asserted the divinity's possibility in some sense in 1526, but he had not developed the theme then (CS III, 356:3–26). He owed much to Crautwald and Hilary (CLM 718, 219v).

of their unity. He feared that Crautwald had fallen into Nestorian-ism.[31] Schwenckfeld's own position was quite clear. Christ's divinity could and did suffer. If God could be born and the Virgin Mary be addressed as *Theotokos*, then God could die. And if he could die, he could suffer.[32] Schwenckfeld used this reasoning to counter charges of Patripassianism. If it was possible for only the second person of the Trinity to be incarnated, then it was equally possible for only the sec-ond person to suffer.[33] The relationship was something like that exist-ing between body and soul. Though the soul was immaterial, it shared in its own way the suffering of the material body. In the same way, just as the soul continued to exist and live after the body had died, so too the divinity experienced death without actually dying.[34]

Still, Schwenckfeld was not unaware that his efforts to maintain both unity and distinction were fraught with difficulties. He wanted to combat Nestorianism without falling into Hoffmannitism. And like the church fathers of the fourth and fifth centuries who sought to find an orthodox middle between Nestorianism and Eutychianism, Schwenckfeld saw the solution in the *person* of Christ. It was the per-son of Christ, the whole person, that was born, suffered, and died.[35]

> Then when Peter says [1 Peter 4:1]: Since Christ suffered in the flesh . . . I do not understand as [meaning] according to [*nach*] the flesh or by means of [*am*] the flesh. Rather I judge it higher, as you now can see my opinion from the preceding: Quod nempe Christus passus sit in nostra carne, non sola caro nostra in Christo. That is, that Christ suffered in our flesh and not only our flesh in Christ.[36]

It would seem that Schwenckfeld's suspicions concerning Craut-wald's "Nestorianism" were groundless.[37] But Schwenckfeld's rediscov-

31. CS V, 759:32–38, 765:16–27.
32. CS V, 752:1–23, 766:34–768:6.
33. CS V, 752:15–23, 759:32–38, 775:23–776:3.
34. CS V, 758:7–27, 764:15–20, 771:1–22, 775:17–22.
35. CS V, 751:13–23, 757:20–758:6, 766:16–33.
36. CS V, 760:16–24.
37. In Crautwald's letter to Margareta Engelmann (1538), Cod. Aug. 45.9.2, fols. 74v (147)–95r (189), he explained that he had written to persuade her of the Schwenckfeld-Crautwald position, but had presented opposing arguments as a good teacher would. He also gave a clear exposition fully in agreement with Schwenckfeld. Cf. Weigelt 1973, 166–67. But Schwenckfeld remained unconvinced that Crautwald had not strayed, at least for a while, per-

ery of Christ's "personality," of the whole Christ, determined the further development of both his and Crautwald's Christology.

So far we have discussed Schwenckfeld's christological development in the context of the dissidents' intramural disagreements over the nature of Christ. But the final stage of that development was provoked by Schwenckfeld's clash with the South German theologians Butzer and Frecht, thinkers whom he termed "creaturists." The category 'creature' had come to play an important role in Schwenckfeld's thought and polemic only in 1531.[38] Prior to that his vocabulary consisted predominantly of variations on earthly and material in opposition to heavenly and spiritual. Christ was sometimes termed a creature without further comment.[39] The use of the term *creature* in a polemical way also represented a departure from Crautwald's concerns. Crautwald's major christological works to that date had not dealt with the issue.[40]

Schwenckfeld's sudden emphasis on the duality creature/noncreature can be traced to Michael Servetus's visit to Strassburg in June–August 1531. Schwenckfeld admitted having read the Spaniard's works and having spoken with him.[41] These discussions proved fruitful for both men. In *Two Books of Dialogues on the Trinity*, published in early 1532, Servetus wrestled with the question whether or not Christ was in fact a creature.[42] One passage sounds startlingly like Schwenckfeld's own post-1531 position.

This dispensation of the Incarnation was followed by the admirable one of the resurrection, in which the existence of the creature, which he acquired through his Incarnation, was laid aside just as if it were an accidental thing. There is nothing now in Christ which is animal. Christ has been wholly perfected and glo-

haps with good reason. CS V, 746–48; cf. "De cognitione Christi seu diiudicationem" (1529), CLM 718, 429r.

38. The dating on the pertinent citations is often inexact: Schwenckfeld to Bader, ca. 1530–31, CS IV, 18:7–21; "Vom Evangelio Jesu Christi," prior to September 1531, CS III, 360:34–

39. A marginal notation in his letter of 1528 to Johann Rurer (CS III, 219) denying Christ was a "Creaturlicher Mensch" was probably a later addition. It was only published years later. We have other evidence of Schwenckfeld backdating his discovery (Hirsch 1922, 155–56).

39. CS II, 536:30–537:2 (1527); CS III, 249:35–250:5, 258:29–30 (1528–1529). Cf. Hirsch 1922, 155–56.

40. E.g., the "De cognitione Christi seu diiudicatione . . ." (1529) never deals with the question (CLM 718, 422r–458r).

41. CS XVIII, 49.

42. *Dialogorum de Trinitate Libri Duo . . . per Michaelem Serveto . . . Anno M.D.XXXII*, Servetus 1965b. On Servetus's Christology, see Friedman 1978, 65–71.

rified through his resurrection so that he has returned to the original state of the word, and is then God, and is in God, as before.[43]

Citing Hebrews 2:14, Servetus denied that Christ was a creature "absolutely," but was rather a "participant in creatures" (*particeps creaturarum*).[44] Presumably Servetus meant that Christ partook of the flesh during his earthly life in an accidental, non-essential manner.

It is difficult to determine who "influenced" whom on this point. Servetus's book was published after his visit to Strassburg and was meant to answer the objections of his critics.[45] Since Schwenckfeld was suspected of favoring Servetus at the time, it might be that the two men collaborated to a certain extent.[46] At the very least they both drew upon the common matter of their discussions. But since the issue of Christ's creaturehood was more central to Servetus's whole approach to Christology and its insistence on Christ's divine sonhood, it is probable that he and not Schwenckfeld was the prime mover. Servetus also shared Schwenckfeld's conviction that salvation consisted of participation in God through Christ's flesh, and their eucharistic doctrines bore a close resemblance.[47] Both developed their Christologies in opposition to the Zwinglian view; they safeguarded Christ from becoming just another prophet by asserting that Christ was no longer a creature, even in his humanity.[48] Servetus and Schwenckfeld directed their efforts at keeping Christ, the only begotten son of God, at the center of the Christian experience.

Schwenckfeld was vocal in his criticism of Butzer's Christology from 1531 on, but Butzer chose not to pick up the gauntlet.[49] Instead Martin Frecht became the opponent who was the catalyst for Schwenckfeld's thought. Their first clash had taken place at the Tübingen Colloquy, where Frecht attacked Schwenckfeld for denying that the risen Christ was a creature.[50] Frecht had been stirred by Sebastian Franck's

43. Servetus 1965, B8r. Translation from Servetus 1969, 212, slightly revised. Cf. Servetus 1965b, C3r.

44. Servetus 1965b, B7v–B8r.

45. Servetus 1965b, A1v.

46. Butzer was not sure that Schwenckfeld sided with him in his debate with Servetus (Schiess 1, 307). Interestingly, there was also concern for Capito (Scheiss 1, 306).

47. Servetus 1965b, B8r–B8v. Friedman 1978, 93–94.

48. CS IV, 18:7–21.

49. CS IV, 246:3–12, 548:10–31. At the 1533 synod Schwenckfeld brought it up, but Butzer sought to evade the issue (CS IV, 791:26–793:19). Cf. CS V, 260:5–15, 325:14–18. Schwenckfeld had also discussed Christology in Memmingen and Ulm during his travels in 1534 (Schiess 1, 478, 504–05).

publication in Ulm of one of Crautwald's works, for which Franck provided a preface.[51] In it Franck asserted that salvation could neither be earned nor conveyed by creatures.[52] Though Franck himself did not explicitly draw the conclusion that Christ could not be a creature, others did.[53] What had been Schwenckfeld's private teaching restricted to conversation and manuscript had been made public, and in Ulm at that. Even the Tübingen Concord did nothing to lessen Frecht's concern.[54]

When the excitement surrounding the Wittenberg Concord began to settle down in 1537 and 1538, Schwenckfeld took up the cudgels in defense of the "glory of Christ."[55] The arguments he offered for his position that Christ was no longer a creature after his resurrection, however, could just as easily be deployed to argue the proposition that Christ had never been a creature. In fact, they seemed to demand that more radical position.

The new "Arians," by asserting that Christ according to his humanity remained a creature after his glorification, endangered salvation and the assurance which Christians had of it. It was only the divinity that saved.[56] If the humanity had remained a creature, "Christ could thus do no more according to his humanity than had Moses or any other prophets who are also in heaven or with God. How would Christians

---

51. "Von der gnaden Gottes," CS III, 85–98. CS dated it to 1528, which caused Hirsch (1922, 67 n. 3) some difficulty in determining both the author and, as a result, the chronology for Schwenckfeld's Christology. On Franck's role in publishing it, see Weigelt 1970, 11.

52. CS III, 86:2–25.

53. *Iudicium ueber der lutherischen Predicanten Buechlen one namen / wider den herrlichen freien gang der gnaden Gottes aussgangen* (CS III, 269–343). This too must be post-1535 since it is a response to the Lutheran criticism of the published edition of Crautwald's work. It contained a fully developed Schwenckfelder Christology (i.e., Christ was not a creature at birth [CS III, 296:26–33]) and must therefore be post-1539, which is when Crautwald accepted Schwenckfeld's new position (Weigelt 1973, 168). In his *Iudicium* Crautwald countered the Lutheran preachers' conclusions regarding Christ (CS III, 295:14–28).

54. Frecht to Blaurer, June 5, 1535, Schiess 1, 700.

55. "Von der Eer, Herlicheit und erhoehung der menschait Jesu Christi . . . 1537," CS V, 780–97; "Das unser herr Jesus Christus warer got und mensch hinfur kainer lieblicher stelle / bedarff / sonder im himlischen gotlicher wesen ist von aller dimensionen umbschreibung und zufall dises wesens gefreiet" (before June 1538), CS VI, 78–85; "Was fur Irrung / Abfal / von Christo und ungeschuckligkait / uss der leer folget / die Christus den menschen nun fur ein creatur helt" (before June 18, 1538), CS VI, 86–94; "Von der Herrlichait Christi. Das der Mensch Jesus Christus kain creatur. Sonder der Herre von Hyemel sey" (August 5, 1538), CS VI, 119–39; "Von der Menschwerdung Christi, ain Kurtz Bedencken. Wie der mensch Jesus Christus auss Gott dem h. gaiste (nicht auss irgent ainer creatur) sey empfangen undd geporen von Mariam der Junckhfrawen" (fall 1538), CS VI, 231–49. All of these must be used with care since Schwenckfeld and later editors (especially Suderman) interpolated later developments. See, for example, CS V, 793:18–38 margin, 797:12–21.

56. On the consequences of making Christ a creature, see CS VI, 94:1–4, 125:24–126:5, 130:8–13, 538:28–32; on the position that divinity, not humanity, saves: CS V, 768:7–18.

be born out of his flesh and limbs? Yes, how would they be Christians? Or where would Christianity remain?"[57] If Christ continued in part as a creature would it be correct or safe to worship him?[58] Does not the "creaturist" position also bring with it Trinitarian heresy?

> The single simple person of Christ would be divided. Christ would thus be divided and dissolved. He would not totally remain in the substance [wesen] of the Holy Trinity. Rather, his humanity would be placed below his divinity. Yes, there must be a fourth person in God's substance [wesen] if one wants to introduce or set up a creaturely imperfection or inequality in Jesus Christ.[59]

If Christ's flesh remained creaturely, then it could not be life-giving and the Eucharist would be impossible.[60] But to deny that Christ's humanity after the resurrection was a creature, would that not deny Christ's humanity itself?

> The humanity of Christ is not abolished or destroyed (as blind reason imagines) when one speaks of the honor, power, and glory of the glorified flesh of Christ in God—namely that Jesus has become Christ. Rather he remains and is still today a true man (who has a true body, flesh, and blood). But a man in God and of the substance [wesen] of God which he has now received.[61]

This assertion posed the problem of how Christ's humanity could remain human without being a creature. It was a matter of definitions. Schwenckfeld denied that creatureliness pertained to the substance of humanity. What a human being was (flesh and blood) could be distinguished from the method by which it had come to be (creation or generation).[62] If one were to use Aristotelian terminology, *creature* would refer not to the substance, but to the accident of relation.[63] And it was man's ability to achieve a new relationship with God that both set him

57. CS VI, 92:31–93:4.
58. CS VI, 93:22–26.
59. CS VI, 130:26–31.
60. CS VI, 132:4–10.
61. CS VI, 137:4–10.
62. CS VI, 237:15–18, 238:10–14. Cf. 392:10–17.
63. "It cannot be affirmed that predication of relationship by itself adds or takes away or changes anything in the thing of which it is said" (Boethius 1973, 27). In *De Trinitate*, Boethius employs the category of relationship to distinguish the three persons of the Trinity without affecting the divine substance.

apart from all other beings and made the incarnation possible and useful.

> Among all other creatures man alone was created by God for the kingdom of heaven, and that he should become heir to the same, a child of God, equal to and resembling God in joy, honor, and majesty. That he should participate eternally in the divine substance [*wesen*], power, authority, and nature.[64]

Although, in the course of arguing the case for the resurrected Christ, Schwenckfeld had begun to waver somewhat on the creaturely status of the earthly Jesus,[65] the decisive impetus to extend Christ's exemption from creaturehood to cover his life on earth probably came from Frecht's query: "But what of the state of dispensation? Was Jesus not Christ in Bethany? Was he not a creature?"[66] Having prevented a Nestorian division of the natures of the glorified Christ, Schwenckfeld could scarcely approve such a division in the earthly Christ. His argument that Christ need not remain a creature in order to safeguard his humanity was as valid when applied to the earthly Christ as when it was employed for the glorified Christ. In fact, Schwenckfeld's stress on the distinction of creation and generation necessitated a discussion of the conception of Christ and the incarnation of the word.

In the fall of 1538 Schwenckfeld wrote the treatise "On the Incarnation of Christ."[67] Its subtitle reads: "How the man Jesus Christ was conceived out of God the Holy Spirit (not out of any creature) and borne by the Virgin Mary." In it Schwenckfeld denied for the first time that Christ as a human had ever been a creature.[68] The treatise represented a careful attempt to distinguish Schwenckfeld's position from

---

64. CS V, 782:4–8.

65. In "Von der Herrlichait Christi" (August 5, 1538): "Dweil aber der h. gaist in Psalmen / Christum auch noch der menschait / *sonderlich* von seiner aufferstehunge her / den son gottes nennet . . ." CS VI, 128:15–17, emphasis mine. "Wer aber auch ainigerley weise Christum ain creatur nennet (*furnemlich* nachdem er alles was solcher leiplichen Ordnung und des menschlichen wesens an Jhm gewest / nu durch creutz und leiden in seiner verklerung abgeleget) . . ." (CS VI, 129:1–3, emphasis mine). Cf. 136:27–137:3, 137:34–36, 138:19–31.

66. CS VI, 138 n. 2. Cf. "Christus ante Glorificationem quidem fuit terrestis et humane substantie. non vult spiritus iste [Schwenckfeld] creature nomen addere. Ne videatur Christo in dispensatione creature vocem tribuere," CS VI, 136 n. 3. These comments were found on Frecht's copy of "Von der Herrlichait Christi."

67. "Von der Menschwerdunge Christi," CS VI, 231–49. It bears the date 1538 and must have been written after "Von der Herrlichait Christi" (August 5, 1538), CS VI, 119–39, since it argues the noncreaturehood of the earthly Christ, whereas "Von der Herrlichait" does not.

68. CS VI, 238:15–23.

that of Melchior Hoffmann while at the same time it presented an explanation which bore a close resemblance to Hoffmann's.[69] Hoffmann had claimed that Christ had brought his pure sinless body from heaven and that the Virgin served as a mere conduit, contributing nothing.[70] Schwenckfeld argued that Christ's origin, and the origin of his body, was heavenly and divine, but that the flesh itself in its matter or substance came from his mother Mary.

> Since neither the flesh nor the mother (although Mary gave the matter or substance of her holy virginal flesh to such a holy birth) nor any creature was the origin or beginning of this child, but rather the Holy Spirit . . . he was born a true man through the Holy Spirit in faith. Thus will it be obvious to a Christian believer who will assess this in the grace of Christ, that the man Jesus Christ should be called or confessed to be no creature, that is, no old creaturely man according to his order. But rather a new man, a son of God, yes, God and man in one person indivisible, also according to his birth out of the Virgin Mary.[71]

One must distinguish two types of men.

> One, whose origin arises from blood and flesh, is a man of sin who is lost, etc. . . . He is called an old creaturely man who came originally from the earth out of the works of the six days of creation, and who was totally corrupted by the evil spirit. The other Adam is a new man whose origin is his own. He is the savior, for he brings back the first fallen man and makes him similar to him and heir to eternal life.[72]

Mary's flesh was purified through the power of the Holy Spirit in order to make it suitable for Christ.[73] Mary, therefore, provided the passive matter of Christ's humanity. It was God who provided the active force which generated Jesus Christ and gave him life.[74] God was

---

69. CS VI, 237:1–10.
70. Deppermann 1979, 197–202; Schoeps 1951, 37–46; Keeney 1968, 89–90, 214.
71. CS VI, 235:27–236:2.
72. CS VI, 236:3–12.
73. This was a concession to Hoffmann's concerns. CS VI, 237:24–238:4.
74. CS VI, 238:5–14. Schwenckfeld's views on the mechanics of human conception belonged to the Aristotelian tradition. Only the father contributed a "seed" which was the active force. The mother provided passive matter, nourishment, and the womb. The competing Galenic model argued that there were two "seeds," one from each parent. See Bullough 1973; Needham 1959, 18–74; Keeney 1968, 92. Hilary of Poitiers may have been Schwenckfeld's immediate source for this theory as applied to Christ (Keeney 1968, 93).

thus the father of Jesus Christ both in his divinity and in his humanity.[75] And if Christ's humanity was begotten by God, the humanity was
not that of a creature.[76]

In its substance and physical reality Christ's humanity was the same
as that of other men, save for its sinlessness. After the resurrection
it became invisible, immortal, divine, and intangible. It was not destroyed, only improved.[77] And what Christ is by nature, other men
could become by grace.[78]

Once again Michael Servetus was instrumental in Schwenckfeld's
theological development. In both the *Dialogues* (1532) and the *Seven
Books on the Errors of the Trinity* (1531) Servetus had argued forcefully
that Christ was the son of God according to his manhood and that the
Holy Spirit had played the role which the human father does in normal conceptions.[79] God was the origin, the efficient and productive
cause of Christ.[80] Christ was not composed of two half-sons, one coming from Mary alone, the other from God alone.[81] Christ was the son
of God in both his natures.

> With great blasphemy they despise him as a creature. On the con-
> trary, I shall easily persuade you that he is the creator, if with firm
> faith you hold the whole order of the dispensation of Christ's king-
> dom, namely, the word of God, and its going forth into the world
> through the Incarnation, and its return to the Father through the
> resurrection. In the first place, according to the dispensation ac-
> cording to which he was himself the word with God, there is no
> question of creatures, because that word was God himself. More-
> over, Christ came forth into the world not after the manner of
> creatures, but being conceived by the Holy Spirit, being brought
> forth not out of nothing [*non ex nihilo*], but out of the very hypo-
> stasis of God, and being born of God's substance through the sub-
> stance of the word incarnate and made flesh. . . . Bear in mind

75. CS VI, 240:13–241:26, 313:7–9.
76. CS VI, 238:15–23; 315:4–10, 22–25.
77. CS VI, 243:20–245:18.
78. CS VI, 241:4–13, 20–26.
79. Servetus 1965a, 6r, 68r–68v; Servetus 1965b, C3v–C4r.
80. Servetus 1965a, 9r–9v: "Est enim ipse naturalis filius, sed alij non sunt filij originis,
sicut filij dei, non nascuntur filij Dei" and "Sicut terreni patres dicuntur patres suorum fi-
liorum, alias Deus non posset dici causu peculiariter efficiens, & productiva alicuius certi ef-
fectus."
81. Servetus 1965b, B2v.

that one cannot be called a son who has not come forth from the substance of his parent. Here you should ponder the old difference between being created and being begotten, which the philosophers have twisted for us into another thing.[82]

It would seem that Schwenckfeld received fruitful impulses from Servetus on two occasions separated by seven years. Schwenckfeld first held discussions with Servetus in Strassburg in 1531, and he may also have read *On the Errors of the Trinity*. We do not know if he saw the *Dialogues* at the time of their publication in 1532. His knowledge of Servetus's position may thus have been incomplete. In the fall of 1538, however, precisely at the time when Schwenckfeld came to the conclusion that Christ had never been a creature, one or both of Servetus's works were circulating in Ulm and according to the council Schwenckfeld was in some way involved.[83] Servetus's full doctrine was therefore available to Schwenckfeld just as he faced Frecht's challenge on the status of Christ during his earthly existence.

Though both Servetus and Schwenckfeld were concerned that Christ's glory was underestimated by their contemporaries, and both agreed that to deny the creaturehood of the person Christ was the best safeguard of that glory, they did not fully agree either on the details of the divine conception or on the resultant nature of the person Christ. Servetus argued that the word (which was not a person, but really only an expression or "dispensation" of the unitary Godhead) had been transformed in the incarnation. The substance of the word had become the substance of Christ, with the two natures—humanity and divinity—mingling in that substance.[84] For Schwenckfeld the two natures remained distinct even after the resurrection, even though God was the father of both.

The development of Schwenckfeld's Christology owed a great deal to others—Crautwald, Hoffmann, Servetus, and Hilary of Poitiers. But he was neither a mere eclectic nor an anchorless ship buffeted

---

82. Servetus 1965b, B4v. Translation from Servetus 1969, 206, slightly revised.

83. From the Ulm Religion Protocols: "Aftermontag nach Galli (22. Oktober) 1538. Was Schwenckfelden belangt, auch die Buecher Michel Serveten, wie es angebracht, soll weiter also auf Nachgedenken stehen, doch die Handlung fuerderlich (sofort) (bei Rat) angebracht werden," cited in Endriss 1936, 52. The sale of Servetus's books were forbidden on January 2, 1539. As we have seen, Schwenckfeld's first statement of his revised position occurred in "Von der Menschwerdunge Christi," CS VI, 238:15–23, written in 1538. See note 67 above.

84. Servetus 1965b, B5v–B6v. Schwenckfeld rejected Servetus's formulation later (1555), when charged with holding Servetus's position (CS XIV, 347–48).

about by the winds of changing opinion. There were underlying principles and concerns according to which he decided what was, and
what was not, true or useful. The first was that Christ was to be glorified without reserve. Schwenckfeld took the *solo Christo* plank of the
Protestant platform and made it the focus of his entire thought and
life. Few if any in the sixteenth century were more Christocentric than
Schwenckfeld. His compelling desire to worship, praise, and glorify
Christ functioned as a powerful independent motive in his thought
and determined the development of his theology. The splendor of the
glorified Christ tended to overshadow the Bible, the church, and its
ministry. He built his teaching about the freedom of a Christian on his
idea that the glorified Christ was free from all dependence on earthly
factors. The visible sacraments became almost superfluous when compared with the sacrament which was Christ himself. Martin Frecht
understood the importance of Schwenckfeld's attitude for the development of Schwenckfeld's Christology: "When Schwenckfeld said no
one can give great enough glory to Christ, I added that it was possible
to attribute too much glory to Christ, especially if one attributed to
Christ what neither he nor his word acknowledged."[85]

Schwenckfeld set a limitation to his emphasis on Christ's glory.
Christ's continuing humanity must be affirmed, if only to safeguard
man's salvation. Christ's humanity was the bridge between God and
man. As such, it was better than ordinary humanity, and different from
it. But there was no discontinuity, no break with humanity. The saved
would also make the transition. Christ's humanity and theirs would be
different but not inhuman (*non aliud sed aliter*).[86] It must be admitted,
however, that for Schwenckfeld the importance of Christ's glory out-
weighed that of his integral humanity, and one must wonder whether
Schwenckfeld's care in maintaining the latter may owe more to his
desire to remain orthodox than to any innate concerns.

Trying to maintain both principles in the context of Zwinglian
southern Germany gave Schwenckfeld a new appreciation of Luther's
Christology. Though he continued to reject as insufficient the *com-
municatio idiomatum*, he recognized in Luther a fellow defender of
Christ's glory in the face of Zwinglian Nestorianism.[87] Against Butzer,
Schwenckfeld claimed that Luther, Brenz, and all the ancient writers

85. CS VI, 124 n. 2.
86. "Christus uns perpetuo non aliud sed aliter" (CS VI, 81:9).
87. CS IV, 9:11–14.

taught that Christ was not a creature.[88] Against Frecht, he cited passages from Luther's *Christmas Postills* (1522) that glorified the risen Christ.[89] Though Luther was later to repudiate these statments for their failure to give due credit to Christ's humanity, there continued to be real similarities between Schwenckfeld's Christology and Luther's.[90] For Luther it was Christ's divinity working through his humanity that enabled man to partake of a new creation.[91] There is even some talk of the divinization of man.[92] Luther also argued that Christ's sonship was only on the level of his person and not of his two natures; that is, that Christ the person was the son of God and of Mary. He was, therefore, not a creature. As a result, though Christ had a real human nature, it was not entirely like that of ordinary men. He was heavenly, not earthly. Luther also discussed an "unfleshly" flesh. And finally, Luther emphatically distinguished Christ's period of humiliation on earth from his postresurrection glory.[93] "Christ has completely divested himself of the servant-form and put it aside; henceforth he is in the form of God, and is glorified, preached, confessed, honored, and acknowledged as God."[94] Christ remained man, however, and it was through him that the saved shared in everything that was in God.

Both men accentuated Christ's divinity over his humanity and forcefully asserted the continuing distinction between the two natures, while emphasizing the unity in Christ's person. Luther employed *communicatio idiomatum* to explain the relationship, while Schwenckfeld wrote of a penetration of the humanity and a sharing in the glory of God. The humanity dwelt in God's essence; it did not become part of God's essence.

Luther directly addressed Schwenckfeld's Christology only once, in

---

88. Sixth letter to Hans Konrad Thumb, May 1535, CS V, 325:14–23.

89. CS VI, 395:1–396:13. WA 10, pt. 1, 150, 153, 162–63, 173. According to these citations Luther taught that Christ the man was heir to all that was God's and ruled all creation. Christ was now the son of God according to both natures (p. 153). Christ has been made equal to the Father and become God (pp. 163, 173).

90. On Luther's unease with the 1522 *Postills*, see Siggins 1970, 219.

91. Siggins 1970, 166, 169, 197.

92. Siggins 1970, 97–98. But Luther also says that men will not participate in the divine essence (p. 198).

93. On sonship on the level of person, see Siggins 1970, 205, 207. Not a creature: p. 213. Christ's humanity real, but different from that of other men: p. 215. Unfleshly flesh: pp. 220–21. Distinction of humiliation and glory: p. 53.

94. Quoted in Siggins 1970, 219.

a disputation on the humanity and divinity of Christ.[95] As with most christological statements of the Reformation it produced more confusion than clarity. Nonetheless, in it Luther, while explicitly rejecting Schwenckfeld's position, came quite close to its substance. Because Luther was ignorant of Schwenckfeld's latest christological statements concerning Christ's noncreaturely status, he argued against Schwenckfeld's earlier formulation which limited the issue to the glorified Christ.

Luther forthrightly asserted that Christ was a creature according to his humanity, and that God was the father of his divinity alone.[96] His humanity was assumed, not begotten.[97] This seems clear enough, but Luther's position was not really captured in these statements. The problem was that the term *creature* was equivocal. Luther distinguished the old philosophical terminology from a new grammar of the Holy Spirit. Certain terms when applied to Christ, no longer bore the meaning or significance which was commonly accorded them. *Creature* was one of these terms.

> In grammar this analogy is quite valid: Christ was created. Thus Christ is a creature. But in theology nothing is less valid. Which is why eloquence must be restrained and we must remain with the prescribed formulas of the Holy Spirt. We should not depart from them unless by necessity, because the thing is ineffable and incomprehensible. In the language of the ancients a creature is that which the creator created and separated from Himself. But this meaning has no place in the creature Christ. There creator and creature are one and the same. Because of the ambiguity in the word and because men who hear it immediately think of a creature separated from the creator, therefore they avoid using it, though it is permissible to use it sparingly as a new word.[98]

Luther's desire to stress the unity of the person Christ ran counter to his attempt to distinguish the creaturely humanity from the creating divinity.

95. "Die Disputation de divinitate et humanitate Christi" (February 28, 1540), WA 39 part 2, 92–121.
96. WA 39, pt. 2, 99:20–25, 113:18–28, 119:5–8.
97. WA 39, pt. 2, 110:19–24, 113:18–28
98. WA 39, pt. 2, 104:24–105:19. Crautwald also came to the conclusion that Christ was *sui generis* and *tertium quid* (CS VI, 316:6–13).

From eternity he [Christ] was not man, but now he is conceived
from the Holy Spirit, born from the Virgin, made God and man
in one person, which has predicated of it both man and God.
Here was made the union of the person [*unio personae*]. Humanity and divinity enter into each other. The unity, that is what contains it. I confess two natures which cannot be separated. The
unity makes it; a unity which is a greater and firmer joining than
that of body and soul, because these are separated, the other
never. The immortal divine nature and the mortal human nature,
but unity in one person: That is Christ, son of the impassible
God, God and man crucified under Pontius Pilate.[99]

Because the word incarnate was ineffable, words were treacherous,
and even the Bible was insufficient. Luther took refuge in the formulations of the orthodox fathers inspired by the Holy Spirit.[100]

Both Luther and Schwenckfeld found the term and the concept
creature inappropriate for Christ. They agreed it did not apply to
the person. They diverged concerning the human nature. While
Schwenckfeld concluded that the humanity of Christ was not a creature, Luther redefined the term to fit Christ; that is, he too denied that
the human nature of Christ was a creature as that term was understood
by philosophers, grammarians, and ordinary people. While the entire
issue disturbed Luther, and made his answer ambiguous and uneasy,
Schwenckfeld's clear, radical, decisive conclusions exhilarated him
and filled him with a renewed sense of purpose.

Schwenckfeld's Christology was not Lutheran, but then neither was
it drastically different.[101] On the continuum which stretched from
Nestorianism to Monophysitism Schwenckfeld stood between Luther
and Hoffmann, between Luther and Servetus, toward the latter end of
the scale. If judged by the sophisticated standards of the fifth-century
christological debates, he was not orthodox. But, judged by those standards, few if any in the sixteenth century were: not Luther, not

99. WA 39, pt. 2, 101:20–102:8.
100. WA 39, pt. 2, 96:1–4, 98:13–21, 109:11–30.
101. While I agree with Maron 1961a, 161, that in the long run Schwenckfeld's Christology
was founded on a different anthropology from Luther's, his conclusion "hat er doch in Wahrheit
mit Luther nichts gemein" is unacceptable. Hirsch's opinion (1922, 165) that "Schwenckfeld's
Christologie . . . ist doch nur eine Spielart der lutherischen" goes too far, but is closer to the
truth. Schwenckfeld's Christology is not derivative of Luther's, though there is some dependence.

Zwingli, not Calvin. With all of them, however, Schwenckfeld could insist that he confessed two natures in one person.

All the participants in the christological debates of the Reformation were eventually forced to look to the church fathers for guidance. For Schwenckfeld it was at first Hilary (both directly and through the mediation of Crautwald). In later years Cyril of Alexandria and the other Alexandrines would join the cloud of witnesses.[102] Schwenckfeld shared with all of them a concept of physical redemption and a tendency to Monophysitism.

Schwenckfeld's Christology was the capstone of his theology. As such it was widely discussed and accepted by his followers, who came to call themselves the "Confessors of the Glory of Christ."[103] Schwenckfeld also had success with the common man in Ulm, and Frecht himself admitted that some of his truest followers were attracted to Schwenckfeld.[104] Both Bernhard Besserer and eventually Philip of Hesse found Schwenckfeld's Christology appealing and plausible, while the Ulm city council's committee for religion was greatly distressed that the clergy should preach that Christ was a creature.[105]

The Reformation had intensified the worship of Christ by concentrating the attention and hopes of Christians on Christ and Christ alone. The concepts of *sola fide, solo Christo*, and the consolation of oppressed consciences all depended upon Christ, an almighty divine savior. To quote Besserer: "I am sufficiently satisfied and content with the true, unfailing, saving chief article which I incontestably know and believe: that Christ is my God, Lord, Creator, Redeemer, and Savior."[106]

Schwenckfeld's discovery of Christ's glory and the denial of it by his opponents gave him a personal mission. Crautwald reported in 1538: "As you well know, our good friend C. S. [Caspar Schwenckfeld] now

102. On Schwenckfeld's patristic sources: Maier 1959, 33, 66–67; Schoeps 1951, 25–26. See also CS VI, 85:8–15.

103. Hampe 1882, 20. The Schwenckfelder Michael Ludwig von Freyberg had a twenty-five-line poem containing Schwenckfeld's teaching on Christ inscribed on a fireplace mantle in Schloss Justingen just outside Ulm. F. Weber 1962, 49 n. 193.

104. CS VI, 578:12–16. Schwenckfeld's Christology was discussed in the pulpits and the streets (Endriss 1936, 34). Frecht to Blaurer, August 23, 1539, Schiess 2, 31.

105. Besserer to Hesse, August 28, 1539, and October 17, 1539. Walther 1929, 68–69. Note that Besserer rejects new names for Christ, i.e., *creature*, while holding to old ones that emphasize his divinity. On Philip of Hesse, see French 1908, 84–86. On the committee statement, see Endriss 1936, 51.

106. Walther 1929, 69.

plans to write, speak, and confer about the glory of our lord and savior
Jesus Christ with the creaturists and others who stumble on this curb-
stone which has become and has been placed as the cornerstone and
corbel of the spiritual structure."[107] In February 1540 Schwenckfeld
described his newly discovered role.

> Then if I had wished to please men I would not have become the
> minister of the glorified Christ [*des glorificirten Christi diener*]. I
> would not have brought myself to defend his honor. . . . For our
> Christian name demands that we, each Christian according to his
> abilities, defend and rescue the honor and glory of Christ.[108]

It was as minister, knight, and champion of Christ's glory that
Schwenckfeld entered the lists against Frecht and the "creaturists."
Schwenckfeld's commitment to the glory of Christ provided the enthusiasm and fervor which his theology had lacked, because that theology
had been in many ways too "negative" in its deemphasis or disregard
of symbols capable of inspiring fervor. Schwenckfeld's sense of mission
compensated for the absence in his thought of apocalyptic expectations
found in other radical movements. As with the later Calvinists and
Jesuits, *ad majorem gloriam Christi* fueled the crusading zeal which
could create a new sect. The glory of Christ did not allow dissimula-
tion or reticence. In any event, Schwenckfeld's zeal overcame his prudence. It caused his departure from Ulm.

Frecht's renewed efforts to remove Schwenkfeld and his influence
from Ulm began in the summer of 1538.[109] In July, during one of
Schwenckfeld's absences, Frecht and his allies approached the committee for religion, but they received no support. The council as a
whole, when consulted, decided (October 1, 1538) that nothing was
to be done against Schwenckfeld. He was allowed to enter and leave
the city as he wished, and he was to be left in peace while in the city.
If the preachers had any complaints they were to bring them to the
council before whom Schwenckfeld could defend himself. The
preachers were ordered not to attack him from the pulpit.[110]

This did not prevent Frecht from circulating, anonymously, a now

107. Crautwald to Alexander Berner, November 14, 1538, CS VI, 254, 11–19.
108. CS VII, 8:4–11.
109. It was tied to Frecht's campaign to have Sebastian Franck expelled. Franck left in
January 1539. On Franck see Endriss 1935, 23–31. On Schwenckfeld's troubles, see Endriss
1936, 29–41.
110. Endriss 1936, 29–32, 51–52.

lost treatise, "On the Creaturehood of Christ."[111] He also complained to Bernhard Besserer in January 1539 about a polemical letter which Schwenckfeld had sent him.[112] The council ordered the two men to appear before them on January 13 to settle the matter.[113] Once again it was a colloquium, not a trial. Both men spoke at length on the nature of Christ. Frecht submitted a lengthy apology, and Schwenckfeld handed in a "Confession."[114] The council declared itself unable to judge the matter and promised to consult with the Elector of Saxony, Philip of Hesse, Strassburg, Augsburg, and other members of the Schmalkaldic League. It was a promise they never kept. In the meantime both sides were commanded to be silent. The council also ordered that no books were to be written, printed, imported, or sold unless they had been approved.[115]

Schwenckfeld's publication in August of another christological treatise, perhaps at Mainz, provoked another protest from Frecht.[116] When he demanded the right to respond to Schwenckfeld in print, the council once again refused permission and promised to consult with the learned of the Schmalkaldic League. On August 15, 1539, a second work by Schwenckfeld made its appearance in Ulm.[117] Frecht and the other clerics threatened to resign if they were not allowed to publish against Schwenckfeld. Instead, the council simply renewed its offer to consult outside theologians. But, faced with the same choice that the Strassburg authorities had in 1534, it also asked Schwenckfeld unofficially to "spend his penny elsewhere."[118] Though he acquiesced

---

111. He consulted Butzer, Capito, and others for guidance in the construction of counterarguments against Schwenckfeld's Christology. Luther was contacted, but failed to respond. *CS* VI, 384–85, 387–88.

112. But Frecht r eglected to mention his own letters and treatise. *CS* VI, 381–97.

113. *CS* VI, 398–427; Endriss 1936, 34–40.

114. "Caspar Schwenckfelds zue Ulm erregtes geczenck belangende / von der Menschheit Christ" (Ms. Reg. N. 626). This is a substantial fragment of the apology. Schwenckfeld was also able to replace an "imperfect" account of the colloquy with a better one after the event through the good offices of the Schwenckfelder secretary Sebastian Aitinger (*CS* VI, 399, 549–55).

115. Endriss 1936, 36–40.

116. *Ermanunge zum waren und seligmachende Erkanthnus Christi*, *CS* VI, 501–09; Endriss 1936, 36–40.

117. *Summarium ettlicher Argument—Das Christus nach der Menscheyt kein Creatur / sunder der ganz unser Herr unnd Gott sei*, *CS* VI, 530–39.

118. Endriss 1936, 39–41. This was a bold move by Frecht. The council might have taken him up on his offer if Protestant clergy had not been such a rare commodity. He had never been popular with the council. They would have preferred Leo Jud as Conrad Sam's replacement. Schwenckfeld was involved in efforts to get more sympathetic clerics appointed to Ulm, e.g., Bonifacius Wolfhart, Burckhard Schilling (*CS* VI, 361), and Butzer's deposed opponents from Strassburg (*CS* VII, 84:21–85:9).

and left on September 11, 1539, neither he nor Bernhard Besserer considered this a definitive settlement.[119] Schwenckfeld had left merely in order to avoid occasioning Besserer embarrassment. He would spend much of the remainder of his life in the vicinity of Ulm, on occasion even visiting the city itself.

But Frecht did not let the matter rest. In March 1540 copies of Schwenckfeld's works and Frecht's apology were forwarded to a gathering of theologians at Schmalkald. Appealing to the Nicene, Athanasian, and Apostles' creeds, the theologians condemned Schwenckfeld's early teaching that the humanity of Christ after the resurrection was no longer a creature. The condemnation was drafted by Melanchthon and signed by Butzer and others.[120] This was the first quasi-official condemnation of Schwenckfeld, but it had considerably less impact than has often been supposed. In part this was because of its dubious legality.[121] Though Frecht had the condemnation widely circulated, the council in Ulm itself refused to accept it.[122] Schwenckfeld showed proper caution afterward, but his travel was not restricted as a result, and no secular authority followed up the condemnation with one of its own.

Developments in Silesia were much more serious. Friedrich II of Liegnitz had finally achieved his goal of military and political security.[123] He was offered the protection of the Schmalkaldic League in April 1539. The price was the suppression of the *Schwärmer* and the establishment of a Lutheran church order. Pastors and preachers who did not meet the new standard were dismissed; others conformed.[124] Led by Bernhardinus Egetius, some of Schwenckfeld's friends broke with him, fearing that his radical spiritualism posed yet another threat to a ministry already decimated by Friedrich's Lutheran purge.

Mindful of his own position, Schwenckfeld had been very careful in

119. Schwenckfeld's farewell letter is in CS VI, 540–48. He left for Augsburg in the company of Bünderlin. CS VI, 546:28–30; Walther 1929, 69.

120. Endriss 1939, 41–44; CS VII, 455–60. For the text of the condemnation, see CR 3, 983–86. Butzer was the *éminence grise* behind it all (Schiess 2, 35).

121. Schwenckfeld's friend the lawyer Dr. Kneller pronounced it illegal to Melanchthon, who was reluctant to admit his part in it. CS VII, 459.

122. Frecht to Blaurer, January 21, 1542, Schiess 2, 101.

123. On Silesian events in this period, see Weigelt 1973, 169–74.

124. Johann Scaurus to Schwenckfeld, May 23, 1540, Cod. Aug. 37.27.2, 69–72; Scholastica von Kitlitz to Schwenckfeld, June 2, 1540, Cod. Aug. 37.27.2, 57–61; Schwenckfeld to Scaurus, August 1, 1540, CS VII, 105–17; Schwenckfeld to Scholastica von Kitlitz, August 10, 1540, CS VII, 149–60.

his communications with the duke. He had committed nothing of importance to writing and he had even avoided directly contacting Friedrich's clerics for fear of embarrassing the duke.[125] This explains Schwenckfeld's continued good relations with Friedrich. But the dismissal during the summer of 1539 of Johann Sigismund Werner, the last major Schwenckfelder in Liegnitz, and the duke's refusal to allow Schwenckfeld to return home for a visit provoked Schwenckfeld to candor at last. In two letters to Friedrich (February 7, 1540, and May 23, 1540) he remonstrated with the duke for having fired Werner, Eckel, and the other Schwenckfelders.[126] He defended his and their teaching as Christian. They were part of a larger body including many in Switzerland and southern Germany. To be sure, people like Butzer had given in to the Lutherans, but the original message of Liegnitz had been "the common church teaching . . . at Strassburg, Basel, Constance, Memmingen, and elsewhere in upper Germany, as well as still today in part in Switzerland and with some in the empire."[127]

Schwenckfeld was well aware that the times had changed. Chameleons like Butzer and new papists like Luther and Melanchthon were building state churches. Princes and magistrates were caught in the middle. While he scolded Friedrich, he could only sympathize with him.

For out of God's grace I have long seen how it would go, and in part how it must still go. Daily experience out here [as opposed to in Silesia] for eleven years now gives me no little knowledge. But what sympathy I have borne in this time with Your Princely Grace as with My Gracious Prince and Lord because of the division and the divers troubles (especially since Your Princely Grace's Christian disposition for the furtherance of the gospel was well known to me, though it is still not of such a degree as it reasonably should) I leave to our Lord God.[128]

The original freedom, zeal, and doctrine of the Reformation had been betrayed; the public, visible church was being lost. But there was still hope: Christ's wisdom, grace, and power could not be denied forever.

125. CS VII, 12:3–9; 81:4–8.
126. CS VII, 10–13, 77–91.
127. CS VII, 91:9–12.
128. CS VII, 81:10–17. Cf. Schwenckfeld's "Ratschlag" (ca. October 1528) to Friedrich, CS III, 99–118. Friedrich had finally opted to capitulate to the Lutherans.

I greatly hope God has sown his seeds. We must leave them under
the snow with the earth through the winter and then see if they
sprout in the spring. There will be a great persecution of the children of God. Their concord or agreement [that of Butzer, Frecht,
Luther] will be our cross and death. That will not endure which
has not been reborn, Matt. 13 [vs. 23] [129]

Schwenckfeld now entered into a decisively different phase of his
long career as a Reformer. The heyday of the Schwenckfelder movement, whose "seeds" he had helped sow, still lay ahead. The man himself had constructed all the fundamentals of his theology and had
finally found his vocation as prophet, confessor, and minister of
the glorified Christ. Schmalkald, for all the lack of immediate concrete results, nonetheless had branded him as a pariah. Liegnitz's Lutheran church order effectively barred Schwenckfeld's return home.
Schwenckfeld's long journey out of the Egypt of idols, conformity, and
half-measures had brought him into the desert, the isolation which
was radicalism, where he could come face to face with the glory of his
Lord on his own individual Sinai.

---

129. CS VI, 584:8–14.

Maps

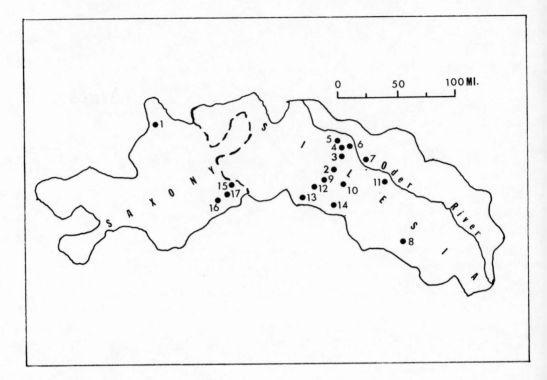

Schwenckfeldianism in Silesia and Saxony

1. Wittenberg	10. Jauer
2. Liegnitz	11. Breslau
3. Ossig	12. Harpersdorf
4. Lüben	13. Hirschberg
5. Raudten	14. Landshut
6. Steinau	15. Görlitz
7. Wohlau	16. Herrnhut
8. Neisse	17. Bertelsdorf
9. Goldberg	

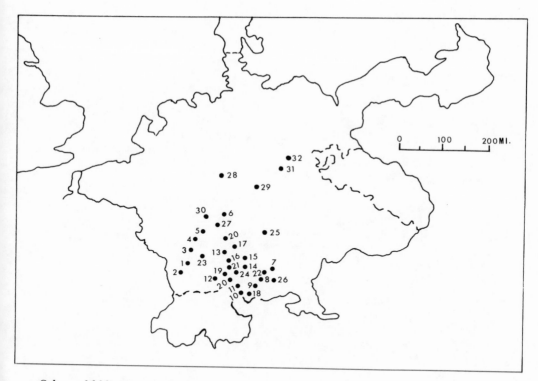

Schwenckfeldianism in Southern Germany

1. Strassburg
2. Rappoltsweiler
3. Hagenau
4. Landau
5. Speyer
6. Frankfurt
7. Augsburg
8. Mindelheim
9. Kempten
10. Isny
11. Memmingen

12. Stetten
13. Koengen
14. Ulm
15. Geislingen
16. Kirchheim
17. Esslingen
18. Wageg
19. Justingen
20. Cannstatt
21. Blaubeuren
22. Kaufbeuren

23. Baden
24. Oepfingen
25. Nürnberg
26. Leeder
27. Heidelberg
28. Marburg
29. Schmalkald
30. Worms
31. Weimar
32. Naumburg

Bibliography

Included are all works cited in the text with the exception of those contained in the list of abbreviations. All works consulted dealing specifically or in large part with Schwenckfeld are also listed.

Manuscript Sources

Berlin, Staatsbibliothek Preussischer Kulturbesitz
  Ms. germ. qu. 162
  Ms. germ. fol. 527
Munich, Bayerische Staatsbibliothek
  CGM 4202a
  CLM 718
Weimar Staatsarchiv
  Ms. Reg. N. 626
Wolfenbüttel, Herzog August Bibliothek
  Cod. Aug. 37.27.2
  Cod. Aug. 45.9.2

Other Sources

Abray, Lorna Jane. 1978. "The Long Reformation. Magistrates, Clergy, and People in Strassburg 1520–1598." Ph.D. diss., Yale University.
Alexander, C. B. 1926. "Kaspar von Schwenckfeld: His Life, Christology and Theology. (An Address delivered . . . before the Society of the Descendants of the Schwenckfeldian Exiles, November 19, 1926)." New York.
Althaus, Paul. 1914. *Zur Charakteristik der Evangelischen Gebetsliteratur im Reformationsjahrhundert.* Leipzig.
Anders, F. G. 1867. *Historische Statistik der Evangelischen Kirche in Schlesien.* Breslau.
Arnold, C. Franklin. 1909. "Zur Geschichte und Literatur der Schwenckfelder." ZVGS 43:291–303.
Arnold, Gottfried. 1703. *Supplementa, Illustrationes und Emendationes zur Verbesserung der Kirchen-Historie.* Frankfurt.
———. 1770. *Unparteyische Kirchen- und Ketzer-Historie.* Vol. 1, pt. 2, bk. 16, chap. 20, 240–61. Frankfurt.
Aubin, Hermann. 1938. *Geschichte Schlesiens, Band I, von der Urzeit bis zum Jahre 1526.* Herausgegeben von der Historischen Kommission für Schlesien unter Leitung von Hermann Aubin. Breslau.
Bahlow, Ferdinand. 1908. "Die Kirchenbibliothek von St. Peter und Paul in Liegnitz." *Mitteilungen des Geschichts- und Altertumsverein für die Stadt und das Fürstentum Liegnitz* 2:140–75.
———. 1918. *Die Reformation in Liegnitz.* Liegnitz.
Bahlow, Hans. 1928. *Die Anfänge des Buchdrucks zu Liegnitz.* Liegnitz.
Bainton, Roland H. 1969. *Erasmus of Christendom.* New York.

————. 1971. *Women of the Reformation in Germany and Italy.* Minneapolis.
Barbers, Meinulf. 1964. *Toleranz bei Sebastian Franck.* Bonn.
Barclay, A. 1927. *The Protestant Doctrine of the Lord's Supper.* Glasgow.
Barker, Sir Ernest. 1948. *Traditions of Civility: Eight Essays.* Cambridge.
Bauch, Gustav. 1892. "Beiträge zur Literaturgeschichte des Schlesischen Humanismus. I." ZVGS 26:213–49.
————. 1901. "Johann Thurzo und Johann Hess." ZVGS 36:193–224.
————. 1902, 1904. "Analekten zur Biographie des Johann Hess." CVGEKS 8:161–85; 9:34–64.
————. 1907. "Schlesien und die Universität Krakau im XV. und XVI. Jahrhundert." ZVGS 41:99–180.
Baur, Ferdinand Christian. 1838. *Die Christliche Lehre von der Versöhnung in ihrer geschichtlichen Entwicklung.* Tübingen.
————. 1843. *Die Christliche Lehre von der Dreieinigkeit und Menschenwerdung Gottes in ihrer geschichtlichen Entwicklung,* 3:219–56. Tübingen.
————. 1848. "Zur Geschichte der Protestantischen Mystik." *Theologische Jahrbücher* (Tübingen), 7:453–528.
————. 1867. *Vorlesungen über die Christliche Dogmengeschichte.* Leipzig.
Beachy, Alvin J. 1963. "The Grace of God in Christ as Understood by Five Major Anabaptist Writers." *MQR* 27:5–34.
————. 1977. *The Concept of Grace in the Radical Reformation.* Nieuwkoop.
Bellardi, Werner. 1934. *Die Geschichte der 'Christlichen Gemeinschaft' (1546/1550). Der Versuch einer 'zweiten Reformation,' ein Beitrag zur Reformationsgeschichte Strassburgs, mit zwei Beilagen.* Leipzig.
————. 1973. "Anton Engelbrecht (1485–1558). Helfer, Mitarbeiter und Gegner Bucers." *ARG* 64:183–206.
————. 1974. *'Abconterfeytung' Martin Butzers (1546).* Münster.
————. 1976. *Wolfgang Schultheiss. Wege und Wandlungen eines Strassburger Spiritualisten und Zeitgenossen Martin Bucers.* Frankfurt am Main.
Bergsma, Wiebe, 1983. "Aggaeus van Albada (c. 1525–1587), schwenckfeldiaan, saatsman en strijder voor verdraagzaamheid." Ph.D. diss., University of Groningen.
Bergsten, Torsten. 1957, 1958. "Pilgram Marbeck und seine Auseinandersetzung mit Caspar Schwenckfeld." *Kyrkohistorisk Arsskrift* (Uppsala), 57:39–101; 58:58–88.
Bernays, J. 1901. "Zur Biographie Johann Winthers von Andernach." ZGO 55:28–58.
Bernhardt, Walter. 1972. *Die Zentralbehörden des Herzogtums Württemberg und ihre Beamten 1520–1629.* 2 vols. Stuttgart.
Bizer, Ernst. 1962. *Studien zur Geschichte des Abendmahlsstreits im 16. Jahrhundert.* Darmstadt.
Boethius. 1973. *The Theological Tractates.* Trans. and ed. H. F. Stewart, E. K. Rand, S. J. Tester. Loeb Classical Library 74. Cambridge, Mass.
Boger, Ernst. 1885. *Geschichte der freiherrlichen Familie Thumb von Neuburg.* Stuttgart.
Borngräber, Otto. 1908. *Das Erwachen der philosophischen Spekulation der Reformationszeit in ihrem stufenweise Fortschreiten, beleuchtet an Schwenckfeld, Thamer, Sebastian Franck von Woerd.* Schwarzenberg.
Bornkamm, Heinrich. 1925. *Luther und Boehme.* Bonn.
————. 1926. *Mystik, Spiritualismus und die Anfänge des Pietismus im Luthertum.* Giessen.
————. 1932. "Äusserer und innerer Mensch bei Luther und den Spiritualisten." In

Imago Dei: Beiträge zur theologischen Anthropologie. Gustav Kruger zum siebzig-sten Gerburtstage am 29. Juni 1932, ed. Heinrich Bornkamm, 85–109. Giessen.

Bossert, Gustav. 1921. "Die Schwenckfelder in Cannstatt und ihre Freunde." *Schwäbische Merkur* nr. 160.

———. 1926. "Hans Ungnads Stellung zu Kaspar von Schwenckfelds Schriften." *Jahrbuch für die Geschichte des Protestantismus in Österreich* 47:159ff.

———. 1929. "Aus der nebenkirchlichen religiösen Bewegung der Reformationszeit in Württemberg (Wiedertäufer und Schwenkfelder)." *BWKG* 33:1–41.

Bossert, Gustav d. J. 1944–48. "Der Beamtenwechsel in Württemberg um 1544." *ZWLG* 8:280–97.

Brady, Thomas A. 1978. *Ruling Class, Regime and Reformation at Strassburg, 1520–1555*. Leiden.

Brecht, Martin. 1964. "Ambrosius Blarers Wirksamkeit in Schwaben." In *Der Konstanzer Reformator Ambrosius Blarer 1492–1564. Gedenkschrift zu seinem Todestag*, ed. Berndt Moeller, 140–71. Constance and Stuttgart.

———. 1966. *Die frühe Theologie des Johannes Brenz*. Tübingen.

Brenz, Johannes. 1868. *Anecdota Brentiana. Ungedruckte Briefe und Bedenken*. Ed. Th. Pressel. Tübingen.

———. 1970, 1974. *Frühschriften*. Ed. Martin Brecht, Gerhard Schaefer, and Frieda Wolf. 2 vols. Tübingen.

Bücher, Otto. 1950. "Adam Reissner: Ein Beitrag zur Geschichte der deutschen Reformation." Ph.D. diss., University of Erlangen.

Bugenhagen, Johannes. 1966. *Briefwechsel*. Ed. Otto Vogt. Hildesheim.

Bullough, Vern L. 1973. "Medieval Medical and Scientific Views of Women." *Viator* 4:485–501.

Butzer, Martin. 1960. *Deutsche Schriften*. Ed. Robert Stupperich. Paris and Gütersloh.

———. 1979. *Correspondence du Martin Bucer*. Vol. 1, *Jusqu'en 1524*. Ed. Jean Rott. Leiden.

Chenu, M. D. 1968. *Nature, Man, and Society in the Twelfth Century*. Chicago.

Chrisman, Miriam Usher. 1967. *Strasbourg and the Reform*. New Haven and London.

———. 1972. "Women and the Reformation in Strasbourg 1490–1530." *ARG* 63:143–68.

Clasen, Claus-Peter. 1965. *Die Wiedertäufer im Herzogtum Württemberg und in benachbarten Herrschaften. Ausbreitung, Geisteswelt und Soziologie*. Stuttgart.

———. 1972. "Schwenckfeld's Friends: A Social Study." *MQR* 46:58–69.

Cohrs, Ferdinand. 1902. *Die Evangelischen Katechismusversuche vor Luthers Enchiridion*. Vol 4. of *Undatierbare Katechismusversuche und zusammenfassende Darstellung*. Monumenta Germaniae Paedagogica 23. Berlin.

Cosack, C. J. 1861. *Paulus Speratus. Leben und Lieder*. Braunschweig.

Courvoisier, Jacques. 1933. *La notion d'église chez Bucer dans son développement historique*. Paris.

Davis, Natalie. 1965. "Strikes and Salvation at Lyons." *ARG* 56:45–64.

———. 1973. "City Women and Religious Change in Sixteenth-Century France." In *A Sampler of Women's Studies*, ed. Dorothy G. McGuigan, 18–45. Ann Arbor.

Deppermann, Klaus. 1977. "Melchior Hoffmann à Strasbourg." In *Strasbourg au coeur religieux du XVIe siècle. Hommage à Lucien Febvre*, ed. Georges Livet and Francis Rapp, 501–10. Strasbourg.

———. 1979. *Melchior Hoffman. Soziale Unruhen und apokalyptische Visionen im Zeitalter der Reformation*. Göttingen.

Dickens, A. G. 1974. *The English Reformation*. New York.

Dollinger. 1937. "Memminger Sektenbewegungen im 16. und 17. Jahrhundert." *ZBKG* 12:129–48.

Dollinger, Philippe. 1953. "La tolérance à Strasbourg au XVIe siècle." *Hommage à Lucien Febvre. Eventail de l'histoire vivante*. Paris.

Dorner, J. A. 1853. *Entwicklungsgeschichte der Lehre von der Person Christi*. Part 2. Berlin.

———. 1871. *History of Protestant Theology*. Trans. Robson and Taylor. Edinburgh.

Eberlein, Gerhard. 1900. "Die kirchliche Volksunterricht nach den Anschauungen der Schwenckfeldischen Kreise in Schlesien im ersten Drittel des 16. Jahrhunderts. Zugleich ein Beitrag zur Würdigung des Valentin Krautwald." *CVGEKS* 7, fasc. 1, 1–49.

———. 1903. "Zur Würdigung des Valentin Krautwald." *CVGEKS* 8:268–80.

Eberlein, Helmut. 1952. *Schlesische Kirchengeschichte*. Goslar.

Eberlein, Paul G. 1955. "Schwenckfelds Urteil über die Augsburger Konfession." *JSKG* 34:58–68.

Ecke, Karl. 1911. *Schwenckfeld, Luther und der Gedanke einer apostolischen Reformation*. Berlin.

———. 1952a. *Kaspar Schwenckfeld, Ungelöste Geistesfragen der Reformationszeit*. Gütersloh.

———. 1952b. *Der Reformierende Protestantismus, Streiflichter auf die Entwicklung lebendigen Gemeinde von Luther bis heute*. Gütersloh.

———. 1965. *Kaspar von Schwenckfeld: Schau einer apostolischen Reformation*. Blaubeuren-Ulm.

Edwards, Mark. 1975. *Luther and the False Brethren*. Stanford.

Eells, Hastings. 1971. *Martin Bucer*. New York.

Eitel, Peter. 1970. *Die oberschwäbischen Reichsstädte im Zeitalter der Zunftherrschaft. Untersuchungen zu ihrer politischen und sozialen Struktur unter besondere Berücksichtigung der Städte Lindau, Memmingen, Ravensburg und Überlingen*. Stuttgart.

Elias, Norbert. 1969. *Die höfliche Gesellschaft. Untersuchungen zur Soziologie des Königtums und der höflichen Aristokratie mit einer Einleitung: Soziologie und Geschichtswissenschaft*. Berlin.

Endriss, Julius. 1931. *Das Ulmer Reformationsjahr 1531 in seinen entscheidenden Vorgängen*. Ulm.

———. 1935. *Sebastian Francks Ulmer Kämpfe*. Ulm.

———. 1936. *Kaspar Schwenckfelds Ulmer Kämpfe*. Ulm.

Engelbert, Karl. 1960. "Die Anfänge der lutherischen Bewegung in Breslau und Schlesien. 1. Teil." *ASKG* 18:121–207.

———. 1961. "Die Anfänge der lutherischen Bewegung in Breslau und Schlesien. 2. Teil." *ASKG* 19:165–233.

———. 1963. "Die Anfänge der lutherischen Bewegung in Breslau und Schlesien. 4. Teil." *ASKG* 21:133–215.

Erb, Peter C. 1976. "The Role of Late Medieval Spirituality in the Work of Gottfried Arnold (1666–1714)." 2 vols. Ph.D. diss., University of Toronto.

———. 1977. "Christian Hoburg und schwenckfeldische Wurzeln des Pietismus, einige bisher unveröffentliche Briefe." *JSKG* 56:92–126.

———. 1980. "Adam Reissner. His Learning and Influence on Schwenckfeld." *MQR* 54:32–41.

———, ed. 1985. *1984 Schwenckfeld Commemorative Colloquium*. 2 vols. Pennsburg, Pa.

Erbkam, Heinrich Wilhelm. 1848. *Geschichte der protestantischen Sekten im Zeitalter der Reformation*. Hamburg and Gotha.

————. 1861, 1877. *Realenzyclopaedie für protestantischen Theologie und Kirche*, S. V. "Schwenckfeldt."

Erdmann, David. 1887. *Luther und seine Beziehung zu Schlesien insbesonders zu Breslau*. Schriften des Vereins für Reformationsgeschichte 19. Halle.

Ernst, Max. 1941. "Bernhard Besserer, Bürgermeister in Ulm (1471–1542)." ZWLG 5:88–113.

Estes, James Martin. 1982. *Christian Magistrate and State Church. The Reforming Career of Johannes Brenz*. Toronto.

Faber, Johann. 1529. *Doctor Johann Fabri. Christenliche ableynung des erschroeckenlichen yrrsal / so Caspar Schwenckfelder in der Schlesy / wyder die warheyt des hochwirdigenn sacraments leibs und bluts Christi / auffzurichten understandenn hat*. M.D.XXIX. Mainz.

Fast, Heinold. 1959. *Heinrich Bullinger und die Täufer. Ein Beitrag zur Historiographie und Theologie im 16. Jahrhundert*. Weierhof (Pfalz).

Febvre, Lucien. 1957. "Une question mal posée, Les origines de la réforme française." In *Au coeur religieux du XVIe siècle*, 1–70. Paris.

Ficker, Johannes. 1891. *Die Konfutation des Augsburgischen Bekenntnisses*. Leipzig.

————. 1941. "Jakob Sturms Entwurf zur Strassburger reformatorischer Verantwortung für den Augsburger Reichstag 1530." *Elsass-Lotharingisches Jahrbuch* 19:149–58.

Fleischer, Manfred. 1975. "The Institutionalization of Humanism in Protestant Silesia." ARG 66:256–74.

Freeman. E. S. 1945. *The Lord's Supper in Protestantism*. New York.

French, James Leslie. 1908. *The Correspondence of Caspar Schwenckfeld of Ossig and the Landgrave Philip of Hesse*. Leipzig.

Friedman, Jerome. 1978. *Michael Servetus. A Case Study in Total Heresy*. Geneva.

————. 1983. "The Reformation in Alien Eyes: Jewish Perceptions of Christian Troubles." *Sixteenth Century Journal* 14:23–40.

Friedmann, Robert. 1949. *Mennonite Piety through the Centuries*. Goshen, Ind.

Fritz, F. 1934. *Ulmische Kirchengeschichte vom Interim bis zum dreissigjährigen Krieg (1548–1612)*. Ulm.

Furcha, Edward J. 1968. "Key Concepts in Caspar von Schwenckfeld's Thought: Regeneration and the New Life." *Church History* 37:160–73.

————. 1970. *Schwenckfeld's Concept of the New Man*. Pennsburg, Pa.

————. 1972. "Schwenckfelder Hymns and Theology." MQR 46:280–90.

Garrett, James Leo. 1958. "The Nature of the Church according to the Radical Continental Reformation." MQR 32:111–27.

Gelbert, J. B. 1868. *Magister Johann Baders Leben und Schriften, Nicolaus Thomae und seine Briefe*. Neustadt.

Gerbert, Camill. 1889. *Geschichte der Strassburger Sektenbewegung zur Zeit der Reformation 1524–1534*. Strassburg.

Gerdes, Egon W. 1967. "Pietistisches bei Kaspar von Schwenckfeld." *Miscellanea Historiae Ecclesiasticae, Bibliothèque de la Revue d'Histoire Ecclésiastique*, fasc. 44, 105–37. Louvain.

Gerdes, H. 1955. *Luthers Streit mit den Schwärmern um das rechte Verständnis des Gesetzes Mose*. Göttingen.

————. 1958. "Zu Luthers Lehre vom Wirken des Geistes." In *Luther-Jahrbuch 1958 Jahrgang 25. Festgabe für Paul Althaus*, 42–61. Berlin.

Germann, W. 1894. *D. Johann Forster der Hennebergische Reformator*.

Gestrich, Christof. 1967. *Zwingli als Theologe: Glaube und Geist beim Zürcher Reformator*. Zurich and Stuttgart.

Grünewald, Johannes. 1964. "Das älteste schlesische Gesangbuch." *JSKG* 43:61–67.

Grützmacher, Richard H. 1902. *Wort und Geist—eine historische und dogmatische Untersuchung zum Gnadenmittel des Wortes*. Leipzig.

————. 1906, 1913. *Realenzyklopaedie für protestantische Theologie und Kirche*, S. V. "Schwenckfeld."

Haaugaard, William P. 1979. "Renaissance Patristic Scholarship and Theology in Sixteenth-Century England." *Sixteenth Century Journal*. 10:37–61.

Hahn, Georg Ludwig. 1847. *Schwenckfeldii Sententia de Christi Persona et Opere Exposita. Commentatio Historico-Theologica*. Breslau.

Hampe, O. 1882. "Zur Biographie Kaspars v. Schwenckfeld." In *Städtisches Evangelisches Gymnasium zu Jauer*, 17 (Ostern 1882): 1–20. Jauer.

Harnack, Adolph. 1961. *History of Dogma*. New York.

Hartmann, Maximilian. 1928. *Die evangelische Kirche Schlesiens in geschichtlicher Entwicklung bis auf die Gegenwart*. Breslau.

Hasel, Gerhard F. 1972. "Capito, Schwenckfeld and Crautwald on Sabbatarian Anabaptist Theology." *MQR* 46:41–58.

Heger, Henrik. 1967. *Die Melancholia bei den französischen Lyrikern des Spätmittelalters*. Bonn.

Held, Friedrich. 1965. "Die Tätigkeit des Ambrosius Blarer im Herzogtum Württemberg in den Jahren 1534–1538. Dargestellt nach seinem Briefwechsel." *BWKG* 65:150–205.

Heyd, A. 1838. "Blauer, Schnepf, Schwenckfeld. Ein Bruchstück aus dem ersten Capital der Reformationsgeschichte Württembergs." *Tübinger Zeitschrift für Theologie* (Tübingen), 4:1–48.

Heyd, Ludwig Friedrich. 1841–44. *Ulrich, Hertzog zu Württemberg*. 3 vols. Tübingen.

Heyer, Fritz. 1939. *Der Kirchenbegriff der Schwärmer*. Schriften des Vereins für Reformationsgeschichte 56, pt. 2. Leipzig.

Heyne, J. 1969. *Dokumentirte Geschichte des Bisthums und Hochstifts Breslau*. Aalen.

Hirsch, Emanuel. 1922. "Zum Verständnis Schwenckfelds." In *Festgabe von Fachgenossen und Freunden Karl Müller zum siebzigsten Geburtstag dargebracht*, ed. Otto Scheel, 145–70. Tübingen.

————. 1951. *Geschichte der neueren Evangelischen Theologie*. Gütersloh.

Hitchcock, William R. 1958. *The Background of the Knights' Revolt, 1522–1523*. Berkeley.

Hofacker, Hans-Georg. 1970. "Die Reformation in der Reichstadt Ravensburg." *ZWLG* 29:71–125.

Hoffmann, Franz. 1897. *Caspar Schwenckfelds Leben und Lehren, Erster Teil*. Wissenschaftliche Beilage zum Jahresbericht der ersten städtischen Realschule zu Berlin, Ostern 1897. Berlin.

Holborn, Hajo. 1937. *Ulrich von Hutten and the German Reformation*. New Haven.

Holl, Karl. 1923. "Luther und die Schwärmer." *Gesammelte Aufsätze zur Kirchengeschichte* (Tübingen), 1:420–67.

Hubmaier, Balthasar. 1962. *Schriften*. Quellen und Forschungen zur Reformationsgeschichte, vol. 19; Quellen zur Geschichte der Täufer, vol. 9. Gütersloh.

Husser, Daniel. 1977. "Caspar Schwenckfeld et ses adepts entre l'église et les sects à Strasbourg." In *Strasbourg au coeur religieux du XVIe siècle. Hommage à Lucien*

Febvre, ed. Georges Livet and Francis Rapp, 511–35. Strasbourg.

Irschlinger, Robert. 1934a. "Die Aufzeichnungen des Hans Ulrich Landschad von Steinach über sein Geschlecht." ZGO 47:205–58.

———. 1934b. "Zur Geschichte der Herren von Steinach und der Landschaden von Steinach." ZGO 47:421–508.

Irwin, Joyce. 1979. *Womanhood in Radical Protestantism 1525–1675*. New York.

Jaeger, C. Stephen. 1977. *Medieval Humanism in Gottfried von Strassburg's Tristan und Isolde*. Heidelberg.

———. 1983. "The Courtier Bishop in *Vitae* from the Tenth to the Twelfth Century." *Speculum* 58:291–325.

Jedin, Hubert. 1963. *A History of the Council of Trent*. Vol. 1. New York.

Jonas, Justus. 1884. *Briefwechsel*. Ed. G. Kawerau. Halle.

Jones, Rufus M. 1959. *Spiritual Reformers in the 16th and 17th Centuries*. Boston.

Kadelbach, Oswald. 1860. *Ausführliche geschichte Kaspar v. Schwenckfelds und der Schwenckfelder in Schlesien, der Ober-Lausitz und Amerika, nebst ihren Glaubensschriften 1524–1860*. Lauban.

Karant-Nunn, Susan. 1978. *Luther's Pastors: The Reformation in Ernestine Saxony*. Philadelphia.

Karlstadt, Andreas Bodenstein von. 1525. *Dialogus oder ein gesprechbuechlin von dem grewlichen und abgottlichen Missbrauch des hochwirdigsten sacraments Christi . . . 1525*.

Keeney, William Echard. 1968. *The Development of Dutch Anabaptist Thought and Practice from 1539–1564*. Nieuwkoop.

Keim, Carl Theodor. 1851. *Die Reformation der Reichstadt Ulm*. Stuttgart.

———. 1855. *Schwäbische Reformationsgeschichte bis zum Augsburger Reichstag. Mit vorzüglicher Rücksicht auf die entscheidenden Schlussjahre 1528 bis 1531*. Tübingen.

———. 1860. *Reformationsblätter der Reichstadt Esslingen*. Esslingen.

Kittelson, James M. 1973. "Martin Bucer and the Sacramentarian Controversy: The Origins of the Policy of Concord," ARG 64:166–83.

———. 1975. *Wolfgang Capito. From Humanist to Reformer*. Leiden.

Klassen, William. 1959. "Schwenckfeld," ME 4:1120–24.

Klaustermeyer, William Henry. 1965. "The Role of Matthew and Catherine Zell in the Strassburg Reformation." Ph.D. diss., Stanford University.

Klibansky, Raymond, Erwin Panofsky, and Fritz Saxl. 1964. *Saturn and Melancholy*. London.

Kliesch, Gottfried, 1961. *Der Einfluss der Universität Frankfurt (Oder) auf die schlesische Bildungsgeschichte dargestellt an den Breslauer Immatrikulierten von 1506–1648*. Würzburg.

Klose, Konrad. 1963. "Schwenckfeld und die Schwenckfelder in Lüben." CVGEKS 11:190–208.

Kluge, A. 1917. "Leben und Entwicklungsgang Schwenckfelds." CVGEKS 15:220–44.

———. 1918. "Caspar Schwenckfelds Stellung zu Theologie und Kirche." CVGEKS 16:7–29.

Knoke, W. 1959. "Schwenckfelds Sakramentsverständnis." *Zeitschrift für Religions- und Geistesgeschichte*. 11:314–27.

Knörrlich, Wolfgang. 1957. "Kaspar von Schwenckfeld und die Reformation in Schlesien." Ph.D. diss., University of Bonn.

Köhler, Walther. 1913a. "Review of Karl Ecke's *Schwenckfeld, Luther und der Ge-*

danke einer apostolischen Reformation." *Theologische Literaturzeitung* 38:209–12.
————. 1913b, 1931. *Religion in Geschichte und Gegenwart*, S. V. "Schwenckfeld." Leipzig.
————. 1913c. "Zu unserem Bilde, das Bildnis Kaspar Schwenckfeld." *Zwingliana* 3:128.
————. 1924, 1953. *Zwingli und Luther. Ihr Streit über das Abendmahl nach seinen politischen und religiösen Beziehungen.* 2 vols. Leipzig.
Koffmane, Gustav. 1885. "Zu Luthers Briefen und Tischreden." *Theologische Studien und Kritiken* 58:131–48.
————. 1887. "Die Wiedertäufer in Schlesien." *CVGEKS* 3:37–55.
Konrad, Paul. 1917. *Die Einführung der Reformation in Breslau und Schlesien.* Breslau.
Köstlin, J. 1864–65. "Johann Hess, der Breslauer Reformator." *ZVGS* 6:97–132, 181–265.
Koyré, Alexandre. 1955. "Schwenckfeld." In *Mystiques, Spirituels, Alchimistes: Schwenckfeld, Séb. Franck, Weigel, Paracelse,* 1–19. Paris.
Krämer, Christel. 1977. *Bezeihungen zwischen Albrecht von Brandenburg-Ansbach und Friedrich II von Liegnitz. Ein Fürstenbriefwechsel 1514–1547. Darstellung und Quellen.* Berlin.
Kreider, Robert. "The Anabaptists and the Civil Authorities of Strassburg, 1525–1555." *Church History* 24:99–118.
Kretschmar, Georg. 1960. *Die Reformation in Breslau.* Ulm.
Kriebel, Martha B. 1968. *Schwenckfelders and the Sacraments.* Pennsburg, Pa.
Krüger, Friedrich. 1970. *Bucer und Erasmus. Eine Untersuchung zum Einfluss des Erasmus auf die Theologie Martin Bucers. (Bis zum Evangelienkommentar von 1530).* Wiesbaden.
Kühn, Johannes. 1923. *Toleranz und Offenbarung.* Leipzig.
Kutscha, Alfred. 1924. *Die Stellung Schlesiens zum Deutschen Reich im Mittelalter.* Historische Studien 159. Berlin.
Lang, A. 1900. *Die Evangelienkommentar Martin Butzers und die Grundzüge seiner Theologie.* Leipzig.
Lashlee, Ernest L. 1969. "The Via Regia: A Study of Caspar Schwenckfeld's Ideas on Personal Renewal and Church Reform." Ph.D. diss., Harvard University.
Lecler, Joseph. 1955a. "Au temps de Luther: Les premiers apologistes du libre examen." *Recherches de science religieuse* 43:56–81.
————. 1955b. *Histoire de la tolérance du siècle de la réforme,* 2 vols., 1:187–95. Paris.
Lienhard, Marc. ed. 1981. *Croyants et sceptiques au XVIe siècle, le dossier des "Epicuriens."* Strasbourg.
Littel, Frank H. 1955. "Spiritualizers, Anabaptists, and the Church." *MQR* 29:34–44.
Locher, Gottfried W. 1979. *Die Zwinglische Reformation im Rahmen der europäischen Kirchengeschichte.* Göttingen and Zurich.
Loetscher, Frederick William. 1906. *Schwenckfeld's Participation in the Eucharistic Controversy of the Sixteenth Century.* Philadelphia.
Loos, Erich. 1955. *Baldassare Castigliones 'Libro de Cortegiano': Studien zur Tugendauffassung des Cinquecento, Analecta Romanica II.* Frankfurt am Main.
Loserth, J. 1925. "Studien zu Pilgram Marbeck." In *Gedenkschrift zum 400 jährigen Jubiläum der Mennoniten oder Taufgesinnten, 1525–1925,* ed. D. Chr. Neff, 134–77. Ludwigshafen.

Lubos, Arno. 1955. "Das schlesische Geistesleben im Mittelalter." *Jahrbuch der schlesischen Friedrich-Wilhelms-Universität zu Breslau* 1:71–111.

———. 1957. "Der Späthumanismus in Schlesien." *Jahrbuch der schlesischen Friedrich-Wilhelms-Universität zu Breslau* 2:104–47.

Luther, Martin. 1961. *Selections from his Writings*. Ed. John Dillenberger. Garden City, N.Y.

———. 1970. *Three Treatises*. Philadelphia.

McLaughlin, R. Emmet. 1979. "Spiritualism and the Bible. The Case of Caspar Schwenckfeld." *MQR* 53:282–98.

———. 1981. "Caspar Schwenckfeld." In *Gestalten der Kirchengeschichte*, ed. Martin Greschat, 14 vols., 5:307–23. Stuttgart.

———. 1983. "The Genesis of Schwenckfeld's Eucharistic Doctrine." *ARG* 74:94–121.

———. 1985a. "Schwenckfeld and the South German Eucharistic Controversy, 1526–1529." In Erb 1985.

———. 1985b. "Schwenckfeld and the Schwenckfelders of South Germany." In Erb 1985.

———. 1985c. "The Schwenckfeld-Vadian Christological Debate." In Erb 1985.

———. 1985d. "Schwenckfeld and the Strassburg Radicals." *MQR* 59:268–78.

McSorley, Harry J. 1969. *Luther: Right or Wrong?* New York.

Maier, Paul L. 1959. *Caspar Schwenckfeld on the Person and Work of Christ—A Study of Schwenckfeldian Theology at Its Core*. Assen.

———. 1963. "Caspar Schwenckfeld—A Quadricentennial Evaluation." *ARG* 54:89–97.

Marbeck, Pilgram. 1929. *Quellen und Forschungen zur Geschichte der oberdeutschen Taufgesinnten im 16. Jahrhundert. Pilgram Marbecks Antwort auf Kaspar Schwenckfelds Beurteilung des Buches der Bundesbezeugung von 1542*. Ed. J. Loserth. Vienna and Leipzig.

Maron, Gottfried. 1959. "Die Anschauungen von der religiösen Unmittelbarkeit bei Caspar v. Schwenckfeld, seine Stellung zu den Sacramenten und sein Urteil über Katholizismus, Reformation und Täufertum." *Jahrbuch der schlesischen Friedrich-Wilhelms-Universität zu Breslau*. 4:25–55.

———. 1961a. *Individualismus und Gemeinschaft bei Caspar Schwenckfeld, seine Theologie dargestellt mit besonderer Ausrichtung auf seinen Kirchenbegriff*. Stuttgart.

———. 1961b. *Religion in Geschichte und Gegenwart*, S. V. "Schwenckfeld." Tübingen.

Maurer, Wilhelm. 1952. "Luther und die Schwärmer." *Fuldaer Hefte. Schriften des theologischen Konvents Augsburgischen Bekenntnisses* 6:7–37.

Mazzeo, Joseph Anthony. 1965. *Renaissance and Revolution. The Remaking of European Thought*. New York.

Meisner, Heinrich, and Reinhold Röhricht. 1878. "Die Pilgerfahrt des Herzogs Friedrich II von Liegnitz und Brieg nach dem heiligen Land." *Zeitschrift des Deutschen Palaestina-Vereins* 1:101–31, 177–209.

Menzel, Josef Joachim. 1964. *Jura Ducalia. Die mittelalterlichen grundlegender Dominialverfassung in Schlesien*. Würzburg.

Meyer, A. O. 1903. *Studien zur Vorgeschichte der Reformation aus schlesischen Quellen*. Munich and Berlin.

Mielke, Heinz-Peter. 1976. "Schwenckfeldianer im Hofstaat Bischof Marquards von Speyer (1560–1581)." *AMKG* 28:77–82.

————. 1977. *Die Niederadligen von Hattstein. Ihre politische Rolle und soziale Stellung.* Wiesbaden.

Mitchell, Charles Buel. 1960. "Martin Bucer and Sectarian Dissent—A Confrontation of the Magisterial Reformation with Anabaptists and Spiritualists." Ph.D. diss., Yale University.

Moeller, Berndt. 1961. *Johannes Zwick und die Reformation in Konstanz.* Gütersloh.

————. 1964. "Ambrosius Blarer, 1492–1564." In *Der Konstanzer Reformator Ambrosius Blarer 1492–1564. Gedenkschrift zu seinem 400 Todestag,* ed. Bernd Moeller, 11–38. Constance and Stuttgart.

————. 1972. "Imperial Cities and the Reformation." In *Imperial Cities and the Reformation: Three Essays,* ed. and trans. H. C. Eric Midelfort and Mark U. Edwards, 41–115. Philadelphia.

Moltmann, J. 1957. "Ein unbekannter Schwenckfeldbrief." *Jahrbuch der schlesischen Friedrich-Wilhelms-Universität zu Breslau* 2:66–72.

Morita, Yasukazu. 1975. "Bullinger und Schwenckfeld." In *Heinrich Bullinger 1504–1575. Gesammelte Aufsätze zum 400. Todestag,* ed. Ulrich Gaebler and Erland Herkenrath, 2:143–56. Zurich.

Müller, Jan-Dirk. 1982. *Gedechtnus. Literatur und Hofgesellschaft um Maximilian I.* Munich.

Naujoks, Eberhard. 1958. *Obrigkeitsgedanke, Zunftverfassung, und Reformation. Studien zur Verfassungsgeschichte von Ulm, Esslingen und Schwäb. Gemünd.* Stuttgart.

Needham, Joseph. 1959. *A History of Embryology.* New York.

Niebuhr, H. R. 1946. "The Doctrine of the Trinity and the Unity of the Church." *Theology Today* 3:371–84.

Nigg, W. 1959. *Heimliche Weisheit, Mystisches Leben, in der evangelischen Christenheit.* Zurich and Stuttgart.

Oberman, Heiko A. 1967. *The Harvest of Medieval Theology.* Grand Rapids, Mich.

Oecolampadius, Johannes. 1525. *Ioannis Oecolampadii De Genuina Verborum Domini, Hoc est Corpus Meum, iuxta vetustissima authores expositione liber. Basilea. Anno. 1525.* Basel.

Osiander (the Elder), Andreas. 1975. *Gesamtausgabe.* Vol. 1. Gütersloh.

Otte, Johannes. 1936. "Die Stellung Kaspar von Schwenckfeld innerhalb der schlesischen Kirchengeschichte." Schwenckfelder Library MS, Pennsburg, Pa.

Otto, Carl. 1872. "Über die Wahl Jacobs von Salza zum Bischof von Breslau und die derselben unmittelbar folgenden Ereignisse (Sept. 1520 bis Sept. 1521)." ZVGS 11:303–28.

Ozment, Steven. 1969. *Homo Spiritualis.* Leiden.

————. 1973a. "Humanism, Scholasticism, and the Intellectual Origins of the Reformation." In *Continuity and Discontinuity in Church History: Essays Presented to George H. Williams,* ed. F. Forrester Church and Timothy George, 133–49. Leiden.

————. 1973b. *Mysticism and Dissent.* New Haven.

————. 1974. "Luther and the Late Middle Ages: The Formation of Reformation Thought." In *Transition and Revolution: Problems and Issues of European Renaissance and Reformation History,* ed. Robert M. Kingdon, 109–53. Minneapolis.

————. 1975. *The Reformation in the Cities. The Appeal of Protestantism to Sixteenth-Century Germany and Switzerland.* New Haven.

Paulus, N. 1911. *Protestantismus und Toleranz im 16. Jahrhundert.* Freiburg.

Pelikan, Jaroslav. 1964. *Obedient Rebels, Catholic Substance and Protestant Principle in Luther's Reformation.* London.
———. 1968. *Spirit versus Structure. Luther and the Institutions of the Church.* New York.
Peschke, E. 1935, 1940. *Die Theologie der Böhmische Brüder in ihrer Frühzeit.* Vol. 1, *Das Abendmahl.* Pt. 1, *Untersuchungen.* Pt. 2, *Texte aus altschechische Handschriften Übersetzt.* Stuttgart.
Pestalozzi, Carl. 1858. *Heinrich Bullinger. Leben und ausgewählte Schriften.* Elberfeld.
———. 1860. *Leo Judae. Nach handschriftlichen und gleichzeitigen Quellen.* Elberfeld.
Peuckert, Will-Erich. 1943. *Sebastian Franck. Ein Deutscher Sucher.* Munich.
Pietz, Reinhold. 1956. "Der Mensch ohne Christus—Eine Untersuchung zur Anthropologie Caspar Schwenckfelds." Ph.D. diss., University of Tübingen.
———. 1959. *Die Gestalt der zukünftigen Kirche: Schwenckfelds Gespräch mit Luther. Wittenberg 1525.* Stuttgart.
———. 1962. *Evangelisches Kirchenlexikon,* S. V. "Schwenckfeld." Göttingen.
Planck, G. J. 1798. *Geschichte der protestantische Theologie von Luthers Tode bis zu den Konkordienformel.* Leipzig.
Pollet, J. V. 1958, 1962. *Martin Bucer. Etudes sur la correspondance avec de nombreux textes inédits.* 2 vols. Paris.
Preger, Wilhelm. 1859, 1861. *Mattias Flacius Illyricus und seine Zeit.* 2 vols. Erlangen.
Press, Volker. 1978. "Adel, Reich und Reformation." In *Stadtburgertum und Adel in der Reformation,* ed. Wolfgang J. Mommsen, Peter Alter, and Robert W. Scribner, 330–83. Stuttgart.
Rachfahl, Felix. 1894. *Die Organization der Gesamtverwaltung Schlesiens vor dem dreissigjährigen Kriege.* Staats- und sozial wissenschaftliche Forschungen 13. Leipzig.
Ranke, Leopold. 1847. *History of the Reformation in Germany.* Trans. Sarah Austin. 3 vols. London.
Rauscher, Julius. 1934. *Württembergische Reformationsgeschichte.* Stuttgart.
Reu, Johann Michael. 1930. *The Augsburg Confession—A Collection of Sources with an Historical Introduction.* 2 vols. Chicago.
Rezek, Anton. 1884. "Eine Unterredung der böhmischen Brüder mit Dr. Joh. Hess im Jahre 1540." ZVGS 18:287–95.
Rieber, Albrecht. 1968. "Das Patriziat von Ulm, Augsburg, Ravensburg, Memmingen, Biberach." In *Deutsches Patriziat 1430–1740,* ed. Hellmuth Roessler, 299–351. Limburg/Lahn.
Roelker, Nancy L. 1972. "The Appeal of Calvinism to French Noblewomen in the Sixteenth Century." *Journal of Interdisciplinary History* 2 (1972): 391–413.
Röhrich, Timotheus Wilhelm. 1830–32. *Geschichte der Reformation im Elsass und besonders in Strassburg.* 3 vols. Strassburg.
Rosenberg, Abraham Gottlob. 1767. *Schlesische Reformations-Geschichte.* Breslau.
Roth, Friedrich. 1902. *Augsburgs Reformationsgeschichte.* Vol. 2, *1531–1537 bzw. 1540.* Munich.
Rothe, K. 1974. *Historisches Wörterbuch der Philosophie,* S. V. "Geist." Stuttgart.
Rothenberger, J. R. 1967. *Caspar Schwenckfeld von Ossig and the Ecumenical Ideal.* Pennsburg, Pa.
Rothmann, Bernhard. 1970. *Die Schriften Bernhard Rothmanns.* Ed. Robert Stupperich. Münster.

Rupp, Gordon. "Word and Spirit in the First Years of the Reformation." ARG 49:13–26.

Sabisch, Alfred. 1938. "Der Messcanon des Breslauer Pfarrers Dr. Ambrosius Moibanus. Ein Beitrag zur Geschichte des protestantischen Gottesdienst in Schlesien in den ersten Jahrzehnten der Glaubensspaltung." ASKG 3:98–126.

———. 1975. Die Bischöfe von Breslau und die Reformation in Schlesien. Münster.

Salig, C. A. 1735. Vollständige Historie der Augsburgischen Konfession, 950–1116. Halle.

Sanders, H. A. 1937. Beiträge zur Geschichte des Lutherischen Gottesdienstes und der Kirchenmusik in Breslau. Die lateinischen Haupt- und Nebengottesdienste im 16. und 17. Jahrhundert. Breslau.

Sattler, Christian Friedrich. 1771. Geschichte der Herzogthums Wuertenberg unter der Regierung der Herzogen. Pt. 3. Tübingen.

Schilling, A. 1880. Die Reichsherrschaft Justingen. Ein Beitrag zur Geschichte von Alb und Oberschwaben. Stuttgart.

Schimmelpfennig, Adolf. 1884. "Herzog Karl I. von Münsterberg-Oels und seine Schwester Margaretha von Anhalt. Nach ungedruckten Briefen aus den Jahren 1503–1530." ZVGS 18:117–61.

Schmidt, Hans Dieter. 1976. "Nürnberg, Schwenckfeld und die Schwenckfelder." In Festgabe für Ernst Walter Zeeden zum 60. Geburtstag, 215–47. Münster.

Schneider, August Friedrich Heinrich. 1857. "Zur Literatur der Schwenckfeldischen Liederdichter bis Daniel Sudermann." In Jahres-Bericht über die königliche Realschule, Vorschule und Elizabethschule zu Berlin. Berlin.

———. 1862. Über den geschichtlichen Verlauf der Reformation in Liegnitz und ihren späteren Kampf gegen die Kaiserlichen Jesuiten-Mission in Harpersdorf. Berlin.

Schoeningh, Franz Josef. 1927. Die Rehlinger von Augsburg. Ein Beitrag zur deutschen Wirtschaftsgeschichte des 16. und 17. Jahrhunderts. Paderborn.

Schoeps, Hans J. 1951. Vom Himmlischen Fleisch Christi. Tübingen.

Scholz, Paul. 1874. "Vertreibung der Bernardiner aus Liegnitz im Jahre 1524." ZVGS 12:359–79.

Schönwälder, K. F. 1855. Die Piasten zum Briege oder Geschichte der Stadt und des Fürstentum Brieg. Brieg.

Schottenloher, Karl. 1908. "Jakob Ziegler und Adam Reissner. Eine quellenkritische Untersuchung über ein Streitschrift der Reformationszeit gegen das Papsstum." Ph.D. diss., University of Munich.

Schroeder, H. J. 1978. Canons and Decrees of the Council of Trent. Ed. and trans. H. J. Schroeder. Rockford, Ill.

Schultz, Christopher. 1942. A Vindication of Caspar Schwenckfeld von Ossig. Allentown, Pa.

Schultz, Selina Gerhard. 1946. Caspar Schwenckfeld von Ossig (1489–1561), Spiritual Interpreter of Christianity, Apostle of the Middle Way, Pioneer of Modern Religious Thought. Norristown, Pa.

Sciegienny, André. 1974. "Réforme erasmienne ou Réforme lutherienne? Caspar Schwenckfeld et Erasme." Revue d'Histoire et de Philosophie Religieuse 54:309–24.

———. 1975. Homme charnel, homme spirituel; Etude sur la christologie de Caspar Schwenckfeld (1489–1561). Wiesbaden.

Scribner, Robert W. 1975. "Memorandum on the Appointment of a Preacher in Speyer, 1538." Bulletin of the Institute of Historical Research 48:248–55.

Scriptores. 1856. Scriptores Rerum Silesiacarum, Vol. 4. Breslau.

Seeberg, Erich. 1929. "Der Gegensatz zwischen Zwingli, Schwenckfeld und Luther." In Reinhold-Seeberg-Festschrift, 43–81. Leipzig.

Seltzer, George Rise. 1934. "Aspects of the Thought of Caspar Schwenckfeld to the End of February 1529." Ph.D. diss., Hartford Theological Seminary.

Servetus, Michael. [1531] 1965a. *De trinitatis erroribus libri septem. Per Michaelem Serveto, alias Reyes ab Aragonia Hispanum. Anno M.D. XXXI.* Reprint, Frankfurt am Main.

———. [1532] 1965b. *Dialogorum de trinitate libri duo. De iusticia regni Christi. Capitula quattuor. Per Michaelem Serveto, alias Reyes, ab Aragonia Hispanum. Anno M.D.XXXII.* Reprint, Frankfurt am Main.

———. [1932] 1969. *Two Treatises of Servetus on the Trinity.* Trans. Earl Morse Wilbur. Reprint, Cambridge, Mass.; New York.

Sessions, Kyle C. 1968. *Reformation and Authority: The Meaning of the Peasants Revolt.* Lexington, Mass.

Seyppel, Joachim H. 1961. *Schwenckfeld: Knight of Faith—A Study in the History of Religion.* Pennsburg, Pa.

Sider, Ronald J. 1974. *Andreas Bodenstein von Karlstadt: The Development of His Thought, 1517–1525.* Leiden.

———. 1978. *Karlstadt's Battle with Luther: Documents in a Liberal-Radical Debate.* Philadelphia.

Siggins, Ian D. Kingston. 1970. *Martin Luther's Doctrine of Christ.* New Haven and London.

Sinapius, Johann. 1720. *Schlesische Curiositäten erste Vorstellung darinnen die ansehnlichen Geschlechter der schlesischen Adels. . . .* Leipzig.

Sippel, Theodor. 1911. "Caspar Schwenckfeld." *Die Christliche Welt* 25:866–71, 897–900, 925–57, 963–66.

Soffner, Johannes. 1885. "Zur Geschichte des schlesischen Schulwesens im 16. Jahrhundert." *ZVGS* 19:271–95.

———. 1889. *Geschichte der Reformation in Schlesien.* Breslau.

Spach, Em. 1872. "Exposé du système christologique de Caspar Schwenckfeld." Master's thesis, University of Strassburg.

Spengler, Lazarus. 1530. *Eyn kurtze ausszug / aus dem Bepstlichen rechten / der Decret und Decretalen / In den artickeln / die ungeverlich Gottes Wort und dem Evangelio gemess sein / oder zum wenigsten mit widerstreben /* 1530. Nürnberg.

Spitta, Friedrich. 1911. "War Caspar Schwenckfeld Dichter?" *Monatschrift für Gottesdienst und kirchlichen Kunst.* 16:209–13.

Spitz, Lewis. 1963. *The Religious Renaissance of the German Humanists.* Cambridge, Mass.

Sporhan-Krempel, Lore. 1958. "Agatha Streicher, die Ärtzin von Ulm." *Ulm und Oberschwaben* 35:174–80.

Staehelin, Ernst. 1939. *Theologische Lebenswerk Johannes Oekolampads.* Leipzig.

Stark, Karl Fr. 1895. *Die Reformation im unteren Allgäu: In Memmingen.* Halle.

Stayer, James. 1972. *Anabaptists and the Sword.* Lawrence, Kansas.

Steck, K. G. 1955. *Luther und die Schwärmer.* Zurich.

Steinmetz, David. 1971. *Reformers in the Wings.* Philadelphia.

Stoegmenn. 1857. "Uber die Briefe des Andrea da Burgo, Gesandten König Ferdinands, an den Cardinal und Bischof von Trent Bernhard Cles." *Sitzungsberichte der Kaiserlichen Akademie der Wissenschaft, Philosophisch-Historische Classe* 24:159–252.

Stoudt, J. J., ed. 1961. *Passional and Prayer Book.* Pennsburg, Pa.

Strauss, Gerald. 1975. "Success and Failure in the German Reformation." *Past and Present* 67:30–63.

———. 1978. *Luther's House of Learning: Indoctrination of the Young in the German Reformation.* Baltimore and London.

Stupperich, Robert. 1958. *Das Münsterische Täufertum*. Münster.

Süss, T. 1967. "Über Luthers 'Sieben Busspsalmen.'" In *Vierhundertfünfzig Jahre lutherische Reformation 1517–1967. Festschrift für Franz Lau zum 60. Geburtstag*, 367–83. Göttingen.

Tappert, Theodore G. 1959. *The Book of Concord*. Ed. and trans. Theodore G. Tappert. Philadelphia.

Troeltsch, Ernst. 1931. *The Social Teaching of the Christian Churches*, vol. 2. 2 vols. New York.

Tschackert, Paul. 1890. *Urkundenbuch zur Reformationsgeschichte des Herzogthums Preussen*, vol. 1. 3 vols. Leipzig.

———. 1910. *Die Entstehung der lutherischen und reformierten Kirchenlehre*. Göttingen.

Uhlig, Claus. 1973. *Hofkritik im England des Mittelalters und der Renaissance. Studien zu einem Gemeinplatz der europäischen Moralistik*. Berlin.

Urner, Hans. 1948. "Die Taufe bei Caspar Schwenckfeld." *Theologische Literaturzeichnung* 23:329–42.

Usteri, Joh. Martin. 1883. "Weitere Beiträge zur Geschichte der Tauflehre der Reformierten Kirche; Joh. Bader, ein weniger bekannter Verteidiger der Kindertaufe." *Theologische Studien und Kritiken*. 56:610–16.

———. 1884. "Die Stellung der Strassburger Reformatoren Bucer und Capito zur Tauffrage." *Theologische Studien und Kritiken* 57:456–525.

Van den Berg, Cornelis H. W. 1981. "Anton Engelbrecht: Un 'epicurien' Strasbourgeois." In Lienhard 1981, 111–20.

Volz, Hans. 1967. "Die Breslauer Luther- und Reformationsdrucker Adam Dyon und Kaspar Libische." In *Gutenberg Jahrbuch 1967*, 104–17.

von Hutten, Ulrich. 1859. *Opera*, vol. 1. 7 vols. Leipzig.

von Velsen, Dorothee. 1931. *Die Gegenreformation in den Fürstentümern Liegnitz-Brieg-Wohlau*. Leipzig.

Vorburger, Max. 1983. "Die Auseinandersetzung Johann Fabris mit Caspar Schwenckfeld." In *Les dissidents du XVIe siècle entre l'humanisme et le catholicisme (Actes du colloque de Strasbourg [5–6 février 1982] publiés par Marc Lienhard)*, 245–59. Baden-Baden.

Wach, Joachim. 1946. "Caspar Schwenckfeld, a Pupil and a Teacher in the School of Christ." *Journal of Religion* 26:1–26.

———. 1951. *Types of Religious Experience, Christian and Non-Christian*. London.

Wachler, Albrecht. 1833. "Leben und Wirken Caspar Schwenckfelds von Ossig während seines Aufenthalts in Schlesien, 1490–1528." *Schlesische Provinzblätter* 97:119–30, 209–21, 301–10, 381–89, 477–83; 98:16–24, 118–27.

Wagner, Johannes Volker. 1966. *Graf Wilhelm von Fürstenberg 1491–1549 und die politisch-geistiger Mächte seiner Zeit*. Stuttgart.

Walther, Heinrich. 1929. *Bernhard Besserer und die Politik der Reichstadt Ulm während der Reformationszeit*. Ulm.

Weber, Franz Michael. 1962. *Kaspar Schwenckfeld und seine Anhänger in den freybergischen Herrschaften Justingen und Oepfingen*. Stuttgart.

Weber, H. E. 1933. *Reformation, Orthodoxie, Rationalismus, Beiträge zur Förderung christlicher Theologie*. Gütersloh.

Weigelt, Horst. 1970. "Sebastian Franck und Caspar Schwenckfeld in ihren Beziehungen zueinander." ZBKG 39:3–19.

———. 1972. *Sebastian Franck und die Lutherischen Reformation*. Gütersloh.

———. 1973. *Spiritualistische Tradition im Protestantismus—Die Geschichte des Schwenckfeldertums in Schlesien*. Berlin.

———. 1974/75. "Das Schwenckfeldischen Gebetsbüchlein 'Bekanntnus der Sünden' und Löhes Gebetssammlung 'Samenkörner des Gebets.'" *Jahrbuch für Fränkische Landesforschung* 34/35:603–16.

———. 1982. "Caspar Schwenckfeld: Proclaimer of the Middle Way." In *Profiles of Radical Reformers. Biographical Sketches from Thomas Müntzer to Paracelsus,* ed. Walter Klaassen, 214–25. Kitchener, Ont., and Scottsdale, Pa. Originally published as *Radikale Reformatoren,* ed. Hans-Jürgen Goetz (Munich, 1978).

———. 1983. "Valentin Krautwald: Der führende Theologe des frühen Schwenckfeldertums: Biographische und Kirchenhistorische Aspekte." In *Les dissidents du XVIe siècle entre l'humanisme et le catholicisme* (Actes du colloque de Strasbourg [5–6 février 1982] publiés par Marc Lienhard), 175–90. Baden-Baden.

Wendel, François. 1942. *L'Eglise de Strasbourg, sa constitution et son organisation 1532–1535.* Paris.

Williams, George H. 1957. "Introduction" to *Spiritual and Anabaptist Writers.* Library of Christian Classics 25. Philadelphia.

———. 1962. *Radical Reformation.* London.

———. 1968. "Sanctification in the Testimony of Several So-Called Schwärmer." *MQR* 42:5–26.

Windhorst, Christof. 1979. "Der 'königliche Weg' des Caspar von Schwenckfeld. Eine Skizze zu seinem Leben und seiner Lehre." In *Wort und Geist. Jahrbuch der kirchlichen Hochschule Bethel,* n.s., 15:133–52.

Wiswedel, Wilhelm. "Zum Problem 'inneres und äusseres Wort' bei den Täufern des 16. Jahrhunderts." *ARG* 46:1–20.

Wolfart, Karl. 1901. *Die Ausburger Reformation in den Jahren 1533/34.* Leipzig.

———. 1902. "Beiträge zur Augsburger Reformationsgeschichte, 3 (Caspar Schwenckfeld und Bonifacius Wolfhart)." *Beiträge zur bayerischen Kirchengeschichte* 8:97–114.

Wotschke, Theodor. 1911. "Zur Reformation in Liegnitz." *CVGEKS* 12:155–64.

Ziegler, Donald J. 1971. "Marpeck versus Butzer: A Sixteenth-Century Debate over the Uses and Limits of Political Authority." *Sixteenth Century Essays and Studies* 2:95–107.

Index